NEW ESSAYS ON THE NORMATIVITY OF LAW

An important part of the legal domain has to do with rule-governed conduct, and is expressed by the use of notions such as norm, obligation, duty and right. These require us to acknowledge the normative dimension of law. Normativity is, accordingly, to be regarded as a central feature of law lying at the heart of any comprehensive legal-theoretical project. The essays collected in this book are meant to further our understanding of the normativity of law. More specifically, the book stages a thorough discussion of legal normativity as approached from three strands of legal thought that are particularly influential and which play a key role in shaping debates on the normative dimension of law: the theory of planning agency, legal conventionalism and the constitutivist approach. While the essays presented here do not aspire to give an exhaustive picture of these debates – an aspiration that would be, by its very nature, unrealistic – they do provide the reader with some authoritative statements of some widely discussed families of views of legal normativity. In pursuing this objective, these essays also encourage a dialogue between different traditions of study of legal normativity, stimulating those who would not otherwise look outside their tradition of thought to engage with new ideas and, ultimately, to arrive at a more comprehensive account of the normativity of law.

Volume 3 in the series Law and Practical Reason

Law and Practical Reason

The intention of this series is that it should encompass monographs and collections of essays that address the fundamental issues in legal philosophy. The foci are conceptual and normative in character, not empirical. Studies addressing the idea of law as a species of practical reason are especially welcome. Recognising that there is no occasion sharply to distinguish analytic and systematic work in the field from historico-critical research, the editors also welcome studies in the history of legal philosophy. Contributions to the series, inevitably crossing disciplinary lines, will be of interest to students and professionals in moral, political, and legal philosophy.

Volume 1: The Normative Claim of Law
Stefano Bertea

Volume 2: Community and Collective Rights: A Theoretical Framework for Rights Held by Groups
Dwight Newman

Volume 3: New Essays on the Normativity of Law
Edited by Stefano Bertea and George Pavlakos

New Essays on the Normativity of Law

Edited by

Stefano Bertea

and

George Pavlakos

• HART •
PUBLISHING

OXFORD AND PORTLAND, OREGON
2011

Published in the United Kingdom by Hart Publishing Ltd
16C Worcester Place, Oxford, OX1 2JW
Telephone: +44 (0)1865 517530
Fax: +44 (0)1865 510710
E-mail: mail@hartpub.co.uk
Website: http://www.hartpub.co.uk

Published in North America (US and Canada) by
Hart Publishing
c/o International Specialized Book Services
920 NE 58th Avenue, Suite 300
Portland, OR 97213-3786
USA
Tel: +1 503 287 3093 or toll-free: (1) 800 944 6190
Fax: +1 503 280 8832
E-mail: orders@isbs.com
Website: http://www.isbs.com

British Library Cataloguing in Publication Data
Data Available

ISBN: 978-1-84946-238-9

Typeset by Hope Services Ltd, Abingdon
Printed and bound in Great Britain by
Lightning Source UK Ltd

Contents

Contributors

Robert Alexy is Professor of Public Law and Legal Philosophy at the Christian Albrecht University, Kiel, Germany. From 1994–1998 he was President of the German Section of the International Association for Philosophy of Law and Social Philosophy. He is known and admired worldwide as a leading legal philosopher.

Stefano Bertea is a Reader in Law at the School of Law of the University of Leicester. He has published widely in the fields of legal philosophy, jurisprudence, political theory and the theory of legal reasoning.

Michael E Bratman is Durfee Professor in the School of Humanities and Sciences and Professor of Philosophy at the Stanford University. He is an internationally-respected philosopher of action. His work is credited with furthering our understanding of moral responsibility, temptation and self-control, shared intention and shared cooperative activity. His research interests also include the nature of agency, practical reason and free will.

Sylvie Delacroix is a Lecturer in Law at UCL and Director of the Law and Ethics Centre. In the past she was a lecturer at Kent University, having previously held a one-year post-doctoral fellowship at Trinity College, Cambridge (Senior Rouse Ball, 2002–2003). She holds a PhD from Cambridge University, Licenses in Law from the University of Louvain-la-Neuve (Belgium), and Candidatures in Philosophy from the Facultés Universitaires Saint Louis (Belgium). From 2004–2005 she was the Evelyn Green Davis Fellow at the Radcliffe Institute for Advanced Study (Harvard University).

Marco Goldoni is a Fellow at the Centre for Law and Cosmopolitan Values at the University of Antwerp. He has a degree in law and a degree in philosophy from the University of Bologna. His present research is on European constitutionalism and in particular on the role of national parliaments seen through a republican perspective. The thesis aims to build a republican model for the principle of political accountability. This model will serve as a compass for proposing specific institutional arrangements.

Dimitrios Kyritsis is a Lecturer in Law at the Sheffield Law School. He undertakes research in jurisprudence, constitutional theory and political philosophy. He is also a member of the Sheffield Institute of Biotechnological Law and Ethics Research Cluster.

Cristina Lafont is Professor at the Philosophy Department of Northwestern University. She holds a PhD and a Habilitation from the University of Frankfurt. She specialises in German philosophy, particularly hermeneutics and critical theory. She has also published in philosophy of language and contemporary moral and political philosophy. She is author of *The Linguistic Turn in Hermeneutic Philosophy* (Cambridge, MA, MIT Press, 1999) and *Heidegger, Language, and World-disclosure* (Cambridge, Cambridge University Press, 2000).

Andrei Marmor earned his BA and MA in philosophy, as well as his LLB, from Tel Aviv University and earned his DPhil from Oxford University. He was a professor at Tel Aviv University, Israel, and taught as a visiting professor at several universities before joining the USC Law and Philosophy faculties in 2002. He concentrates his study on legal and moral philosophy. He is the director of the USC Center for Law and Philosophy, and editor in chief of the *Journal of Ethics and Social Philosophy*, an online peer-reviewed journal in moral, political and legal philosophy.

George Pavlakos is Research Professor in globalisation and legal theory at the University of Antwerp and director of the Centre of Law and Cosmopolitan Values at the same institution. He is also sometime Professor in globalisation and legal theory at the University of Glasgow. His published work, mainly in the area of legal theory and legal philosophy, includes several edited collections and a monograph, entitled *Our Knowledge of the Law*, all published by Hart Publishing, as well as another monograph in German, *Rechtsontologie und praktische Vernunft*, published by Nomos Verlag.

Veronica Rodriguez-Blanco obtained her first degrees in law and philosophy from the Catholic University in Caracas, Venezuela and the Central University of Venezuela (Magister Scientiarium in Logic and Philosophy of Science). She proceeded to study English Law at Balliol College, Oxford (MJur) and Legal Philosophy at Corpus Christi College, Cambridge (PhD). In 2001, she joined Birmingham Law School. Her present research aims to advance a better understanding of the relationship between legal and moral objectivity. She is also interested in, and has written on, the methodological problems in legal theory such as the distinction between normative and descriptive jurisprudence.

Corrado Roversi is a Lecturer in Law at the University of Bologna. His research interests include the study of social and legal ontology, legal epistemology, the theory of argumentation and the philosophy of normative language. Currently, he is focusing on the concept of constitutive rules and on the general phenomenon of normatively constituted concepts.

Katrien Schaubroeck is a post-doctoral Fellow at the faculty of philosophy of the University of Leuven. She has published in the fields of practical philosophy including meta-ethics, normative ethics, theory of action and moral psychology.

Scott Shapiro is Professor of Law and Philosophy at Yale Law School. Before his appointment at Yale, he was Professor of Law and Professor of Philosophy at the University of Michigan. His areas of interest include jurisprudence, family law, constitutional law, criminal law, constitutional theory, philosophy of action and authority and rationality. He is the editor (with Jules Coleman) of *The Oxford Handbook of Jurisprudence and Philosophy of Law*.

Introduction

STEFANO BERTEA AND GEORGE PAVLAKOS

HLA HART ONCE argued that a theory suppressing the normative component of law 'fails to mark and explain the crucial distinction between mere regularities of human behaviour and rule-governed behaviour'.[1] This is a serious drawback for a theory of law, since an important part of the legal domain has to do with rule-governed conduct and so may be expressed only by use of such notions as those of norm, obligation, duty and right. These notions require us to acknowledge the existence of a normative dimension in the legal domain. As a result, a number of different legal traditions regard normativity as a central feature of law and so a notion lying at the heart of any comprehensive legal-theoretical project.[2] This collection of essays is intended to contribute to the study of normativity in law. By building on a debate initiated at an UCSIA International Academic Workshop that took place on 3–4 June 2009 at the University of Antwerp, the book stages a thorough discussion of the normativity of law, as this notion is approached from three strands of legal thought that nowadays are particularly influential and play a key role in shaping the current debate on the normative dimension of law: the theory of planning agency, legal conventionalism and the constitutivist approach. This way the collection of essays presented here does not aspire at giving an exhaustive picture of the current debate on the normativity of law – aspiration that would be, by its very nature, unrealistic, especially in consideration of the width and complexity of such debate – but rather is meant to provide the reader with some authoritative statements of some widely discussed families of views of legal normativity. Thus, the volume has the ambition to encourage a dialogue between different traditions of study of legal normativity and to stimulate those who would not otherwise look outside their tradition of thought to engage with new ideas with a view to arriving at a more comprehensive account of the normativity of law.

In performing those tasks the volume instantiates a distinctive interdisciplinary and multidisciplinary character. The idea underlying the collection is that no

[1] H Hart, *Essays in Jurisprudence and Philosophy* (Oxford, Clarendon, 1983) 13.

[2] *cf* S Perry, 'Hart's Methodological Positivism' in *Hart's Postscript* (J Coleman (ed), Oxford, Oxford University Press, 2001) 311–54) 330, where it is claimed that 'the provision of an account of the normativity of law is a central task of jurisprudence, if not the central task'.

general theory of normativity can be put forward unless it deals with a number of issues pertaining to distinct, albeit interrelated, disciplines such as the philosophy of mind, metaphysics, theory of action, meta-ethics, social philosophy, political theory, ethical theory and jurisprudence. The volume should, thus, be regarded, among other things, as an opportunity for generating a genuinely interdisciplinary discussion in which will be compared theories and ideas that, albeit worked out in different disciplines, are unified by the common aspiration to cope with the whole range of puzzles set by the existence of a specifically normative dimension in legal practices.

The book opens with Part I, 'Law, Normativity and Plans', devoted to the discussion of the theory of planning agency, a general philosophical approach that owes its popularity and significance to the work of Michael Bratman,[3] and how that theory can shed light on key aspects of law and its normativity. The entire Part can be regarded as a sustained discussion of Scott Shapiro's contribution 'Planning Agency and the Law', where the basic principles of Bratman's theory of planning agency are creatively applied to legal contexts and, as a result, Bratman's original insights are expanded from one-to-one situations of shared agency to situations where small-scale group planning, as well as large-scale social interactions requiring no direct relationships between the individuals involved, take place.[4]

In Chapter 1, Shapiro relies on a narrative – the cooking club tale – to introduce and elaborate on the basic idea underpinning his view, to wit, the thesis that social interaction generates a need for collective planning and law is best viewed as a device enabling planning at social level. In a nutshell, Shapiro's view is that social planning is a standard method for guiding, coordinating and monitoring behaviour in society, a method, in addition, that proves to be indispensable on several occasions. Insofar as one acknowledges that legal institutions too play an essential role in guiding social conduct as well as coordinating social interaction, a framework for the study of the law shaped by the idea of social planning seems to be a most natural option. On this view, legal institutions are collective units that perform planning functions for the communities over which they claim authority. This role is performed in either of two basic forms, namely, by telling members of the governed community what they may or may not do, and by identifying those who are entitled to affect what others may or may not do. Legal rules, once they are taken to be issued from such kind of institutions, can accordingly be conceived as generalised plans, or plan-like norms. Similarly, legal adjudication is, from this perspective, a process involving the application of the generalised plans to legal subjects on the part of (a subset of) legal authorities. The picture stemming from this theoretical approach is a general theory of law as the source of organisation of

[3] See the essays collected in M Bratman, *Faces of Intention* (Cambridge, Cambridge University Press, 1987), especially Pt II, and those in M Bratman, *Structures of Agency* (Oxford, Oxford University Press, 2007).

[4] Other arguments to the same effect have been expressed in S Shapiro, 'Law, Morality, and the Guidance of Conduct' (2000) 6 *Legal Theory* 127 and S Shapiro, 'Law, Plans, and Practical Reason' (2002) 8 *Legal Theory* 387.

individual and collective behaviour. The law, once understood as a paradigmatic instance of institutionalised social planning, enables those who live together to structure their shared activities, solve possible coordination problems, settle their disputes and ensure that their individual pursuits do not frustrate one another. The law, then, institutionalises a fundamental human need: the need for planning, coordinating and organising one's activities over time. This institutionalisation brings some degree of complexity and sophistication with itself: as the number of interacting individuals grows (and so we pass from situations of personal social interaction to large-scale cases of social interaction where only few people enter into direct contact one with another) the need for more structured and sophisticated methods of planning arises, to the effect that simple techniques of social coordination give way to more complicated and efficient structures of planning. The end result is the creation of a legal system, which, thus, for Shapiro should be conceived, at its core, as a highly sophisticated planning organisation. The law is, then, to be constructed not as a morally-coloured practice that embodies some values widely shared within a certain community, but rather as the end product of a process that has the practice of planning as its starting point. This is to say that a legal system need not appeal to any moral legitimacy to impose obligations and confer rights: the origin of legal authority resides in the mere ability to plan. Accordingly, existence and authority of law simply reflect the fact that human beings are planning creatures, endowed with the cognitive and volitional capacities and dispositions required to organise their behaviour over time and across persons in order to achieve highly complex ends. This frames the planning theory of law as a version of legal positivism, for, on this approach, moral facts are not needed in order to establish and reiterate a system of laws, and moral norms are not essential to law to the same extent that the principles of planning rationality are.

In the other essays in Part I, Michael Bratman, Veronica Rodriguez-Blanco and Katrien Schaubroeck engage closely with Shapiro's ambitious and comprehensive legal theory. Bratman's contribution may be regarded as a token of internal criticism. Bratman agrees with Shapiro's basic tenet that the planning theory of agency can be fruitfully extended beyond cases of personal shared agency and so that the law does involve norms of rational planning. To that extent Bratman supports the basic steps leading Shapiro to construct his theory of law. However, Bratman also argues that reliance on the theory of planning agency does not suffice to explain the capacity of law to give members of a community – legal officials and law-subjects – normative, or justifying, reasons for acting (call it the 'normative thesis'). For, whilst the planning theory has the potential to set constraints relative to the inner rationality of law – which, then, is a kind of rationality that can be defined independently of morality – it is silent as to whether one has a reason to (continue to) play the legal game. And it is only to the extent that reasons for participating in legal settings are provided that the existence is warranted of normative reasons to do what the law prescribes. The theory of planning agency, then, on the one hand, can be profitably used to account for the social existence of the law, yet, on the other hand, it does not appear to provide a ready-made explanation of whether and why law brings with it distinctive normative reasons. The reason why the planning theory cannot advance us that far lies in its character of a theory that transmits, in the means–end fashion, the normative force of general considerations to solve the problems emerging from social interaction to the specific legal structure. The latter is hence normative only to the extent that the former are. But, those general considerations are normative by virtue of substantive claims that go beyond – although they are compatible with – the planning theory. The upshot of Bratman's argument is that the exclusive reliance on the framework provided by the planning theory does not enable us to vindicate the normative thesis, as it applies to law. All the planning theory can do is to help us single out and articulate the relation between a legal system and the considerations justifying one's action in accordance with the law. This way, Bratman's contribution provides an insightful synthesis of the power as well as the limits of the planning theory of agency when it is applied to the understanding of the law.

The critique that Veronica Rodriguez-Blanco raises in respect of Shapiro's proposal seems to have a more radical impact on that proposal. In her chapter, Rodriguez-Blanco explicitly targets Shapiro's account of legal authority. In Rodriguez-Blanco's reconstruction Shapiro shares with other contemporary scholars (most notably Joseph Raz) the 'constitutive argument', according to which the idea of legitimate authority is taken to be as given, on which basis the conditions that make possible the existence of practical authorities are explored. This argument connects up with, and is completed by, the premise that authority of law constitutes a good ('special status argument') to the effect that obeying the authority's directives is prima facie commendable or something that ought to be done. Shapiro's planning theory of law relies on the same elements and, indeed, purports to perform the role of a bridge between them: by defending the claim that we are planning creatures Shapiro's construction makes it perspicuous that authorities – being functional to our planning agency and plan-based practices – are good. This way, Shapiro's planning theory of law is meant to be in the position to solve the fundamental puzzle of legal authority, which arises when constitutive argument and special status argument are combined. Put shortly, the puzzle arises from the conflict possibly obtaining between the demands stemming from legal authority and the reasons for actions that an agent works out by herself from the deliberative viewpoint. Given the potential for a conflict between legal authority and personal deliberation the puzzle arises as to how one can justify the practice of an agent's surrendering her judgment to legal authority. Shapiro's proposed way out is centred on the thesis of the existence of a distinctively legal point of view that enables one to look at the two kinds of demands – those coming from the legal authority and those internal to one's agency – from some distance. This solution, which amounts to the conclusion that ultimately there is no requirement for one to endorse the authority's commands, is criticised by Rodriguez-Blanco. She argues that, insofar as it distances itself to any commitment to values, the legal point of view is not a deliberative or practical point of view, but merely a theoretical viewpoint. This means that what one concludes from the legal point of view has no direct bearing on action – for, constitutively, it is not the source of reasons for action and so has no independent force in deliberation – and is, by contrast, a mere report of a state of affairs, which at most warrants the establishment of theoretical reasons. As such, Shapiro's legal point of view makes no practical difference and so should be regarded as secondary to, and parasitic upon, the deliberative viewpoint. The secondary and parasitic quality of the legal point of view makes that point of view conceptually incapable of providing the core of an account of legal authority, which unfolds in the practical sphere. The treatment of legal authority associated with the planning theory of law – in Shapiro's version, at least – can, then, be criticised through the argument that it takes as its main explanatory reference a practically-inert perspective and, as a result, ends up presenting legal authority in terms that can make no sense of its action-guiding dimension.

The discussion devoted to the planning theory of agency is concluded by Katrien Schaubroeck's essay. Schaubroeck begins her argument by eliciting the connection between the rationality of planning and the instrumental principle; for, the activity of planning entails one setting ends for oneself and organising one's conduct over time. This process is subject to several norms of rationality, among which the instrumental principle takes a prominent position, for fleshing out and filling in one's plan is tantamount to adopting the means necessary to the planned ends. Accordingly, accepting the authority of plans involves, first and foremost, conforming to the instrumental principle. This way, Shapiro can be interpreted as establishing the normativity of law, qua institutional framework enabling social planning, on the normativity, or authority, of the instrumental principle. However, Schaubroeck notices, despite its apparent attraction, this strategy is problematic at a deep level because the normativity of the instrumental principle cannot be taken for granted. Not only are there competing theories about how to explain the normative force of the instrumental principle, but there are also philosophers who doubt whether the instrumental principle really is a normative, reason-giving principle: the question as to why an agent should take the means to his ends finds, thus, no ready-made answer in the existing philosophical literature. This difficulty applies to the planning theory of law too, at least insofar as that theory relies heavily on the instrumental principle to account for the normativity of law.

Part II of the book, 'Law, Normativity and Conventions', opens with an essay by Andrei Marmor, which in fact constitutes the focus of the discussion of the whole Part II. Marmor's essay, which was originally published as Chapter 7 of his *Social Conventions*,[5] is a thorough discussion of HLA Hart's thesis that in every developed legal system there are certain rules of recognition determining what counts as law in a given society, namely, how law is created, modified or repealed in the relevant legal order. Whilst this thesis is one of the most influential contributions to contemporary legal philosophy, it has proved to be problematic too, for a satisfactory account of the rules of recognition (originally presented as customary social rules

[5] A Marmor, *Social Conventions: From Language to Law* (Princeton, NJ, Princeton University Press, 2009).

that are accepted by the relevant population) is difficult. In order to cope with certain difficulties some theorists have relied on David Lewis' theory of conventions and in fact have come up with a conventionalist account of the rules of recognition. Far from being generally endorsed, even in the positivist camp, this solution has generated as many problems as it solves. Accordingly, Marmor goes back to the question whether the conventional account of the rules of recognition is sound or not. In his contribution he claims that, while conventionalism should be regarded as an adequate approach to the problem to the effect that the nature of the rules of recognition can be shown to be that of social conventions, the traditional conventionalist view should be radically revised. More specifically, the standard conventionalist construal of the rules of recognition needs to undergo two crucial modifications before it can be shown to be insightful. First, Marmor claims that the rules of recognition are constitutive conventions, and not, as previous advocates of conventionalism claimed, coordination conventions; secondly, he argues that a distinction between conventions – the distinction between deep conventions and surface conventions – can be employed to solve some of the puzzles about the nature of the rules of recognition. In this context, the role of deep conventions in law is discussed in great detail and the thesis is defended that between the general reasons for having law in our societies, and the surface conventions of recognition constituting what counts as law in a given legal system, there is a further layer: the deep conventions of law.

Marmor's confidence in the potential of legal conventionalism to solve basic legal puzzles is not shared by Marco Goldoni, who adopts instead a more critical approach to what has been defined, in recent years, the 'conventionalist turn'.[6] Goldoni acknowledges the strengths of Marmor's version, which undoubtedly is one of the most elaborated and challenging theories within the conventionalist realm and, in fact, may be regarded as the best accomplishment in this stream of thought. This is due in large part to the fact that central to Marmor's innovative version of legal conventionalism is the distinction between different levels of conventions. This grants that Marmor's conventionalism can provide us with a much more complex and stratified representation of the law than the one given by traditional conventionalist accounts shaped exclusively by the idea of coordinative conventions. Marmor's multilayered conventionalism, however, is open to certain criticisms, especially when the ensuing theory of the normativity of law is taken into account. In particular, Goldoni focuses on Marmor's thesis of involuntary membership, which, when applied to law, turns out to be substantially reductive, and on the relation (which is argued to be uneasy) between sources thesis and multilayered conventionalism. The analysis of these arguments leads to the conclusion that even in Marmor's sophisticated version the conventionalist approach can better explain the social aspect of law than its normativity. This is not surprising, to a certain extent, because it is part of the project of legal conventionalism to concentrate mainly on the social aspect of law, yet – one may add – this under-

[6] L Green, 'Positivism and Conventionalism' (1999) 12 *Canadian Journal of Law and Jurisprudence* 35.

estimating of the normative dimension of the legal domain is puzzling, at least insofar as legal conventionalism aspires to be considered a general theory of law. For, to the extent that we interpret legal conventionalism as an account concentrating mainly on the sociality of law, it can hardly be regarded as a successful attempt to explain how social thesis (the thesis that law is a social fact) and normativity thesis (the thesis that law gives members of a community reasons for acting) combine and coexist. And it is the explanation of this combination and coexistence which constitutes the bare bones of any comprehensive theory of law.

Finally, Dimitrios Kyritsis builds on an earlier contribution where he attempted a partial reconciliation between two jurisprudential traditions, legal conventionalism and natural law theory.[7] He did so there by accommodating the basic insights of the contemporary legal conventionalist literature – literature that is generally regarded as being positivist in nature – within a robust version of natural law theory. In the contribution included in this volume, Kyritsis further elaborates on and deepens his original argument by clarifying the significance that his project has for a better understanding of legal systems where different categories of legal officials with limited competences operate. Kyritsis focuses, in particular, on the relationships between two categories of legal officials: legislatures and courts. The standard conventionalist characterisation of the relationships between legislatures and courts can be described as follows: the legislature is essentially a rule-creating institution and a court is essentially a rule-applying one. Accordingly, the rules created by the legislature are legal by virtue of the fact that courts in their rule-applying function have a conventional practice of treating the legislature as a source of valid law. Endorsing this assumption lends support to a positivist theory of law; since, if it is accepted that the identification of law is a matter of how a set of rules created by an institution (the legislature) is regarded by another institution (a court), then the stage of moral evaluation of those rules envisaged by natural law theories appears largely redundant to the qualification of those rules as legal – and, thus, establishes a direct connection between positivism and conventionalism. For Kyritsis, however, this characterisation is misguided and should be replaced by a different view whereby the legislature and courts are involved in a common institutional endeavour and, more specifically, perform shared cooperative activity in Bratman's sense. This alternative framework gives us a yardstick for understanding the different institutional roles legislature and courts are assigned, as well as their mutual relationships, which does not imply positivist tenets. Working within this framework we can reconcile what we might call the receptive aspect of the role of courts towards the legislature – the idea that courts apply rules created by the legislature – with the more active aspects of that role that courts perform, for instance, in so-called 'hard cases' and in legal systems that follow a practice of constitutional review of legislation for its conformity with higher-order legal standards. Most importantly, this reconceptualisation of the relationship between legislature and courts in terms of participants in a joint

[7] D Kyritsis, 'What is Good about Legal Conventionalism' (2008) 14(2) *Legal Theory* 135.

activity enables Kyritsis to give a natural-law interpretation of the institutional setting most common in Western legal systems. The picture resulting from the alternative philosophical framework argued for by Kyritsis, on the one hand, casts the point of the joint activity in morally laden terms, on the other, shows that moral principles pertaining to the point of the joint activity play an essential role in the determination of judicial or legislative duty and, in fact, have a bearing on the truth of propositions of law. Therefore, in Kyritsis' reconstruction the basic conventionalist insights and legal positivism do not imply one another.

Part III of the book, 'Law, Normativity and Autonomy', focuses on constitutivism about practical normativity, ie the strategy that derives the normativity of certain propositions – here legal directives – from certain traits constitutive of agents or basic human activities. The first essay of this Part is Stefano Bertea's. The initial assumptions of the essay are that a theory of obligation features as a central element of jurisprudence and that an integral part of any theory of obligation in law aspiring to achieve any degree of comprehensiveness will have to be an explanation of the grounds of the obligatory force of law. The essay is meant to specifically contribute to such explanation. With this aim in view, Bertea discusses some preliminary notions that can be used in setting up an argument on the basis of which to construct a foundation for the obligation-imposing capacity of law. The treatment, rooted in the Kantian tradition of practical philosophy and conditioned to the endorsement of the thesis of the conceptual continuity between law and practical reason, proceeds from the belief that if we are to adequately explain the connection between law and obligation, we will have to take up some contemporary discussions of Kant's conception of humanity as the source of the normativity of practical reason. This gives the essential rationale for the contribution, where the author confines himself to laying the groundwork for a Kantian argument for the foundation of the obligatoriness of law by fleshing out a notion of action derived from the notion of human agency, in turn understood as the source of the normativity of practical reason. While in defending this foundation of the obligatoriness of law Bertea tries to achieve something that is Kantian in spirit, he does not mean this to be simply a restatement of Kant's view. The resulting view argued in the chapter amounts, then, to a kind of revisionary Kantian approach recasting in pragmatic terms the concept of humanity that Kant posits as the notion grounding practical normativity – we no longer have a metaphysical attempt to define the essence of humanity, but a pragmatic one to single out the conceptual features of human agency. In turn, human agency is taken to be the key of explaining the normativity of practical reason. And once the overall foundation of the normativity of practical reason is worked out, then it can be extended to grounding the bindingness of law, at least insofar as the law is regarded as continuous with practical reason, to the effect that the normativity of law shares the same foundation with the normativity of practical reason, and legal obligation is a specific case of the normativity of law.

This argumentative strategy is critically addressed by Robert Alexy, who in his chapter 'Normativity, Metaphysics and Decision' takes issue with Bertea's argument as it has been developed in *The Normative Claim of Law*,[8] where the revisionary Kantian approach summarised and further elaborated on in the contribution included in this volume is put forward and discussed at greater length. Alexy notes that at the core of Bertea's project we find the attempt to develop a conception of normativity that follows Kantian lines but apart from any metaphysics. The elimination of metaphysics is achieved by substituting for Kant's metaphysical notion of humanity a concept of human agency that refers to a 'pragmatic unit' defined by a set of capacities related to action and agents. Alexy rejects this claim on the argument that normativity necessarily presupposes metaphysics. In his view, metaphysical abstinence notwithstanding, Bertea's pragmatic approach carries with it very strong conclusions, among which, the thesis figures prominently that normative requirements express a certain necessity, or non-optional character. This thesis too is rejected by Alexy, who argues that in this way the practical nature of legal normativity is underestimated. In fact, the normativity of law, by virtue of its practical nature, is a kind of normativity essentially connected with the concept of decision but this connection escapes Bertea's account. The more general and constructive argument which, in his critical contribution, Alexy indirectly deploys is, thus, twofold: for Alexy, on the one hand, normativity is not possible without metaphysics, on the other hand, practical normativity – normativity of law included – is not possible without decision.

The Kantian strategy of dealing with normative issues is tested in Cristina Lafont's chapter too, where an attempt is made to move from the normativity of morality and practical reason as it is applied to, and by, single individuals to the normativity of institutional practices such as the law. Lafont invites us to focus our attention specifically on Kantian constructivism in moral theory, which is taken to be a most promising starting point to understand the connection between the autonomy of agents and the validity, or authority, of norms. In Lafont's interpretation, the idea underlying Kantian constructivism is that the validity of norms depends on the reasonable agreement of those to whom the norms apply. The centrality of the notion of free and reasonable agreement makes Kantian constructivism seem particularly apt for an extension from moral into legal contexts, also in consideration of the fact that that notion fits well with the democratic ideal, an ideal that is distinctively based on the idea of the 'consent of the governed'. Yet, the relationship between the notion of agreement operative in Kantian constructivist approaches and democratic decision-making procedures is, Lafont argues, by no means unproblematic. For, in the constructivist framework any appeal to agreement as the source of the validity of norms must include some normative constraints in order to be plausible. This suggests that the normative notion operative in constructivist approaches is merely a notion of hypothetical agreement and not a notion of actual consent. And appealing to a notion of hypothetical agreement may mean, on the one hand, that to the extent that the suitably ideal conditions can never be met in real social contexts, the actual

[8] S Bertea, *The Normative Claim of Law* (Oxford, Hart Publishing, 2009).

agreements reached by democratic procedures cannot confer genuine legitimacy on collective political decisions, and, on the other hand, that nothing else is needed for the legitimate enforcement of collective norms. Therefore, so long as legal norms track the interests and views of reasonable persons, those norms would be considered legitimate, even in lieu of asking citizens, or their representatives, for their actual agreement through democratic decision-making procedures such as elections or referenda. The upshot of this state of affairs is that Kantian constructivism, once extended from moral settings to legal contexts, does not lend any straightforward support to a defence of democracy and, in fact, can have pretty disquieting implications from the point of view of a democratic mind.

A different variant of constitutivism is defended by George Pavlakos who in his chapter argues that a complete account of legal normativity rests on the possibility of (legal) obligations *simpliciter*. Pavlakos' essay builds on and continues previous work, where positivist accounts of legal obligation *from a point of view* had been rejected as leading to semantic contextualism, which threatens the fragmentation of normative meaning and communication.[9] This chapter aims to put forward a positive account of the conditions that make possible obligations *simpliciter*. These conditions are developed within the framework of a 'model of norms', which purports to offer a unified account of the normativity of practical reason, of which legal normativity is considered to be a distinct layer only. In a nutshell the model of norms conceives reasons for action as resting on normative facts (norms) that are independent of the subjective mental states of the agents ('mind-independent'). At the same time such normative facts are grounded on rational deliberation, hence they are not external or heteronomous in Bernard Williams' sense[10] – call them, for that reason, 'reason-dependent'. This means, roughly, that anything that counts as a normative reason may count as such only if it can pass a deliberative test that takes into account the point of view of every rational agent – call this cumulative point of view 'the point of view of agency'. The norms comprising the inventory of an agent's reasons materialise, according to the model of norms, in a two-layered structure. At the top layer we have a set of general norms that are *a priori* true – call them norms *simpliciter*. Norms *simpliciter* are general propositions that specify *the content* of our most general normative terms – such as 'ought', 'right', 'wrong', 'obligation', 'duty', and so on. Notwithstanding their abstract character, norms *simpliciter* function as a reliable compass for determining the grounds of deliberative endorsement of more concrete norms by 'projecting' their evaluative point upon the context of particular social practices. This leads to the second layer of norms. This specifies the content of normative reasons with respect to some relevant (social) practice. Reasons are given, in this context, by the normative facts that correspond to true normative propositions (call these norms in a domain). Norms in a domain are *a posteriori* propositions and amount from the projection of norms *simpliciter* onto the particular facts of a practice. Norms in a

[9] G Pavlakos 'Practice, Reasons, and the Agent's Point of View' (2009) 22(1) *Ratio Juris* 74.

[10] B Williams, 'Internal and External Reasons' reproduced in B Williams, *Moral Luck: Philosophical Papers 1973–1980* (Cambridge, Cambridge University Press, 1981) 101–13.

domain are worked out against the various particular social, moral and legal practices which nevertheless are constituted in light of the agent's point of view as specified by the layer of norms *simpliciter*. Through the interplay between the two layers of norms, Pavlakos' constitutive account defends the existence of obligations *simpliciter* without losing sight of the variety of institutional normativity that pertains to human societies. Finally, Pavlakos' account is presented as an alternative to Ronald Dworkin's interpretivism, mitigated by an analysis of obligation *simpliciter* that eschews reference to any robust moral reality, such as is assumed by that theory.

Constitutivism, in both the variants introduced so far, is the target of Corrado Roversi's contribution, which establishes conceptual connections between the different versions of the approach seeking for the ultimate grounds of practical normativity by showing that these grounds are to be found in the constitution of agents or certain human practices. This solution, typically championed by Christine Korsgaard,[11] is clearly and explicitly the offspring of a Kantian approach to normativity, based on an explanation of the inner constitution of the capability to act and on a series of transcendental arguments. Roversi sets the stage for his argument by noticing that the constitutivist strategy presents striking similarities, which often go unnoticed, with the 'discourse ethics', a view brought forward by Karl-Otto Apel and Jürgen Habermas, and aimed at grounding moral normativity in discoursive rationality.[12] Building on this remark Roversi takes Korsgaard's and Apel's work as paradigmatic instances of the two perspectives and discusses their mutual relationship. After arguing that Korsgaard's constitutivist strategy and Apel's discourse ethics revolve around transcendental arguments, Roversi argues that, aptly analysed, they are two faces of the same coin and so are mutually dependent. More specifically, in an argument that is both insightful and highly original, Roversi shows that some central problems faced by discourse ethics can be solved by appealing to the constitutivist strategy, and that the converse is true as well, that is, one can appeal to discourse ethics to rescue constitutivism from certain criticism. The result is a merged approach combining some of the main tenets of the constitutivist strategy with some of those of discourse ethics. Whilst the approach so constructed is stronger than the single independent constituents from which it results, Roversi claims that it nonetheless falls short of answering other crucial problems of those views and (which is most relevant to the issue to which the essays contained in this book are devoted, normativity) it fails to answer the question as to why one should accept the constitution of agency or the fundamental trait of discourse as normative. This point can be framed in terms of a hidden normative regress; namely, normativity, as it is derived from the strategy here criticised, is relative to that which is constituted (agency or discourse); yet it is not made clear why 'that which is constituted' should be taken to be normative

[11] See C Korsgaard, *The Sources of Normativity* (Cambridge, Cambridge University Press, 1996) and C Korsgaard, *Self-constitution: Agency, Identity, and Integrity* (Oxford, Oxford University Press, 2009).

[12] See KO Apel, *Transformation der Philosophie* (Suhrkamp, Frankfurt am Main, 1973) and J Habermas, *Moralbewußtsein und kommunikatives Handeln* (Suhrkamp, Frankfurt am Main, 1983).

unless, of course, one assumes that it is already grounded and so can by itself provide reasons for action; but, insofar as this ground is not shown to be unavoidable or necessary in the relevant (ought-related) sense, it is in need of some further ground; as a result, the claim made by the constitutive strategy hides a normative regress. This problem, as Roversi acknowledges, may well not be a conclusive argument against constitutivism, but it is certainly one still in need of a satisfactory treatment.

Finally, Sylvie Delacroix's chapter is likewise critical of the constitutivist enterprise. Delacroix aims at tracing a genealogy of legal normativity; namely, it does not focus on the impact of this specific kind of normativity and its relations with other forms of normativity, but is rather concerned with the conditions of possibility of legal normativity. From this perspective, legal normativity is explained by referring to the network of social and cultural practices that make it the case that the law has a claim on our action and judgement. This means that any search for one principle from which the normativity of law stems is illusory. In fact, a genealogical enquiry can show that diverse processes, not mutually reducible or open to be reconstructed as one, lie at the origin of the normative force of law. This awareness has the potential of downplaying the perceived legitimacy of the law as a normative phenomenon: by challenging the common perception that normativity is solidly grounded on some element the binding force of which is taken for granted (such as morality, universal truths, or other) the genealogic account departs from the classical models, such as the natural law theory, as well as the constitutivist model. In both cases, we assist in some attempt to establish the ultimate grounding of the normativity of law and this is exactly the endeavour that genealogy condemns as futile and illusory. The disenchanted view underpinning Delacroix's genealogical account leads her to the thesis that the normativity of law emerges out of the desires and aspirations of the members of the law-governed community. As a result, from this perspective, the normativity of law is derivative from the capacity of legal practice to serve a social project that in its day-to-day interactions those who live within a social setting contribute to shape, bring about, and constantly revise. The origin of the normativity of law, thus, is neither mysterious nor puzzling, for it ultimately presents a social nature. This way Delacroix lays the basis for making sense of the dual character of law that still puzzles most comprehensive legal theories, namely, law's social existence and its justification. For the law has a dual character that escapes most traditional legal theories: on the one hand, it presents a factual side to the extent that it is regarded as an institutional arrangement; on the other, the law possesses an ideal aspect that refers to the claim made by those who act in law's name to exercise a legitimate form of authority. Delacroix's account, which depicts the two basic elements of legality as conceptually interlinked and interdependent, seems to have the resources to explore, and make sense of, the otherwise problematic combination of sociality and value that lies at the foundation of law.

We would like to thank the board of directors of UCSIA (University Centre Saint-Ignatius Antwerp) for organising, funding and hosting the conference 'The

Normative Dimension of Law' on the 3 and 4 June 2009 at the University of Antwerp, during which the majority of the papers were presented. The members of the advisory academic panel of the same organisation provided us with valuable suggestions throughout the organisation of the event, which made our task especially rewarding. Further, we are grateful to the many friends and colleagues who have contributed to this volume and, with their helpful remarks and comments, have both made possible and improved the overall work. In particular, we thank Triantafyllos Gouvas most warmly for his assistance and constructive attitude during the editing of this volume. Mel Hamill at Hart Publishing, in her effortless manner, has turned once again the huge task of production into fun.

Finally, we acknowledge the permission of Princeton University Press and Harvard University Press to reprint chapter five and portions of chapter one respectively.

Part I

Law, Normativity and Plans

1

Planning Agency and the Law

SCOTT SHAPIRO

I HOW TO DO THINGS WITH PLANS

A A Fresh Start

FROM CHILDHOOD ON, we are taught that there is a crucial difference between what others think is right or wrong and what *is* right or wrong. Just because everyone does it does not mean that we should do it. We are repeatedly told that the rules of ethical behaviour apply to us regardless of whether other people accept them as well.

But in the realm of law, the legal positivist claims, this admonition is out of place. What is *legally* right or wrong *does* depend on other people and certain other people in particular. According to HLA Hart, if judges accept a rule requiring you to jump off the proverbial bridge, then it is legally wrong for you *not* to plunge into the icy waters below.

This claim follows from the positivist's picture of morality and law as distinct domains with correspondingly distinct ground rules. According to this picture, the proper way to establish the existence of moral rules is to engage in substantive moral argument. It is never enough simply to say: 'That's what we do round here'. While a convention may of course be morally relevant, it is because some moral fact ultimately deems it to be so. In the case of law, on the other hand, rules must satisfy the specific criteria for legal validity, and these criteria can only be discovered through empirical observations of the relevant legal communities. To divine the set of legally valid rules, in other words, one must know what legal officials think, intend, claim and do. For the legal positivist, it is simply irrelevant to point out that these criteria of validity are morally illegitimate, or that they sanction undesirable rules. Regardless of the merits, the law is just what certain people think, intend, claim and do around here.

Here I want to present an argument that, I believe, captures the power of the positivistic picture of law while also showing that there is another realm whose norms can only be discovered through social, not moral, observation, namely, the realm of *planning*. The proper way to establish the existence of plans, as I argue below, is simply to point to the fact of their adoption and acceptance. Whether I have a plan to go to the store today, or we have a plan to cook dinner together tonight, depends not on the desirability of these plans, but simply on whether we have in fact adopted – and not yet rejected – them. In other words, positivism is trivially and uncontroversially true in the case of plans: the existence of a plan is one thing, its merits or demerits quite another.

As I hope will become clear in what follows, my purpose here is not to draw an analogy between laws and plans, but to flesh out an implication. The existence conditions for law are the same as those for plans because the fundamental rules of legal systems *are* plans. Their function is to structure legal activity so that participants can work together and thereby achieve goods and realise values that would otherwise be unattainable. For that reason, the existence of legal authority can only be determined *sociologically*: the question of whether a body has legal power is never one of its moral legitimacy; it is a question of whether the relevant officials of that system accept a plan that authorises and requires deference to that body.

I am going to argue here that understanding fundamental laws as plans not only vindicates the positivist conception of law, but provides a compelling solution to our earlier question about how legal authority is possible. For the picture that emerges is one in which the creation and persistence of the fundamental rules of law is grounded in the authority that all individuals possess to adopt plans. As I attempt to show, this power is not conferred on us by morality. On the contrary, it follows from the fact that we are planning creatures. As the philosopher Michael Bratman has shown in his groundbreaking work on intention and action, human beings have a special kind of psychology: we not only have desires to achieve complex ends, but we also have the capacity to settle on such goals and to organise our behaviour over time and between persons to attain them.

Building on Bratman's insights, I want to show that understanding the law entails understanding our special psychology and the norms of rationality that regulate its proper functioning. For that reason, I am going to spend a significant amount of time describing the activity of planning, the structure of plans, the motivation for creating plans and the rationality constraints that attend this activity. I will begin by constructing simple hypotheticals involving one person planning his own actions and then move on to more complicated examples, such as group planning in hierarchical and non-hierarchical contexts among both small and large numbers of people.

One of my main goals in this chapter is to show that planning is a surprisingly diverse activity. Not only can it be carried out in very different ways, but it comprises many distinct stages. In fact, multiple individuals can engage in the planning process at the same time: one person can formulate a plan, another can adopt it, a third can apply the plan and the fourth can enforce it. Plans are also complex entities: they have a rich structure and assume diverse forms. As our hypotheticals will illustrate, planners are able to combine different kinds of plans to construct new and sophisticated technologies of planning, which enable participants in shared activities to navigate complex, contentious and arbitrary environments.

In the next chapter, I want to develop my central argument that legal activity is best understood as social planning and that legal rules themselves constitute *plans*, or *plan-like* norms. I realise that this claim is not self-evidently true and the relationship between legality and planning is not yet apparent. But as the nature of planning becomes more explicit, and our examples become more complex, the connection between the two phenomena will become clearer. Or at least that is the plan.

B Individual Planning

The Partiality of Plans

I am sitting at my desk in my office and thinking about what to do for dinner tonight. Should I eat out or cook dinner at home? Since I feel a bit guilty about having frequented restaurants so often lately, I decide on the latter option. I now have a plan – namely, to cook dinner at home tonight. Admittedly, it is not much of a plan, because I have no food at home to cook. So the question with which I started – where to eat? – has been replaced with a new query – where should I get food to cook?

I respond to this new query by forming an intention to buy the food from a supermarket. And so I now have two plans: one to cook dinner tonight and one to buy food at the supermarket. These plans are clearly related to one another. Buying food at the supermarket is a means to cooking dinner at home tonight. When one plan specifies a means for accomplishing, or a way of realising, the end fixed by another plan, we will say that it is a 'sub-plan' of the second. Thus, the plan to buy food at the supermarket is a sub-plan of the initial plan to cook dinner tonight.

Of course, by adopting these two plans, I have also created a third plan, namely, the plan to cook dinner *by* buying food at the supermarket. This larger plan (we might say) has two parts to it: the first is the plan to cook dinner tonight and the second is the plan to buy food for dinner at the supermarket. These parts are related as means to end: the second part is a sub-plan of the first.

As Michael Bratman has shown, planning typically involves the creation of these larger plans.[1] When I initially form my intention to cook dinner tonight, my plan simply identifies my end goal. But if my plan is going to work – that is, if it is to organise my behaviour so that I may attain the goal I set for myself – I have to specify the means as well. I must decide which meal to make, what kind of food to buy, where and when to buy it, whether to make enough for leftovers, which knife to use when preparing the food, and so on.

Bratman notes that these larger plans are typically partial. They begin as empty shells and, as more details are added, they become more comprehensive and useful. Plans are almost never exhaustive because there is rarely a need for a full

[1] M Bratman, *Intention, Plans and Practical Reason* (Cambridge, MA, Harvard University Press, 1987) 28–30.

specification of every step necessary to achieve a goal. My plan to cook dinner tonight will not specify the correct way to hold the knife when I cut the food because I have the skills necessary to accomplish the task without deliberation or reflection.

As plans are filled in, they thus naturally assume a nested structure. My plan to make dinner tonight specifies the overall goal I wish to achieve. My plan to buy food from a supermarket, as we mentioned, is a sub-plan of the overall plan of making dinner. My intention to buy chicken at the supermarket after work is, in turn, a sub-plan of the plan to buy food at the supermarket and, thus, a sub-sub-plan of the overall plan to cook dinner tonight.

The nested structure of plans explains how past deliberation shapes present planning. When constructing my plan, I take my prior decisions about means and ends as given. These plans and sub-plans are settled and not up for reconsideration. Rather, my present deliberation is confined solely to those options that are not ruled out by past decisions. If I have decided to go to Stop & Shop to buy food, I figure out how to get there, not whether it might be better to go to Pathmark instead.

As Bratman points out, plans not only organise our behaviour, they also organise our thinking about how to organise our behaviour.[2] The planner sets ends to be achieved and determines which means are best suited to achieve those ends. Once selected, these means are treated as new ends and lead the planner to determine which new means ought to be adopted. By fleshing out plans in this manner, the planner ensures that, according to his beliefs, he will perform all the necessary actions in the right sequence and thus realise the overall ends of the plan.

Planning Ahead

Clearly, if we did not seek to achieve complex ends, there would be no need to engage in planning about the future. Non-human animals have little or no use for plans, whether because they do not have goals that require significant degrees of behavioural organisation or because they do but are hard-wired with the proper instincts to fulfil them. It is plausible to suppose that dogs, cats and mice act purposely insofar as they have desires and that they act on those desires in light of their beliefs. But they probably do not *plan* since they lack both the need and capacity to do so.

We are planning creatures in part because we have desires for many ends that demand substantial coordination. But there is another aspect of our psychology that compels us to planning, namely, that our rationality is limited. If we were like chess computers, able to look ahead millions of moves on each turn and choose the best play among the myriad alternatives, we might have little use for planning. Since we are not, however, mentally omnipotent and rational deliberation is costly, we must conserve our energies. I cannot spend every second of the day thinking about what to do and reviewing every one of my past judgements or I

[2] ibid 32–35.

would never get anything done. It is generally far more efficient to decide on a course of action beforehand and follow it when the time for action arrives.

Planning ahead is not, however, a solely economising measure; we often plan out of paternalistic concerns for our future selves. Deliberation is a risky endeavour. If I were to engage in perpetual reasoning about what I ought to do, I would almost certainly find myself in a poor state to make decisions. I would lack the composure, energy and will either to think through all of the possibilities or to resist temptation. Making up my mind well in advance allows me to pick a good occasion for reflection, provides ample time to puzzle things out and saves me from choosing a course of action deemed less than ideal from my current perspective.

We have good reason, therefore, to be planners: planning guides and organises our behaviour over time, enabling us to achieve ends that we might not be able to achieve otherwise. As Bratman has argued, this pragmatic rationale for planning suggests that the activity is subject to several different norms of rationality.[3] Suppose that having decided to make dinner at home tonight, I do not give that decision any more thought. I do not contemplate how I am going to pull off this feat; eg where to get the food, what to eat, when to cook and so on. These omissions would be irrational because I would not be able to achieve the end that I set for myself. I cannot just *cook dinner*. Cooking dinner is not a simple action like raising my arm – it is a multistep process, requiring that I make preparations, string numerous actions together and perform them in the proper order.

When we set ends for ourselves, rationality thus demands that we flesh out our plans. Of course, we need not settle all outstanding issues at once. While I should soon decide when to buy the food for dinner, I can probably wait until I arrive at the supermarket to decide what to make and how much to cook. And I certainly can wait until I get to the kitchen before settling on which knife to use. Indeed, there is a pragmatic argument for leaving certain aspects of plans open until the time for action nears. Settling on a course of conduct far ahead of time in the absence of complete information is a risky thing to do. By leaving our plans for future actions somewhat sketchy, we provide the measure of flexibility necessary to enable us to fill in the details as our visibility substantially improves.

Strictly speaking, rationality does not demand that the planners formulate courses of action *themselves*. Others may tailor the means and communicate the plan to the person committed to the end in question. My foodie friend may tell me what food to buy and how to cook it. Rationality does not forbid taking instruction from others; indeed, it requires it when they are more reliable or when doing so is economical.

[3] See ibid 30–32. It should be noted that the pragmatic justification for the requirements of rationality, as well as the content of the requirements themselves, set out in the text is the subject of philosophical controversy. For alternative accounts, see J Broome, 'Normative Requirements' (1999) 12 *Ratio* 398; RJ Wallace, 'Normativity, Commitment, and Instrumental Reason' (2001) 1 *Philosophers' Imprint* 1 and K Setiya, 'Cognitivism about Instrumental Reason' (2007) 117 Ethics 649. For Bratman's rejoinder, see his 'Intention, Belief, Practical, Theoretical' in S Robertson (ed), *Spheres of Reason: New Essays in the Philosophy of Normativity* (Oxford, Oxford University Press, 2009) 29–61 and 'Intention, Belief and Instrumental Rationality' in D Sobel and S Wall (eds), *Reasons for Action* (Cambridge, Cambridge University Press, 2009) 13–36 .

When we say that planners are rationally obligated to 'fill in' their plans, we mean they are required to *adopt* the means to their ends, not that they are required to figure out what those means are themselves.

Rationality not only demands that we fill in our plans over time; it also counsels us to settle on plans of actions which are internally consistent and consistent with each other. In this respect, plans are different from desires. Desires typically conflict, but plans must not. There is nothing irrational about wanting to lose weight and wanting to have dessert, but it is incoherent to go on a no-dessert diet and, at the same time, order dessert. In the same way, one's plans must be consistent with one's beliefs about the world. One should not adopt a plan that one believes cannot successfully be carried out. Again, these consistency demands are supported by the pragmatic rationale for planning: consistency within plans is necessary if we are to achieve the ends of the plan; consistency between plans is necessary if we are to achieve the ends of all our plans; and consistency with one's beliefs ensures that the plans we have adopted can be achieved in the world in which we find ourselves.

Finally, if planning is to compensate for our limited cognitive capacities and reduce deliberation costs, our plans must be fairly stable, which is to say that they must be reasonably resistant to reconsideration. Suppose on my way home from the office I ask myself: 'Should I eat out or at home?'. After thinking about the issue, and weighing the ease of dining out against the economy of eating in, I settle on the same option I chose earlier, namely, cooking dinner at home. My reconsideration of the issue of where to eat, therefore, rendered my prior decision moot. I did not derive any benefit from my earlier planning, for I ended up engaging in the same thought processes that I followed earlier.

To be sure, choosing a plan does not set it in stone. Reconsideration is rational when, but only when, there is good enough reason to do so. If I find out, for example, that the power is off at home, then I *should* of course reconsider my earlier decision. If nothing much has changed, however, it would be irrational to up-end my earlier judgement. It would defeat the purpose of having plans if I were to review their wisdom without an otherwise compelling reason to do so.

Top-Down versus Bottom-Up Planning

As we saw in the last section, planning never occurs in a vacuum. Past decisions form a framework that constrains and guides present deliberation. When a rational planner contemplates whether to pursue a certain end, she attempts to determine whether the goal can be achieved in a manner compatible with this framework of prior decision-making.

In fleshing out her plans, the planner may pursue one of two options: 'top-down' or 'bottom-up' planning. In instances of top-down planning, the planner starts with the overall action to achieve – cook dinner – and breaks it up into a few major tasks – buy food, cook food, clean up. She then refines each major task into its component parts – buy food → drive to store, pick up food, buy food, load car and drive home. The planner continues this process of refinement at each step until she reaches a point at which the relevant actions can be accomplished without further planning – get in car, start car, make right at State Street, etc.

In cases of bottom-up planning, the planner starts with a vague sense of the goals to be achieved – I want to eat some soup for dinner – and proceeds to think through the lower-level tasks in great detail – make the stock → fill pot with water, throw in carrots, celery, onions and chicken, skim when boils, simmer for one hour. Any decision to carry out a simple task in a certain way constrains how other simple tasks will be carried out – making chicken stock requires going to a market that sells chickens. Once other basic tasks are planned, she attempts to combine them to see whether they fit together. They might fail to connect up for two reasons: either they are inconsistent with each other – it may not be possible to get to Safeway and cook the soup in the available time – or they are consistent, but insufficient, to accomplish any higher-level task – something more must be added to the stock to make soup. In the first case, consistency must be restored through fiddling with one or both of the conflicting tasks – go to Pathmark instead. In the second case, new lower-level tasks must be added to achieve the necessary effect – add rice to stock. Once the sub-plans are adjusted, the new higher-level tasks are then combined to see whether they fit together: is there enough time to make the rice?; is soup enough for dinner?. The process of planning ends when all the tasks settled on are sufficient to achieve the ultimate goal.

Bottom-up planning is especially useful when the planner is unsure which tasks she must undertake or how they all will hang together. In such cases, she cannot start from her main aim and methodically work her way down the planning tree because she lacks an abstract appreciation of how the various tasks connect up. By starting with lower-level tasks whose contours she understands, her detailed planning of one part of the project constrains how the closely-related tasks must be performed. She can proceed to fill in adjacent slots, moving slowly across and up the planning hierarchy and eventually establishing a coherent and complete plan of action.

The downside of bottom-up planning is that the ordering of tasks is not informed by a full sense of the overall structure of the activity. Too much attention to low-level detail may unwittingly cause the planner to lose the forest for the trees and result in plans that are riddled with inconsistencies, gaps and redundancies. By contrast, if the functional shape of the project is well-understood, a top-down approach is usually more appropriate. To be sure, planning in real-life usually combines both elements of top-down and bottom-up planning, with the best mix determined by how well the planner understands the nature of the activity she intends to perform.

Applying Plans

There would be little point in making plans if we did not use them to guide our conduct. If my cooking plan is to be useful to me, it is not enough to formulate and adopt it: it must be applied as well.

As I employ the term, to 'apply' a plan means to use it to guide or evaluate conduct. A plan is applied prospectively when it is used to determine which actions are required, permitted or authorised in the circumstances; a plan is applied retrospectively when it is employed to assess whether an action conformed, or failed to conform, to the plan in question. A note of caution: sometimes, when we say that we are 'applying' a plan, we mean that we are carrying it out. Thus, I apply my chicken-on-sale plan when I actually buy the chicken because it is on sale. When I speak of 'applying' plans, however, I will be referring to the use of plans to guide or evaluate action, reserving 'carrying out' for the process of following through on them.

Applying a plan is a three-step process. The plan-applier must determine: (1) the content of the plan; (2) the context of its application; and (3) how to conform to the plan in that context. Thus, if I apply my plan during the afternoon, I must decide what that plan is – ie 'to cook dinner tonight' – , what the world is like – eg 'do I have enough food to cook?' – and what I should do to execute the plan at that point – ie 'must head out soon to buy food'. The planner might find out that the plan is not applicable to a particular situation, in which case there is nothing that the plan requires, permits or authorises the subject to do or not to do.

Just as someone need not formulate a plan she adopts, she need not apply it herself either. If I ask the butcher for a pot roast at the supermarket, my friend might say to me: 'Wait, I thought you told me that you were going to buy the chicken if it's on sale, and look, it is on sale'. My friend, thus, applied my plan for me.

Regardless of who applies the plan, rationality requires that the plan-adopter make sure that *someone* does. To adopt a plan and not use it, or use it incorrectly, is irrational. In other words, a planner is subject to criticism when she forgets that she adopted a certain plan, cannot figure out the content of the plan, does not bother to find out what the world is like, fails to use her beliefs to determine the application of the plan, uses these beliefs incorrectly, or simply does not carry out the plan that she believes applies.

In order to determine the content of the plan, the planner must be careful not to engage in deliberation about its merits. As we have seen, the value of a plan is that it does the thinking for us. If, in order to determine the content of my cooking plan, I had to deliberate about whether I should cook dinner tonight, then adopting my plan would have been useless. Plans cannot do the thinking for us if, in order to discover their counsel, we are required to repeat the same sort of reasoning.[4]

[4] Similarly, it follows that when a planner recognises that her plan applies, she should not deliberate about the merits of the case at hand. The plan is supposed to settle the matter of whether she should act in a certain way and, thus, to deliberate before execution undermines the fundamental purpose of the plan. The planner rationally executes the plan because she adopted it and it applies and for no other reason.

Plans and Norms

Let me end this section on individual planning by saying a few words about what I mean by the term 'plan'. By a 'plan', I am not referring to the mental state of 'having a plan'. Intentions are not plans, but rather take plans as their objects. For my purposes, plans are abstract propositional entities that require, permit or authorise agents to act, or not act, in certain ways under certain conditions.

A norm can be characterised as an abstract object that functions as a guide for conduct and a standard for evaluation. In keeping with this characterisation, plans too are norms. They are guides for conduct, insofar as their function is to pick out courses of action that are required, permitted or authorised under certain circumstances. They are also standards for evaluation, insofar as they are supposed to be used as measures of correct conduct, if not by others then at least by the subjects of the plans themselves.

When a person adopts a personal plan, she thus places herself under the governance of a norm. This power of self-governance is conferred on her by the principles of instrumental rationality. Planning creatures, in other words, have the rational authority to subject themselves to norms. Indeed, this authority explains the efficacy of planning. Planning psychology is unique not only because it enables planners to form mental states that control future conduct, but insofar as it enables them to recognise that the formation of these states generates rational pressure to act accordingly. Thus, when an individual adopts a self-governing plan, the disposition to follow through is not akin to a brute reflex; it is instead mediated by the recognition that the plan is a justified standard of conduct and imposes a rational requirement to carry it out.

While all plans are norms, not all norms are plans. The laws of logic and the principles of morality, for example, are norms but they are not usually considered plans. Plans are 'positive' entities – they are created via adoption and sustained through acceptance. By contrast, logical and moral norms exist simply by virtue of their ultimate validity. They are not created by anyone. Plans are also typically partial norms which are supposed to be fleshed out over time, whereas it makes no sense to talk about incrementally developing the laws of logic or morality.

Plans are also purposive entities. They are norms that are not only created, but are created *to be norms*. I adopted a plan to cook dinner tonight precisely so that it would guide my conduct in the direction of cooking dinner. Customary norms, on the other hand, may exist even though they were not created in order to be used in decision-making. The custom to eat turkey on Thanksgiving, for example, may have arisen spontaneously and not for the purpose of getting people to choose to eat turkey on Thanksgiving.

In general, we can say that a norm is a plan as long as it was created by a process that is supposed to create norms. In the case of individual planning, the process is the psychological activity of intending. In institutional contexts, however, as we will see in Part II of this chapter, a plan may be created even though the one who adopted it did not intend to create a norm. As long as the institutionally prescribed procedure is followed, he will be acting in accordance with a process that is supposed to create norms and will therefore be capable of adopting a plan.

While all plans are positive purposive norms, not all positive purposive norms are plans. Threats, requests and advice are created by human action, and are created to guide action, but they are not typically structured norms: unlike plans, they are not characteristically partial, composite or nested. More importantly, these norms do not aim to guide conduct by settling questions about how to act. Threats, requests and advice merely purport to be one factor among many to be considered. It shows no irrationality or disrespect to deliberate about whether to capitulate to a threat, grant a request or accept advice. By contrast, when one has adopted a plan, for oneself or for another person, the plan is supposed to preempt further deliberations about its merits.

Finally, a norm is a plan only if it is created by a process which disposes the subjects of a norm to follow it. If I plan to cook dinner tonight, I will be disposed to cook dinner tonight. This does not entail that I *will* cook dinner, only that under normal conditions I will. It follows then that decisions that do not instill dispositions in their subjects to comply do not generate plans. If a madman 'plans' to withdraw the United States Army from Iraq, no withdrawal plan exists because the madman's decisions have absolutely no effect on troop movements.

To conclude, a plan is a special kind of norm: first, it has a typical structure, namely, it is partial, composite and nested; secondly, it is created by a certain kind of process, namely, one that is incremental, purposive and disposes subjects to comply with the norms created.

C Planning for Small-Scale Shared Activities

My Part and Your Part

Having decided that I will cook dinner at home, it occurs to me that it would be fun to cook with someone else. I therefore call up my friend, Henry, invite him over to cook together, and he agrees. We now have a plan: that is, to cook dinner together tonight.

Of course, this plan won't be of much use to us unless we fill it in. But here matters become complicated. Whereas I was previously able to resolve all issues regarding cooking by myself, I must now consult Henry, at least with respect to the major tasks. It would be unfair, let alone rude, to decide unilaterally what we are going to eat, when we should start cooking, and so on. In addition, we have a new set of questions that must be answered, such as who should get the food, who should cook which part of the meal, who should clean up, and so on. Planning for two involves organising behaviour not only across time but between persons as well.

Let's say that Henry and I decide to cook fish and make a salad. I opt to get the fish and he opts to get the ingredients for the salad. How many plans do we now have – or, as I will sometimes say, how many plans do we now *share*? Again, the answer depends. In one sense, we have adopted five plans: we cook dinner together tonight; we cook fish together tonight; we make a salad together tonight; I get the fish before dinner; you get the salad ingredients before dinner.

In another sense, we share only one plan, namely, the plan to cook dinner together tonight. Cooking fish and making salad together are sub-plans of the overall plan of cooking dinner together. We cook dinner together *by* cooking fish and making salad together. Likewise, my purchasing the fish before dinner is a sub-plan of our cooking fish together tonight, Henry's procuring the salad ingredients before dinner is a sub-plan of our making salad together, and each is a sub-sub-plan of the overall plan of cooking together tonight.

As the foregoing suggests, the structure of shared plans is similar to that of individual plans. Shared plans too are typically partial: they are developed over time, beginning with a settling of ends and a progressive divvying up of steps each member is to take. Shared plans are also normally composite: they have parts which are themselves plans. Our plan to cook dinner, for example, includes plans to buy and cook the food. Finally, shared plans are usually nested: they identify the overall end to be achieved by the group and specify in their sub-plans the parts that everyone is to take. When fleshing out how we are to cook dinner together, we take our cooking together as settled and deliberate only about which courses of action each of us should take so that our combined activity adds up to tonight's dinner.

Planning for the Group

Although planning for a group can be a complicated affair, especially when it is also performed *by* a group, the benefits of planning normally outweigh the costs. As with individual planning, participants in a group activity will not always be able to ponder the optimality of their next move. Since Henry and I are not hi-tech deliberation machines, programmed for precisely this purpose, we need to map out some of our actions beforehand so that when the time for execution arrives we can each consult our respective parts of the shared plan and proceed accordingly.

There are, nonetheless, reasons to plan for the group which are quite independent of these benefits of planning ahead. To see what they are, let us begin by considering the advantages of acting together. According to David Hume:

> When every individual person labours a-part, and only for himself, his force is too small to execute any considerable work; his labour being employ'd in supplying all his different necessities, he never attains a perfection in any particular art; and as his force and success are not at all times equal, the least failure in either of these particulars must be attended with inevitable ruin and misery.[5]

[5] David Hume, *A Treatise of Human Nature* in DF Norton and MJ Norton (eds), *A Treatise of Human Nature* (Oxford, Oxford University Press, 2000, (1739)) Pt II, section II.

As Hume points out, individual effort is often too feeble, amateurish and/or risky to accomplish many of the ends we wish to accomplish – think of building a house all by yourself. By pooling efforts in an orderly fashion, we are able to supplement our energies, engage in specialisation and minimise the risk of failure.

In a shared activity, then, the actions of the participants must be coordinated with one another in order to benefit from the pooling of talent. The utility of any course of action cannot be evaluated in isolation but only as part of a total vector of concerted effort. Rational deliberation in a shared activity is, therefore, inherently strategic: what one person ought to do depends on what others will do.

We can imagine two basic ways in which participants to a shared activity might attempt to order their affairs. The first way is completely improvised: at each moment, each person assesses the various options open to them based on their predictions about how the others will act and chooses the option that they judge to be best. When an activity is completely improvised, no guidance is provided to any participant; each is left to their own deliberative devices.

While this kind of improvisation is effective in many contexts, such as leisurely walks, doubles tennis and jazz riffs, there are a number of reasons why it cannot be a universal method for coordinating shared activity. First, participants might not always be able to trust one another to make the right decisions: some participants might be less informed and mistakenly judge certain choices to be the best; some might have all the necessary information, but become overwhelmed at the moment of choice and pick the wrong option; or some might have different preferences and, as a result, choose courses of conduct that work at cross purposes. Without some method for correcting or guiding behaviour, information asymmetries, cognitive incapacities and divergent preferences threaten to plunge joint ventures into chaos.

Secondly, improvisation of this kind might also fail to coordinate behaviour due to problems of predictability. Since rational deliberation in shared activities is strategic, improvisers must be able to predict what their fellow improvisers will choose. Predictions, however, may be hard to come by. Participants cannot assume that others will do what they want them to do because group members might have different wants. Although participants might be able to predict behaviour if they knew what everyone believes and desires, they will not typically have that sort of information, and even if they did, it might be very time-consuming to figure out what they will do by calculating what it would sensible for them to do given everything they believe and want.

The problems of predictability are especially acute when the group faces a coordination problem. Recall that in these strategic situations, the solutions to the games are arbitrary. When solutions are arbitrary, each player's preferences are determined exclusively by their expectations of what the other players will do. For example, I may not care whether I get the fish and Henry the salad ingredients or he gets the fish and I the salad ingredients. He may be similarly indifferent. The right strategy for each of us, therefore, depends entirely on which strategy the other chooses. Unless we have some basis for predicting each other's choices, our attempt to coordinate our actions is likely to be thwarted.

Unconstrained improvisation is not a robust method for coordinating shared activities because it is appropriate only when there is a very high degree of trust and predictability among participants. When either breaks down, some form of advanced planning will be the preferred strategy. Thus, if I have worries about Henry's abilities or preferences, I should raise them with him prior to action; for if I can convince him that it would be best for him to choose one option and me another, or bargain to some form of compromise, we can settle on the same joint strategy and implement a good plan when the time for action rolls around.

Planning in the context of shared activities, thus, serves a crucial control function. It enables some participants to channel the behaviour of others in directions that they judge to be desirable. The need to guide the behaviour of the other members will be pressing whenever members have jaundiced attitudes toward each other's intelligence, character or knowledge, or when their preferences significantly diverge. In such circumstances, participants cannot simply assume that others will be able to coordinate their behaviour properly. They must use plans to direct their fellow participants to act in the way that they want them to or believe they should.

Planning in group contexts also alleviates problems of predictability. The adoption of shared plans by members of the group obviates the need for detailed knowledge about everyone's beliefs and desires. I don't have to *know* that Henry wants to choose some option in order to be able to expect that he will choose it. Notice here that the function of planning is not to improve choices, but rather to render them legible to others. By having a common blueprint that each of us accepts, each of us can reasonably forecast that the others will do their part. In these circumstances, it is better to settle for a decent plan than to hope for the best solution.

Complex, Contentious, Arbitrary

As we have seen, group planning is unnecessary for shared activities when it seems clear that the members of the group, if left to their own devices, will end up coordinating their behaviour effectively. However, if participants harbour reasonable worries that order will not appear extemporaneously, or that it will be significantly defective, then they ought to formulate and adopt shared plans. Such fears will naturally arise in three kinds of scenarios: when the activities to be shared are complex, contentious or possess arbitrary solutions.

In the absence of guidance, *complex* activities demand significant knowledge and skill, tax cognitive capacities, and consume precious intellectual resources. Completely improvised attempts at coordination are thus bound to lead participants to distrust their own judgements or those of their fellow group members. Plans aim to resolve these doubts and disagreements by greatly simplifying the decision-making procedure. Instead of having to arrive at an all-things-considered judgement about what to do, participants can focus on the same few variables and, as a result, make better choices, or at least ones that cohere well with those of others.

In the case of *contentious* activities, there is a threat that, without planning, some participants will choose poorly, or worse, act at cross-purposes. The contentiousness of an activity might stem from its complexity, or from the simple fact that the members of the group have different preferences or values. In either case, it is crucial that potential conflicts be identified and resolved ahead of time. The function of planning here is to settle disputes correctly and definitively before mistakes are made and become irreversible.

Finally, the *arbitrariness* of many aspects of shared activities generates coordination problems which render the behaviour of the other participants difficult, if not impossible, to predict. Plans pick one solution out of a multiplicity of options, enabling the group to converge on that solution and hence to coordinate its actions successfully.

To be sure, a shared activity may be *so* complex that planners may be unable to map out a sequence of events that will lead to the desired outcome. A standard critique of planned economies, for example, is that allocation decisions are so intricate that no central body can gather all the necessary information, process it correctly and optimally direct production and consumption.[6] This does not, however, mean that planning plays no role in market economies. As I will show in the next chapter, the rules of property, contract and tort can be understood as general plans whose function is to create the conditions favourable for optimal order to emerge spontaneously. Rather than acting as visible hands directly guiding economic decisions, they provide market actors with the facilities to carry out their own profit-maximising plans so that overall economic efficiency will be maximised in the process.

Similarly, if a shared activity is too contentious, participants will be unable to agree on a common plan to order their affairs. Imagine, for example, trying to use the political process to distribute food, shelter, education, childcare, sneakers, books, shampoo, laptops, iPods, DVDs, beer, candy bars, paper clips, and so on. Aside from being impossibly complicated, questions about optimal levels of production and fair distribution are simply too contentious to be resolved in a collective manner. The plans that structure market interactions, on the other hand, allow individuals who fundamentally disagree with one another to place values on goods and services and to engage in mutually advantageous trades. The benefits that are unavailable through collective action can thus be had through the spontaneous interaction of group members following their own conceptions of the good life.[7]

[6] See eg L von Mises, 'Economic Calculation in the Socialist Commonwealth' in F von Hayek (ed), *Collectivist Economic Planning: Critical Studies on the Possibilities of Socialism* (London, Routledge, 1935) 87–130; this article appeared originally under the title 'Die Wirtschaftsrechnung im sozialistischen Gemeinwesen' (1920) 47 *Archiv für Sozialwissenschaft und Sozialpolitik* 86; F von Hayek, *Individualism and Economic Order: Essays* (Chicago, IL, University of Chicago Press, 1948) chs 7–9.

[7] See eg J Raz, *The Morality of Freedom* (Oxford, Oxford University Press, 1986); J Coleman, *Risks and Wrongs* (Cambridge, Cambridge University Press, 1992) 62–64.

D Shared Plans and Shared Agency

In the last section, we saw why a group would want to converge on a common plan when engaged in a shared activity. We said that the value of planning stems not only from its ability to lower deliberation costs and compensate for cognitive incapacities, but also from its power to coordinate the participants' behaviour. Insofar as the utility of an individual action is a function of the choices made by other participants, it is imperative that the behaviour of the group members be channelled in the right direction and made predictable to one another. In complex, contentious and arbitrary environments, however, doubts and disagreements about the best way to proceed thwart the prospect of coordination through complete improvisation. Shared plans resolve these doubts and disagreements, harnessing and focusing the individual efforts of the participants so that they may accomplish together what they could not achieve separately.

Having argued for the importance of plans in joint ventures, we might ask how exactly groups have or share plans. For example, what makes our plan to cook dinner tonight *our* plan?

Clearly, when we speak of a group sharing a plan, we don't mean that the group has a collective mind which has adopted a plan. A plan is shared by a group only if each of the members of the group in some sense 'accepts' the plan. Henry and I would not share a plan to cook dinner if both us of did not accept the plan to cook dinner.

By the same token, two people cannot be said to share a plan simply because each intends to engage in the same generic activity. I intend to cook dinner tonight and my neighbour intends to cook dinner tonight, but my neighbour and I do not share a plan to cook tonight. To say that a group has a plan to A is to say more – and, as we will soon see, sometimes less – than that each member of the group plans to A.

One reason that Henry and I can be said to share a plan, but my neighbour and I cannot, is that Henry and I designed the plan for ourselves, and not for my neighbour. This suggests that a group shares a plan only if the plan was designed, at least in part, with the group in mind, as a joint activity constituted by our individual actions.

The requirement that shared plans be designed for members of the group does not, however, require that every member play a role in the design of the plan. One group member could take the lead and design the plan for others. In fact, someone who is not even a member of the group could take on this role. My wife could plan for Henry and me to cook dinner tonight for all three of us. Henry and I would then share a plan in part because it would have been designed with Henry and me in mind.

But simply designing a plan for a group is not enough for plan sharing. For even though my neighbour might have designed a plan with me in mind, my neighbour and I do not yet have a plan unless I agree to it. In order for a group to share a plan, then, each member of the group must accept the plan. And 'acceptance' of a shared plan does not mean simply that each member accepts *their* particular part of the plan. To accept a plan entails a commitment to let the other members do their parts as well. Thus, if our plan requires that I cook the fish and Henry make the salad, I am committed to acting in a manner consistent with your making the salad. If you need the big knife to cut the carrots, I must at some point during our cooking let you have it. The acceptance of a plan does not require that the participants actually know the full content of the shared plan; the commitment may simply be to allow others to do their parts *whatever they happen to be.*

Because a plan can be shared only if it is accepted by all participants, shared plans will rarely be complete. I can plan on Henry making the salad without having any commitment to let him use the big knife first. In this case, the shared plan will specify only who makes what, but not who uses the knife first. In fact, there may be no accepted plan apart from the commitment to engage in the joint venture, in which case the shared plan will be virtually blank. 'We cook dinner tonight' can be its only content. Wherever the shared plan is unspecified in this way, participants may be required to design individual sub-plans in order to execute the plan itself. Unless these sub-plans come to be accepted by others, these parts will not be shared and may be contested some time in the future. If these problems are anticipated, prudence dictates that efforts be undertaken to resolve them ahead of time by negotiating and accepting new provisions to the shared plan.

Thus far, we have said that a group shares a plan only if the plan was designed, at least in part, with the group in mind and the group accepts it. It seems nevertheless that one more condition is required. Because a plan that is completely secret cannot be shared, it should be insisted that a shared plan be at least 'publicly accessible', namely, that the participants could discover the parts of the plan that pertain to them and to others with whom they are likely to interact if they wished to do so.

At the same time, it should also be noted that plan sharing does *not* require that members of the group *desire* or *intend* the plan to work. Let's say I want my house painted and hire my two sworn enemies, Dudley and Stephens, to paint my house. I offer US$1,000 dollars to Dudley if Dudley does what I tell him to do. I offer Stephens the same terms. Dudley and Stephens both agree because they need the money. I then tell Dudley to scrape off all the old paint and Stephens to paint a new coat on the scraped surface. Despite the fact that Dudley and Stephens hate me and loathe the idea that my house will be freshly painted, and, as a result, do not intend that the house be painted, they nevertheless share a plan, namely, one that directs Dudley to scrape and Stephens to paint.[8] They

[8] How would we know that Dudley and Stephens did not intend to paint the house? Suppose that halfway through his painting the fresh coat, Stephens announces that he quits. Dudley replies that it doesn't matter to him – after all, he will get his money regardless. If we assume that Dudley is rational, sincere and hasn't changed his mind once he accepted the job, we can infer from this exchange that Dudley never formed a plural intention. This is so because to intend that they paint the house entails a

share a plan because I designed the plan for them, it is accessible to them and they accept it.[9]

Acting Together

In the last section, we tried to explain why Henry and I shared a plan to cook dinner, but my neighbour and I did not. We said that in the former case, the plan to cook dinner was designed with Henry and I in mind, we accepted it and the plan was accessible to us. In the latter case, however, none of these conditions obtained. No plan was designed to enable my neighbour and me to cook dinner together. And since there was no such plan, we could not accept it and it could not be publicly accessible.

Suppose now that Henry and I cook dinner together. One might ask: why is it the case that Henry and I cooked dinner together but my neighbour and I did not? A plausible response is to say that Henry and I acted together because we shared a plan to cook dinner and this plan enabled us to cook dinner, whereas my neighbour and I did not share such a plan. Shared agency – ie acting together – is distinguished from individual agency – ie acting alone – by virtue of the plans of the agents. Even if my neighbour used my kitchen to cook and cooked it at the same time as Henry and I cooked, and even if we cooked the same food, our cooking was distinct from his cooking because we did not share a plan to cook with him and he did not share a plan to cook with us. Shared plans, we might say, bind groups together.

Shared plans are constitutive of shared agency because they explain how groups are able to engage in the activity.[10] By appealing to them, group members are relieved, at least partially, from deliberating about proper action. Shared plans do the thinking for the group, enabling participants to know what they should do and what others will do. They not only coordinate the behaviour of each participant,

rational commitment on the part of Dudley to the joint activity of their painting the house. This commitment, if present in a rational participant, must express itself in some form of action designed to result in their painting of the house. Dudley might pick up the brush and paint the house himself, or notify me of Stephens' departure, or try to convince Stephens that he shouldn't leave. The fact that Dudley does nothing indicates that he is not so committed. He has the singular intention to do as I say and, hence, to scrape the paint off the house, but not the plural intention that *they* paint the house. Yet, despite the fact that Dudley is not so committed to the joint activity, it will be true that they share a plan if Stephens changes his mind and returns to the job.

[9] Because Dudley and Stephens do not intend to act together, they are not subject to the same rationality constraints as Henry and I are. Dudley must fill in all his sub-plans related to scraping, ensure that they are consistent with all his other sub-plans and not reconsider prior decisions absent a good reason. Dudley must also make sure that he does not totally interfere with Stephens' painting. But beyond that, Dudley need not worry about Stephens' sub-plans. Suppose Stephens does not know how to paint. Dudley is under no rational obligation to help Stephens paint the house; after all, Dudley gets paid regardless of whether Stephens paints. Of course, since I know that Dudley is not rationally obligated to help Stephens, I should give Stephens very detailed instructions on how to paint the house. Unlike them, it is rationally incumbent on me to ensure that the house painters know what they are doing.

[10] The analogy here is to individual agency: just as individual action is individual behaviour explained by an individual plan, shared action is group behaviour explained by a shared plan.

they organise their further planning, directing them to fill in their sub-plans in manner consistent with their own and other participants' sub-plans.

But while sharing a plan is necessary for shared activity, it is clearly not sufficient. For even if Henry and I shared a plan to cook dinner, we will not have cooked dinner together unless we acted on the plan and successfully carried it out. This suggests that a group intentionally acts together only when each member of the group intentionally plays their part in the plan and the activity takes place because they did so. Henry and I cooked together because we played our respective parts in the shared plan and, in so doing, managed to cook dinner.

In addition to sharing a plan, acting on the plan and achieving it, it seems that two more conditions are necessary for a group to act together. First, the existence of the shared plan must be common knowledge. We could hardly be said to have acted together intentionally if it were not plain to each of us that we shared the same plan. Second, members of a group intentionally act together only if they resolve their conflicts in a peaceful and open manner. If Henry and I disagree with one another about who gets to use various pots and knifes and, instead of talking our problems out, we wrestle each other over, or hide, every piece of cooking equipment, our activity would be more competitive than cooperative. Force and fraud not only destroy trust, but they render shared intentional activities impossible as well.

E Reducing Planning Costs

As we have seen, the function of shared plans is to guide and coordinate the behaviour of participants by compensating for cognitive limitations and resolving the doubts and disagreements that naturally arise in strategic contexts. Indeed, shared activities are partially constituted by the acceptance of shared plans precisely because the existence of shared plans explains how agents can work together in complex, contentious or arbitrary environments.

However, many of the same reasons that make shared plans necessary for shared activities also make them costly to produce. If shared plans are needed to regulate behaviour in complex and contentious environments, it is likely that they will be expensive to create ahead of time through deliberation, negotiation or bargaining. Fortunately, it is often possible to reduce these costs. As we will see, policies, customs and hierarchy are three ways in which shared plans can be forged without the members of the group having to engage in the time-consuming process of plan formulation and adoption.

Policies

Having enjoyed our collaboration, Henry and I decide to invite several of our friends over to cook with us. Cooking in this larger group turns out to be even more entertaining and, as a result, we start to make dinner together every week. We call ourselves the 'Cooking Club'.

Initially, we find planning these culinary events the least fun part of the process. Each week we make many phone calls and send numerous emails to club members trying to work out the details of our get-together: the day, time and location of our dinner, what we will make, who is to get what, who is to cook what, and so on.

Slowly, though, we start to learn ways to avoid having to consult each other on every issue. In particular, we begin developing 'policies', ie general plans. For example, instead of selecting the menu each week, we decide instead to follow the recipes set out in the Wednesday edition of the *New York Times*. This general plan radically cuts down on our deliberation and bargaining costs. We simply follow this sub-policy of our shared plan every week and know what each of us should and, hence, will do.

Policies have their downsides, however. While planning every week was tiresome, at least it allowed our choice to suit our then-current tastes. By deciding to follow the recipes in the *New York Times*, we tie our hands to courses of action that may be less than ideal. In this respect, adopting policies involves a trade-off: planners must decide whether the risks of sub-optimal outcomes by following a plan outweigh the costs of repeated deliberation and bargaining.

Custom

Another way planning costs are reduced in ongoing shared activities is through the development of customs. When we began the club, for example, we chose a different person's house to cook the dinner every week. Once we went through the entire club roster, we followed the same pattern again. Eventually, we begin to treat this pattern as the norm. In other words, the group regards the choice of venue for our cooking as settled and, thus, not something normally up for reconsideration. Likewise, because everyone always agreed to make three courses for dinner – appetiser, main course and dessert – we eventually take this pattern as the standard for our dinners and act accordingly.

These customs turn out to be quite beneficial. We do not have to deliberate, negotiate or bargain about these matters in order to apply our shared plan. The customs, in other words, coordinate our behaviour spontaneously. My sub-plans about venue and menu are consistent with my friends' sub-plans about venue and menu because we always fill out our shared plans in the customary way.

It is tempting to say that our past practice has led us to adopt a 'plan' for venues and menus. After all, we regard alternating houses and three-course meals as the right way to cook dinner together. But this temptation should, I believe, be resisted since our customs were not created *for the purpose* of settling questions about proper conduct but instead emerged spontaneously. Each of us independently found it advantageous to act in accordance with the pattern set by past practice and eventually took the matter as settled.

When customary standards arise in a non-purposive manner, I will not refer to them as 'plans', but rather as 'plan-like' norms. They are plan-like because they do what plans normally do: they economise on deliberation costs, compensate for cognitive incapacities and organise behaviour between participants. Like plans, and unlike other norms such as the rules of morality and logic, they are created and sustained by human action. Moreover, they are also typically partial and hierarchical. Our custom to alternate houses does not specify the time that we are supposed to show up at each others' houses. And if we were to fill in this custom by setting a time, this decision would act just as a sub-plan, ie specifying the means by which we carry out the end of alternating houses.

Although some customary standards might not be plans, I will nevertheless consider them as eligible to be part of shared plans. Shared plans, then, need not contain only plans, but may incorporate plan-like norms as well. Customary standards are part of a shared plan just in case they are accepted by the members of the group and are seen as specifying the means by which they are to engage in the shared activity.

Introducing Hierarchy

While adopting policies and developing customs did lessen some of the burden associated with planning our dinners, we were nevertheless forced to engage in extensive deliberation and negotiation each week to set up our club meetings. In order to reduce the costs of planning more radically, we decided to let one person take charge of planning the whole meal for the rest of us. The 'head chef' for the week would direct the 'sous chefs' on what to make and buy, where, when and how to cook the food, and so on. We decided to select our leader randomly: the head chef for the next week is the one who draws the longest straw at the end of each week's dinner.

As expected, most of our planning problems disappeared. When I am head chef, I am able to plan the shared activity without having to worry about winning an argument, striking a deal or forging a consensus. Regardless of whether my friends agree with me, I can get them to do what I think they should do straightaway. That is, I can *order* them to do so. Similarly, when I am the sous chef, I need not enlist the others in filling out our shared plan. I can just sit back and take instruction from the head chef. To be sure, this scheme does not totally relieve me of responsibility for planning. The head chef never completely plans out my actions and hence I am required to fill in the gaps of the shared plan that apply to me.

When the head chef orders a sous chef to perform some action, we might say that he 'adopts a plan' for the sous chef. By issuing the order, the head chef places the sous chef under a norm designed to guide his conduct and to be used as a standard for evaluation. Moreover, the head chef does not intend her order to be treated as one more consideration to be taken into account when the sous chef plans what to do. Rather, she means it to settle the matter in her favour. And because the sous chef accepts the hierarchical relationship, he will adopt the content of the order as his plan and revise his other plans so that they are consistent with the order. He will treat the order as though he formulated and adopted it himself and, as a result, will be disposed to apply and comply with it.

In setting up our hierarchy, therefore, we 'vertically' divide our labour. Instead of everyone deliberating and negotiating with each other, we entrust one person with the responsibility to fashion the shared plan for us. When accepting the role of sous chef, club members thus surrender their exclusive power to plan. Put somewhat more precisely, when accepting their subordinate position, the sous chefs *use* their power to plan to outsource various stages of planning to the head chef. Instead of formulating and adopting their own plans, they accept a plan to defer to someone else's planning. In turn, when one of us assumes the role of head chef, we agree to play the role of planner for other members of the group. Instead of simply planning our own affairs, we plan to formulate and adopt plans for others.

In this context, it is possible to see hierarchy as a major technological advance in behavioural organisation. By dividing labour between those who plan and those who follow through on such plans, group members are no longer limited to arduous deliberations and unpleasant squabbling on the one hand, and precarious attempts at improvisation on the other. When doubts or disagreements arise with respect to the proper way to proceed, superiors can resolve these conflicts quickly and cheaply by issuing orders and thus changing the shared plan that subordinates are required to follow. Leaders are useful, in other words, because they are efficient 'planning mechanisms'. They can simplify complexity, settle controversy and disambiguate arbitrariness without having to engage in costly deliberations, negotiations or bargaining.

Self-Regulating Shared Plans

But hierarchy is not only an efficient tool for producing shared plans; it is often the product of shared plans as well. In the cooking case, for example, part of our shared plan authorises one member of the group to adopt plans for the others. Thus, the reason I become the *head chef* after drawing the longest straw is that our shared plan authorises the longest straw drawer to do the groups' planning.

In a shared activity involving hierarchy, then, shared plans are self-regulating; that is to say, they regulate the manner of their own creation and application. Parts of the shared plan authorise certain members of the group to flesh out or apply the other parts of the shared plan. These 'authorisations' are accepted when members of the group agree to surrender their exclusive power to plan and commit to follow the plans formulated and applied by the authorised members. Thus, when someone authorised by the shared plan issues an order, she thereby extends the plan and gives members of the group new sub-plans to follow.

The fact that someone adopts a plan for others to follow does not, of course, mean that, from the moral point of view, those others *ought* to comply. The plan might be foolish or evil and, thus, unless there are substantial costs associated with non-conformity, the subjects morally should not carry it out. However, if the subject has accepted the shared plan which sets out the hierarchy then, from the point of view of instrumental rationality, he is bound to heed the plan. For if someone submits to the planning of another, and yet ignores an order directed to him, he will be acting in a manner inconsistent with his own plan. His disobedience will be in direct conflict with his intention to defer.

While acceptance of a subordinate position within a hierarchy creates rational requirements of obedience, it may of course be the case that participants were irrational for acquiescing to the shared plan in the first place. Their superiors may be ignorant, unethical or irresponsible. Nevertheless, there are often good reasons to defer. For example, others might know more than the subordinates do about what the group should do and can be trusted to point them in the right direction. As we have also seen, the complexity and contentiousness of shared activities not only increases the benefits of planning, but also its costs. By vertically dividing labour between those who adopt plans and those who apply and carry them out, participants are able to resolve their doubts and disagreements without having to engage in costly deliberations or negotiations. It should also not be overlooked that an individual might accept a subordinate role in a shared activity because they have no other viable option. They might desperately need the money or fear that they will be harmed if they do not. Even in cases of economic or physical coercion, once an individual forms an intention to treat the superior's directives as trumps to his or her own planning, he or she has transformed their normative situation and are rationally – if not morally – committed to follow through unless good reasons suddenly appear that force them to reconsider.

F Planning for Massively Shared Agency

While concentrating the power to plan in the hands of a few is often useful for small-scale shared activities, it is absolutely indispensable when large collections of individuals act together. On the one hand, the complexity, contentiousness and arbitrariness of shared activities grow with the size of the group participating, leading to a corresponding increase in the need for and cost of planning. Without economical methods for adopting and applying plans, it is unlikely that the members of the group will be able to organise themselves through sheer improvisation or group deliberation and bargaining. Even more importantly, hierarchy is necessary because of the need to hold members of the group accountable. If an activity is to be shared in a group of considerable size, those who are committed to the success of the activity must have some way of directing and monitoring those who fail to share their enthusiasm.

As we will see, the simple forms of planning and hierarchy we have been exploring are insufficient for these larger scale tasks. To manage instances of massively shared agency, it is imperative to divide labour horizontally, develop a dense network of plans and erect sophisticated planning structures so that the participants can navigate their way through unfamiliar and challenging terrain and others can chart their progress.

Plans and Alienation

The Cooking Club has been going strong for so long that one day one of us suggests that we open up a catering company. Why not make money doing something that we enjoy doing for free? We all find the idea appealing and thus decide to turn the Cooking Club into the Cooking Club, Inc.

Our initial venture into business turns out to be hugely successful. Word of mouth spreads the news quickly and soon we can no longer meet the demand for catering services. We know that we must hire more workers to help us with our business. Expanding the business in this way, however, requires us to change the way that we run it. Because the new workers know little or nothing about the complexities of the catering business, we must provide them with detailed instructions if they are to be productive.

But lack of catering experience is not the only reason forcing us to plan for them. Unlike the founders and owners of the Cooking Club, Inc, a large percentage of these workers are not committed to seeing the business prosper. Many are aspiring actors waiting for their big break and care only about picking up their paycheck. Relying on them to organise themselves, therefore, would be foolish. If they get paid as long as they merely appear to help, there is no reason to think that they will in fact be helpful. Given their alienation from the activity, they will not do what really needs to be done if doing it is too demanding.

The natural solution is for those who care about the success of the endeavour to direct the actions of those who do not. Having all read Adam Smith and knowing about the gains to productivity that the division of labour enables, we decide to assign to each worker separate roles, eg cook, dishwasher, waiter, driver, bartender, bookkeeper, and so on. The benefits of specialisation, we anticipate, will be considerable: instead of teaching the staff how to perform every single task, we can simply train each to do one job well; because each worker only performs one job, they are able to perfect their skills; given that workers stay at their posts, they waste no time shifting and retooling from one task to another; and since each staff member is assigned a specific task, we are able to determine whom is responsible, and should be held accountable, for shortfalls in performance.

In order to divide the labour in the horizontal direction, we adopt policies that direct staff members to act, or not act, in certain ways. For example, the bartender policy states: 'During a job, the bartender is to stand behind the bar and prepare the drinks that the guests request'. In addition to these role-specifications, we also adopt company-wide directives, such as 'Waiters, cooks and bartenders must wear the Cooking Club, Inc uniform' and 'All employees must wash their hands after using the restroom'.

Since the policies allocating roles are highly general, we adopt further policies to help guide the staff in applying them. For example, we provide the bartender a book of drink recipes. These recipes stipulate the 'right' way to mix various drinks. When a guest requests, say, a Bloody Mary, the bartender is required to carry out the bartender policy by using the Bloody Mary recipe as his guide. If the bartender does not use that recipe, he will not have performed his job correctly.

Call these types of policies *stipulations*. Stipulations do not demand that their subjects believe the stipulated propositions to be true; rather, they are merely required to *treat them as true* for the purpose of applying certain plans. Suppose that the Bloody Mary recipe uses mango nectar. The bartender need not believe that Bloody Marys should be made with mango nectar. Rather, he should regard the stipulated recipe as the right way to make a Bloody Mary only for the purposes of preparing drinks for the guests. Another stipulation is that the customer is always right. Regardless of whether the customer is actually justified on some matter, workers are required to treat what they claim as correct for the sake of doing their job.

In addition to stipulations, we promulgate *factorisations*. Factorisations specify the factors that should be taken into account when planning how to act. For example, we direct the staff to be cost-conscious. This plan directs the staff to give weight to the cost of various actions and adopt plans in part based on this consideration. Like stipulations, factorisations do not require that their subjects actually value the factors specified by the plan; rather, they merely direct them to *treat them as valuable* for the sake of doing their jobs.

In addition to plans that direct planning and action, we also introduce *permissions*. Permissions are best understood as 'anti-directives': they do not direct the staff to do, or not do, any action; rather, they inform their addressees that they are *not* required to perform, or refrain from performing, some action. Thus, the permission to take home leftover food instructs the staff members that they are not required to leave leftover food, which is useful to know if one is concerned that taking food home may be forbidden.

These general plans, stipulations, factorisations and permissions constitute subplans of the shared plan to engage in the catering business together. Their function is to guide and organise the behaviour of the group. Instead of staff members having to design a shared plan themselves, each can simply appeal to the parts of the shared plan formulated and adopted for them. The promulgated policies also serve a crucial monitoring function. Once they have been adopted and disseminated, the lines of responsibility become clear, rendering it difficult for workers to shirk or blame failure on ignorance. If they do not perform their assigned role or carry it out in the manner specified by the plans, they can be held accountable for any omissions, mishaps or abuses that resulted from their waywardness.

Decentralised Planning Mechanisms

Assigning roles to the staff is necessary, but it is by no means sufficient. While the adopted directives set out the basic division of labour, most of the operational details are left unresolved. Moreover, given the staff's indifference to our success, we need a way of checking that they are indeed doing their jobs. Unfortunately, we cannot organise and oversee day-to-day operations because there are simply too many problems to solve and too much activity to supervise. We are able to allocate roles and set broad institutional objectives but our group is too slow and unwieldy to effectively run the day-to-day aspects of the business.

As a result, the owners develop a more elaborate vertical division of labour. First, we empower individuals who we deem trustworthy to adopt detailed plans for the day-to-day operations of the company. They are authorised to determine who to staff on which job, where trucks should be parked when at catering sites, when the soup gets served during the meals, and so on. Second, we direct them to supervise the staff. They are, in other words, to 'apply' company policies to the staff to see whether they are carrying them out properly. If they are not, we direct the supervisors to notify the staff members of the shortfall and respectfully insist that the job be done correctly.

By appointing these supervisors, we *decentralise* the process of group planning. Instead of direction coming exclusively from the centre, multiple planning mechanisms are available to create and administer the company's shared plan on a distributed basis. When the supervisors create new plans for daily operations, they are engaged in decentralised plan-adoption; when evaluating staff behaviour using existing company policies, they are engaged in decentralised plan-application. Because of decentralisation, doubts and disagreements about the best plans to adopt, or the proper way to apply existing plans, need not make their way to us. Nor must we supervise every aspect of the business. Local supervisors who are close to the action can resolve conflicts and monitor behaviour in an agile fashion.

To decentralise our planning hierarchy, we adopt various *authorisations*. Thus, the authorisation which empowers supervisors to apply plans to others can be formulated as follows: 'Supervisors have the power to apply those company plans that are directed to staff members'. By accepting this authorisation, staff members commit themselves, for the purpose of applying company plans, to treat as correct their supervisors' judgements about the applications of company plans.

We also adopt plans that specify how supervisors are to exercise their authorised powers. For lack of a better term, I am going to call plans of this sort *instructions*. One instruction, for example, requires the supervisor to issue a warning before he docks a staff member for failures to comply with company policies. This plan has the following form: 'In order to dock pay from a staff member, a supervisor must first issue a warning'. The instruction does not actually require the supervisor to issue a warning; rather, it specifies the proper procedure that the supervisor is to follow if he wishes to validly exercise the power to dock pay. Thus, if the supervisor fails to issue a warning, the worker cannot be denied wages.

Authorisations, instructions, stipulations and factorisations are special types of plans. Unlike the bartender directive or the smoking permission which regulate *action*, these types of plans guide *planning*. Authorisations specify *who* is to plan, while instructions, stipulations and factorisations specify *how* to plan. We might say that these plans are 'plans for planning'. They constitute the self-regulating parts of shared plans which specify the manner in which the shared plan is to be formulated, adopted, applied and enforced.

Affecting Plans

One of the powers conferred on supervisors is to hire and fire employees. But this power is not the same as the power to adopt or apply any plan. If a supervisor fires a waiter for being rude to a patron, he is not directly telling anybody to do anything: he is simply letting the waiter go.

Of course, by firing the waiter, the supervisor affects the applicability of numerous company plans. For example, the bookkeeper is no longer required to pay the fired employee and other employees are not permitted to let him in the kitchen. We might say, therefore, that the authorisation to fire employees involves the power to *affect* certain pre-existing company plans.

At the risk of some artificiality, I will consider the exercise of an authorisation to affect plans to be a form of planning. For although affecting plans does not involve the creation of any new plans, it is the functional equivalent. When someone affects plans in an authorised manner, he generates the same normative consequences as if he adopted a new set of plans himself. Indeed, affecting pre-existing plans is typically a more efficient way of organising behaviour than adopting new plans. Instead of separately directing the bookkeeper not to pay the waiter, the employees not to let him back in the kitchen, and so on, the supervisor can accomplish the same ends by simply firing the waiter.

Modernity and Massively Shared Agency

As we have seen, we respond to the challenge of managing a large group of inexperienced and unmotivated individuals by requiring them to hand over vast amounts of planning power to us. By accepting the shared plan, they not only assume certain roles, but transfer their powers to adopt and apply plans in case where their plans conflict with the planning of the supervisors. This dense horizontal and vertical division of labour channels the behaviour of the staff in such a way that they eventually end up doing what we want them to do. The beauty of the scheme is that the workers themselves need not care a wit about helping us; their interest can lie simply in earning enough money to make it to the next audition. Nor do they have to understand how the whole enterprise hangs together. As long as they do what they are told, our business prospers.

That individuals can be made to work together in pursuit of ends that they do not value is critically important in understanding how the modern world is possible. For the world that we encounter in day-to-day life is distinguished by the enormous scale of social life. Business corporations, consumer cooperatives, trade unions, research universities, philanthropic organisations, professional associations, standing armies, political parties, organised religions, governments and legal systems, not to mention the collaborative ventures made possible by the digitally networked information and communication technology (such as Wikipedia, massively multimember online games (MMOGs), open-source software and the World Wide Web itself) all harness the agency of multitudes in order to fulfil certain objectives. The modern world, we might say, is one defined by 'massively shared agency' – the agency of crowds.

Because the modern world is also characterised by diversity, it is extremely unlikely that large-scale ventures can be staffed with individuals who are all committed to the same goals. The Cooking Club, Inc, for example, simply could not find enough truly dedicated people to staff our services. Ultimately, we had to rely on others who were willing to do what was demanded of them but no more. In the modern world, alienation and massively shared agency almost always go hand-in-hand.

As we have seen, shared agency is indeed possible in the face of alienation. In order for a group to act together, they need not intend the success of the joint enterprise. They need only share a plan. That plan, in turn, can be developed by someone who does intend the success of the joint activity. As long as participants accept the plan, intentionally play their parts, resolve their disputes peacefully and openly, and all of this is common knowledge, they are acting together intentionally.

To be sure, some participants may be so apathetic, lazy, selfish, misguided, rebellious or, in some cases, honourable that they will not be committed to acting on their part of the plan or letting others do likewise unless they are forced to do so. In such cases, the only alternative is to direct others who do accept the shared plan to enforce the group policies through sanctions. At least in these kinds of cases, plan-enforcement is a distinct stage of group planning; for only by enforcing the shared plan can some participants bring others to accept it as well and dispose them to act accordingly.

Although alienation does not confound the possibility of shared agency, the case of the Cooking Club, Inc illustrates that its existence presents difficult logistical problems for planners. Because alienated participants are not usually committed to the success of the joint activity, it is likely that they will have to be given detailed guidance on how to act. It may also be necessary to create hierarchical structures so that conflicts are resolved and performance monitored. Finally, those in supervisory positions might need to be authorised to enforce the group's policies through the imposition of sanctions. The task of institutional design, in other words, is to create a practice that is so thick with plans, plan-adopters, -affecters, -appliers and -enforcers that alienated participants end up acting in the same way as non-alienated ones. The fact that activities can often be structured so that participants intentionally achieve goals that are not *their* goals accounts for the pervasiveness of massively shared agency in the world around us.

G Living Together

We began this chapter by exploring individual planning and why we need it. We saw that human beings plan their individual actions because they typically pursue ends that can only be achieved by taking several, sometimes myriad, different actions over time sequenced in just the right order. Our desire to achieve complex ends outstrips our capacity to deliberate continuously and arrive at the optimal choice for every moment. We compensate for this cognitive failing by thinking through the best course of action in advance, settling on it, and then relying on this judgement when the time comes to carry it out.

We then proceeded to explore why and how small groups plan their shared activities. Aside from the deliberative demands that complex activities place on us, we saw that shared activities require constituent action to be coordinated in certain ways. When faced with complex, contentious or arbitrary activities, it is unlikely that completely improvised attempts at ordering will result in synergistic patterns of behaviour. Group planning is an improvement over simple improvisation insofar as it enables participants to control behaviour and render it predictable to others. By having a common blueprint to guide them, members of groups need no longer guess what part they should play.

While shared plans are often essential to the success of shared activities, we also saw that they are costly to produce. We, therefore, went on to examine several strategies that participants normally use to reduce their planning costs. Adopting policies enables participants to guide their conduct over a whole class of cases; developing customs permits groups to take advantage of plan-like norms in order to settle questions about how to act without anyone formulating or adopting them for the group; and consolidating and concentrating planning power in the hands of a few circumvents the need for the many to deliberate, negotiate or bargain about how to conduct their shared activity.

We also considered the challenges posed by massively shared agency. We saw that the complexity, contentiousness and arbitrariness of shared activities tend to increase with group size to the point that planning and hierarchy becomes not only desirable but absolutely indispensable. But massively shared agency brings with it a pressure for planning not typically present in the small case. As a group enlarges, the odds that some members will be alienated from the joint activity grow. Developing a dense network of plans and establishing decentralised plan-adopters, -affecters and -appliers are essential to supply alienated participants with correct instructions for how to proceed, as well as standards for holding them accountable.

I would like to end this long discussion of planning by noting one other occasion in which members of groups plan for one another. Most room-mates, for example, have policies about how they are to behave in their shared dwelling. These policies usually prohibit playing loud music late at night, require certain cleaning duties and responsibilities, specify who must buy communal items such as toilet paper, butter and beer, identify the proper place to put the key when they leave the house, and so on. While some of these plans regulate shared activity, eg stocking the house with essentials, others concern solely individual pursuits, eg playing music in one's room late at night.

There is no mystery about why plans are needed to regulate individual actions in communal settings. When people occupy the same space and share a common pool of resources, certain courses of action will result in clashes between individual pursuits, while others will avoid them. Planning is often necessary to ensure that those who live together do not undermine each other's ends.

As with cases involving individual and shared agency, plans that regulate individual pursuits in communal contexts aim to harness the benefits of thinking ahead. First, plans enable the group members to figure out the best ways to avoid conflict and hence eliminate the need to deliberate at every turn about how to steer clear of trouble. Second, they allow group members to anticipate possible mistaken choices that negatively affect others and to prevent them before they happen.

As we saw with shared activities, plans are also useful in communal settings because they are capable of coordinating behaviour in complex, contentious and arbitrary environments. Social life presents numerous ethical quandaries about personal and social rights and responsibilities. People not only have doubts about the proper way to live together but, more perilously, often find themselves at odds with one another about how such doubts should be resolved. The contentiousness of living together, let alone its complexity, increases the costs of deliberation, negotiation and bargaining and threatens to generate additional emotional and moral costs should the parties fail to talk through their problems.

Plans are vital for groups because they are capable of resolving many of the ethical problems of communal life. Members of the group who live together and face conflict need not litigate every dispute, disagreement or perceived act of disrespect. Nor need they try to overpower or deceive each other in order to circumvent the difficulty. They may rely instead on plans that were adopted in anticipation of the conflict. Prior planning allows the community members to treat questions of fairness and what they owe to each other as settled, as matters not up for reconsideration. And in this way they are not only able to economise on costs and increase predictability of behaviour, but also to facilitate an ethic of respect among the entire community.

II THE MAKING OF A LEGAL SYSTEM

A The Idea of Social Planning

The twentieth century was not very kind to the activity often referred to as 'social planning'. Any list of social engineering projects of the past hundred years tends to read like a veritable Who's Who of Unmitigated Human Disasters: eg the collectivisation of Russian agriculture after the Bolshevik revolution, the command economy of the Soviet Union, the Great Leap Forward, the deurbanisation of Cambodia under the Khmer Rogue, the villagisation of Tanzanian farmers after independence, the totally planned city of Brasilia, and so on.[11] At the very least, it

[11] For a fascinating discussion of these colossal failures of social planning, see JC Scott, *Seeing Like a State: How Certain Schemes to Improve the Human Condition Have Failed* (New Haven, CT, Yale University Press, 1998).

seems safe to say that the social planners responsible for these tragedies – Lenin, Stalin, Mao, Pol Pot, Julius Nyerere and Le Corbusier – have fared far worse in history's estimation than their critics – Karl Popper, Friedrich Hayek, George Orwell, Jane Jacobs and (depending on your politics) Rosa Luxemburg and Ronald Reagan.

But, in truth, there is no reason that these notorious large-scale public projects should be taken to represent and thus discredit the practice of social planning in general. As we have seen, planning is an excellent – often indispensable – method for guiding, coordinating and monitoring behaviour in social settings. What the above list *does* bring into disrepute is a very specific mode of social planning. What distinguishes these disastrous political experiments is the hubristic and coercive use of an untested ideology to radically transform communities purely through directives issued from the centre. These social planners conducted themselves as experts whose monopoly on superior scientific, technological and ethical knowledge entitled them to ruthlessly impose their vision of society on everyone else.

Most social planning, however, is not revolutionary, centralised, top-down and directive in nature. In fact, most attempts at group planning in general, and social planning in particular, combine centralised and decentralised mechanisms for progressive and conservative ends; use bottom-up, as well as top-down, practical reasoning; and rely on authorisations in addition to directives. As Hayek himself complained, socialists hijacked the term 'social planning' to suggest that socialism is 'the only rational way of handling our affairs'.[12] But as Hayek reminded us, liberals engage in social planning as well:

> The dispute between the modern planners and their opponents . . . is *not* a dispute . . . on whether we ought to employ foresight and systematic thinking in planning our common affairs. It is a dispute about what is the best way of doing so. The question is whether for this purpose it is better that the holder of coercive power should confine himself in general to creating conditions under which the knowledge and initiative of individuals is given the best scope so that *they* can plan most successfully; or whether a rational utilisation of our resources requires *central* direction and organisation of all our activities according to some socially constructed 'blueprint'.[13]

Hayek's point here is uncontroversially right. Socialism is hardly unique in advocating that the state engage in social planning. With the exception of certain extreme forms of anarchism, *all* political theories do so to some degree. What distinguishes these various theories is *how* they understand the planning process: to whom they allocate planning authority, the moral ends of planning and which activities should be subject to social planning in the first place.

In this chapter I will begin to argue that legal activity is a form of social planning. Legal institutions plan for the communities over which they claim authority, both by telling members what they may or may not do, and by identifying those who are entitled to affect what others may or may not do. Following this claim,

[12] F Hayek, *The Road to Serfdom*, 2nd edn (London, Routledge, 2001) 37.
[13] ibid 36–37.

legal rules are themselves generalised plans, or plan-like norms, issued by those who are authorised to plan for others. And adjudication involves the application of these plans, or plan-like norms, to those to whom they apply. In this way, the law organises individual and collective behaviour so that members of the community can bring about moral goods that could not have been achieved, or achieved as well, otherwise.

In order to motivate these claims, I begin with a narrative – the Cooking Club narrative – drop the club members into the 'state of nature' and describe their various reasons for creating a legal system. As I show, communal life generates a need for social planning. Those who live together must be able to organise shared activities, solve coordination problems, settle disputes and ensure that individual pursuits do not thwart one another. As the group attempts to cope with these pressures, they develop simple social planning mechanisms. The success of these mechanisms, nevertheless, inevitably leads to population growth and hence the need for further planning. In order to meet this increased need, simple techniques give way to more complicated and efficient structures of planning. The end result is the creation of a highly sophisticated planning organisation – otherwise known as a legal system.

I should emphasise, of course, that I am not making an empirical claim about the evolution of legal systems or why they were originally created. My claim is conceptual: I use the state of nature narrative as an analytical device for developing a more general account about the identity and foundations of law. By examining the reasons that one community has for developing legal institutions, I hope to show that these pressures are hardly unique to this particular fictional setting. Any human community of modest size will experience similar needs for social planning which can only be met by highly sophisticated technologies of plan adoption and application.

My aim in what follows is also to demonstrate that *technologies of planning* – even the highly complex ones that are mobilised by the law – *can be constructed through planning alone*. In other words, to build or operate a legal system one need not possess moral legitimacy to impose obligations and confer rights: one need only have the ability to plan. The existence of law, therefore, reflects the fact that human beings are planning creatures, endowed with the cognitive and volitional capacities and dispositions to organise their behaviour over time and across persons in order to achieve highly complex ends.

B Private Planning

The Cooking Club, Inc eventually becomes so successful that Wall Street approaches us with an offer to take the company public. Unable to resist the lure of obscene wealth, we agree to turn our business over to the public markets. We will still participate in the business at the management level but our cooking days are over.

As it turns out, however, the thrill of being executives in a multinational corporation nevertheless proves to be extremely short-lived. None of us went into the catering business in order to push paper in a corporate office. We soon decide to sell our shares, use the money to buy an island in the South Pacific and start a new community. Alienated by our brief experience of corporate life, we plan to live off the land, treat each other with equal concern and respect, eschew coercive means of social control, and live happily ever after.

The island that we purchase (and rename 'Cooks' Island') appears to be an ideal location for hunting and gathering. It is inhabited by wild boar, deer and game birds, has a wide variety of fruit trees, numerous species of wild grains and cereals, and a natural lagoon filled with fish, crab and edible seaweeds. We move to Cooks' Island in the Spring, finding plenty of food to eat and abundant materials with which to build huts.

From the outset, small-scale group planning is crucial to our ability to live peacefully and productively together. The main features of our lives – building shelter, collecting fuel, finding food, preparing meals, raising children, playing and entertaining – are shared activities and so we need a way to organise them. The hunters among us must decide where to go, what to hunt, who should flush, shoot, gut, and so on. We will also need designated caretakers to look after the children while the hunters are on an expedition. Since everyone has plenty of time on their hands, group members are free to negotiate with one another about who will perform which tasks. In instances of group planning such as this, no one has the authority to tell everyone else what to do: each individual decides which course of action to take and then finds ways to coordinate his or her chosen course of action with those who wish to join them.

Group planning is not always necessary, however; in some cases, order is spontaneously generated. Coordination problems, such as where to dispose of our refuse or which side of the road to ride our bikes on, are usually solved through the emergence of coordination conventions. We find others disposing of their refuse in a certain location or riding on one side of the road and we simply follow suit. No one plans for this result – it simply happens through 'spontaneous ordering'.

In this respect, we might say that Cooks' Island is an *unplanned* community. All issues concerning how members should act are resolved solely through the unilateral decisions of individuals or small subgroups. Questions about which individual and shared activities ought to be required, prohibited and regulated are not resolved on a community-wide basis, either through unanimous consensus or exercises of authority, but rather exclusively through private ordering. In other words, while there is plenty of *group* planning, there is no *social* planning.

Internalising Costs

Notwithstanding the absence of social planning, members of our unplanned community are able to work and live together in harmony throughout the Spring, Summer and Fall. Winter, however, is a different story. Many of the animals hibernate for the winter and the game birds migrate north. The fish move farther offshore in order to take advantage of richer feeding grounds. The fruit trees bear fruit only in the Spring and Summer and the wild grains refuse to germinate in the winter. Each of us anticipates this shortage to some extent by privately storing smoked meat and surplus grain, but there is not nearly enough food to feed us all. We are ultimately able to survive only by importing food from the mainland.

After this first difficult Winter, we all recognise that hunting and gathering is not a sustainable way of life and that community-wide action is necessary if we are to survive on the island. In keeping with this, the community decides to pool its resources and buy domesticated grains and livestock from the mainland. Together, we clear large portions of the island to plant the domesticated strains of grains and cereals and graze our newly purchased sheep, goats and cows. We abandon hunting and gathering and take up farming and ranching instead.

Before we are able to embark on this new agricultural lifestyle, however, we have to make an important choice. Until now, the island has been treated as common property. Everyone was entitled to harvest the game animals, lagoon fish, wild berries, fresh water and hardwood timber and use them in any way they saw fit. Now we must decide whether to maintain common ownership of resources, holding the new livestock, crops and pastures as joint owners and engaging in a shared activity of farming, or whether we should instead create a system of private property in which a share of animals, seeds and land is allocated to each individual in order that they will be able to grow food for themselves.

Since all of the inhabitants of Cooks' Island have taken basic economics, we know what economists would advise us to do in this situation. In a collective property regime, there is always a danger of free-riding. If each islander must work the fields in order to produce food for all (the economist warns), each are likely to be tempted by the following calculation: to do my fair share is to work very hard; if I do not do my fair share, there will be a little less to eat; I would rather eat a little less and not work very hard than eat a little more but work very hard; therefore, I ought not do my fair share. But, of course, if each islander reasons in this way and acts accordingly, everyone will starve.

The economically efficient decision is to switch from a system in which each enjoys the benefits of other's labour to one in which each gain only from their own efforts. In economic terms, the socially optimal decision involves instituting an arrangement whereby each 'internalises' the costs and benefits of their actions. If I benefit from my labour alone, and not from anyone else's, then I have no incentive to be lazy. For if I do not work, I will be the one to starve.

In an effort to make good on this economic insight, we assemble together and engage in another act of social planning. We agree as a community to allocate the newly arable land, seeds and livestock on the basis of family size. The larger the family, the greater the share received. This allocation is accomplished through the adoption of stipulations of the form: 'For the purposes of complying with island land-use policies, Family X is to be deemed the owner of Plot A, Seed lot B and Livestock lot C'.[14] In addition to these specific plans, we also adopt several general policies that govern the use of the allocated land. For example, one policy permits owners to use and enjoy the property as they see fit, while another forbids a non-landowner from taking the grain or livestock of another without the owner's consent. A third policy permits anyone to cross another's field in order to reach the village square, but a fourth one requires that anyone who does so must compensate the landowner for the destruction of any crops or injury of any livestock on that property.

A principal purpose of these plans is to force each member of the group to internalise the costs and benefits of their actions. The first policy, for example, permits owners to enjoy the fruits of their labour, while the second one attempts to avert free-riding by directing non-owners not to benefit from the agricultural labour of owners without their permission. The third and fourth policies permit non-owners to use another's land when the alternatives are particularly costly, but incentivise them to exercise reasonable precautions by requiring them to pay for what they damage. Insofar as a major aim of these policies is to prevent free-riding, it is imperative that the policies govern the activities of the whole community; that is to say, in order to be effective, they must be *social* plans.

We also adopt plans that allow for the transfer of property rights. A fifth policy, for example, authorises owners to alienate their property, whereas a sixth instructs the owners of movable property as to how to exercise this power. It states that in order for ownership to pass, there must be physical delivery and acceptance, unless the parties agree otherwise. These policies, in other words, confer power on owners to affect the previous four policies. By alienating property in the proper manner, owners affect who falls within and without these pre-existing policies and hence who may use and enjoy the alienated property.

Planning for Spontaneous Order

Fortunately, our shared plan fulfils its intended purpose. The new property regime leads to a substantial crop yield and livestock supply and provides the community with plenty of food to eat and store for the winter. In fact, each of us has more goods than we can possibly use. And – as a result – markets emerge in which the islanders trade their surplus goods.

Not surprisingly, the participants in these markets are able to adjust their production to aggregate demand and their consumption to aggregate supply without engaging in social planning. Our group does not, for example, decide in advance that the cheese-makers will make more or less cheese. The cheese-makers instead take their cues from the demand they find in the market. If more cheese is demanded, more cheese is supplied. If the amount of cheese demanded cannot be

[14] The reason that the stipulation is prefaced with 'For the purposes of island land-use policies' is that the plan does not require the group to consider the family in question to be owner for, say, tithing purposes. As is the case in many jurisdictions, someone can be deemed the owner (to have title) for the purpose of determining who bears the risk of loss, but not for whether they owe property or sales tax.

met, the cost of the cheese goes up until the amount of cheese demanded equals the amount of cheese available.

To say that market decisions about supply and demand proceed in the absence of social planning should not be taken to mean that the existence of the market itself is independent of social planning. For the regime of private property that makes our market possible – the allocation of ownership rights to members of the group, the policies for how to treat the items allocated and the power to affect these policies through voluntary exchange – is the product of plans developed *by us for us*. That group members can only procure one set of goods by trading them for another, and cannot simply appropriate them without permission, is a requirement imposed by our shared plan. This plan seeks to boost agricultural output by creating the conditions favourable for spontaneous order to emerge.[15]

Nevertheless, as more goods are produced and traded, the possibility of economic loss through mishaps grows. These accidents raise numerous questions of responsibility. Let's say that my cow wanders from my pasture and eats some of your crops. Am I responsible for the damage? Or should you bear the costs of not having built a fence?

Even though our group has no shared plan about liability in these circumstances, the various parties find themselves able to resolve the conflict through private deliberation and bargaining. Each person relies on their sense of fairness and neighbourliness in determining how to reach a just settlement. For example, neighbours normally choose to overlook small damage to their crops caused by grazing livestock. Because they are aware that their own animals probably inflict similar damage to their neighbour's property, they figure that it all evens out in the long run. As for large losses, which tend not to net out over time, livestock owners generally feel obligated to compensate their neighbours for the damage.[16]

C The Supply and Demand for Plans

The Need for Social Planning

Although our shared plan solves important social problems, it generates new ones as well. For it turns out that the move to a system of private property exponentially increases the range of matters over which we can quarrel. When property was held in common, everyone was permitted to plan their own actions on any

[15] Moreover, since we designed our system of private property and market exchange to increase the amount of food available for the group to eat, our policies are sub-plans of the overall shared plan to boost the agricultural output of the island. They organise the behaviour of the group so that the goal of the shared plan can be achieved. It turns out, then, that market activity – an activity that has traditionally been thought to be the paradigm of individualism – on our island is a shared activity. As long as we seek to maximise our own wealth subject to the cost internalisations mandated by our shared plan, we will collectively maximise food production.

[16] Robert Ellickson's *Order Without Law: How Neighbors Settle Disputes* (Cambridge, MA, Harvard University Press, 1991) is the locus classicus for how communities are often able to order their affairs without resorting to law. The discussion in the text is much indebted to Ellickson's discussion.

aspect of island life. The land, water, air, animals, fruit, grains, and so on were freely available to all. The private property regime changed all that, rendering previously abundant resources instantaneously scarce. Our shared plan has rendered most of the land, and the goods it yields, inaccessible to almost everyone. Moreover, while the incentives to create and innovate that were generated by the new property regime increase the overall production of goods, the prevailing system of ownership dictates that these goods are under the exclusive control of only certain members of the group.

As a result of our shared plan, therefore, questions of rights become extremely urgent and, at the same time, increasingly contentious as well. For we now have an incentive to dispute which objects we own and what we are permitted to do with them. Thus, we bicker about whether islanders are authorised to acquire new land, and, if so, how they can or should do so. Owners who live upstream assert the right to use the water for irrigation, even if this means that there is less water for downstream farmers to use. Downstream farmers hotly contest this claim. Those who find fresh water on their property assert exclusive control over this precious resource, while the bulk of the group denies their right to do so. The merchants claim that the islanders should have the ability to condemn private property for public purposes, such as building roads, while another portion of the group, mainly the farmers, vehemently rejects this position.

Our private property regime has not only rendered our communal life more contentious but also greatly increased its complexity. For in an effort to innovate economically, we start to unbundle the property rights allocated to each family under the original shared plan and recombine them with various promises to create new packets of claims and duties. In this way, gifts, leases, easements, bailments, consignments, life-estates, loans, assignments, mortgages, partnerships, trusts, wills, negotiable instruments and other types of contractual and property arrangements, are formed. But, while successful in certain respects, these new measures once again raise further questions about the content and scope of the normative relationships created. For example, if a farmer enters into an agreement with, say, the baker to supply a certain quantity of wheat at harvest and then, due to bad weather, the crop fails, does the farmer owe the baker damages and, if so, what kind? If one farmer sells a cow to another but, unbeknownst to both, the cow is barren, can the purchaser get his money back? And what if someone builds a hut for someone else but fabricates the roof of that hut out of an inferior material that makes it less durable than the other huts in the village? Can the purchaser insist on a better roof? Can an unsecured creditor foreclose on property if the debtor becomes bankrupt? In what circumstances can a tenant refuse to pay rent and, if those circumstances do not obtain, at what point can a landlord evict a tenant?

Not only have our private transactions become more complex and contentious, but our public projects have done as well. For example, our new economy has generated much material prosperity but it has also skewed its distribution. As a result, we are eager to institute a programme of income redistribution.

Unfortunately, however, this particular shared activity turns out to be too complicated and presents too many coordination problems for us to be able to bring them about exclusively through improvisation or planning in small groups. Furthermore, while we all agree on the broad outlines of the redistributive programme, we disagree about its precise implementation, thus increasing the costs of resolving our conflicts through private deliberations and negotiations.

It is important to note at this point that the doubts and disagreements that arise on Cooks' Island are entirely sincere. Each of us is willing to do what we ought to do – the problem is that none of us knows or can agree about what that is. Customs cannot keep up with the evolving conflict because they develop too slowly to regulate rapidly changing social conditions and are too sketchy to resolve complex disputes and coordinate large-scale social projects. While private negotiation and bargaining are able to quell some conflicts, this process can be very costly, not only in terms of time and energy but emotionally and morally as well. With many more ways to interfere with one another's pursuits and many more goods to fight over, there is a danger that disputes will proliferate and fester, causing the parties to refuse to cooperate in the next communal venture or, worse, to become involved in ongoing and entrenched feuds. Some projects, such as income redistribution, are so complex, contentious and arbitrary that they are simply not feasible through private planning alone.

To compensate for this failure of private ordering, we revive our earlier experiment in social planning and regularise it as an ongoing shared activity. We get together several times a week to discuss how best to handle the social issues that arise within our group. We discuss not only how to structure our interactions in the market but also how to collect and redistribute wealth, educate our children, protect ourselves against droughts, hurricanes and wild animals, and so on. Though our deliberations and negotiations are sometimes long and protracted, dealing as they do with weighty matters of political morality and group morale, we eventually settle on plans that we believe will enable us to live together on the island for the foreseeable future.

Failure of Consensus

The disadvantages of social planning via consensus, nevertheless, become apparent very quickly. Not only is it time-consuming and emotionally draining, but it is extremely unstable. For the plans are useful only so long as they are accepted by almost everyone. As soon as people start to reconsider their wisdom, the plans lose their ability to guide behaviour and settle conflict and the group must start deliberating and negotiating once again.

Eventually, as the island economy booms and its population multiplies, this consensual method of governance becomes intolerable. Economic prosperity makes it possible to sustain a greater number of people, and family size increases along with this new capacity. At the same time, people from the mainland immigrate to the island in search of the good life. More people engage in more interactions, more interactions lead to more doubts and disagreements, and more doubts and disagreements generate higher planning costs.

The increase in conflict is not only a function of the increased number of interactions. Population growth also entails a more intricate division of labour, with group members engaging in ever more complex activities; the cheese-maker, for example, recently hired 10 workers and incorporated his business, with the bread-maker and meat-smoker as the chief equity investors. Simply relying on untutored judgements of fairness and neighbourliness tends to be a poor method for resolving the complicated disputes that arise from these arrangements. And the expansion of the population makes it increasingly unlikely that these untutored judgements will be shared among the contestants or that losses from any particular interaction will balance out in the long run. Social life has become extremely complex and more contentious as well. Community-wide shared activities are less and less amenable to large doses of improvisation.

On the one hand, then, population growth enhances the need for plans in order to guide and organise the behaviour of the islanders. This *increased* demand for shared plans, however, coincides with a corresponding *decrease* in our community's ability to supply them through consensus. We simply can no longer get everyone to agree to particular solutions to many social problems and, when we can, the time and expense incurred in the course of forging a consensus is enormous.

Nor do our difficulties end here. Experience has shown us that the mere existence of shared plans is not a panacea. For in order for a plan to resolve doubts or disagreements, the relevant parties must agree about how to implement it. Not only has the number of disputes unregulated by prior plans increased, so have the number of disputes about the application of prior plans. Yet, as the demand for adjudication has increased so, once again, has the cost of supplying it. If the parties must agree on the application of plans in order to settle their disputes, the expense of conflict resolution will rise with the quantity and complexity of the disagreements.

The Solution: Hierarchy

Recognising that our need for plans and adjudication exceeds our ability to generate them, the inhabitants of Cooks' Island converge on the idea of *hierarchy*. At one of our weekly meetings, we decide to divide the social labour vertically by outsourcing various stages of social planning to a small group of trusted islanders. First, we identify three people who will be the chief plan-adopters for the island. They will act together as a unit to develop social plans for our community. Second, we identify three islanders who serve as plan-appliers for the island. When a dispute arises between islanders as to the proper application of some social policy and one of the parties wants the dispute resolved, he or she may ask one of these appliers to do so. The plan-applier will determine by herself which course of action is required by the island policies and her decision will be binding on both parties.

In addition to this vertical division of labour, which delegates the social planning to a small group of islanders, our newly hierarchical approach also distributes the planning labour horizontally among those few designated social planners. The new plan authorises three people to *adopt* plans for the islanders and three other people to *apply* these norms whenever a conflict arises and their services are sought. Our hierarchy, in other words, involves a separation of planning powers. Moreover, the plan centralises plan-adoption, but decentralises plan-application: the adopters must act together in order to make plans, but the appliers can resolve conflicts on a solo basis. Only one body can adopt plans, but multiple bodies can apply them.

Notice that the plan which establishes the hierarchy for the island is a shared plan: it has been designed for the social planners, it is accessible to them and they accept it. This shared plan regulates the activity of social planning. It guides and organises the behaviour of the social planners so that each knows which part they are to play in the shared activity. *It is a shared plan for social planning.*

Notice further that since the shared plan was designed for the handful of social planners, it is they who share the plan, not the islanders as a whole. This means that it is not necessary for the community to accept the shared plan in order for it to obtain – though, as a matter of fact, we do accept the plan. Since we consider the social planners to be morally legitimate, we plan to allow the adopters and appliers to adopt and apply plans for us. For this reason, we consider the shared plan to be the 'master plan' for the group.

As expected, the master plan does solve many of the planning difficulties we encountered earlier. Now social policies can be adopted simply by the adopters proclaiming that such-and-such shall be the case – no one has to agree with the wisdom of the policies themselves. As a result, we have an agile protocol for guiding and organising our community's behaviour and for resolving any disputes that might arise. When one of the designated appliers determines that a policy has been satisfied or violated, his or her judgement does not need to be regarded as wise or right by anyone involved. It is binding simply because it was applied by the authorised individual.

The newly adopted plans prove to be durable as well. In our revamped system, the persistence of plans does not depend on whether members of the community accept their wisdom. As long as they are approved in accordance with the requirements of the shared plan, the plans will be deemed binding, both by the planners and the islanders generally, and followed accordingly.

The Office

Unfortunately, our saga does not end here. For while the islanders find that their original master plan drastically reduces the costs of social planning, it is nonetheless a crude prototype which suffers from several significant flaws.

It turns out that the plan's *most* significant flaw is that it is limited to a particular set of individuals. The plan specifies those who are currently authorised to plan for the community, ie 'Bob, Ted and Jane have the power to adopt plans for the residents of Cooks' Island', but says nothing about who is to succeed them if they step down, become physically or mentally incapacitated, or die. As a result, when one of them vacates their post, we have to deliberate again about whether we want hierarchy and, if so, who should possess the power to plan for others. What we learn from this frustrating duplication of effort is that it would be far more convenient to devise policies that create an abstract structure of control and specify in impersonal terms who should occupy which role at which time. In this way, when one planner quits, another person can assume his or her structural role but the master plan itself will remain unaffected.

With this in mind, we develop new policies that define various structural roles and identify their occupants in less personal and more general terms. With respect to the adopters, for example, three new policies are adopted: an authorisation of the form: 'Adopters have the power to adopt plans for residents of Cooks' Island'; a directive of the form: 'Appliers are required to apply the plans adopted by adopters in cases that arise before them'; and a stipulation of the form: 'A person shall be deemed an "adopter" if and only if they have lived on the island for more than a year and receive the most votes in the latest island election'.

This hierarchical structure establishes what is otherwise known as an 'office', an indefinite, non-ad hoc position of power. The office of 'adopter', for example, carries with it various rights and responsibilities, all of which persist over time and attach to whoever happens to occupy the office at the given moment. Because the authorisation to adopt plans does not single out planners by name, but rather defines a class of individuals who meet the appropriate qualifications (eg they were elected by a majority of islanders), the master plan does not need to be amended each time a new person seeks to acquire the power to plan for the island. As long as that person satisfies the impersonal qualifications associated with the office, they will immediately inherit all of its powers as determined by the relevant parts of the master plan.[17]

And we soon discover another advantage of offices. Instead of requiring succeeding adopters to readopt every plan adopted by their predecessors, the master plan is amended to mandate that the policies of past holders of the office are to be followed whenever a new occupant takes over, unless and until the new occupants change the policies in question. In this way, the plans of previous office holders acquire a normative inertia that renders them even more durable.

Institutionalising Plans

But while the introduction of offices does depersonalise our hierarchy, we soon find that it is still not impersonal enough. For example, when the adopters wish to adopt a plan, they must gather us in the village square and issue proclamations of

[17] On the importance that offices play in routinising authority, see Max Weber, *Economy and Society: An Outline of Interpretive Sociology* (G Roth and C Wittich (eds), New York, Bedminster Press, 1968, (1921)) chs 11and 14.

the form: 'We hereby direct all farmers to erect fences on their land no lower than two metres' or 'In order to discharge debts, debtors must use clamshells'. These proclamations are commands that direct the community to comply with the proclaimed policies.

Needless to say, this face-to-face mode of social planning proves to be tedious for all and so the adopters eventually switch to a less intimate system. This process involves writing down their plans and deliberating on the proposed edict before them. If at the end of the deliberations all of the adopters form an intention to settle the matter in favour of following the order, then the edict is valid. The document is then posted in the village square as a written record for all to see.

The problem with *this* method is that it ties the validity of an edict to the private mental state of the plan-adopters. An edict is binding only if the adopters *intend* the edict to settle the matter in its favour and for others to guide their conduct by it. In many cases, however, the islanders have legitimate concerns about whether the posted decree truly represents the will of the planners, eg when the plan was long and complex, or contained provisions that led to absurd recommendations. These doubts lead some residents to question whether they are in fact required to follow certain of the posted orders.

In an effort to make the plans more robust, the master plan is amended to include new provisions that specify the formal conditions for the exercise of planning power. For example, in order to enact a new plan, the master plan merely requires that a majority of the adopters say 'Aye' when polled. The master plan, in other words, does not mandate that the plan-adopters *intend* that others follow the plan. Instead, plan-adoption has become *institutionalised*: the adopters' votes have normative significance for the islanders regardless of the specific intentions with which they were carried out.

By institutionalising our social planning in this way, the governance system of the island attains a very high degree of impersonality. Not only can those who hold the office of adopters adopt plans outside the earshot of the islanders, they can do so regardless of the intentions with which they performed their actions. As long as they follow the procedures set out in the master plan, their actions will have binding force. And so the islanders no longer need to divine the intentions of the planners in order to know which plans they must follow.

D Law as Social Planning

Sanctions?

At this point, it seems safe to say that Cooks' Island has developed a legal system. The planners are the legal officials; the plan-adopters are the legislators; and the plan-appliers, the judges. The master plan is the constitution that defines their offices. The plans created and applied by these officials pursuant to the shared plan are the laws of the system: the policy directives are the duty-imposing rules and the authorising policies are the power-conferring ones. Finally, the islanders all act according to plan. They are law-abiding citizens.

Some might object and deny that Cooks' Island has a genuine legal system because its plans make no provision for penalties in cases of disobedience. But it seems to me a mistake to consider sanctions to be a *necessary* feature of law. There is nothing unimaginable about a sanctionless legal system; in fact, we have just imagined one. The Cooks' Island legal system makes no provisions for sanctions but it has a constitution, a legislature and judges. It has norms that confer powers and impose duties. It maintains order, redistributes wealth, protects the moral rights of parties, provides facilities for private ordering, solves coordination problems and settles disputes. This legal system is sanctionless not because it could not impose sanctions; after all, to impose sanction merely requires that certain types of plans be adopted. Rather, sanctions are not imposed because its designers did not think them necessary. The islanders all accept the legitimacy of the group plans and, as a result, abide by them. And when they make mistakes, they voluntarily make amends. Sanctions would simply be otiose in such a setting.

Sanction-oriented theorists often discount the possibility of sanctionless legal systems because they cannot imagine *why* such a legal system would exist. What would be the point of a community having law if its members are willing to listen to the existing social or moral norms regardless? The story of Cooks' Island rebuts this concern. The islanders' decision to develop a legal system was not motivated by distrust. They had no problem relying on one another to follow the policies they created. Their problem was that they could not create enough policies to follow.

As we saw, the Cooks' Islanders were motivated to develop a legal system as part of their effort to break a potentially destructive dynamic. On the one hand, population growth on the island led to an increase in the need for policies to guide and coordinate behaviour. Yet, the same growth also amplified the cost of producing and applying such policies. At some point, the costs associated with improvisation, spontaneous ordering, private bargaining and communal consensus became so great that the demand for policies outstripped the island's ability to supply them. In an effort to radically reduce the costs of planning, the islanders were led to construct a hierarchical, impersonal and shared form of social planning. In doing so, they were able to adopt and apply the policies they needed and thereby solve the moral problems that more expensive or risky methods of planning could not.

The Circumstances of Legality

The residents of Cooks' Island may be atypical in their level of communal spirit and moral virtue, but their social problems are hardly unusual. For it is plausible to suppose that any modestly sized community will face similar questions about ownership, contractual obligations, duties of care to one another, proper levels of taxation, limitations of public power, legitimacy of state coercion, and so on. Moreover, like the islanders, it will find that resorting exclusively to non-legal forms of planning is an inefficient or inadequate way of resolving these questions. To settle the doubts and disagreements of its members in a cost-effective manner – or even at all – requires sophisticated techniques of social planning such as those provided by legal institutions.

I am going to refer to the social conditions that render sophisticated forms of social planning desirable as the 'circumstances of legality'.[18] The circumstances of legality obtain whenever a community has numerous moral problems whose solutions are complex, contentious or arbitrary. In such instances, the benefits of planning will be great, but so will the costs and risks associated with non-legal forms of ordering behaviour, such as improvisation, spontaneous ordering, private agreements, communal consensus or personalised hierarchies. Indeed, the costs and risks of non-legal planning may be so large as to be prohibitive. Communities who face such circumstances, therefore, have compelling reasons to reduce these associated costs and risks. And in order to do so, they will need the sophisticated technologies of social planning that only legal institutions provide.

Although the circumstances of legality emerged on Cooks' Island due to its system of private property, we can easily imagine similar conditions cropping up in a system of common ownership as well. In fact, in a collectivist regime where mass mobilisation of the community is needed to produce the necessities of daily life, the value of sophisticated technologies of social planning will be especially great. Massively shared activities can only be managed through the development of a dense network of plans and planners. Relying solely on non-legal methods to coordinate collective action on such an immense scale will eventually prove to be inferior to legal forms of social planning.

Once we recognise the extent to which even modestly sized human communities require sophisticated methods for guiding, organising and monitoring conduct, we can begin to see legal institutions in a new light. According to what I will call the 'planning theory of law', legal systems are institutions of social planning and their function is to compensate for the deficiencies of alternative forms of

[18] The term 'circumstances of legality' is a reference, of course, to David Hume's famous doctrine of the 'circumstances of justice'. Hume argued that the justice is a virtue only in situations of moderate conflict. He identified the circumstances of justice as ones of (1) modest scarcity, (2) limited altruism, (3) rough equality and (4) moderate social interdependence; see eg D Hume, *An Enquiry concerning the Principles of Morals*, edited by LA Selby-Bigge, 3rd edn revised by PH Nidditch (Oxford, Clarendon Press, 1975) section 3, Pt I. Other philosophers have added further conditions. Rawls, for example, claims that justice is appropriate also where people have divergent conceptions of the good life; see J Rawls, *A Theory of Justice*, revised edn (Cambridge, MA, Harvard University Press, 1999) 109–12. See also HLA Hart, *The Concept of Law*, 2nd edn (J Raz and P Bulloch (eds), Oxford, Oxford University Press, 1994) 193–200. The planning theory of law does not take the circumstances of justice to be sufficient for rendering law valuable. For the circumstances of justice can obtain for a certain community, but the problems of justice posed may be resolvable through non-legal forms of social ordering. Jeremy Waldron speaks of the 'circumstances of politics', which he identifies as obtaining whenever a group of people must act together over time but persistently disagree about the principles of justice that will regulate their joint activities; see eg J Waldron, *The Dignity of Legislation* (Cambridge, Cambridge University Press, 1999) 153–54. On the planning theory, the circumstances of legality include the circumstances of politics, but are not exhausted by it. Waldron's account unfortunately neglects the importance that complexity and arbitrariness play in rendering legal institutions valuable.

planning in the circumstances of legality. Legal institutions are supposed to enable communities to overcome the complexity, contentiousness and arbitrariness of communal life by resolving those social problems that cannot be solved, or solved as well, by non-legal means alone.

Of course, the aim of the law is not planning for planning's sake. If legal systems were merely supposed to adopt and apply plans regardless of method or content, the task would be better served by flipping a coin. Rather, the law aims to compensate for the deficiencies of non-legal forms of planning by planning in the 'right' way, namely, by adopting and applying morally appropriate plans in a morally legitimate manner. Legal systems are improvements over alternative forms of planning, and hence serve their function, whenever the total reduction in the costs of planning more than offsets any increase in the moral costs engendered by the switch. The task of institutional design, therefore, is to ensure that the legal process does not render mistakes so likely, or use methods that are so unsavoury, that the moral benefits of switching to law vanish. Indeed, legal systems are sometimes designed to *increase* the cost of adopting plans so as to *decrease* the risk that bad plans will be adopted. The worry here is that social planning may be *too* easy and, thus, overly responsive to the momentary passions of the electorate or self-interest of politicians. Throwing some sand in the gears may slow down the legal process enough to improve its ultimate reliability.

The planning theory of law's central claim – that the law is first and foremost a social planning mechanism – is supported by two considerations. First, it explains why we consider law to be valuable. It is, for example, a widely shared assumption of political theories that agree on virtually nothing else that the law is an indispensable social institution in the modern world. This belief is, of course, entirely sensible when we consider the benefits and costs of various methods of planning in such settings. Given the complexity, contentiousness and arbitrariness of modern life, the moral need for plans to guide, coordinate and monitor conduct are enormous. Yet, for the same reasons, it is extremely costly and risky for people to solve their social problems by themselves, via improvisation, spontaneous ordering or private agreements, or communally, via consensus or personalised forms of hierarchy. Legal systems, by contrast, are able to respond to this great demand for norms at a reasonable price. Because of the hierarchical, impersonal and shared nature of legal planning, legal systems are agile, durable and capable of reducing planning costs to such a degree that social problems can be solved in an efficient manner.

On the other hand, when the net savings in planning costs engendered by the switch to law are low or non-existent, we tend not to judge legal institutions to be necessary or even desirable. For example, it would be quite odd to pity hunter-gatherers for not having law. Hunter-gatherers, after all, need very few rules. Since they do not cultivate land or domesticate animals, they have no need for a fixed system of property rights in real property. Moreover, because the food collected is perishable, hunter-gatherers accumulate little or no surplus and hence have no need for rights in personal property as well. Rules for the voluntary transfer of property and compensation for their damage are similarly useless to them. Not only are the benefits of social planning low but so too are the costs. For when hunter-gatherers require rules, they can either rely on custom or create them straightaway. They can deliberate among themselves about how they ought to live and arrive at some consensus or, failing that, the discontents can separate and merge with other groups. Determining whether the rules have been broken is easy both insofar as there are very few of them and collective deliberations are possible. And when a rule has been violated, communal responses are not difficult to organise. In short, hunter-gatherers do not need law because they do not face the circumstances of legality and, hence, have no need for sophisticated technologies of social planning.

Attributing a planning function to law is further supported by the observation that legal systems can be criticised not only for being evil, but also poorly designed. The Articles of Confederation of the first United States, for example, were roundly condemned for their inability to regulate interstate commerce, impose taxes, raise an army, establish a system of federal courts, etc. They were also assailed for their amendment procedures which required unanimous consent to change any article. In other words, the former colonists considered their legal system defective precisely because it was an inadequate response to the circumstances of legality. Confederation following Independence generated so much complexity, contentiousness and arbitrariness that the system could not meet the nation's new demands for social planning.[19]

[19] To say that the function of the law is to resolve those moral problems that cannot be solved as efficiently by custom, tradition, persuasion, consensus and promise is not to suggest, of course, that the law *never* relies on these other mechanisms. When simpler methods of organising behaviour work, it would be irrational to abandon or overturn them in favour of accomplishing the very same ends through more sophisticated methods. Thus, when customs or contracts solve moral problems, the law will typically let them stand. And the master plan may itself be filled out through customary means or private agreements as well. In other cases, the law will interfere with private orderings in a modest way, by supporting them when they emerge, such as when it enforces certain types of customs and contracts, and by empowering others to form when they would not otherwise, such as when it authorises persons to engage in various types of property and contractual relationships. In these cases, the task of the law is to use minimally invasive forms of social planning in order to promote the solution of moral problems through private ordering. To say that the function of the law is to resolve those moral problems that cannot be solved as efficiently by custom, tradition, persuasion, consensus and promise is not to suggest, of course, that the law *never* relies on these other mechanisms. When simpler methods of organising behaviour work, it would be irrational to abandon or overturn them in favour of accomplishing the very same ends through more sophisticated methods. Thus, when customs or contracts solve moral problems, the law will typically let them stand. And the master plan may itself be filled out through customary means or private agreements as well. In other cases, the law will interfere with private orderings in a modest way, by supporting them when they emerge, such as when it enforces certain types of customs and contracts, and by empowering others to form when they would not otherwise, such as when it authorises persons to engage in various types of property and contractual relationships. In these cases, the task of the law is to use minimally invasive forms of social planning in order to promote the solution of moral problems through private ordering.

E Law as a Universal Means

According to the planning theory of law then, the function of law is not to solve any *particular* moral quandary. Its function is to solve a higher-order problem, namely, the problem of how to solve moral quandaries *in general*. A community needs law whenever its moral problems (whatever they happen to be) are so numerous, and their solutions so complex, contentious or arbitrary, that non-legal planning is an inferior way of guiding, coordinating and monitoring conduct.

In this sense, laws, like intentions, are 'universal means'.[20] Just as there are no specific ends that intentions are supposed to serve, there are no substantive goals or values that laws are supposed to achieve or realise. They are all-purpose tools that enable agents with complex goals, conflicting values and limited abilities to achieve ends that they would not be able to achieve, or achieve as well, without them.

The Problem of Bad Character

It is worth noting at this point that the planning theory of law contrasts sharply with a more conventional view of the law, famously expressed by James Madison in *Federalist* 51, when he wrote that 'if men were angels, no government would be necessary'.[21] Following this popular view, the function of the law is to solve a particular social problem, namely, *the problem of bad character*. Legal institutions are created not as general purpose technologies of social planning but rather as antidotes to the infirmities of human nature that inevitably lead people to transgress existing social or moral norms.

The problem of bad character is perhaps the most salient theme running through the classical social contract theories of the early modern period. Hobbes argued, for example, that the state of nature is a state of war because men are greedy and vain.[22] In their desire to dominate others as well as protect themselves, they inevitably disregard their covenants of non-aggression and launch preemptive attacks against those who might attack them first. Locke also thought that individuals in the state of nature would act aggressively.[23] Unlike Hobbes, however, he did not think they would do so out of callous disregard for the natural law but rather as a result of self-deception. Since people are often biased in their own favour, each side in a dispute will judge themselves justified and hence be unwilling to yield. Unable to settle their conflicts peacefully, individuals in the state of nature will resort to violence, leading to destructive cycles of feuding.

[20] M Bratman, *Faces of Intention: Selected Essays on Intention and Agency* (Cambridge, Cambridge University Press, 1999) 5.

[21] J Madison, 'The Federalist No 51' in JE Cooke (ed), *The Federalist* (Middletown, CT, Wesleyan University Press, 1961) 347–53.

[22] See eg T Hobbes, *Leviathan* in E Curley (ed), *Leviathan, with selected variants from the Latin edition of 1668* (Indianapolis, Hackett, 1994 (1668)) chs 13–15.

[23] See eg J Locke, *Second Treatise of Government* in P Laslett (ed), *Locke: Two Treatises of Government*, 3rd edn (Cambridge, Cambridge University Press, 1988 (1690)) chs 2–3, 8–9.

Similarly, Hume believed that, in the absence of government, people will tend to ignore the principles of justice.[24] Hume attributed this non-compliance largely to irrationality: people often heavily discount the future and seek to maximise short-term benefit over long-term gain. As a result, they routinely fail to recognise the benefits of abiding by the principles of justice.

For each of these three political theorists, the state of nature is undesirable because human nature is corrupt in some way. And, correspondingly, the law is a necessary social institution precisely because it compensates for the infirmities of human nature by ensuring that individuals abide by the existing norms. For Hobbes and Hume, the law secures compliance by threatening coercion and sanctions, whereas for Locke, it acts as a third party adjudicator, providing impartial resolution of disputes for those who consent to its authority.

In view of our earlier discussion however, this general account of the law is obviously flawed. For if the principal aim of law is to solve the problem of bad character, we would expect law to be deemed unnecessary in situations where everyone has good character. But as we saw in the last section, legal institutions can be highly desirable even though everyone in the community is willing to abide by the existing norms. The residents of Cooks' Island, for example, were committed to following their shared plan, and acting in accordance with morality. The complexity and contentiousness of these normative questions, however, rendered that task difficult and costly to accomplish. Moreover, the complexity and arbitrariness of many large-scale shared activities rendered it impossible for members of the group to do what they had good ethical reasons to do. Even when they knew what moral problems they ought to rectify, they could not figure out how to coordinate their behaviour so as to resolve these problems. Their sterling characters did not, in other words, diminish their need for law.

The Plan is Mightier than the Sword

Following the planning theory of law, it is a mistake to suppose that the function of the law is to solve the problem of bad character or any other particular social or moral quandary. As a contingent matter, of course, the law serves a number of important social aims. It builds roads and bridges, educates the population, finances and organises communal self-defence, sets up markets, regulates imports and exports, controls the money supply, standardises weights and measures, collects and redistributes wealth, arbitrates and mediates disputes, constitutes national identity, and so on. It also ensures that people listen to its rules. Indeed, it would be absurd to deny that, in the modern world at least, social deviance caused by vicious character is one of the reasons why law is an indispensable social institution. It is indeed likely that life would be poor, nasty, brutish and short without legal systems maintaining order through threats of coercion.

[24] See eg David Hume, *A Treatise of Human Nature* in DF Norton and MJ Norton (eds), *A Treatise of Human Nature* (Oxford, Oxford University Press, 2000 (1739)) Part II, section VII.

The essential point, however, is that whenever the law properly addresses a particular social problem, it does so because (given current social conditions) alternative methods of planning are somehow deficient. Thus, when the law is needed to combat bad character, it is because, and only because, coercion in the absence of sophisticated forms of social planning would be expensive, ineffective or dangerous. To appreciate this, it is important to remember that law enforcement is a shared activity and, in modern states, a quite massive one. In some cases, the roster of officers who are engaged in enforcement (police, judges, magistrates, bailiffs, clerks, wardens, guards and lawyers) contains millions of names. It is hard to imagine such groups acting together in such complex and contentious environments without an extensive network of social plans to regulate their behaviour. These inherent problems can be further aggravated when alienated participants are asked to play roles that they cannot be trusted to perform in the absence of guidance and monitoring. Add to these difficulties the enormous number of coordination problems that arise in such large-scale contexts and it becomes evident that improvisation, spontaneous ordering, private planning and simple forms of social planning are not adequate to guide, organise and monitor such activities.

Kelsen once described law as an 'organisation of force'.[25] Although I disagree with this claim that the law necessarily uses force, I agree that, when the law does use force, it is always organised. Both to maximise its effect and control its power, the law organises a coercive response to social deviance through an interlocking set of social plans. The master plan which regulates all official conduct controls the procedural aspects of coercion: it selects those whose role it is to enforce the law and the procedures that they must follow in order for coercion to be permissible. The directives that are created pursuant to the master plan concern the substantive aspects of coercion: they identify those actions that warrant a coercive response. Legal officials know which behaviours to punish because other officials have issued directives informing members of the group of their rights and obligations. When enforcement personnel follow this dense network of social plans, they are able to act collectively to subdue members of the community. Thus, despite the fact that legal officials are almost always a small minority of a population, the shared agency made possible by social planning harnesses and magnifies their power, thereby enabling them to enforce the will of the law.

F The Primacy of Social Facts

As we have seen, the planning theory not only maintains that legal activity results *in* planning; it maintains that it results *from* planning as well. Legal institutions are structured by shared plans that are developed for officials so as to enable them work together in order to plan for the community. These norms set out the

[25] H Kelsen, *General Theory of Law and State* (A Wedberg (trans), New York, Russell & Russell, 1961) 21.

vertical and horizontal divisions of social labour, specifying who is authorised to formulate, adopt, affect, apply and enforce the plans and instructing them about how to engage in these various stages of social planning. These shared plans can be thought of as *the law's plans for planning.*

Once we recognise the central role that shared plans play in the law, we can begin to address the following questions: Why might one claim (as legal positivists do) that law and morality do not share the same basic ground rules? and Why is the determination of legal validity a matter of a sociological, rather than moral, inquiry?

I hope that my answer to these questions is now apparent; namely, that the fundamental rules of a legal system constitute a shared plan and, as we have seen, the proper way to determine the existence or content of a shared plan is through an examination of the relevant social facts. A shared plan exists just in case the plan was designed with a group in mind so that they may engage in a joint activity, it is publicly accessible and accepted by members of the groups in question. As a result, if we want to discover the existence or content of the fundamental rules of a legal system, we must look only to these social facts. We must look, in other words, only to what we think, intend, claim and do round here.

Notice further that the existence of the shared plan does not depend on any moral facts obtaining. The shared plan can be morally obnoxious: it may cede total control of social planning to a malevolent dictator or privilege the rights of certain subgroups of the community over others. Nevertheless, if the social facts obtain for plan sharing, then the shared plan will exist. And if the shared plan sets out an activity of social planning that is hierarchical and highly impersonal and the community normally abides by the plans created pursuant to it, then a system of legal authority will exist as well.

The crucial point here is that the determination by social facts is not some necessary, but otherwise unimportant, property of shared plans. Shared plans must be determined exclusively by social facts *if they are to fulfil their function.* As we have seen, shared plans are supposed to guide and coordinate behaviour by resolving doubts and disagreements about proper action in complex, contentious and arbitrary environments. If a plan with a particular content exists only when certain moral facts obtain, then it could not resolve doubts and disagreements about the right way of proceeding. For in order to apply it, the participants would have to engage in deliberation and bargaining that would recreate the problem that the plan aimed to solve. The logic of planning requires that plans be ascertainable by a method that does not resurrect the very questions that plans are designed to settle. Only social facts – not moral ones – can serve this function.

The purpose of the master plan, we have said, is to guide, organise and monitor the shared activity of legal officials. It seeks to overcome the enormously complex, contentious and arbitrary problems associated with arranging a system of social planning. Because reasonable (and unreasonable) people can have doubts and disagreements about which social problems to pursue and who should be trusted to pursue them, it is essential to have a mechanism that can settle such questions, creating a mesh between legal officials and leading them all in the same direction. To seek to discover the existence or content of such a mechanism by looking to moral philosophy, as the natural lawyer recommends we do, would frustrate the function of the master plan. It would require members of the community to answer the very sorts of questions that the master plan aimed to circumvent.

This objection to natural law theory might helpfully be put in a slightly different way. Consider a theory called 'plan positivism'. Plan positivists believe that the existence and content of plans never depends on moral facts. Plan positivism is uncontroversially true. Everyone, even natural lawyers, accepts that people can have morally bad plans. Terrorist plots, for example, exist even though they should not be carried out from the moral point of view; rather, they exist just because terrorists share certain plans. Indeed, plan positivism must be true if plans are to fulfil their function. Plans can do the thinking for us only if we can discover their existence or content without engaging in deliberation on the merits.

Since plan positivism is uncontroversially true, natural law theory will be false *if the fundamental rules of a legal system are plans*. Since the planning theory of law claims that all law is grounded in shared plans, it follows that if the planning theory of law is true, then natural law theory cannot be.

My objection to natural law theory, therefore, stands or falls based on the planning theory of law. For once it is conceded that legal systems are grounded in shared plans, natural law theory can be maintained only on pain of contradiction. I hope that I have given the reader at least some reason to think that the planning theory of law is a reasonable jurisprudential theory. And if the reader has been convinced, he or she will be logically compelled to accept some form of legal positivism as well.

G The Possibility of Legal Authority

A crucial test for any jurisprudential theory is its ability to solve what we can call the 'possibility puzzle'. The possibility puzzle purports to show that legal authority is impossible. On the one hand, legal authority must be conferred by legal norms; yet, on the other, legal norms must be created by legal authority. From these two assumptions, we get a classic chicken–egg paradox. Any time we try to establish a claim of legal authority, we either enter into a vicious circle (the authority created the norm which conferred the power on the authority to create that very norm); or an infinite regress (the authority got his power from another authority, who got his power from another authority, and so on).

In this final section, I want to show that the planning theory of law does indeed provide a convincing solution to this apparent paradox. Before I can do so, however, I need to say a bit more about how legal authority is generated by the plans of a legal system.

The Ability to Plan

According to the planning theory of law, someone has legal authority only if they are authorised by the master plan of a particular legal system. But while authorisation is necessary for legal authority, it is clearly not sufficient. The reason is simple: if legal authority entails the ability to plan for others, as the planning theory claims, then the norms adopted and applied by legal authorities must be plans. Plans, as I have argued, are a special kind of norms. They are not only positive entities that form nested structures, but they are formed by a process that disposes their subjects to comply. As a result, unless the members of the community are disposed to follow the norms created to guide their conduct, the norms created will not be plans.

Thus, being authorised to plan for others does not entail that one actually has the *ability* to plan for others. A group of poor deluded souls can share a plan authorising one of them to plan for the withdrawal of US forces from Iraq. But the one authorised will not have the ability to adopt a plan for US forces because he cannot dispose them to act in accordance with his directives.

The disposition instilled by the legal process is obviously not a brute causal one – it must be tied in some way to human motivation. Legal authorities have the ability to plan for others, in other words, only if they are able to motivate their subjects to obey under normal conditions. Of course, not every official with legal authority need be able to instill this disposition; rather, they must be part of a group of individuals who, by planning together in accordance with the master plan, can dispose most of the people to comply with most of the plans most of the time.

When members of the community consider legal authorities to be morally legitimate, encouraging compliant behaviour will be relatively straightforward. By designating a standard as *the* standard to be used to guide and evaluate conduct, their subjects will take themselves to have reasons to defer and, in the normal course, will obey. If members of the community are less 'cooperative', legal authorities can dispose them to comply through various forms of intimidation. When these threats are strong and credible enough, even those who do not accept the law's moral authority will nevertheless be motivated to follow the adopted plans.[26]

Legal Authority and Planning Authority

As we have seen, the planning theory of law claims that a body has legal authority in a particular legal system when two conditions are met: (1) the system's master

[26] Notice that while the authorisation to plan for others merely depends on the mental states of legal officials, the ability to plan depends on the mental states of ordinary citizens as well. Legal authorities can motivate obedience in the normal course only if members of the community are sufficiently virtuous, submissive or cowardly. Trying to plan for a 'stiff-necked people' may simply not be possible and, when this is so, legal authority will not be possible either.

plan authorises that body to plan for others; and (2) the members of the community normally heed all those who are so authorised. Legal authority will be possible, therefore, just in case it is possible for both of these conditions to obtain. Let us, then, consider each of these two conditions in turn.

First, is it possible that a shared plan authorises some body to plan? Of course it is! As we have seen, shared plans exist when certain social facts obtain. A shared plan can authorise some person to plan for another just in case some person or persons designed the plan (at least in part) for a group, part of the plan authorises some body to plan for another, the plan is publicly accessible, and the members of the group accept it. When these conditions obtain, a shared plan will be created and will authorise some to plan for others.

On this account, the question of how the Queen of England is the Queen is no more perplexing than the question of how my friend can be the head chef during a meeting of our club. My friend is authorised to adopt plans for club members because we have committed ourselves to defer to him. Similarly, the Queen is legally authorised to plan for others because British legal officials have accepted a shared plan which authorises her to play a certain role in adopting legal policies and, hence, requires them to defer to her in the circumstances specified in that plan.

In the end, shared plans are able to authorise legal officials to plan for others because human beings are planning agents and are capable of guiding and organising their actions both over time and across persons. Not only can we figure out how others should act in order to achieve some complex goal, but we can form intentions to do what we are instructed to do. In other words, we are able to create law because we are able to create and share plans.

Notice that the planning theory of law is able to secure the existence of fundamental legal rules without generating vicious circles or infinite regresses. Legal officials have the power to adopt the shared plan which sets out these fundamental rules by virtue of the norms of instrumental rationality. Since these norms that confer the rational power to plan are not themselves plans, they have not been created by any other authority. They exist simply in virtue of being rationally valid principles. Instrumental rationality, therefore, constitutes the normative bedrock on which every legal system rests.

Having shown that shared plans authorising bodies to plan for others are possible, we should consider the second condition of legal authority, namely, whether those so authorised can motivate their subjects to comply under normal conditions. As we have just seen, there is nothing perplexing about this condition obtaining either. Members of the group might all accept a general policy to obey the law or deem those in authority to be morally legitimate. In such cases, the adoption of plans by legal officials will induce a rational requirement for those individuals to comply. Even when members of the group are not predisposed to conform to the law, the commitment of officials to carry out parts of the shared plan that direct punishment in case of disobedience may be sufficient to motivate ordinary citizens to obey.

We can see, therefore, that legal authority is possible because certain kinds of agents are capable of (1) creating and sharing a plan for planning, and (2) motivating others to heed their plans. Legal systems are possible, in other words, because certain states of affairs are possible, namely, those that underwrite the existence of a legal system's master plan and those that account for the disposition of the community to comply with the plans created under normal conditions.

It might be thought that this solution is one that the legal positivist would whole-heartedly endorse since it maintains that the authoritative status of any official does not derive from any moral fact. Even if the shared plan is morally odious and the citizens are as servile as sheep, the authorised individual will have legal authority within the existing system.

Upon closer inspection, however, the planning theory of law poses problems for legal positivism. For according to the traditional formulation, legal positivists claim that the existence and content of the law rests on social facts alone. Yet, according to the planning theory, the existence of the law actually depends on a normative fact as well, namely, the fact that planning agents have the rational authority to give themselves plans. To be sure, the rational authority of planners is not a form of moral authority: terrorists, as we have said, have the rational authority to create evil plots among themselves. But the fact that planners are so empowered is nonetheless a normative fact because it affects, in a very important sense, what individuals ought to do.

It turns out, then, that the conventional debate between legal positivism and natural law theory has presented legal theorists with a false choice. It is true neither that the law ultimately rests on social facts alone nor that it rests on social *and* moral facts. The planning theory of law shows that there is a third alternative, namely, that legal facts ultimately rest on social and non-moral normative facts. To be sure, this third alternative is clearly within the spirit of legal positivism, because it denies a role to moral facts in determining the existence or content of the law. But this version also departs from the letter of legal positivism by recognising that the law does indeed rest on irreducible norms of practical rationality.

The Legal Point of View

Natural lawyers might respond to this defence of a moderate version of legal positivism in the following way: they might concede that moral facts are not needed in order to establish a social planning system. Planning agents have the rational authority to plan their social planning and the resulting shared plans are indeed created by a combination of social and non-moral normative facts. Yet, they will surely deny that these facts are sufficient *for establishing legal authority*.

Someone possesses legal authority, natural lawyers will point out, only if they have the ability to impose legal obligations. But how can anybody have this normative power simply because certain of their cronies authorise them to have such a power and members of the community acquiesce? To generate relations of legal authority, the objection goes, a group needs more than social and non-moral normative facts: it needs *moral facts* as well. In the case of Cooks' Island, it is plausible to suppose that the adopters and appliers possessed legal authority because their planning system is morally legitimate. After all, it was set up in a democratically appropriate manner and designed to serve moral aims. Their plans do confer legal authority and impose legal obligations. Once we remove the assumption of moral legitimacy, however, the claim of legality becomes highly dubious.

In order to address this objection, we should examine claims of legal authority in more detail: what are we imputing to someone when we say that they have 'legal authority'? One possibility is that we are imputing a type of moral authority. On this reading, the word 'authority' means the same as it does in moral contexts, namely, the power to impose moral obligations, and the word 'legal' functions as an adjective, identifying this kind of moral power. We are saying, then, that the person in question has moral authority in virtue of being an official in a legal institution. Call this the 'adjectival' interpretation.

It appears that the natural law objection interprets claims of legal authority adjectivally. For on the adjectival interpretation, legal authority entails moral authority and since morally illegitimate shared plans do not confer moral authority they cannot confer legal authority. To be sure, this implication would be devastating for the planning theory of law if we were compelled to accept the adjectival interpretation of legal authority claims as the only possible one. I do not, however, think we are. The problem with the adjectival interpretation is that it ties legal authority too tightly to moral authority and thus precludes the possibility of morally illegitimate governments: not only are such cases possible, but they are actual. Stalin, Hitler and Mao (to use three paradigmatic examples) all had legal authority but were morally illegitimate. The adjectival interpretation, therefore, does not permit us to make the claims about legal authority that we customarily make.

Fortunately, there is another interpretation that does permit the ascription of legal authority to morally illegitimate bodies. The key here is to recognise that, although the term 'authority' in legal authority claims refers to a moral power, the word 'legal' often functions as a *qualifier* rather than a modifier. When we ascribe legal authority to someone, we are not necessarily imputing any kind of moral authority to them. To the contrary, we are qualifying our ascription of moral legitimacy. We are saying that, *from the legal point of view*, the person in question has morally legitimate power. Similarly, to say that one is legally obligated to perform some action need not commit the asserter to affirming that one is really obligated to perform that action, ie has a moral obligation to perform that action. The statement may be understood to mean only that from the legal point of view one is (morally) obligated to perform that action.

To understand the discourse of legality, therefore, one must recognise that it typically performs a *distancing* function. It enables us to talk about the moral conception of a particular legal system without necessarily endorsing that conception. Sure (one might say) sodomy is wrong from the legal point of view. But this assertion does not imply anything about whether sodomy is in fact wrong. In some cases, the word 'legal' registers our agnosticism: we do not know or care whether the law's normative judgements are correct, we are simply reporting these judgements – in effect, bracketing them off in a special kind of invisible inverted commas. At other times, the word 'legal' signals our alienation from the legal point of view. Sodomy, we can say, is legally wrong, but it is wrong *only legally*. From our own point of view, sodomy is morally permissible.

What, then, is the legal point of view? It is not necessarily the perspective of any particular legal official. No official may accept the law's conception of itself. The legal point of view, rather, is the perspective of a certain normative theory. According to that theory, those who are authorised by the norms of legal institutions have moral legitimacy and, when they act in accordance with those norms, they generate a moral obligation to obey. The legal point of view of a certain system, in other words, is a theory that holds that the norms of that system are morally legitimate and obligating. Thus, communism is the point of view of communist legal systems, individualism the point of view of laissez-faire capitalist systems, democratic theory the point of view of democratic systems, and so on.

The normative theory that represents a system's point of view may, of course, be false from a moral perspective; that is, the legal point of view may not coincide with the true moral point of view. Those authorised by legal institutions to act may be morally illegitimate and their actions may generate no moral obligations to obey. The point of view of a particular legal system may be like the phlogiston theory of combustion – a scientific theory that aimed to be true but missed the mark. In short, the legal point of view always *purports* to represent truly the moral point of view, even when it fails to do so.

Given this interpretation of legal authority and obligation claims, we can easily see how morally illegitimate shared plans can confer legal authority. For to ascribe legal authority to a body in a particular legal system is to assert that, from the point of view of that legal system, the body in question is morally legitimate:[27]

> (1) X has legal authority over Y in system S ↔ From the point of view of S, X has moral authority over Y.

The point of view of that legal system will ascribe moral legitimacy to a body just in case its norms confer legal power on that body. Since on the planning theory of law the legal norms that confer legal authority are sub-plans of the system's master plan, the legal point of view will ascribe moral legitimacy to a body when its master plan authorises that body to so act:

> (2) From the point of view of S, X has moral authority over Y ↔ The master plan of S authorises X to plan for Y.

[27] Since a legal system exists only when it is generally efficacious, ie members of the community normally obey the law, X will have legal authority over Y in S only when S is generally efficacious. The legal point of view, therefore, ascribes moral legitimacy only to those who are authorised by a master plan of a generally system.

It follows from (1) and (2) that a body will have legal authority in a particular legal system just in case the system's master plan authorises that body to so act:[28]

> (3) X has legal authority over Y in system S $\leftrightarrow$ The master plan of S authorises X to plan for Y.

We can see thus that the truth of legal authority claims is not dependent on the moral legitimacy of a system's master plan. A body has legal authority in a system because the master plan authorises it. And, as we have seen, master plans are capable of authorising someone to plan for another just in case the members of a group exercised their planning authority in the right sort of way.

[28] As mentioned in the previous note, X will have legal authority over Y in S only when S is generally efficacious. Hence, it will not be sufficient for a master plan to authorise someone to plan in order for that person to have legal authority. The master plan must be the plan of a generally efficacious planning system.

2

Reflections on Law, Normativity and Plans

MICHAEL E BRATMAN

IN HIS 1982 essay Gerald Postema considers the following:

> *The Normativity Thesis*: . . . We understand law only if we understand how it is that laws give members of a community, officials and law-subjects alike, reasons for acting. Thus any adequate general theory of law must give a satisfactory account of the normative (reason-giving) character of law.[1]

Postema accepted this normativity thesis, and wanted to know how a positivist theory could combine it with the 'social thesis' that 'law is a social fact'.[2] His answer, very roughly, was that law is a structure of coordination conventions, and such conventions provide each participant with reasons for action that depend in a characteristic way on the regularities of the behaviour of most or all. The purported reasons cited by Postema are what we can call, following Bernard Williams, internal reasons, since they depend on the preferences of each of the participants.[3] Indeed, the underlying view is that these preferences ensure corresponding normative reasons.

Let's step back. Talk of the normativity of law covers a wide range of ideas. We can begin with a fairly weak, though fundamental, idea:

(a) Law essentially involves *legal-norm guidance* – that is, guiding one's activities by appeal to legal norms/standards – at least on the part of legal officials.

This was one of HLA Hart's basic points – and a fundamental advance from Austin's appeal solely to habits of obedience – in emphasising the internal acceptance of relevant social rules, including rules of recognition.[4] And this is an idea that is also central to Scott Shapiro's 'planning theory of law'.[5] According to that theory, law is, very roughly, a union of a hierarchy of shared social plans for social

[1] GJ Postema, 'Coordination and Convention at the Foundations of Law' (1982) 11 *Journal of Legal Studies* 165.

[2] ibid 165.

[3] B Williams, 'Internal and External Reasons' in his *Moral Luck* (Cambridge, Cambridge University Press, 1981) 101–13.

[4] HLA Hart, *The Concept of Law*, 2nd edn (New York, Oxford University Press, 1994).

[5] My essay is to a large extent a commentary on Shapiro's theory. References are to Chapter 1 of this volume.

planning.[6] These shared plans are publicly accessible, each official intends to conform and play their roles, and each official is committed to allowing the others to play their roles. And the relevant conformity with these shared social plans essentially involves the guidance of thought and action, on the part of those legal officials, by appeal to these shared plans.

Turn now to a second, and stronger idea:

(b) Given the nature of a legal system, the officials in that system are subject to distinctive constraints of *rationality*. There is, in this sense, an *inner rationality of law*.[7]

This is in the spirit of Hart's views. Though (to my knowledge) Hart did not formulate his view in quite this way, I take it that he would agree that in taking the internal point of view on, and so accepting, a social rule, eg a rule of recognition, an official intends to reason and to act in accordance with that rule; and such an intention brings with it constraints of consistency, and what I call means–end coherence with other relevant intentions, eg intentions concerning particular legal cases.[8] And this point about the inner rationality of law is central to Shapiro's planning theory of law: according to that theory officials are subject to characteristic consistency and coherence constraints on the shared plans they accept, and these constraints are at work in legal-norm guidance.

On Shapiro's planning theory of law, the officials have intentions, plans and policies with distinctive contents, and the inner rationality of law is primarily the inner rationality of planning. For example, a lower court judge will likely have a policy of treating the rulings of the higher court as binding on him. Given the inner rationality of plans and policies, this lower court judge is then rationally constrained in his relevant practical reasoning and further decisions. And similar points can be made about the various other types of plans and policies that Shapiro describes as elements in law, including, for example, policies that define offices.

Now, Donald Davidson famously claimed that the very phenomenon of mind essentially involves norms of rationality.[9] Davidson's argument for this claim depended on his views about interpretation. But let's just consider the claim itself. What is interesting in the present context is that the planning theory of law has a somewhat analogous view about law: the very phenomenon of law essentially involves the norms of rational planning. This view about law is, however, not grounded in a background view about interpretation. It is, rather, grounded (I take it) in a kind of inference to the best explanation: this model of law best

[6] Shapiro, Chapter 1 of this volume, 55.

[7] *cf* Lon L Fuller's talk of 'the internal morality of law itself' in his 'Positivism and Fidelity to Law: A Reply to Professor Hart' (1958) 71 *Harvard Law Review* 630.

[8] These norms of consistency and means-end coherence play a basic role in my planning theory of intention and our agency. See my *Intention, Plans, and Practical Reason* (Cambridge, MA, Harvard University Press, 1987) (reissued Stanford, CA, CSLI Publications, 1999).

[9] See eg D Davidson, 'Psychology as Philosophy' in his *Essays on Actions and Events*, 2nd edn (Oxford, Oxford University Press, 2001) 229–44.

captures its important features and complexities. And Shapiro's further idea (I take it) is that while norms of planning rationality are essential to law, distinctively moral norms are not in the same way essential to law – where this last claim is one he shares with the positivist tradition. As we might say, the legal positivist rejects the extension of a Davidsonian idea of the status of norms of rationality as partly constitutive of mind to the case of moral norms and legality.

One way to think of this is as a view about our knowledge of law. Investigators into the nature of law will need, on this view, to agree about the basic rationality norms associated with planning: this is part of what is involved in the idea of the inner rationality of law. But they need not (though of course they may) agree in their moral assessments either of specific legal systems, or even (a point I return to below) of the functions that law normally serves. Consider an analogous view about our knowledge of religion: different researchers can converge in their understanding of religious practices, the reasoning internal to those practices, and the characteristic functions of those practices, while disagreeing in their assessments of the value of these practices.

These ideas of the inner rationality of law are important. But now we need to note (though here I am unsure whether I am disagreeing with Shapiro) that these ideas do not yet get us to Postema's idea that law provides normative reasons for action. To see this let's turn to one version of that idea, a version I flag with a '*' for reasons that will become clear:

(c*) Law, quite generally and by its nature, induces *normative/justifying reasons* for legal officials to act in ways mandated by the law.

(c*) does not say that these reasons for action need be the same across the different officials. All that is claimed, so far, is that each official has some normative reasons to act as mandated by the law, reasons that somehow flow from the nature of a legal system.

Even though there is as yet no claim that the relevant reasons are the same across the different officials, (c*) nevertheless goes beyond (b). Appreciating this point will lead to important complexities in our understanding of what (as I see it) the planning theory of law should say about the normativity of law; in particular, it will lead to a somewhat complex story of the ways in which law may be 'reason-giving'.

Now, the basic reason for seeing (c*) as going beyond (b) is that you might think that law brings with it distinctive rationality constraints – there is an inner rationality of law – but still wonder if you have any reason at all to (continue to) engage in the practice of law. You might even think you have good reason not to engage in this practice, though the practice itself has its own inner rationality. This is a basic way in which the inner rationality of law differs from the Davidsonian idea of, so to speak, the inner rationality of mind. There is a sense in which having a mind is not a matter of choice (though, of course, suicide remains an option). But it is more or less a matter of choice whether to participate as an official in a legal system. So you can sensibly ask what reason there is for you to participate.

Let's reflect on this point by considering a toy example.

A Toy Example Suppose there is a game that involves a rule that says: if you make move A you cannot also make move B, and you must, as a preliminary to A, make either move C or move D. This game has a kind of inner rationality, one which you violate if, knowing the rules, you intend to make move A and intend to make move B, or intend to make move A without either intending to make move C or intending to make move D. But you could know all this and still think there is no reason at all to play this game and, indeed, good reason not to. After all, perhaps this is a 'game' of torture.

But what if you are now intentionally playing the game? If you were to intend to make move A when it is your turn would you, quite generally, thereby have a normative reason to either make move C or make move D? Well, we can assume that it remains up to you whether to continue to play. So even if you now intend to make move A it still seems a real question whether to continue to play or to withdraw. And suppose you think there is no reason at all to continue and good reason to withdraw. Then it seems that what you should think is that you do not have reason either to make move C or to make move D. You should think that what you have reason to do is, rather, to withdraw from the game.

Should we say that simply by intending to play the game and intending to make move A you thereby do, quite generally, have a normative reason to play the game and make move A? If we were to say this then we could go on to say that, given the inner rationality of the game, and given that you do intend to play the game and to make move A, you do now have a reason not to make move B. So we need to ask whether it is true that simply by intending to play the game and intending to make move A you thereby, quite generally, have a normative reason to play the game and make move A.

Well, I do think that many times your intention to engage in some activity induces a new normative reason for engaging in that activity. In Sartre's famous example, if the boy arrives at the intention to devote his life to his mother, rather than to the Free French, he thereby comes to have a reason to devote his life to his mother, a reason that he would not have had if he had instead arrived at an intention in favour of the Free French. And many career decisions are less dramatic examples of this.

But it does not follow that *whenever* one intends to A one thereby has a new normative reason to A. And indeed that seems to me implausible. Suppose one makes a decision that is contrary to one's better judgement. It seems odd to suppose that, quite generally, such a weak-willed intention provides a new reason for action. After all, if it did provide such a new reason then it might tilt the scales in favour of acting against one's better judgement; and that would be an odd kind of boot-strapping.[10] Again, suppose I decide to do something that is horrendous:torture the captives, say. Should we say that, quite generally, I thereby create a new normative reason for torturing? I doubt it.

[10] See my 'Intention and Means-End Reasoning' (1981) 90 *Philosophical Review* 252.

In doubting this I am assuming that when we judge that there is a normative reason for action we are endorsing its role as a positive consideration in relevant deliberation. Such a view about judgements about reasons is available to a range of theories about such judgements. I myself am inclined in the direction of a theory that is broadly in the spirit of Allan Gibbard's expressivism.[11] But what I say here does not depend on this specific view but only on the general thought that judgements about normative reasons involve endorsement.

I also intend these remarks to be neutral concerning the question whether all normative reasons for action are internal reasons in roughly Williams' sense. Even if we were to suppose that all normative reasons for action are internal reasons, it would be a further question whether just by forming a new intention one quite generally comes to have a new reason. And it is that question that I have answered in the negative. So we are so far without an argument that if you intend to play the game and to make move A, you have a reason not to make move B.

Now, in talking of planning rationality I have so far highlighted demands of consistency and means–end coherence. These are demands of synchronic rationality. But there is also, I think, a norm of diachronic rationality of planning. There is some sort of rationality demand not to change one's settled plans, from moment to moment, absent reason to do this. Without trying to provide a careful formulation, let's just call this a demand for rational plan stability. Does our recognition of this idea of rational stability support the claim that merely by intending some end you do in general come to have a new normative reason to intend necessary means and to eschew intending options you know are incompatible with that end?

Return to your intention to play the game and make move A. If you go on to intend to make move B you will either be plan-inconsistent, or you will give up your prior intention to make move A. If the latter were in general a violation of rational plan stability then we would have an argument that if you do intend to make move A, then plan rationality provides *pro tanto* support for the specific option of refraining from intending to make move B. This is not yet to say that your intention in favour of A gives you a normative reason to eschew intending B. But it does highlight a kind of rational pressure specifically against intending B.

An initial problem here, however, is that if your intention in favour of A is a weak-willed intention then it may well be that a plausible principle of rational plan stability would allow or even require giving up that intention. So we cannot say that, quite generally, rational stability supports retaining a prior intention. So we are still without a general argument in favour of the *pro tanto* rationality of sticking with intending to make move A.

But now suppose that your intention to play the game and to make move A is not weak-willed but is, rather, a whole-hearted intention. In the absence of relevant new information, will rational stability support its retention? Well, rational

[11] As Gibbard puts it: 'when a person calls something – call it R – a reason for doing X, he expresses his acceptance of norms that say to treat R as weighing in favor of doing X' (A Gibbard, *Wise Choices, Apt Feelings* (Cambridge, MA, Harvard University Press, 1990) 163).

stability, I take it, will be broadly a function of your other plans, valuings, and the like, as well as your relevant factual beliefs. And given that your intention is whole-hearted it seems that rational stability, so understood, will support, *pro tanto*, its retention in the absence of relevant new information.

What happens, however, if this whole-hearted intention favours something horrendous? Given our understanding of rational stability it may be rationally stable of you to stick with your horrendous intention. But I think that it still is not true that you have a normative reason to engage in the horrendous activity that you intend. After all, a judgement that there is such a normative reason so to act would involve (or so I am supposing) an element of endorsement.

If this is right, then recognising a diachronic norm of rational stability does not entail that intentions, even whole-hearted intentions, are, quite generally, reason-creating.

So we need to distinguish two ideas. There is, first, the idea of a normative reason for action. And I have said that one aspect of this idea is that in judging that R is a normative reason in favour of your acting in a certain way I am endorsing R as favouring your so acting. Second, there is the idea of something to which you could coherently give significance in your practical deliberation, given how you are now and rational transitions from how you are now. We can understand one of Bernard Williams' claims to be that the second idea induces a necessary constraint on the first idea. I am sympathetic to this claim; but it is important to note that it does not follow from this claim that the second idea provides a *sufficient* condition for the first idea. And in rejecting the thought that, in the last example, you have a normative reason to engage in the horrendous activity that you whole-heartedly intend, I am rejecting this claim of sufficiency.

There is also a related distinction to be made concerning intention stability. There is, first, the idea of rational stability. And rational stability, I have said, will be broadly dependent on the agent's other plans, valuings, and the like. A second idea is that of (as Kieran Setiya puts it) a 'good disposition of practical thought'[12] for, in particular, the case of intention-retention. Standards of rational stability will, I think, be a part of any story of such good dispositions of intention-retention. But it seems to me that a judgement of a practical disposition as good, like a judgement of normative reasons, involves a substantive endorsement. So there is a substantive step (one we may not want to make in a particular case) in moving from the judgement that retaining your whole-hearted intention is supported by norms of rational stability, to the judgement that such retention involves a good disposition of intention-retention. In particular, we may think that sticking with your whole-hearted but horrendous intention is not a manifestation of a good disposition of practical thought, even though it is a case of rational stability. A good planner, we might think, would reassess and revise his intended end in such a case.

[12] K Setiya, *Reasons Without Rationalism* (Princeton, Princeton University Press, 2007) 12.

My conclusion, then, is that in our toy example you could be playing the game and intend to make move A, and yet still not have a normative reason to refrain from intending to make move B, or to make one of the preliminary moves, C or D.

THE LEGAL 'GAME'

Turn now from our toy example back to the legal officials. They are participating in the 'game' of law; and so they are subject to the inner (planning) rationality of law. But the lesson of our discussion of our toy example is that claim (c*) – the claim that law quite generally, and by its nature, induces normative reasons for action on the part of the officials – does not quite follow. To arrive at (c*) we would need some further claim about reasons for participating/continuing to participate in law.[13]

Now, at various points Shapiro says things like the following:

> if the subject has accepted the shared plan which sets out the hierarchy then, from the point of view of instrumental rationality, he is bound to heed the plan. For if someone submits to the planning of another, and yet ignores an order directed to him, he will be acting in a manner inconsistent with his own plan.[14]

If we understand, as I think Shapiro does understand, the appeal here to instrumental rationality as the appeal to the rationality constraints built into structures of planning, then we can understand Shapiro here (and elsewhere) as highlighting the inner rationality of law, as that inner rationality is understood within the planning theory. However, we need to be careful about Shapiro's talk of being 'bound'. As I am understanding things, a rational agent is 'bound' to have consistent plans. But given some prior intention (eg one involved in accepting the shared, hierarchical plan cited in Shapiro's example), there are, normally, two routes to consistency. In Shapiro's example the two routes are: (1) intend to conform to the subsequent order, or (2) give up the prior intention. As John Broome would say: this consistency demand is a 'wide scope' requirement.[15] And so far, solely by appeal to the inner rationality of law, we do not have a reason that favours (1) over (2). So it might be misleading to say simply that the agent in Shapiro's example is 'bound to heed the plan', since that suggests a 'narrow scope' reading that has not yet been supported.

This returns us to the conclusion we have drawn from our discussion of our toy example, namely, that to support the claim that the legal officials have, quite generally, normative reasons to make certain legal moves we cannot simply cite the inner rationality of law. To support this claim we would need some account of the reasons these officials have, quite generally, to continue to play the legal 'game'.

[13] This is in the spirit of aspects of Andrei Marmor's discussion in chapter 7 of his *Social Conventions: From Language to Law* (Princeton, NJ, Princeton University Press, 2009), esp 161 and 168–69.

[14] Shapiro, n 6 above, 37–38.

[15] J Broome, 'Normative Requirements' in J Dancy (ed), *Normativity* (Oxford, Blackwell, 2000) 398–419.

Now, both Hart and Shapiro emphasise that the reasons legal officials have to continue to participate in the legal system can simply be personal reasons – a good salary, say. But if we are looking to defend a very general claim like (c*) we cannot lean on such personal reasons, since we cannot assume that such reasons will be present in all cases. Instead, we need to find reasons that are associated quite generally with there being a legal system.

Postema thought that the normative reasons that are associated quite generally with a legal system are like the reasons we have to drive on the right given that most others do. This is what is built into Postema's use of a concept of a coordination convention broadly due to David Lewis. And Shapiro argues that this is an overly limited model of the plan-like social organisation associated with a legal system. Shapiro notes that for there to be the kind of convention Postema cites, the participants need to see things in a certain way. In particular, they need to think that this convention is just one of two or more possible solutions to the relevant coordination problem, where a possible solution is one that each prefers to act in accord with so long as others do so as well. But, Shapiro notes, it is possible to have a legal system in which officials both think the system is uniquely sensible and would not prefer to act in accordance with an alternative system even if others were to act in accordance with it. Such 'fundamentalist' officials could still have a shared social plan for planning of a sort that, according to Shapiro, is foundational for law. In this way Shapiro aims to provide a model of the sociality basic to law that goes beyond the special case of a coordination convention.

Shapiro's idea of shared social plans for planning also aims at giving us a clearer understanding of the sense in which the legal officials accept basic rules as (in Hart's terms) 'common public standards'.[16] To see the problem note that there might be a convergence in the personal policies of everyone in the group even though the participants do not accept their policies as 'common public standards'. In a version of an example from Hart,[17] perhaps everyone has a personal policy of having tea at breakfast. It still may be true that no one accepts his policy as a common public standard, even if it is common knowledge, and a good thing, that everyone has this personal policy.

What then is involved in the acceptance of a policy as a common public standard? This is where Shapiro, and I, would appeal to an idea of a shared intention, plan or policy. On Shapiro's version of this idea, shared plans are designed, at least in part, for the group, the plan is accessible to all, and each intends to do his part and is committed to letting the others do their part. Shapiro also alludes to the condition that the existence of the shared plan is common knowledge.[18] We might argue about the details of this specific account of a shared intention, plan or policy. And there are differences here between the details of Shapiro's model of shared plans and what I have said, in reflecting on small-scale cases of shared

[16] Hart, n 4 above, 116.

[17] ibid 9.

[18] Shapiro sees this as a condition of a group acting together, rather than a condition on their sharing the plan on which they act; but I put this nicety aside here.

agency, about shared intentions.[19] But I agree that this appeal to shared intention is an advance over the mere use of the idea of a common public standard without a theory of what the public commonness of a standard involves.

So I think we can see Shapiro's planning theory of law as having a trio of advantages: it gives us a more general story of the underlying sociality than do coordination-convention accounts; it makes progress in understanding acceptance of a rule as a common pubic standard; and it gives us a clearer account of the inner rationality of law by understanding it as the rationality of planning structures. There remains a worry, along lines that Ronald Dworkin has emphasised, that this model is overly sanguine about the degree of agreement that will in general be present within law.[20] But I put this issue aside here. What I do want to emphasise is that even given these advantages of Shapiro's planning theory of law we are still without a settled view about (c*), and so we are still without a settled view about Postema's normativity thesis. We do have a view of the inner rationality of law, and an associated view of the reasoning of the legal officials that is guided by their participation in relevant shared intentions and associated norms of consistency, coherence and stability. But this is not yet a view about whether and why law brings with it distinctive normative reasons.

At this point we need to turn to a theme that Shapiro shares with Hart (and others). Both see a legal system as a social solution to a characteristic range of problems that can be expected to emerge given basic facts about human beings and human sociality. For Shapiro these are problems of complexity, contentiousness and the need for choice among arbitrary solutions: problems that characterise the 'circumstances of legality'. Just as Shapiro's underlying model of the sociality central to law aims to be more general than the model of a coordination convention, so his conception of the problems to be solved by law aims at the more general idea of the problems posed in the 'circumstances of legality' – though he will grant that among these problems can be Postema-type coordination problems. Shapiro sees these problems as, in a broad sense, moral problems since (I take it) he assumes that their solution can contribute significantly to people living good lives. A legal system (that is, a system of hierarchical social plans for planning) will almost always make some, albeit perhaps limited, contribution to a solution to these problems, though we learn from history that in some cases this solution brings with it horrors of its own.

This suggests that one thing the planning theory of law does is provide a model of a kind of sociality that helps solve these characteristic problems and thereby transmits, in means–end fashion, the normative force of the general reasons we have to solve those problems to the specific legal actions mandated by the relevant planning structures. The inner rationality of law is an essential aspect of what supports this transmission of reasons. But this transmission of reasons also requires a

[19] See the quartet of essays on shared agency in my *Faces of Intention* (New York, Cambridge University Press, 1999) and, for a recent overview, my 'Modest Sociality and the Distinctiveness of Intention' (2009) 144 *Philosophical Studies* 149.

[20] See eg R Dworkin, 'Thirty Years On' (2002) 115 *Harvard Law Review* 1655, 1663.

background story of the reasons for law – this is, so to speak, the major premise in the transmission. The Shapiro story of the reasons for law, by appeal to the 'circumstances of legality', depends on the idea that the planning structures he highlights are, normally, solutions to the cited problems. And these planning structures essentially involve norms of plan rationality. But the cited reasons for law are not just a matter of plan rationality.

The idea that structures of law can help transmit general reasons for law to specific legally mandated actions is (I take it) implicitly shared among Hart, Postema and Shapiro. I will take this idea as given here, though it can be challenged. An advantage of the planning theory is that it gives us, arguably, a better model of the social mechanisms through which such a transmission of reasons proceeds.

This does raise the question of the status, within Shapiro's positivist theory, of the substantive normative claim that we have normative reasons to solve these problems. This normative claim goes beyond the norms of plan rationality that Shapiro sees as essential to law; and I take it that if this is to be a positivist theory it cannot say that this normative claim about reasons to solve these problems is in the same way essential to law. It seems to me that what Shapiro should say here is that you do not need to accept that normative claim about reasons in order to accept his planning model of law. You do need to accept the claim that law has the *function* of helping to solve the cited problems. But you can grant this claim about function whether or not you think it a good thing that the law succeeds in playing this function. You can study social institutions and understand them in part in terms of the functions they play in the social world, without thinking that it is a good thing that they play those functions[21] – think about a person who claims that religion is the opiate of the people. However, if you want to establish something along the lines of (c*) you will need some normative premises about reasons. And I am supposing that one normative premise that Shapiro would appeal to is that we have reasons to solve these problems.

Even given this normative premise, do we have enough to support (c*)? There are two reasons why we should answer in the negative. First, we have not ruled out the possibility of a system of social structures characteristic of law that is horrendous in ways that block any normative support that may come from going some way to solving problems of the 'circumstances of legality'. Second, even in those (extremely common) cases in which there really are reasons of the cited sort for the legal system in question, it is misleading to say that, on the current picture, law by its nature *induces* reasons for specific legal actions. What it is more accurate to say, so far, is that law *transmits* such reasons; that is, there are, independently of law, reasons to solve the cited problems (or so we are supposing). Law, we are now supposing, is a means to solving those problems. Law requires certain forms of conduct. So the reasons for solving those problems are transmitted by law to reasons for that conduct.

[21] I am here disagreeing with John Searle when he suggests that to assign a function to something, I need to value what that thing supports as a matter of its function. See J Searle, *The Construction of Social Reality* (New York, The Free Press, 1995) 15–19.

So, what we can now say is:

(c) It is usually true that law, by its nature, transmits normative reasons for solving the problems inherent in the circumstances of legality to normative reasons for legal officials to act in ways mandated by the law.

Further, since these reasons are grounded in general reasons that will apply both to legal officials and law subjects, we are also in a position to say:

(d) It is usually true that law, by its nature, transmits normative reasons for solving the problems inherent in the circumstances of legality to normative reasons for legal officials and law-subjects to act in ways mandated by the law.

Though (d) takes us closer to Postema's normativity thesis, it does not say (as, I take it, Postema wants to say) that law *always* transmits such normative reasons. There remains the possibility of a legal system so corrupt that it is not supported by these reasons. Further, while (d) depends on the planning theory of law, it also depends on substantive normative claims about reasons for action, claims that fit with the planning theory but are, on the theory, not essential to law in the way in which norms of plan rationality are.

Now, as I have emphasised, (d) says that law usually *transmits* normative reasons that favour solving the cited problems. Does law also, at least usually, induce its own, distinctive normative reasons? I think that the planning theory of law lends support to an affirmative answer.

Return to Sartre's case of mom and the Free French, but let's consider a less dramatic example of a career decision. Suppose you decide on a career in creative writing rather than a career in environmental science. You normally thereby come to have a new reason for action. As noted, intentions and decisions do not always induce such reasons: if your decision is significantly weak-willed, or if you plump for a career as a torturer, then your decision may well fail to induce a new reason. But non-akratic intentions in favour of options that are not beyond the pale do seem normally to induce new normative reasons. We can call these *reasons of specification.*[22]

Similarly with law. Specific legal systems are one among multiple possible solutions to the problems characteristic of the circumstance of legality. This is true even when the participants are 'fundamentalists' who think their solution is unique. So long as a specific solution is not itself beyond the pale, we can see it as analogous to a career decision in the face of multiple, more or less sensible alternatives: the specific solution constituted by the actual shared plans of law induces new normative reasons of specification, reasons that can then transmit to specific, legally-mandated courses of action.

[22] This is in the spirit of Henry Richardson's thought that 'specification can set up new final ends'. See H Richardson, *Practical Reasoning about Final Ends* (Cambridge, Cambridge University Press, 1997) 82.

Turn now to a second idea. If law involves shared plans for planning then the officials (and perhaps many law-subjects) can sensibly think what they might express as: *we* are *together* solving problems characteristic of the circumstances of legality. The solution of which they are a part is not just a coordination convention, but a shared intentional, and perhaps a shared cooperative, activity. In solving these problems together as a shared activity they are part of the way toward a kind of social self-governance.[23] And we might well think that there is a distinctive value in such social self-governance, where the legal system is a potential constituent of such self-governance. Since the shared planning and shared activity characteristic of law can itself help realise or constitute this social self-governance, we could then say that there is, at least usually, a *reason of social self-governance* in favour of these forms of sharing.

Consider now *cross-temporal* self-governance. If there is going to be cross-temporal social self-governance involving law then there needs to be some stability in the basic shared plans of law. If we suppose, as is plausible, that there is normally a distinctive value in such cross-temporal social self-governance, then we can suppose that there will normally be a reason in favour of such legal stability as partly constitutive of such cross-temporal social self-governance. So once the legal system is up and running there will usually be *reasons of cross-temporal social self-governance* in favour of a kind of stability of the shared plans that help constitute the legal system.

So we have uncovered three kinds of (purported) normative reasons commonly induced by law, as understood within the planning theory. Given certain background conditions, a legal system induces reasons of specification, reasons of social self-governance, and reasons of cross-temporal social self-governance for conforming to and maintaining the legal system. And these reasons can then be transmitted to reasons for specific, legally-mandated courses of action. While the claim that there are such normative reasons goes beyond the planning theory of law, strictly speaking, the planning theory helps us articulate the relation between a legal system and these (purported) normative reasons.

We are now in a position to supplement (c) and (d) with a claim about reasons induced by law:

(e) Suppose that L is a legal system that is supported by normative reasons that favour solving the problems of the circumstances of legality. L will induce normative reasons of specification and normative reasons of social (cross-temporal) self-governance that favour L and its persistence; and these induced reasons will transmit to reasons for specific, legally-mandated courses of action.

(e) depends on several substantive normative premises about reasons. While these normative premises are not essential to law in the way in which norms of planning rationality are, they are plausible (if so far not fully spelled-out) normative premises, ones that fit with, even if they are not entailed by, the planning theory of law.

[23] Other conditions may include, for example, the absence of certain kinds of coercion.

(e) does not say that law *always* induces normative reasons for action. (e) explicitly limits its claims to cases in which L is supported by a background of reasons. So (e) does not yet give us (c*). But once we have (e) on board we may wonder about the cited reasons of social self-governance. Should we say that even a horrendous legal system engages these reasons of social self-governance. Is there a reason in favour of social self-governance even when that self-governance is in the pursuit of terrible ends? And, if there is, what follows for claims, like that in (c*), that law quite generally provides reasons for the legal officials to do their legal duty? But these are issues for another occasion.

3

The Moral Puzzle of Legal Authority

A Commentary on Shapiro's Planning Theory of Law

VERONICA RODRIGUEZ-BLANCO*

Doctor Ferreiro: 'But Captain, obedience for obedience's sake . . . that's something only people like you do' *Pan's Labyrinth*, Guillermo del Toro

I INTRODUCTION

THE CLAIMS OF authority are part of our everyday life. For example, parents demand certain conduct from their children and legal officials command or forbid us to act in specific ways. In all these cases we say that authority is practical because it changes the practical situation of the agent. For example, a child intends to run after a ball that has landed on the road, but the mother stops the child and demands that she do something else such as wait on the pavement until she can safely cross the road to rescue the ball. A lecturer, driving quickly to his first lecture of the morning, is asked by the police to pull over, and he obeys. At first sight – from the first person or the deliberative point of view – neither the child nor the lecturer has a reason to act.[1] The child does not

* This chapter is based on a paper presented at the Centre for Cosmopolitan Values at Antwerp, the Legal Theory Seminar at the University of Girona and at the Centre for Law and Society, University of Edinburgh. I am grateful to the audiences for their comments and especially to Jules Coleman, Jordi Ferrer, Claudio Michelon, Nicola Muffato, Maribel Narvaez and Scott Shapiro. I also would like to thank George Pavlakos and Stefano Bertea for their suggestions which helped me to improve this chapter.

[1] Reasons here are understood as good-making or desirability characteristics: see especially GEM Anscombe, *Intention*, 2nd edn (Oxford, Blackwell, 1963) paras 20–27; J Raz, 'Agency, Reason, and the Good' in his *Engaging Reason: On the Theory of Value and Action* (Oxford, Oxford University Press, 1999) 22–45; W Quinn, 'Rationality and the Human Good' in his *Morality and Action* (Cambridge, Cambridge University Press, 1993) 210–27; Aristotle, *Nicomachean Ethics* in T Irwin (trans), *Aristotle: Nicomachean Ethics*, n 10 below, 1094a1; T Scanlon, *What We Owe to Each Other* (Cambridge, MA, Harvard University Press, 1998) 18–19. For a criticism of the idea that a reason for action ought to be presented as a good-making characteristic, see R Hursthouse, 'Arational Actions' (1999) 87 *Journal of Philosophy* 57; M Stocker, 'Desiring the Bad: An Essay in Moral Psychology' (1979) 76 *Journal of Philosophy* 738 and K Setiya, *Reasons Without Rationalism* (Princeton, Princeton University Press, 2007) 62–67. *cf* Raz, 'Agency, Reason and the Good', above. For a helpful discussion of the idea of values as part of our actions see G Watson,

'have' a reason to stop. As an answer to the question 'why did you do that?'[2] neither the child nor the lecturer is able to formulate a reason in terms of good-making or desirability characteristics. However, if asked to reflect on it, they might formulate such reason. Thus, the child might say that she obeyed her mother because she loves her and the lecturer might say that he obeyed the police because the law is good at enabling us to organise our lives, and pursue and realise ends. The lecturer's justification for obeying authority relies on the 'special status'[3] of the authority. Law has authority because it is good[4] and parents have authority because children love their parents. Let us consider the latter reason. If we ask a child 'why do you love your mother?', the child might reply that it is because they purport to do good. Parents and law have authority because they purport to do good. But is it the case that if I purport to do good, I also can have authority rather than the law, for example? The 'special status' argument needs refinement. This is provided by the idea that such authorities purport to do good and they endeavour to do it in such a special way[5] as to guarantee the success of the enterprise. In the case of parents, they have a special commitment to their children, they love them and this provides a guarantee (in principle) that the parent will act for the good of the child. Similarly in the case of the law, human goods and human ends can only be achieved through the very special institutional character of law.

A different strategy of argumentation to explain practical authority has been adumbrated by some scholars, who appeal to a 'constitutive argument'. This argument takes the idea of 'legitimate authority' and aims to explain the conditions that make possible the existence of practical authorities. For example, in the political and legal domain, Raz[6] takes legitimate authority as given, which is evidenced by the claims of legal authorities. The question that arises is how legitimate authority might be possible. What are the conditions that make possible the legitimate authority claimed by legal officials? Raz establishes two constitutive

'Free Agency' (1975) 72 *Journal of Philosophy* 205, last reprinted in G Watson (ed), *Free Will* (Oxford, Oxford University Press, 2003) 337–51.

[2] Anscombe in *Intention* (n 1 above) engages in the task of describing 'an intentional action'. She believes that to act intentionally is to act according to reasons for actions and affirms that if an act is done with an intention then the question 'why' is applicable.

[3] The 'special status' view might be interpreted as an extended notion of the inspirational conception of authority discussed by Raz in the Morality of Freedom, n 6 below.

[4] I follow P Geach, ' Good and Evil' (1956) Analysis 32 on the view that the term 'good' is an attributive adjective rather than a predicative adjective. *cf* CR Pidgen, 'Geach on Good' (1990) *Philosophical Quarterly* 129. Therefore, I will use the terms 'good' and 'a good sort of thing' as interchangeable.

[5] Arguably, the 'special way' of the law is through the rule of law. See N Simmonds, *Law as Moral Idea* (Oxford, Oxford University Press, 2007).

[6] J Raz, *Practical Reason and Norms*, 3rd edn (Oxford, Oxford University Press, 1999); *The Morality of Freedom* (Oxford, Clarendon Press, 1986); 'The Problem of Authority: Revisiting the Service Conception' (2006) 90 *Minnesota Law Review* 1003, reprinted in J Raz, *Between Authority and Interpretation: On the Theory of Law and Practical Reason* (Oxford, Oxford University Press, 2009) 126–65. For some early criticism of Raz see D Regan, 'Authority and Value: Reflections on Raz's Morality of Freedom' (1989) 62 *Southern California Law Review* 995; C Gans, 'Mandatory Rules and Exclusionary Reasons' (1986) *Philosophia* 373 and M Moore, 'Law and Razian Reasons' (1989) *Southern California Law Review* 827.

conditions for the possibility of legitimate authority: (1) the pre-emptive and (2) the dependence thesis. Arguably, from the deliberative viewpoint, the 'constitutive argument' is not independent of the 'special status' argument. The authority of law is possible because it purports to do good and is a good sort of thing. Therefore, from the deliberative viewpoint, the agent has reasons to follow the law. This is the role that Raz's normal justification thesis is meant to play: it justifies the surrendering of our judgement. In other words, for Raz, authority is a good because if we follow the law, we are likely better to comply with reasons which apply to us rather than by trying to follow the reasons which apply to us directly. Shapiro's planning theory of law, in common with Raz, offers a hybrid of 'constitutive arguments'[7] and 'special status arguments' to explain legal authority. I will explain both arguments in the second section of this chapter. For now, I need to point out that the bridge between both arguments is the idea that we are planning agents. The background premise that connects the constitutive and the special status argument in Shapiro's planning theory of law is the meta-principle: legal authority is a good because we are planning agents. From the deliberative viewpoint, law has authority because it is a good sort of thing and in the same way that a mother does, it performs its function in a specific way. In clear contrast to Raz's normal justification thesis, Shapiro does not consider that a condition for a legitimate authority is to purport to do good. He asserts that there can be evil legitimate authorities with evil intentions. The fundamental question that arises is how Shapiro solves the 'moral puzzle' of legal authority.[8] The moral puzzle states that there is a conflict between the legal authority of the law – a heteronomous force on the agent – and the reasons for actions that the agent from the deliberative viewpoint has. Why should the agent surrender his/her judgement to an authority? There is a tension here between personal autonomy and authority. What Shapiro calls the 'possibility puzzle'[9] of legal authority is a corollary of the 'moral puzzle'. Authority seems impossible because norms are the outcome of the human will since they are a human creation and they cannot therefore confer legitimate power to obligate. If we assume that there is a basic authoritative norm that confers power to legitimate authorities, we enter an infinite regress, as it could similarly be assumed that there is a more basic norm that gives power to the basic norm. As Shapiro describes it, we get the chicken–egg paradox.

In our previous examples of both the child and the lecturer, the justification for their surrendering of judgement is the 'special status' of the authority. In both cases, the authority purports to do good and is, presumably, a good *sort of thing*. But then we might also ask, if law can be immoral and plans do not need to purport or aim to do good, how can we explain the moral legitimacy of legally

[7] See S Shapiro 'Planning Agency and the Law' (Chapter 1 of this book, from now onwards 'PAL'), at 18: 'I am going to argue here that understanding fundamental laws as plans not only vindicates the positivist conception of law, but provides a compelling solution to our earlier question about how legal authority is possible'.

[8] Raz, 'The Problem of Authority', n 6 above, 1012, 1015; Raz, *The Morality of Freedom*, n 6 above, 38–41.

[9] S Shapiro, 'PAL' n 7 above, at 66.

authoritative directives exemplified in 'ought' statements? Shapiro argues that we can do this from the legal point of view – a distance viewpoint that does not commit itself to action. I criticise this idea and advance arguments to show that the 'legal point of view' is not a deliberative or practical point of view, but merely a theoretical viewpoint. In other words, what we say from the 'legal point of view' is a mere report. If law moves us to action and guides us, it needs to have practical authority; it needs to change our practical situation. Should it not be that the deliberative viewpoint is primary over the theoretical?

Shapiro's insight is significant and in my view, sound: law is necessarily connected to practical rationality. However, I attempt to show that the consequences of this important insight are not compatible with a middle way theory between legal positivism and natural law as he envisages it. But perhaps this is not important: we should be slaves to truth, not to theories about truth. The subject matter itself is our guiding star and it is palpable that this is what Shapiro is guided by.

This chapter is divided into three sections. The first section explains the role of the deliberative viewpoint and the transparency condition. The second evaluates Shapiro's argument on solving the 'moral puzzle' of legal authority in terms of a 'legal point of view' and shows that the latter conflicts with the deliberative viewpoint. It is also shown that the 'legal point of view' is parasitic upon the deliberative viewpoint which should be at the core of the planning theory of law. The third part considers five possible objections to my criticism of Shapiro and examines some tentative – hopefully convincing – replies to such objections.

II THE TRANSPARENCY CONDITION AND THE DELIBERATIVE[10] VIEWPOINT

The key to explaining legal authority and to solving the moral puzzle is to understand how we act for reasons in following practical authorities. This is substantially different from understanding how we act according to practical authorities. In the latter case, action takes place not for reasons, but rather because of threats, sanctions and so on. Legal positivism finds itself between the Scylla of coercion and the Charybdis of practical reason. A common strategy of contemporary legal positivism is to sail the boat so close to the Charybdis of practical reason that it possesses a plausible emaciated side that presents no real danger or threat to the main tenets of legal positivism. Shapiro's planning theory aims to unmask the emaciated side of practical reason in law. Legal positivists have learned from Hart's *Concept of Law* that the real threat lies in either the model of coercion or the

[10] For an explanation of the 'deliberative point of view' see J Finnis, 'Law and What I Truly Should Decide' (2003) 48 *American Journal of Jurisprudence* 107. Aristotle asserts: 'A voluntary act would seem to be an act whose origin lies in the agent, who knows the particular circumstances in which he is acting' (Aristotle, *Nichomachean Ethics*, III i 20–21, (H Rackham (trans), Cambridge, MA Harvard University Press, 1934). 'For a man stops enquiring how he shall act as soon as he has carried back the origin of action to himself, and to the dominant part of himself, for it is this part that chooses' (NE, III iii 17–18).

crude empirical model of prediction. To understand action in the circumstances of legal authority as merely predictive or coercive action entails abandoning our self-understanding as agents in the circumstances of law. Furthermore, Hart has shown that both Austin's sanction theory of law and the Scandinavian Realists' predictive theory of law are not satisfactory accounts of the different orders, complexities and multiple functions of legal rules. In the 1970s, contemporary scholars, such as Raz and Finnis, recovering the Aristotelian classical view on reasons, began to develop a conception of law in continuity with practical reason.

We first need to understand the distinction between practical and theoretical knowledge. Let us take a modified version of the example provided by Anscombe in *Intention*.[11] A man is asked by his wife to go to the supermarket with a list of products to buy. A detective is following him and makes notes of his actions. The man reads in the list 'butter', but chooses margarine. The detective writes in his report that the man has bought margarine. The detective gives an account of the man's actions in terms of the evidence he himself has. By contrast, the man gives an account of his actions in terms of the reasons for actions that he himself has. However, the man knows his intentions or reasons for actions not on the basis of evidence that he has of himself. His reasons for actions or intentions are self-intimating or self-verifying. He acts from the deliberative or first person perspective. There is an action according to reasons or an intention in doing something if an answer to the question 'why' is applicable. It is in terms of his own description of his action that we can grasp the reasons for actions of the man. In reply to the question 'why did you buy margarine instead of butter', the man might answer that he did so because it is better for his health. This answer (following Aristotle's theory of action[12] and its contemporary interpretations advanced by Anscombe and Raz) *provides a reason for action as a desirability or good-making characteristic*. According to Anscombe, the answer is intelligible to us and inquiries as to why the action has been committed stops. However, in the case of the detective, when we ask 'why did you write in the report that the man bought margarine', the answer is that it is the truth about the man's actions. In the case of the detective, the knowledge is theoretical – the detective reports the man's actions in terms of the evidence he has of it. In the case of the man, the knowledge is practical. The

[11] Anscombe, n 1 above, paras 32–33.

[12] Aristotle, *Nicomachean Ethics*, n 10 above, I i 2; III V 18–21. See Thomas Aquinas, *Summa Theologiae* in Thomas Gilby (ed and trans), *Summa Theologiae*, vol 17, *Psychology of Human Acts* (London/New York, Blackfriars/Eyre & Spottiswoode/, McGraw-Hill, 1970) Ia2æ 12, I. See also A Kenny, *Aristotle's Theory of the Will* (London, Duckworth, 1979); R Pasnau, *Thomas Aquinas on Human Nature: A Philosophical Study of Summa Theologiae 1a, 75–89* (Cambridge, Cambridge University Press, 2002); J Finnis, *Aquinas: Moral, Political, and Legal Theory* (Oxford, Oxford University Press, 1998) 62–71 and 79–90. For contemporary formulations of the Aristotelian theory of intentional action see Raz, 'Agency, Reason and the Good', n 1 above; W Quinn, 'Putting Rationality in its Place' in his *Morality and Action* (Cambridge, Cambridge University Press, 1993) 228–55; C Korsgaard, 'Acting for a Reason' in her *The Constitution of Agency: Essays on Practical Reason and Moral Psychology* (Oxford, Oxford University Press, 2008) 207–29; R Moran and M Stone, 'Anscombe on the Expression of Intention' in C Sandis (ed), *New Essays on the Explanation of Action* (Basingstoke, Palgrave MacMillan, 2009) 132–68; M Thompson, *Life and Action: Elementary Structures of Practice and Practical Thought* (Cambridge, MA, Harvard University Press, 2008).

reasons for action are self-verifying for the agent. He or she does not need to have evidence of his own reasons for actions. This self-intimating or self-verifying understanding of our own actions from the deliberative or practical viewpoint is part of the general condition of access to our own mental states that is called the 'transparency condition' (TC).[13] Its application to reasons for action can be formulated as follows:

> (TC for reasons for actions) 'I can report on my own reasons for actions, not by considering my own mental states or theoretical evidence about them, but by considering the reasons themselves which I am immediately aware of'.

The direction of fit in theoretical and practical knowledge are also different. In the former case, my assertions need to fit the world, whereas in the latter, the world needs to fit my assertions. The detective needs to give an account of what the world looks like, including human actions in the world. He relies on the observational evidence he has. The detective's description of the action is tested against the tribunal of empirical evidence. If he reports that the man bought butter instead of margarine, then his description is false. The man, by contrast, might say that he intended to buy butter and instead bought margarine. He changed his mind and asserts that margarine is healthier. There is no mistake here.

The Aristotle/Anscombe conception of intentional action is very different from the Humean and Neo-Humean approaches to intentional action which are the predominant views in moral psychology. Let me take a detour to clarify the differences. The standard view of intentional action advocated by Humeans, and in its more sophisticated form by Donald Davisdon, presupposes an inward-looking approach to action as opposed to an outward-looking or 'transparent' approach. The latter examines intentional actions as a series of actions that *are justified in terms of other actions* and in view of the purpose or end of the intentional action as a *good-making characteristic*. Let me illustrate this position with an example. I intend to make tea and in order to make tea I need to focus on the kettle, the water, the plug and the cup. Thus, I put on the kettle *in order to* boil the water, *in order to* make tea *because* it is pleasant to drink tea. By contrast, the inward-looking

[13] See G Evans, *The Varieties of Reference* (J McDowell (ed), Oxford, Oxford University Press, 1982) 225. The most extensive and careful contemporary treatment of the 'transparency condition' is in R Moran, *Authority and Estrangement: An Essay on Self-Knowledge* (Princeton, NJ, Princeton University Press, 2001). For discussions on Moran's notion of transparency, reflection and self-knowledge see B Reginster, 'Self-Knowledge, Responsibility and the Third Person' (2004) 69 *Philosophy and Phenomenological Research* 433; G Wilson 'Comments on Authority and Estrangement' (2004) 69 *Philosophy and Phenomenological Research* 440; J Heal, 'Moran's Authority and Estrangement' (2004) 69 *Philosophy and Phenomenological Research* 427; J Lear, 'Avowal and Unfreedom' (2004) 69 *Philosophy and Phenomenological Research* 448; R Moran, 'Replies to Heal, Reginster, Wilson and Lear' (2004) 69 *Philosophy and Phenomenological Research* 455; S Shoemaker, 'Moran on Self-Knowledge' (2003) 11 *European Journal of Philosophy* 391; L O'Brien, 'Moran on Self-Knowledge' (2003) 11 *European Journal of Philosophy* 375; R Moran, 'Responses to O'Brien and Shoemaker' (2003) 11 *European Journal of Philosophy* 402; C Moya, 'Moran on Self-Knowledge, Agency and Responsibility' (2006) 38 *Critica: Revista Hispanoamericana de Filosofia* 3; T Carman, 'First Persons: On Richard Moran's Authority and Estrangement' (2003) 46 *Inquiry* 395. For a critical view on the transparency condition see B Gertler, 'Do We Determine What We Believe By Looking Outward?' in A Hatzimoysis (ed), *Self-Knowledge* (Oxford, Oxford University Press, 2010).

approach examines the mental states that rationalise the actions; however, at the ontological level, it is argued that these mental states cause the actions. The mental states are the pair belief/pro-attitude towards the action. For Davidson, if someone does something for a reason he can be characterised as (a) having some sort of pro-attitude towards actions of a certain kind, ie desires, and (b) believing (or knowing, remembering, and so on) that this action is of that kind.[14] According to Davidson, I intend to make tea because I have the *desire* to make tea and the *belief* that the action of putting the kettle and boiling the water is of that kind. Let me exemplify this point with a more complex example. Let us suppose that a man drives his vehicle, stops it at a parking space and get out of his vehicle because he wants to go to the supermarket. On the way to the supermarket he meets a friend. What he has done for a reason and intentionally is only to park his vehicle and go to the supermarket; he did not intentionally meet his friend. His desire to go to the supermarket and his belief that driving his vehicle will get him to the supermarket constitute the reasons for his actions. The pair belief-desire is a mental state. *The presupposition that is operating here is that to understand the mental state of desiring and the mental state of believing is the same as to understand the content of the belief and the content of the desire.* In other words, to establish whether I believe that I am intentionally driving, I need to look introspectively at my mental state of desiring and believing.

The main criticism that has been raised against the pair belief/pro-attitude view is that this conception cannot explain deviations from the causal chain[15] between mental states and actions. The problem with this view is that it needs to specify the 'appropriate causal route'. Let us suppose that the man who is driving to the supermarket intends to kill his enemy later on that day. Whilst he is driving his car, and by mere coincidence, he sees his enemy walking on the pavement and the man suffers a nervous spasm that causes him to turn the wheel of the vehicle and run over his enemy. Obviously, he did not kill his enemy intentionally. However, according to Davidson's view, in order to have an intentional action we need two conditions: (a) a pro-attitude or a desire for the action, and (b) the belief that the action is of that kind. In our example, the man has the desire to kill his enemy and has the belief that driving his vehicle will result in the death of his enemy. Nevertheless, although in this case the conditions of intentional action as advanced by the pair belief/desire are met, the man did not act intentionally. There is clearly something wrong with this view of intentional action as it cannot explain cases where there is deviance from the causal chain. My argument is that we can only understand intentional actions if we examine the description of the action *as advanced by the agent, not in terms of his own mental states, but in terms of the ends of the action.* In this case, we will ask the man, why did he drive his vehicle, why did

[14] D Davidson, 'Actions, Reasons and Events' in *Essays on Actions and Events* (Oxford, Clarendon Press, 1980) 3–19. This analysis is modified in his essay 'Intending' which is published in the same collection. However, he still maintains the causal account of intentions. For an illuminating critique of introspection or the inward approach see R Hursthouse, 'Intention' in *Logic, Cause and Action* (R Teichman (ed), Cambridge, Cambridge University Press, 2000).

[15] The first to discuss deviant causal chains was R Chisholm in 'Freedom and Action' in K Lehrer (ed), *Freedom and Determinism* (New York, Random Hous, 1966) 28–44.

he turn the wheel and why did he run over his enemy. The answers respectively will be 'to go to the supermarket'; 'because I had a nervous spasm; and 'I did not intentionally run over my enemy'. These reasons are transparent, ie self-evident to him, and he does not need any evidence of his own mental state to understand *why* he accidentally killed his enemy. Because of his own description of the action we understand that it is not an intentional action and we can grasp the meaning of the action.

Davidson has made much effort in specifying the 'attitudes that cause the action if they are to rationalise the action':[16]

> And here we see that Armstrong's analysis like the one I propose a few pages back, must cope with the question *how* beliefs and desires cause intentional actions. Beliefs and desires that would rationalize an action if they cause it in the right way – through a cause of practical reasoning, as we might try saying – may cause it in other ways. If so, the action was not performed with the intention that we could have read off from the attitudes that caused it. What I despair of spelling out is the way in which attitudes must cause actions if they are to rationalize the action.

In the following paragraph, Davidson seems to fear that the idea of attitudes causing action might lead to *infinite regress*:

> A climber might want to rid himself of the weight and danger of holding another man on a rope, and he might know that by loosening his hold on the rope he could rid himself of the weight and danger. This belief and want might so unnerve him as to cause him to lose his hold, and yet it might be the case that he never *chose* to loosen his hold, nor did he do it intentionally. It will not help, I think, to add that the belief and the want must combine to cause him to want to loosen his hold, for there will remain the *two* questions how the belief and the want caused the second want, and how wanting to loosen his hold caused him to loosen his hold.

Here we see Davidson struggling with his own proposal.[17] He asks *how attitudes must cause actions if they are to rationalise actions*? Davidson's model of intentional action does not help us to determine whether there is an intentional action, it only help us to determine the *conditions* that would explain the existence of an intentional action. The intentional action is already *given*.

III A CRITICISM OF SHAPIRO'S PLANNING THEORY ARGUMENTS IN FAVOUR OF THE PRIMACY OF THE DELIBERATIVE VIEWPOINT

Let us now examine Shapiro's example of Cooks' Island. Let us suppose that the planners of the island – ie the authority of the island – ask a man to go to the nearest town by boat and buy some products, including butter. He buys butter as commanded, though he believes that margarine is healthier. What are the conditions

[16] D Davidson, 'Freedom to Act' in *Essays on Actions and Events* (Oxford, Clarendon Press, 1980) 79.

[17] For an illuminating discussion of this point see C Vogler, 'Modern Moral Philosophy Again: Isolating the Promulgation Problem' in *Proceedings of the Aristotelian Society* (2007) 347–64.

that make this action an action according to reasons? The reasons for actions are not his. What does it mean that the reasons for actions are not his reasons? He can still describe his own actions, but not in terms of his own reasons – he could say that he bought some products in the supermarket, including butter, because the planners have asked him to do so. However, he thinks that he has better reasons to buy margarine instead of butter and therefore he acted contrary to his reasons. Raz calls this the 'moral puzzle' of legal authority. Any account of legitimate authority needs to justify the 'surrendering of my own judgement'. How can we assert that the man acted for reasons? From the deliberative viewpoint, reasons for buying butter are not transparent for him. Nor can he answer the question 'why did he buy butter' by providing reasons in terms of good-making characteristics. He could, however, provide a justification in terms of the 'special status' of authority. He might intelligibly say that the planners purport to do good for the community and therefore such authority is good. This is why he bought butter instead of margarine. This is why he has surrendered his judgement to the planners. The fundamental premise in his reasoning is 'authority is a good' and it can be formulated as follows:

> (I) Legitimate authority is a good thing.
> I ought to obey the authority's commands.
> The planners have asked me to buy butter.
> The planners are the authority.
> I ought to obey the planners' commands.
> Conclusion: I ought to buy butter.

This answer is transparent to the agent and in terms of good-making characteristics. This is the answer that Raz provides. In normal cases – ie, central cases – authority is a good and purports to do good because if the agent obeys the law, she will be complying with the reasons that apply to her. However, if she decides to act following her own reasons, she will probably not succeed in complying with the reasons that apply to her – Raz's normal justification thesis. Given that Shapiro argues that legal officials do not need to purport to do good to have legitimate authority, he cannot provide an answer along Raz's lines, or so I will argue.

Notice that the previous reasoning is not different from the following:

> (II) Vitamin C is good for *my* immune system.
> I have a cold, therefore, I need to boost my immune system.
> This orange contains Vitamin C.
> Conclusion: I ought to eat this orange.

There is no difference between premises (I) and (II). If we follow Raz, legal authorities present a similar structure. In the normal case, authority is a good and Raz explains what it means to say that 'legitimate authority is a good thing and purports to do good'.

Let us examine Shapiro's answer to the moral puzzle of legal authority. For Shapiro's planning theory we are asked to follow a plan; let us suppose that this plan states that I ought to pay my taxes. This plan has been authorised by a master plan which has been designed as a shared plan by the planners. Shapiro advances an explanation of why we surrender our judgement to legal norms. He conceives such norms as plans that enable us to achieve our different goals or ends, though they are not necessarily good, intrinsically valuable or moral.[18] He engages in an explanation of authority as both 'special status' and 'constitutive argument'. On the former point he makes the following set of assertions:

(a) The planning theory of law's central claim – that the law is first and foremost a social planning mechanism – is supported by two considerations. First, it explains why we consider law to be valuable. It is, for example, a widely shared assumption of political theories that agree on virtually nothing else that the law is an indispensable social institution in the modern world. Given the complexity, contentiousness and arbitrariness of modern life, the moral *need* for plans to guide, coordinate and monitor conduct are enormous.[19]
(b) As we will see, policies, customs and hierarchy are three ways in which shared plans can be forged without the members of the group having to engage in the time-consuming process of plan formulation and adoption.[20]
(c) There is no mystery about why plans are needed to regulate individuals' actions in communal settings. When people occupy the same space and share a common pool of resources, certain courses of action will result in clashes between individual pursuits, while others will avoid them. Planning is often *necessary* to ensure that those who live together do not undermine each other's ends.[21]
(d) Even when they knew what moral problems they ought to rectify, they could not figure out how to coordinate their behaviour so as to resolve these problems. Their sterling characters did not, in other words, diminish their need for law.[22]
(e) The essential point, however, is that whenever the law properly addresses a particular social problem, it does so because, given current social conditions, alternative methods of planning are somehow deficient.[23]

[18] 'Everyone – even natural lawyers – accept that people can have morally bad plans. Terrorist plots, for example, exist even though they should not be carried out from the moral point of view; rather they exist just because terrorists share certain plans' (Shapiro, 'PAL', n 7 above, 66). See also in the same text: 'Even if the shared plan is morally odious and the citizens are as servile as sheep, the authorised individual will have legal authority within the existing system' ('PAL', at 69).

[19] Shapiro, 'PAL' n 7 above, at 60 (emphasis added). Probably, what he means here is some kind of 'Aristotelian necessity' in terms of human needs. See GEM Anscombe, 'Rules, Rights, and Promises' (1978) 3 *Midwest Studies in Philosophy* 318, reprinted in her *Ethics, Religion and Politics: Collected Philosophical Papers of G.E.M. Anscombe* (Oxford, Blackwell, 1981) 97–103; for the notion of 'Aristotelian necessity' as opposed to the internal necessity of rules such as chess, see Anscombe's account of authority qua practical necessity in her 'On the Source of the Authority of the State' (1978) 20 *Ratio* 1, reprinted in *Ethics, Religion and Politics: Collected Philosophical Papers of G.E.M. Anscombe*, above, 130–55.

[20] Shapiro, 'PAL', n 9 above, 34.

[21] ibid 44–45 (emphasis added).

[22] ibid 63.

[23] ibid 64.

We can conclude that for Shapiro authority is a good. Additionally, Shapiro's 'constitutive' argument[24] establishes the conditions that make possible legal authority. Five conditions are identified: (a) plans are shareable by a group in the community, planners;[25] (b) plans are publicly accessible;[26] (c) plans are accepted;[27] (d) plans are hierarchical;[28] and (e) the existence conditions of plans and some legal norms (ie basic norms) are the same.

The bridge between the 'special status' argument and the 'constitutive' argument is made by the following meta-principle:

(M) Authority is a good because we are planning creatures.[29]

But, what does it mean that we are 'planning creatures'? Michael Bratman's work on practical reason and action might help us here. According to Bratman,[30] following the Lockean notion of personal identity, our personal identity is determined by our psychological experiences: in other words, loving our children and partner, memories with friends, parents, brothers, etc. For example, if there is another Veronica on planet X with the same memories and psychological experiences as Veronica on planet Earth we cannot differentiate between her and me. We are the same person, though we have different bodies.[31] These Lockean ties go over time and they are therefore continuities and connections between my past, present and future psychological experiences. How is this possible? Bratman advances the view that plans and policies play a crucial role in ensuring our identity over time. Shapiro aims to show that plans also play a significant role in our identity across persons. We need plans when we do things together. Plans, following Shapiro, enable us to coordinate the different goals that we have in the community. But we also need to stick to our plans to create a continuity of the things that we do together and their correlative experiences. We share goals and ends, and to ensure their realisation we need sophisticated planning. This can only be done if we accept the need for authority. Such authorities plan for us and help us to achieve our goals. The lurking idea here is our view as self-determining agents. We can rationally impose plans on ourselves to ensure our desired ends and goals. Shapiro tells us: 'Yet, according to the planning theory, the existence of the law actually depends on a normative fact as well, namely, the fact that planning agents have the rational authority to give themselves plans'.[32] We can then say that authority is a good, though according to Shapiro (in clear contrast to Raz) we do not need to say that authorities purport to do good.

[24] ibid 18.
[25] ibid 36–37.
[26] ibid 32.
[27] ibid, 32, 33, 36, 53, 65 and 68.
[28] ibid 54.
[29] ibid at 18, 20, 25, 47.
[30] M Bratman, *Structures of Agency: Essays* (Oxford, Oxford University Press, 2007) 28–32 and 118–20.
[31] See D Parfit, 'Why Our Identity is Not What Matters' in Raymond Martin and John Barresi (eds), *Personal Identity* (Malden, MA, Blackwell, 2003) 115–43.
[32] Shapiro, 'PAL', n 7 above, 69.

In this way, Shapiro would tell us, the moral puzzle is solved. We surrender our judgement because we need plans in order to be who we are – in other words, persons with an identity over time and across persons. Planning is a complex activity, Shapiro argues, and it necessitates authority. Briefly, we surrender our judgement to legal authority because it enables us to be creatures whose identity can survive over time as connected with the past and the future[33] (obviously, this is a very rough and bold sketch of the subtle background premises of the planning theory of law advanced by Shapiro, but it will suffice for our discussion).

However, Shapiro emphasises that this does not mean that legal authority collapses into moral authority. On the contrary, he promptly points out that there is a 'legal point of view' that distances itself from any commitment to values or moral reasons.

Let us illustrate with an example how 'the legal point of view' might be applied. Let us go back to our example of the man who lives in Cooks' Island. Everyone on the island knows that the planners are corrupt and that they do not purport to do good. This is evidenced by their claims and their actions. They have designed a master plan that is considered the basic norm of the island. This plan imposes intensive labour work upon the elderly population and the children of the island, it authorises the rape of women and men, and the execution of people without fair trial. The master plan also authorises the planners to kill babies who have been born with physical or mental disabilities. It is customary that the planners do this with poisoned dairy products. A man is asked to go to the nearest town by boat and buy many kilograms of butter and milk. Is it intelligible to say that the planners have legitimate authority and that, therefore, the man ought to buy the butter and surrender his judgement? Shapiro would say that 'from the legal point of view, he ought to buy the milk and the butter'. But this is not an answer to the moral puzzle of why the man ought to surrender his judgement. I think that Shapiro's legal point of view underestimates the parasitic relationship between the 'legal point of view' and the 'deliberative viewpoint'. This is my main objection to Shapiro's planning theory of law. I will proceed to explain this objection.

What is the 'legal point of view'? Shapiro[34] asserts that when we refer to legal authority, the word legal is a qualifier. This means that it qualifies[35] our ascription of moral legitimacy. When we say 'X has legal authority' what we are truly saying is that 'from the legal point of view, X has morally legitimate authority'. It has a dis-

[33] 'For the picture that emerges is one in which the creation and persistence of the fundamental rules of law is grounded in the authority that all individuals possess to adopt plans. As I attempt to show, this power is not conferred on us by morality. On the contrary, it follows from the fact that we are planning creatures' (Shapiro, 'PAL' at 18, n 7 above).

[34] ibid 69–72.

[35] Raz rejects the 'qualified' view which he assimilates to Bentham's conception of law as sanction-based. See J Raz, *The Authority of Law* (Oxford, Oxford University Press, 1979) 154. Raz puts this as follows: 'Thus qualified, they mean no more than that the rule or duty is recognised by a generally efficacious legal system. But this is essentially no more than a more sophisticated version of Bentham's view'. It seems, therefore, that Shapiro's legal point of view is different from Raz's legal point of view.

tancing function; it enables us to talk about the moral conception of a particular legal system without necessarily endorsing that conception.[36]

Let us go back to our previous imaginary example of Cooks' Island. The evil master plan is the basic norm that is shared by the planners. The man has been asked by the planner, the legal official Z, to buy butter and milk and the man is conscious of the evil purposes of this request. He asks for advice from his lawyer, who states: 'from the legal point of view, Z has moral authority' and will probably add: 'from the legal point of view, you ought to buy the milk and the butter'. If this proposition has any practical force on the man, it needs to be part of the practical reasoning of the agent – as in the case of the child or the speeding lecturer, it needs to change the practical situation of the agent. But how can a mere theoretical reason do this? Arguably, unlike the case of the man who is asked to buy butter but buys margarine because it is healthier, the second man of the Cooks' Island example has neither (a) a transparent reason nor (b) a reason in terms of good-making characteristics. The authoritative reasons of Z are presented to him as a theoretical reason. Let us think about the following analogy: when as an A-level student of physics you were given reasons for believing in the truth of classical mechanics, the reasons were presented on the evidence given. Some classical laboratory experiments were performed during that time and you came to have these reasons 'on observation'. Similarly, the lawyer provides reasons in terms of the evidence she has. She has read and carefully studied the master plan (ie the basic norm of the island's legal system) and knows that the order that has been given to her client is compatible with the master plan. She merely reports the reasons that she has learned by evidence. But the man does not 'have' these reasons as practical reasons because he simply cannot acquire reasons for actions by observation. For these reasons to make a change in the practical situation, he needs to 'have' them. Let us suppose that, after the consultation with his lawyer, he declares: 'I intend to buy the butter and the milk as ordered by Z'. If it is an act that follows a practical authority for reasons, then the question 'why' is applicable. We ask the man why and he responds: 'because it is the point of view of the law'. But he has now probably misunderstood the question. We are looking for a reason for action. We can continue our inquiry and ask why he intends to buy the butter and the milk and follow the 'point of view of the law' and his answer might be because 'authority is good'. The man can continue: 'Though the authority does not purport to do good, it is good'. We can now stop our inquiry. The reason provided is both (a) transparent and (b) it is presented by the agent as a good-making characteristic. But now we see that the only reason he can give is from the deliberative viewpoint. The phrase of the lawyer 'from the legal point of view' has no independent force in the deliberation. If I am asked whether 'X believes that p', I need to assess X's beliefs about p. However, if I am asked to do something because 'X believes that p', I do not assess X's beliefs and her mental states, I rather look outward and assess p. Similarly, if someone asks me whether a legal official

[36] Shapiro, 'PAL', n 7 above, 71.

believes that the law has moral legitimate authority, I need to examine her mental state. However, if I am asked by the legal official to do p, I need to look outward and assess whether I should do p in terms of reasons for p. The phrase 'according to the law' simply indicates who issues the alleged authoritative command, but to solve the moral puzzle, the only authority is the agential authority. This means that only the agent can justify the command and surrender his judgement. The legal legitimacy of authority is primarily from the deliberative viewpoint. Of course, the agent can be mistaken about his reasons, as in our example of Cooks' Island it is not the case that this particular authority is good. Furthermore, how can it be good? How can it coordinate the different goals and ends of the community in a good way, without purporting to do good?

IV. OBJECTIONS TO THE ARGUMENT THAT IN ORDER TO SOLVE THE 'MORAL PUZZLE' OF LEGAL AUTHORITY THE DELIBERATIVE POINT OF VIEW HAS PRIMACY OVER THE 'LEGAL POINT OF VIEW'

(1) The 'legal point of view' is neither deliberative, nor theoretical, but rather a 'third point of view'. However, this 'third point of view' is, like the deliberative one, a practical point of view; the difference lies in the fact that it is formulated from a third person perspective.

The 'legal point of view', an objector might point out, is neither a deliberative viewpoint (ie from the first person perspective) nor a theoretical viewpoint. Statements made from the 'legal point of view' cannot be reduced to either. Following Raz, an objector might say that I have presented a very narrow interpretation of the practical point of view and have reduced the 'legal point of view' to the deliberative point of view. According to Raz, 'the legal point of view' has two core features and should be characterised as follows.

First, statements are true or false according to whether there is, in the legal system referred to, a norm which requires the action which is stated to be one which ought to be done; secondly, if the statement is true and the norm in virtue of which it is true is valid, then one ought to perform the action which according to the statement ought legally to be performed. Such statements are widespread in legal contexts. It should be emphasised again that statements from a point of view or according to a set of values are used in all spheres of practical reason, including morality. Their use is particularly widespread when discussing reasons and norms which are widely believed in and followed by a community. There are always people who accept the point of view and want to know what ought to be done according to it in order to know what they ought to do.[37]

Let us first think about examples outside the law as suggested by Raz. When you give advice to a friend who, for example, is vegetarian, you do not, according to Raz, consider your reasons for actions, but rather her reasons. You probably

[37] Raz, *Practical Reason and Norms*, n 6 above, 177.

love meat, but you give advice to your friend within the framework of her normative system, ie vegetarianism.

My reply to this objection is as follows: in the example used by Raz, being vegetarian is good and if you tell your friend when you go to a restaurant that she has to eat either the spinach or the cabbage (the only vegetables on the menu), both are good things to eat *qua* vegetarian and *qua* human being. In this example you can tell her 'you'd better have the cabbage as you are vegetarian'. There is no further question why that advice has been given. The goodness of eating either cabbage or spinach is obvious in the context. Thus, it is given as a good-making characteristic and is transparent to you and her. It is, I argue, parasitic on the deliberative viewpoint. The reasoning is not different from (I) and (II):

> (III) Cabbage is a good sort of thing for vegetarians.
> You are vegetarian.
> This is a cabbage.
> Conclusion: You ought to eat cabbage.

The dependence or parasitic relationship of the 'third point of view' on the deliberative viewpoint is also apparent in examples very different from premises I, II and III. Franz Stangl[38] was the commander of Treblinka. When he first was appointed as head of a euthanasia clinic, he was morally repelled by the actions of the Nazis. But then he was afraid that he would lose his job and career. He began to think that euthanasia was a necessary evil and it was a favour to those killed. Let us suppose that Stangl was my friend in 1943 and that before he began his process of self-deception, he asked me for advice on what to do. According to Shapiro, I could have replied to Stangl 'according to the normative system of National Socialism, you ought to continue being head of the clinic'. But, according to Raz,[39] like a vegetarian who has accepted the normative framework of being vegetarian, Stangl has already accepted the 'normative point of view of National Socialism'. His question is like the question of a chess player: given the rules of chess, how ought I to play? He has already surrendered his judgement.

But let us suppose that Stangl wishes to know what he ought to do (according to the Nazi law, without surrendering his judgement to it yet). In response to my assertion 'according to Nazi law, you ought to remain head of the euthanasia clinic', Stangl would might sensibly have asked why. The 'why' is directed to the action that I have given as advice. He has asked for advice in terms of a reason for action, not just in terms of an action *simpliciter* (for example, a voluntary action that is done for no reasons) and my answer needs to be also in terms of reasons for actions. When people look for practical advice they are seeking for reasons. Children do this all the time. They ask parents, teachers, relatives, friends how to

[38] Example given by Eleonore Stump to explain the interrelation between intellect and will in Aquinas, see E Stump, *Aquinas* (London, Routledge, 2003) 355. See also G Sereny, *Into That Darkness: An Examination of Conscience* (New York, First Vintage Books Edition, 1983).

[39] My analysis is limited to Raz's notion of a detached point of view and does not aim to establish any conclusion concerning Raz's conception of legal authority as exclusionary reasons.

do this and this, why to do this and this. They learn that some ends are valuable and worth pursuing and others not. To give advice to Frank Stangl in terms of reasons for actions, as in the case of the vegetarian friend, I need a premise like (III) – vegetables are good. What kind of premise can play this role? My argument is that only a premise that (a) is transparent and (b) describes the action as a good-making characteristic could play this role. In this case, the premise 'legitimate authority is a good sort of thing' plays the role of III. The reasoning could be as follows:

> (IV) Legitimate authority is a good sort of thing.
> Nazi law has legitimate authority.
> A Nazi official has commanded that
> 'you ought to remain head of the euthanasia clinic'.
> Conclusion: You ought to obey the command.

But here my advice is mistaken. I know that Nazi law has no authority because it is not an instance of 'authority as a good sort of thing'. The second premise is false. It is similar to the case of vitamins and oranges, as follows:

> Vitamin C is good for one's immune system.
> This synthetic orange without vitamins is good.
> You have a cold, you ought to boost your immune system.
> Conclusion: You ought to eat this synthetic orange.

As in the case of Nazi law, my advice is mistaken because my reasoning is defective as the second premise is false. Stangl has no reason to surrender his judgement. If my advice stops at the moment of expressing 'from the legal point of view, you ought to obey the law', my advice is incomplete. He can legitimately demand reasons for actions, namely, an answer to the question 'why'. Then I need a premise like I, II, III or IV.

(2) In extreme cases of injustice law has no legitimate authority; however, in less extreme cases of injustice law has legitimate authority. In the latter case, the 'legal point of view' can explain the normative or moral character of such authority.

Shapiro could make the following move: we have discussed *en passant* that we can reconstruct his 'special status' argument in terms of a kind of 'Aristotelian necessity'.[40] Authority therefore is a necessity and the 'legal ought' is different from the 'ought' of the rules of chess, because human good is involved. Therefore, his fundamental premise is 'authority is a good sort of thing', but now in a stronger sense: as an Aristotelian necessity. He could reject his initial view that in cases of extreme injustice – Nazi law – law has legitimate authority. The consequences of an unjust system trump any possible benefits obtained from authority. It does not matter how much we try, there is no way we can describe the authority embodied in Nazi law, for example, as good. However, Shapiro could continue arguing that law in less extreme unjust cases is still legitimate as 'authority is a

[40] See n 19 above.

good sort of thing'. But then the question is 'what is the threshold of "defectiveness" that law can tolerate and still be a good?'. Is it possible for law not to purport to do the good and still be good? Arguably, the case is different from the previous example of an orange. An orange does not purport to do the good. An orange is good because it provides Vitamin C or not because, for example, it is rotten, or because it is a synthetic orange without vitamins. *But the law is not a natural kind.* Law is created by officials exercising practical judgements and in many cases they get it wrong. If this is true, however, the problem with Shapiro's view is the denial that authorities purport to do the good. Imagine a mother who does not purport to do the good. Does she have legitimate authority over her child? Imagine a mathematician who does not purport to get it right. In most of the cases, he will not get it right. Does he have theoretical authority? Similarly with legal authorities. If they do not purport to do the good, it is very unlikely that they will be a good sort of thing. The law that purports to do the good and is good can be described as a paradigmatic example of authoritative law. Other kinds of law as authoritative but that do not purport to do good can be described, using the methodology of the central case advanced by Finnis[41] and Aristotle,[42] as authoritative in a secondary sense.

(3) The moral legitimacy of authority should be explained as belief-based and not as value-based.

There might still be a further worry. In the only and short sentence on this issue in the manuscript, Shapiro asserts: 'Since we *consider* the social planners to be morally legitimate, we plan to allow the adopters and appliers to adopt and apply plans for us'(emphasis added).[43] This sentence might seem to rescue Shapiro from my objection. Shapiro might say that it is sufficient if the citizens *consider or believe* that the social planners are morally legitimate and that, therefore, they believe that the master plan is morally legitimate, even though in reality it is not. How might this work? Let us rethink our example of a man who is asked to buy butter and milk for evil purposes. The majority of the islanders believe and consider the planners to have legitimate authority. We might say that at one point they have examined their acts and evaluate them as desirable. In their reasonings, the islanders use this as evidence to place trust in the authorities' commands and attribute moral legitimacy to them. It is desirable (they might say) that disabled children are killed after birth as there are not sufficient resources on the island to support them; this is very similar to the process of self-deception suffered by Stangl, but what is involved here is collective self-deception. In the eyes of the islanders, the authority is a good sort of thing; it replaces their judgement with effective plans to coordinate the complexity of the plural and conflicting goals and ends of the islanders; it minimises the cost of deliberation, and so on. But at some point one can ask the man 'why did you surrender your judgement and obey the authority?' and the man could answer 'because authority is a good sort of thing

[41] J Finnis, *Natural Law and Natural Rights* (Oxford, Clarendon Press, 1980) ch 1, 3–22.
[42] Aristotle, XIX, *Nicomachean Ethics*, n 10 above.
[43] Shapiro, 'PAL', n 7 above, 55.

and purports to do the good'. But here, as in the case of false beliefs, we have a mistaken judgement. He had no reason to surrender his judgement. Similar mistakes are made when we consider the information provided by theoretical authorities. Let us suppose that a friend, who is a mathematician but barely passed his final exams and actually failed his geometry exam, tells me that there are not non-Euclidean geometries. I have evidence that he is a good mathematician because he has helped me with some difficult equations. I believe that the results are correct, though in fact they are wrong. He is really an incompetent mathematician. In my view, however, he has shown that he is a skilful mathematician and I place my trust in him. I now believe that there are not non-Euclidean geometries, but, of course, I am mistaken. I had, therefore, no reasons to surrender my theoretical judgement to him.

(4) The 'legal point of view' is given to someone who has already accepted a specific normative system. But it is not merely this acceptance which explains the binding force of legal authorities; it is rather that we accept hierarchical plans, ie master plans, because we are planning creatures.

Shapiro could argue that I have overlooked his argument that as planning creatures, it is rational to accept hierarchical plans, and the 'legal point of view' might be advanced as a sound one. Shapiro could argue that once a normative system has been accepted,[44] the answer to the question what I ought to do should be given within the accepted normative framework. Consequently (the objection might continue) the answer to the question of why to accept hierarchical – second-order – plans is because we are planning creatures. To achieve ends and first-order plans, we need to accept second-order plans, that is to say, master plans. We are human beings whose identities lie in psychological connections. The achieving ends can only be guaranteed by the temporal and interpersonal continuity of first- and second-order plans. This is (Shapiro might remind us) the basis of the meta-principle: 'authority is a good because we are planning creatures'. The sense of 'good' (this objection might continue) is neither axiological nor moral. 'Good' here is a predicate attributed to the satisfaction of our ends and desires, whatever they are. Authority is good because it enables us to achieve our ends, desires and goals. Mistakenly (the objector might say) I have used a robust conception of 'good'.

So let us suppose that the objector is right and that we can conceive goodness in terms of degrees. The minimal level refers to the satisfaction of our desires and preferences. Let us examine the meta-principle: 'authority is good because we are planning creatures'. On Cooks' Island, islanders have the common preference that all their children will be educated. The planners of the island coordinate all the different activities to achieve such end. Their schools are inspiringly designed eco-buildings and provide all the required equipment. But the planners decide to segregate schools and separate the children between those who are left-handed and those who are right-handed. All preferences are satisfied since all the children receive an adequate education.

[44] The term 'acceptance' here does not mean 'acceptance in terms of reasons for actions'.

Let us remember that, according to Shapiro, legal authorities can be good, without purporting to do the good. The planners of Cooks' Island do not aim to do the good. Organising and coordinating the different activities and conditions that will guarantee the satisfaction of the different preferences of the members of the community is their only aim. Indeed, in the example, the preferences are achieved. Let us suppose that I am a mother living in Cooks' Island and my right-handed daughter is ordered to attend school. I ask for your advice on what I ought to do. Following the objection, the answer should be: given that I have accepted the master plan and the hierarchical structure of the planners, 'from the legal point of view, you ought to obey the order'. In other words, 'from the legal point of view, the order has morally legitimate authority'. According to the proposed objection, my question is limited within the normative framework of what I have already accepted, but not because I have accepted it, but because of who I am, ie a planning creature. But let us think again about the argument of personal identity. If there is a twin Veronica on planet X with the same memories and psychological experiences as Veronica on planet Earth over time, then there is complete identity between the twin Veronica and me. However, let us suppose that the twin Veronica has slightly different values. For example, twin Veronica actually dislikes truth and knowledge, she could not care less about what is true and she only teaches and researches philosophy because she loves to be recognised and to be praised. Can we say that twin Veronica is the same as me? The answer is negative. We are not only a bundle of psychological experiences. We are not only planning creatures, but creatures who value values. Therefore, arguably, one can affirm that not only plans, but also values are constitutive of who we are. If I am also a planning and a valuing creature, why would I accept a plan that does not reflect my valuing – ie that laws should be designed according to principles of justice. If this is sound, then Shapiro's meta-principle should be formulated as follows: 'Authority is good because I am a valuing and planning creature'. This means that there are important connections between legitimate authority, values and conceptions of personhood. It is, unfortunately, not possible to fully develop these ideas here and thus what has been presented is merely an outline of how this objection might be refuted.

(5) We do not, and cannot, commit ourselves to all the different normative systems that coexist in our practical experience. In other words, we act following different norms that we do not fully endorse. A citizen of a state does not commit a contradiction in saying 'I ought to do what the legal official has commanded, but I do not believe they have legitimate authority'. The 'legal point of view' aims to explain the cogency of the latter statement.

The objection raises a sound point. True, there is no logical contradiction in such a sentence, but it nevertheless has a paradoxical nature. There is a parallel between Moore's paradox[45] types and the statement 'I ought to do what the legal

[45] For discussions on Moore's paradox, see R Sorensen, 'The All-Seeing Eye: A Blind Spot in the History of Ideas' in M Green and JN Williams (eds), *Moore's Paradox: New Essays on Belief, Rationality, and the First Person* (Oxford, Oxford University Press, 2007) 37–52; J Adler and B Armour-Garb, 'Moore's

officials have ordered, but I do not believe they have legitimate authority'. Moore's paradox can be found in statements such as 'it is raining, but I do not believe it'. The oddness is caused by an assertoric sentence and its negation such as 'x, but I do not believe x', 'I ought to x, but I do not believe "I ought to x"'. To believe or assert is to *look outward* to the world and determine whether the object of your belief or assertion is true or not. Presumably, when a person says 'I ought to do what the legal officials have ordered' she conveys, in the normal case, the idea that she has surrendered her judgement on the basis of believing that the authority is legitimate, otherwise she will use sentences such as 'I am obliged', 'I am ordered', 'I am coerced', and so on. Then she adds, 'I do not believe they have legitimate authority'. This clause can be replaced by 'I do not believe "I ought to do what the legal officials have ordered"'. The paradox arises because propositional attitudes are outward looking and we are required to look at the object of our beliefs. The paradox, arguably, might be explained because the person takes a 'distance' or 'detached' viewpoint on herself. It is as if there were two subjects in her[46] – the one who believes in the legitimacy of the 'ought' demanded by the legal officials, and the one that denies that the 'ought' of the officials has any legitimacy. This problematic arises only from the first person perspective, both deliberative and theoretical viewpoint. There is no paradox in asserting 'she ought to do what the legal officials have ordered, but she does not believe it'.

Arguably there is some kind of alienation when, from the deliberative viewpoint, the citizen engages in such a thought as 'I ought to obey the law', but then denies avowal or practical endorsement of his own thoughts by asserting 'I do not believe that I really ought to obey the law, because it does not have legitimate authority'.

(6) The possibility puzzle is not a corollary of the moral puzzle since the possibility puzzle is about the *existence conditions* of a norm or rule whereas the moral puzzle is about the *legitimacy conditions* of norms or rules.[47]

My reply to this objection might be as follows. When one explains the existence conditions of an organ of the body – the heart, for example – one is also providing an explanation of the existence conditions of its function – namely, it pumps the blood. We can establish here an analogy between 'heart' and 'norm'. To explain what a heart is without explaining what it is for, is to provide an incomplete explanation of its existence conditions. Similarly, when one explains the existence conditions of norms or rules, it seems to me that one also needs to explain the existence conditions of their functions. A norm exists to guide our conduct – this is one of its core function – but then the question that arises is why should my

Paradox and the Transparency of Belief' in ibid 146–64; A Gallois, 'Consciousness, Reasons and Moore's Paradox' in ibid 165–88, and J Heal, 'Moore's Paradox: A Wittgensteinian Approach' (1994) 103 *Mind* 5.

[46] See S Shoemaker, 'Introspection and the Self', 'On Knowing One's Own Mind' and 'First-Person Access' in his *The First-Person Perspective and Other Essays* (Cambridge, Cambridge University Press, 1996) 3–24, 25–49 and 50–73, respectively.

[47] Jules Coleman formulated this objection to me at the Conference where the paper on which this chapter was based was presented.

conduct be guided by a norm or rule that is external to me? How is it that norms and rules are able to guide my behaviour, and how do they compel me to surrender my own judgements? A complete and satisfactory explanation of the existence conditions of norms needs also to explain how they perform their function; in other words, we need to provide an answer to the moral puzzle. One can say, therefore, in the terms of our previous example, that the existence conditions of a heart are a corollary of the existence conditions of its function. Similarly, the existence conditions of a norm are a corollary of the existence condition of its function. Consequently, puzzling features of the former are a corollary of the puzzling features of the latter. We can assert, then, that the possibility puzzle formulated by Shapiro is a corollary of the moral puzzle formulated by Raz.

4

Legal Normativity and the Instrumental Principle

KATRIEN SCHAUBROECK

THERE IS AN old, classic question in jurisprudence which one could call – adapting somewhat an expression from Christine Korsgaard – *the normative question.* The normative question is what launches Korsgaard's examination of moral theory. It asks 'what justifies the claims that morality makes on us'.[1] According to Korsgaard, the normative question arises when an agent acknowledges the truth of a moral claim but fails to feel the force of that claim. Agents who do not feel the force of their duty fail to recognise the normativity – or authority – of morality. These agents know right from wrong, they know what morality requires but they challenge the common view that moral requirements make a claim on us. The combination of these two attitudes towards morality should not be puzzling. For almost any action, there is a plurality of evaluations possible: a decision can be good for an agent's career but bad for his family life, an action can be morally good but problematic when judged from the standpoint of etiquette, and so on. What matters for the agent is whether the evaluative standard in question is normative for him. In this sense the normative question is also applicable to law. After it is established what the law requires you to do, there remains a question to be answered: in what way is this fact significant for or binding on you? Should you do as the law requires? Has the law authority over you? In other words, is law normative?

Three preliminary remarks should shed light on the meaning and significance of the normative question as applied to law. First, the sense of 'should' as it is used in the normative question needs clarification. When asking 'should one do as the law requires?' the 'should' must be understood in terms of reasons, so the question equals: 'does one have a reason to do as the law requires?' It is common in contemporary philosophy to understand normativity in terms of reasons. Joseph Raz, for instance, writes: 'The normativity of all that is normative consists in the way it is, or provides, or is otherwise related to reasons'.[2] Reasons are understood as

[1] C Korsgaard, *The Sources of Normativity* (Cambridge, Cambridge University Press, 1996) 9.

[2] J Raz, 'Explaining Normativity: On Rationality and the Justification of Reason' in J Raz, *Engaging Reason: On the Theory of Value and Action* (Oxford, Oxford University Press, 1999) 67–89 at 67.

considerations, or facts, that speak in favour of a certain response of the subject. Theoretical reasons are considerations in favour of believing something, while practical reasons recommend certain actions, or at least intentions. The question whether legal requirements are normative is not identical to the question whether they are requirements, because obviously they are, be it in a limited sense, namely as *legal* requirements. To ask whether legal requirements are normative is to ask whether they provide us with reasons to act, whether they guide or bind our decisions and behaviour in such a way that if we don't follow them, we are criticisable.

Secondly, in some interpretations of law, the question whether a legal requirement has authority is already answered once confirmed that the requirement is a legal requirement. In this interpretation normativity is built into the concept of law. The way in which I frame the debate is different: I imagine someone who recognises that something is ordered by the law but wonders why that should make a difference to his intentions and decisions. This set-up of the problem assumes, indeed, that there is a conceptual distinction between law and its normative force, that it at least makes sense to ask 'it is law, but is it normative?', whereas for instance 'it is a triangle, but does it have three angles?' is nonsensical because of the conceptual connection between triangles and the property of having three angles. I assume that law and normative force can be pulled apart at least far enough to give content to the question 'it is law, but is it normative?'

And thirdly, it is important to understand the question 'should one do as law requires?' as a question about normativity, not about motivation. A parallel question in meta-ethics is the one raised by the amoralist. The amoralist is sceptical about the normative force of morality. He has correctly identified his moral obligations (for instance, on the basis of considerations about human welfare) but wonders whether these obligations are normative, whether they give him the kind of reasons that would make it irrational for him not to act on them. He asks: 'Why should I care about moral demands?'. Rationalists and anti-rationalists offer different strategies to deal with the amoralist question, exposing a deep disagreement about the foundation of morality.[3] A different challenge from the amoralist one is raised by the free-rider. His challenge concerns the *motivational* power of morality. A free-rider realises that he should do as morality requires, that is why he keeps his disobedience secret. At first, he recognises the claims that morality makes on him, but, after second thoughts, he believes he can get away with breaking the rules. Applied to the legal context, the free-rider invites reflection on the necessity of punishment as a part of law: by raising the costs of disobedience, one might increase the motivational power of the law. But punishment and the threats

[3] For rationalist theories, see M Smith, *The Moral Problem* (Oxford, Blackwell, 1994) and Korsgaard, *The Sources of Normativity*, n 1 above. They analyse moral requirements in terms of rational requirements so that it becomes an a priori truth that one has reason to do as morality requires. Anti-rationalists, like David Brink and Peter Railton, insist that the question whether it is rational to be moral can only be answered through empirical, thus *a posteriori*, argumentation. See D Brink, 'Moral Motivation' (1997) 108 *Ethics* 4 and P Railton, 'Moral Realism' (1986) 95 *Philosophical Review* 163, reprinted in S Darwall, A Gibbard and P Railton (eds), *Moral Discourse and Practice: Some Philosophical Approaches* (Oxford, Oxford University Press, 1997) 137–63.

of coercion do not need to play a role in an account of the *normativity* of law. They do not seem to provide the answer that the normative sceptic (the amoralist in meta-ethics) is looking for. In fact, the legal theory that will be central to this article, the planning theory of law of Scott Shapiro, is an illustration of this latter point. Shapiro does not relate the normativity of law to reasons to avoid punishment because Shapiro denies that the principal aim of law is to solve the problem of bad character. In his theory, law is basically a social planning mechanism. The instrumental reasons that set this mechanism in motion have social cooperation as their end, not the avoidance of punishment.[4]

In the second section we will have a closer look at Shapiro's account of the identity and foundation of law, and the instrumental principle. In the third section I will refine the instrumental principle but in the meantime it suffices to treat it as a requirement that has something to do with taking the means to our ends. But first I will juxtapose Shapiro's account to the non-positivist account that defines law and its authority in relation to morality. I interpret Shapiro's choice of the instrumental principle as the foundation of law as an alternative to the much more contested attempts to ground the authority of law in morality's authority. Despite the many attractive features of the planning theory of law, I will use the remaining sections of the chapter to point to a lacuna in the theory with regard to its explanation of the instrumental principle. A survey of recent literature on instrumental rationality shows that the normativity – or reason-giving force – of the instrumental principle cannot be taken for granted. Not only are there competing theories about how to explain the normative force of the instrumental principle, and not only have these theories far-reaching consequences for the application of the instrumental principle in jurisprudence, there are also philosophers who doubt whether the instrumental principle really is a normative, reason-giving principle. The normative question which threatened legal authority will arise again, with regard to the instrumental principle: why an agent should take the means to his ends, is a question not as easy to answer as it might seem. The difficulty to ground the instrumental principle in general affects the planning theory of law in particular because it presupposes the normativity of the instrumental principle. In the end, this chapter does not argue that it is impossible to rescue instrumental rationality from scepticism; it just aims to show what is required in order to do so. It wants to show that instrumental rationality does not offer an exit out of the discussion on law's normativity as quickly and easily as one might hope.

I NON-POSITIVISM AND THE AUTHORITY OF MORALITY

Law is thought to be a normative phenomenon, offering reasons for action to its subjects. But explaining the normative purport of the law has proven to be extremely

[4] Subsequent citations are from S Shapiro, 'How to Do Things with Plans', Chapter 1 of this volume. At the end of this chapter I will explain why I integrate Shapiro's planning theory into a story about the normativity of law and why Shapiro might object to it.

hard and the problem divides the landscape of general jurisprudence into two camps: theorists who believe that legal authority depends to some degree upon moral authority, and others who firmly deny this dependence. According to natural law theories, law is an array of values, not a social fact. Their view is summarised – and simplified – in Aquinas' statement *lex iniusta non est lex* (an unjust law is not law). Also on Ronald Dworkin's interpretivist account law and morality are deeply connected. He draws attention to the amount of interpretation that takes place in legal practice. Judges often have to appeal to extra-institutional principles to know which rule to apply, and how. These principles prove morally laden because interpretation of the law is driven by a conception of what makes the law valuable. Insofar as these principles are part of the legal system, law essentially rests on morality.[5]

When the identification of law is considered to be driven by moral aspirations, it paves the way for an interpretation of the duty to obey the law as a moral duty. To ground legal normativity on morality's authority has some prima facie advantages. If law were based on morality, it could profit from the allegedly universal and unconditional applicability of moral laws. Moral rules are supposed to provide reasons for everyone, unlike for instance the rules of tennis, as is effectively illustrated in the following passage from Ludwig Wittgenstein's 'Lecture on Ethics':

> Supposing that I could play tennis and one of you saw me playing and said 'Well, you play pretty badly' and suppose I answer 'I know, I'm playing badly but I don't want to play any better', all the other man could say would be 'Ah, then, that's all right'. But suppose I had told one of you a preposterous lie and he came up to me and said 'You're behaving like a beast' and then I were to say 'I know I behave badly, but then I don't want to behave any better', could he then say 'Ah, then, that's all right'? Certainly not; he would say 'Well, you ought to want to behave better'.[6]

The same thought is expressed in calling moral imperatives 'categorical'. Their application is unconditional, independent of personal objectives or contingent desires. In this sense they differ from hypothetical imperatives like the one that says: 'If you want to play tennis, you must get the ball over the net'.

But grounding the normativity of law on morality's authority also has disadvantages, not the least because it gets us into the deep waters of jurisprudence. The debate between positivists and non-positivists about the relevance of morality to law is such a complicated, fundamental debate that I cannot possibly do justice to it within the scope of this chapter. Legal positivism distinguishes sharply between law's existence and its moral merit, as it was put in a quotation from John Austin which has become the dogma of legal positivism: 'the existence of law is one thing; its merit or demerit is another'.[7] By this, he did not mean to deny that moral opinions often influence the development of legal systems, nor that moral

[5] R Dworkin, *Law's Empire* (Cambridge, MA, Harvard University Press, 1986).

[6] L Wittgenstein, 'A Lecture on Ethics' (1965) 74 *Philosophical Review* 3, 5, reprinted in JH Gill (ed), *Philosophy Today*, No. 1 (New York, Macmillan, 1968) 4–14.

[7] J Austin, *The Province of Jurisprudence Determined* (W Rumble (ed), Cambridge, Cambridge University Press, 1995) (first published 1832), Lecture V, 157.

principles can be brought into a legal system and form part of its rules. Rather, as H Hart emphasises:

> What . . . Austin [was] anxious to assert were the following two simple things: first, in the absence of an expressed constitutional or legal provision, it could not follow from the mere fact that a rule violated standards of morality that it was not a rule of law; and, conversely, it could not follow from the mere fact that a rule was morally desirable that it was a rule of law.[8]

Insisting on the separation of law and morality eliminates morality as a possible source of legal normativity. Positivists have to look elsewhere in order to answer the normative question.

But even for non-positivists who feel comfortable fusing morality and legality, the foundation of law in morality does not fully answer the normative question. There remains an assumption to be vindicated. Morality can pass normative authority on to the law only if it possesses this authority itself. Despite the prima facie plausibility of Wittgenstein's illustration of the special authority of morality, morality's allegedly unconditional authority is doubted by many philosophers. Philippa Foot, for instance, argues that morality is a system of hypothetical, rather than categorical imperatives. She opposes the widespread view that morality consists of unconditional requirements that provide reasons to everyone. Foot does not see why moral considerations should possess any more 'automatic reason-giving force' than, for instance, considerations of etiquette. She argues:

> [M]oral judgements have no better claim to be categorical imperatives than do statements about matters of etiquette. People may indeed follow either morality or etiquette without asking why they should do so, but equally well they may not. They may ask for reasons and may reasonably refuse to follow either if reasons are not to be found.[9]

Non-positivists cannot take morality's authority for granted. Even if it was accepted that law's authority reflects the authority of the underlying moral requirements, the assumption that morality requires things of us in a specific, unconditional way needs to be argued for. That is, by the way, exactly what Korsgaard aims to do in her attempt to answer the normative question – for morality. Whether non-positivists would want to adopt her Kantian construction of moral authority or prefer a more robust moral realism is up to them. In any case, as long as it is an open question whether – and why – we should take morality's demands seriously, the non-positivist's case is not closed.

The difficulty to provide a foundation for morality speaks in favour of legal theories that try to minimise the assumptions on which they rest. One such attempt is offered by Scott Shapiro, who grounds the legal system on something less disputed than moral normativity, namely, on the normativity of the instrumental principle.

[8] HLA Hart, 'Positivism and the Separation of Law and Morals' (1958) 71 *Harvard Law Review* 593, 599, reprinted in his *Essays in Jurisprudence and Philosophy* (Oxford, Clarendon Press, 1983) 49–87, as well as in A Kavanagh and J Oberdiek (eds), *Arguing About Law* (Abingdon, Routledge, 2009).

[9] P Foot, 'Morality as a System of Hypothetical Imperatives' (1972) 81 *Philosophical Review* 305, 312, reprinted in P Foot, *Virtues and Vices and Other Essays in Moral Philosophy* (Oxford, Clarendon Press, 1978).

After outlining Shapiro's theory, I will examine the instrumental principle upon which his construction heavily relies.

II THE PLANNING THEORY OF LAW: POSITIVISM AND THE AUTHORITY OF INSTRUMENTAL RATIONALITY

Shapiro starts with an observation that provides prima facie support for the positivist paradigm. He observes how the existence of moral rules is never established simply by saying 'that is what we do around here', whereas the rules that define what is legally right or wrong do depend on the practices of people. Referring to Austin's 'dogma', Shapiro writes 'Regardless of the merits, the law is just what certain people think, intend, claim and do around here'.[10] In the positivist picture of law that follows from this observation 'rules must satisfy the specific criteria for legal validity, and these criteria can only be discovered through empirical observations of the relevant legal communities'.[11] Non-positivists deny that things are that simple and emphasise that moral legitimacy also plays a role in the legal validity of rules. Shapiro's simple but brilliant move is to point out that, though legal conceptions are subject to controversy, there is no controversy with regard to *plans*: in our conception of what a plan is, we are all positivists. He writes:

> Whether I have a plan to go to the store today, or we have a plan to cook dinner together tonight, depends not on the desirability of these plans, but simply on whether we have in fact adopted (and not yet rejected) them. In other words, positivism is trivially and uncontroversially true in the case of plans: the existence of a plan is one thing, its merits or demerits quite another.[12]

The central thesis of the theory is that law is a form of planning, that the fundamental rules of a legal system are plans. If the existence conditions for law are the same as for plans, positivism provides the right approach to law as well as to plans. Thus:

> the existence of legal authority can only be determined *sociologically*: the question of whether a body has legal power is never one of its moral legitimacy; it is a question of whether the relevant officials of that system accept a plan that authorizes and requires deference to that body.[13]

Law does not receive its authority through moral vindication but through being accorded authority by agents who possess the capacity to accept plans and to accept the authority of plans.

Plans have authority in the sense that they guide and direct the courses of action that the agent *should* take. In this sense plans are embedded in a normative discourse. The activity of planning is subject to several norms of rationality, the

[10] Shapiro, n 4 above, 17.
[11] ibid 17.
[12] ibid 17–18.
[13] ibid 18.

most important of which is the instrumental principle. Planning is a matter of setting ends for ourselves and organising our behaviour over time so that we achieve ends that we might not be able to achieve without planning. When we set ends for ourselves, rationality demands that we adopt the means to those ends, or in Shapiro's words, rationality demands that we 'flesh out' or 'fill in' our plans.[14] Accepting the authority of plans thus involves, among other things, conforming to the instrumental principle.

As Shapiro spells out, planning, or the closely related attitude of intending – in Shapiro's terminology, intentions have plans as their object – is very different from the attitude of desiring. There is nothing irrational about desiring to lose weight and to have dessert at the same time, because desires can conflict – they typically do. But plans are different from desires in the sense that they must be coherent and consistent. If one intends to lose weight and therefore plans to go on a no-dessert diet, it is incoherent to intend to have dessert at the same time.[15] Moreover, intentions must be consistent not only with each other but also with beliefs that the agent holds. If one believes that it is impossible for humans to fly, one should not intend to fly – although there might be nothing irrational about *wishing* one could fly, or *desiring* to fly. In short, when a person adopts a plan, she must accept all the requirements that come with that plan, such as the requirement to take the means to realise the plan. Adopting a plan is like placing oneself under the governance of a norm. An agent who performs an action contrary to the plan he adopts opens himself to criticism. This way, a plan functions as 'a guide for conduct and a standard for evaluation' and that is why Shapiro even claims that plans *are* norms.[16]

Once established that adopting a plan is like installing a norm which the planner should conform to, what is further required in order to accept Shapiro's account of the identity and foundations of law is a defence of the claim that law is a form of planning. Using the state of nature narrative as an argumentative device, Shapiro explains the reasons that a community has for developing legal constitutions. Life in a community, however small, generates coordination problems, and social planning is one way to solve those problems. If a community has cooperation as a shared end, one way to achieve this end is by adopting a shared plan. Moreover, the shared plan also provides ways to settle disputes and to deal with disagreements in complex, contentious and arbitrary environments. The bigger a community, the more sophisticated the shared plan must be. The need for further planning, together with the realisation by members of the community that social planning via consensus in plenary meetings is slow and inefficient, ends up in outsourcing various stages of social planning to a small group of trusted

[14] ibid 21.

[15] The example is Shapiro's, ibid 22.

[16] Ibid 25. To *identify* plans with (a certain type of) norms goes further than to *relate* plans to independent normative principles, such as the instrumental principle. It sounds more plausible to me to say that plans activate norms, and in this way create reasons, rather than to say that plans really are norms. But this probably depends on how flexible one's use of the concept of 'a norm' is. Insofar as plans guide and evaluate action, one can understand why Shapiro wants to call them norms.

members. They become the social planners of a community, who will adopt and apply a variety of norms that are called for by the circumstances and whose activity of social planning is regulated by a shared master plan. Making social planning hierarchical, impersonal and institutional basically amounts to the creation of a legal system including legal officials (the social planners), and a constitution that defines their offices (the master plan). The legal system plans for the community over which it claims authority, 'both by telling members what they may or may not do, and by identifying those who are entitled to affect what others may or may not do'.[17] In this way, legal activity can be understood as a form of social planning, and legal rules, issued by those who are authorised to plan for others, as plan-like norms.

This conception of law as a social planning mechanism allows for a positivist theory of the identity and foundation of law. Since the proper way to determine the existence and content of a shared plan is through observing the relevant social facts (is the plan designed for a group, is it publicly accessible, is it accepted by the members of the group?, etc), the existence and content of the rules of a legal system are determined through sociological inquiry as well. No moral inquiry is required because the validity of legal rules does not depend on the moral permissibility of the content of the rules or on the moral legitimacy of the officials that issued them. The shared plan that constitutes the law may be morally obnoxious because:

> Just as there are no specific ends that intentions are supposed to serve, there are no substantive goals or values that laws are supposed to achieve or realise. They are all-purpose tools that enable agents with complex goals, conflicting values and limited abilities to achieve ends that they would not be able to achieve or achieve as well, without them.[18]

And the legal officials need not do their job out of morally good intentions; their authoritative status does not derive from any moral assessment. All that is required is that there is a shared plan designed for a group and accepted by the members of the group, which authorises the legal officials to plan for others. As Shapiro says:

> In other words, to build or operate a legal system one need not possess moral legitimacy to impose obligations and confer rights: one need only have the ability to plan. The existence of law, therefore, reflects the fact that human beings are planning creatures, endowed with the cognitive and volitional capacities and dispositions to organize their behaviour over time and across persons in order to achieve highly complex ends.[19]

Legal rules are plans created in order to achieve complex ends like social cooperation. In this approach, reference to moral values is neither necessary nor relevant to explain how law comes about.

[17] Shapiro, n 4 above, 46.
[18] ibid 62.
[19] ibid 47.

The form of legal positivism that the planning theory of law amounts to, is different from traditional forms of legal positivism according to which the existence and content of law rests on social facts alone. According to the planning theory, legal facts rest on social facts as well as a normative fact, be it a non-moral normative fact. This normative fact is articulated in two ways by Shapiro: on the one hand, he describes it as 'the fact that planning agents have the rational authority to give themselves plans';[20] on the other hand, he refers to the authority possessed not by the agent but by the irreducible norms of practical rationality. In a crucial passage, Shapiro explains how the planning theory succeeds in explaining legal authority without generating vicious circles (the body creates a norm which confers authority to that body to create that very norm), or infinite regresses (the body gets its authority from another body which gets its authority from another body, and so on). Imagine that legal officials accept a shared plan that authorises the queen to play a certain role in adopting legal policies. The queen thus receives legal authority, but where exactly does this authority come from? Do the legal officials have the legal authority to defer authority to the queen through a shared plan? Is their authority passed on to the queen? But where does the authority of these legal officials come from? An infinite regress looms. A vicious circle is the only outcome, *unless* we can invoke an irreducible kind of authority upon which the existence and authority of legal rules rest. The planning theory provides exactly this kind of solution as Shapiro explains:

> Legal officials have the power to adopt the shared plan which sets out these fundamental [legal] rules by virtue of the norms of instrumental rationality. Since these norms that confer the rational power to plan are not themselves plans, they have not been created by any other authority. They exist simply in virtue of being rationally valid principles. Instrumental rationality, therefore, constitutes the normative bedrock on which every legal system rests.[21]

If one identifies law with a plan, one can also invoke the kind of normativity that gives authority to plans, namely the normativity of the instrumental principle. Once an agent accepts a plan, he accepts the norms that come with it. He puts himself under the authority of the plan, which means that he ought to attempt to fill in or flesh out the plan. This kind of 'ought' is irreducible to, for instance, moral normativity because the morally assessable content of the plan does not affect the normative force of the principle that one should take the means to realise the plan.[22] That is why Shapiro remarks that 'the rational authority of planners is not a form of moral authority: terrorists . . . have the rational authority to create evil plots among themselves'.[23] So even if the fundamental legal rules are

[20] ibid 69.

[21] ibid 68.

[22] At least, that is the commonsense opinion adopted by Shapiro. Upon closer inspection, however, the instrumental principle is not that unproblematic when applied to immoral ends. As we will see, philosophers struggle with the normativity of the deceptively simple requirement to take the means to our ends.

[23] Shapiro, n 4 above, 69.

morally odious, and the legal officials are cruel dictators, the legal system has authority as long as there is a shared plan – a constitution – which authorises the officials to plan for the community. Whether there is such a plan solely depends on whether certain social facts obtain. Moral facts are denied any role in determining the existence, content and authority of the law. Therefore the planning theory of law is a positivist account.

Summing up, the positivist claim that one can know whether a body has legal authority through sociological observation alone is defended by Shapiro on the basis of a particular explanation of legal authority: the law has authority because it is a plan. Like the existence of plans, the existence of law is an empirical, sociological matter. Like the authority of plans, the authority of law is grounded in the ability of planning agents to bestow authority on plans by adopting them. Plans have authority in the sense that we act irrationally if we don't take the means to our planned ends. The normative force possessed by plans is captured by the instrumental principle. Now, how exactly does this principle capture the normativity possessed by law? How does it support legal authority? What is exactly the connection between legal requirements and the requirements to take the means to our ends? Are the former applications of the latter? Shapiro does not spell this out in great detail. In order to get a better grip on the alleged connection between legal normativity and the instrumental norm, let us first fine-tune the instrumental principle. Afterwards, we will examine whether 'the normative bedrock of every legal system' is indeed such a firm foundation. If the instrumental principle is without ground or contested itself, the positivist's model built upon it becomes shaky.[24]

III THE NORMATIVITY OF THE INSTRUMENTAL PRINCIPLE

The content of the instrumental principle is controversial. In an established version, formulated by Immanuel Kant, the principle says this:

> Whoever wills the end also wills (insofar as reason has decisive influence on his actions) the indispensably necessary means to it that are within his power.[25]

There are two restrictions built into the principle as it is formulated by Kant: it does not apply to less than necessary means nor to desires on which one does not yet intend to act – 'willing an end' means 'intending an end' and is different from desiring in the Kantian vocabulary, as will be explained in the next section on Korsgaard. But a third restriction is called for: the agent who wills the end must know that certain means are necessary, or even more precisely: the principle

[24] In footnote 3 of Chapter 1 (p 21), Shapiro acknowledges that the justification for the requirements of practical rationality as well as the content of the requirements is the subject of philosophical controversy. Therefore, it would not be fair to accuse Shapiro of making hasty, false assumptions. I suggest one reads this chapter as a critical exposition of what still has to be done if Shapiro aims for a complete account of law's identity and formation.

[25] I Kant, *Groundwork for the Metaphysics of Morals* in MJ Gregor (ed and trans), *Immanuel Kant: Practical Philosophy* (Cambridge, Cambridge University Press, 1996 (1785)) AK 417.

applies to those means that the agent *judges* to be necessary – even if, in reality, they are not. The revised instrumental principle, which I will further refer to as IP, is:

(IP) If you intend to E and judge that M-ing is a necessary means to E, you should intend to M.

The principle expresses a requirement. It says more than that intending an end provides a *pro tanto* (and thus defeasible) reason to take the necessary means. It is not that there is *a* reason to take the necessary means to one's ends, rather one must do so. Insofar as a person intends to see the Mona Lisa, and judges that going to Paris is necessary in order to see the Mona Lisa, he must intend to go to Paris.[26]

Kant insisted that the hypothetical imperative 'requires no special discussion' since it is 'analytic'.[27] And many agree with Kant. R Jay Wallace writes in an encyclopaedia entry on practical reason: 'Among the substantive norms of practical reason, those of instrumental rationality have seemed least controversial to philosophers . . . In the modern era, this form of rationality has widely been viewed as the single unproblematic requirement of practical reason'.[28] One of the key articles on instrumental rationality in recent years, written by Christine Korsgaard, opens with: 'Most philosophers think it is both uncontroversial and unproblematic that practical reason requires us to take the means to our ends'. But, Korsgaard continues, 'philosophers have, for the most part, been silent on the question of the normative foundation of this requirement'.[29] Since the publication of Korsgaard's 'The Normativity of Instrumental Reason' a lot has changed. Over the last decade the instrumental requirement has become a popular research topic in contemporary theory about practical reasoning. *Pace* Kant, IP does seem to require a lot of discussion.

In an attempt to clarify, or even justify, the authority of the law, legal philosophers who invoke or implicitly rely on instrumental rationality might do so out of

[26] Instrumental rationality involves more than the core requirement to take the means that one believes to be necessary to one's ends. For instance, it enjoins us to take the means that facilitate the realisation of our ends: practical reason tells us that it is wise to make a Thalys reservation beforehand, though it is not strictly necessary in order to achieve the end. Practical reason also requires us to do those things that realise an end, without strictly speaking being a means to the end. If you want to make 'coq au vin' for instance, you must marinate the chicken in red wine. But marinating the chicken is not really a means to making 'coq au vin', it is rather a part of the process of preparing this dish. For reasons of simplicity, I will limit the instrumental principle to the means that are believed to be necessary for the achievement of intended ends. Also for reasons of simplicity, I will ignore a condition that limits IP to those means that one can bring about by intending. For instance, the agent in the example probably also believes that normal blood circulation or normal weather conditions are necessary to realise the end of seeing the Mona Lisa, but this does not create an instrumental obligation because blood circulation nor good weather are things that the agent can bring about by intending.

[27] Kant, *Groundwork for the Metaphysics of Morals*, n 25 above, AK 417.

[28] RJ Wallace, 'Practical Reason' in EN Zalta (ed), Stanford Encyclopedia of Philosophy (Summer 2009 edn) available at http://plato.stanford.edu/entries/practical-reason/.

[29] C Korsgaard, 'The Normativity of Instrumental Reason' in G Cullity and B Gaut (eds), *Ethics and Practical Reason* (Oxford, Oxford University Press, 1997) 213–54 at 215.

the Kantian assumption that the hypothetical imperative 'whoever wills the end also wills the means' requires no discussion. More precisely, they might take its normative authority for granted. In recent years, however, the normativity of IP has come to seem problematic to many philosophers. The problem is that there is no obvious answer to the following question: does an agent have a reason to take the means to his end, or would the agent be irrational in failing to take the means to his end, if it is irrational for the agent to hold that end? Many authors tackling this vexed question start by pointing out their ambiguous feelings about it – they are torn in both ways. As Raz expresses his ambivalence:

> On the one hand, we feel that the value of the means derives from the value of the ends. If there are reasons to take the means, they must be none other than the reasons to pursue the ends, or at least they must derive from them. On the other hand, we also feel that failure to take the means to one's ends is a distinct kind of failure, different from the failure to have proper ends.[30]

Now, what does the dilemma consist in exactly? On the one hand, it sounds wrong to confirm that a frustrated neighbour creates for himself a reason to sharpen the kitchen knife just by making it his goal to stab the crying baby next door. If the instrumental principle generates a reason to take the means to any end an agent sets oneself, it leads to implausible consequences. Adopting Bratman's useful terminology, I will call this 'the boot-strapping problem': it seems as if the instrumental principle 'boot-straps' reasons into existence out of nothing.[31] One way to avoid this problem is to interpret the value of the means as derivative from the value of the end – which would imply that irrational, weak-willed or horrible ends don't create reasons to take the means. But this strategy has implausible consequences too; because, on the other hand, it seems also true that the failure to take the means to one's ends is a failure apart from, and in addition to, the failure to have rational or proper ends. Wallace uses the word 'cleverness' to denote the kind of intelligence that is displayed by agents who are in the grip of akrasia and who do not endorse the ends they set themselves, yet exhibit great intelligence and skill in pursuing these ends.[32] What is more: we expect these agents to do so, in the sense that not taking the means to one's end, regardless of how worthy the end is, is always regarded as a failure, which one could plausibly describe as a failure of instrumental rationality. Kieran Setiya illustrates this particular form of irrationality by describing someone who intends to count the blades of grass in his garden but is not bothered with bookkeeping and has to start

[30] J Raz, 'The Myth of Instrumental Rationality' (2005) 1 *Journal of Ethics and Social Philosophy* 1, 2.

[31] See M Bratman, *Intentions, Plans and Practical Reason* (Cambridge, MA, Harvard University Press, 1987) 24–27. The boot-strapping problem resonates the problem that David Hume detected in accounts that derive an 'ought' from an 'is': how could the mere fact that I have a certain end affect what I *should* do?

[32] RJ Wallace, 'Normativity, Commitment and Instrumental Reason' (2001) 1 *Philosophical Imprint* 1, reprinted in his *Normativity and the Will: Selected Essays on Moral Psychology and Practical Reason* (Oxford, Oxford University Press, 2006) 82–120.

all over again each morning.[33] The intention to count blades of grass is crazy enough, but the failure to take the means to realise this end makes our judgement about this agent even worse. And Raz gives the example of someone who akratically intends to buy a car yet does not intend to make an offer. He wonders: 'It appears that just by failing to intend to pursue the means to her end she is behaving irrationally. But if her end is no reason for her to facilitate its realization, how can that be?'[34] Does the mere fact that an agent has a certain end make a normative difference after all? But how can we articulate this normative difference without falling prey to boot-strapping? Thus, the challenge for a theory of instrumental reason is to specify the sense in which a person 'should' take the means he believes necessary to his end while (i) avoiding boot-strapping and (ii) explaining the distinctive form of rationality called 'cleverness'. Different theories have been proposed by Christine Korsgaard, Stephen Finlay, R Jay Wallace and Kieran Setiya, John Broome, Niko Kolodny and Joseph Raz, and Michael Bratman. All their attempts to explain the normative force of IP are structured by the double task of explaining the phenomenon of cleverness while avoiding boot-strapping. I will analyse and compare their accounts, in order to point out the implications they would have if they were plugged into the planning theory of law. It will turn out that none of the accounts provides a foundation for IP that allows it to play the exact role it is supposed to play in Shapiro's planning theory of law.

IV CHRISTINE KORSGAARD'S VIEW OF THE INSTRUMENTAL REQUIREMENT AS CONSTITUTIVE OF RATIONAL AGENCY

Christine Korsgaard's influential article 'The Normativity of Instrumental Reason' is a reaction against these philosophers who hold that instrumental reasons exhaust the domain of practical reasons – 'the instrumentalists', often identified with 'the Humeans'. Korsgaard's argument is designed to show that the requirement of instrumental rationality cannot stand on its own but presupposes other requirements of practical reason. She resists the Humean assumption, as it resonates in Philippa Foot's earlier mentioned scepticism, that 'hypothetical imperatives do not require any philosophical justification, while categorical imperatives are mysterious and apparently external constraints to our conduct'.[35] As part of her defence of the Kantian foundation of morality, her goal is to show that the constraints on human conduct imposed by morality are not more problematic than those imposed by instrumentality. Or, conversely, she argues against Humeans that the justification of the instrumental principle is not less problematic than that of the moral law, and that actually, they are interdependent.

[33] K Setiya, 'Cognitivism about Instrumental Reason' (2007) 117 *Ethics* 649.
[34] Raz, n 30 above, 11.
[35] Korsgaard, n 29 above, 217.

On the Humean picture, practical reasoning is instrumental.[36] It is there to serve the passions, and more precisely to help fulfil the agent's ends. These passions or ends are themselves considered immune to rational assessment. Yet they determine the actions the agent has reason to perform, because the reasons an agent has are revealed by deliberating on the means necessary to achieve the ends. In this desire-dependent theory of practical reasons, all reasons for action are reduced to instrumental reasons. It is pretty uncontroversial to affirm that instrumental reasoning can reveal reasons. But many resist the Humean reduction of all practical reasons to instrumental reasons. Korsgaard argues against this reduction by showing that a purely instrumental conception of practical reason is incoherent in the following way.

According to the Humeans, our ends are determined by what we desire. There is nothing extra required of a desire for it to become our end, because there are no other practical requirements besides the instrumental principle. The instrumental principle tells us to take the means to our ends, but if our ends are our desires, and our desires determine our actions, the instrumental principle could just as well have ordered us to do what we are going to do anyway – which turns it into a poor normative requirement. Korsgaard's argument rests on this claim: as long as the instrumental principle is the only principle of practical reason, then to say that something is an agent's end is not to say that he has a reason to pursue it but that he is going to pursue it. For the instrumental principle to function as a requirement there must be a way to distinguish between what we ought to do and what we factually do, or, between our ends and the desires that we will actually pursue. Another reason to look for a way to distinguish ends from desires is that it is just not true that we ought to take the means to our desires. We desire all sorts of, often inconsistent, things. If we want to make sense of the idea that we have reason to take the means to our ends, ends must differ from desires. Therefore (Korsgaard's argument goes) if practical reason is to deliver any reasons at all, as is presupposed by the Humeans (in contrast perhaps to Hume himself), the instrumental conception must be supplemented.

What is needed is a theory of practical reason that includes principles that determine ends. As Korsgaard explains it, there are two options:

> If we allow reason a role in determining ends, then the instrumental principle will be formulated this way: 'if you have a *reason* to pursue an end then you have a reason to take the means to the end'. But if we do not allow reason a role in determining ends,

[36] The Humean view might not be Hume's view. In fact, many Hume-interpreters agree that Hume's view is more aptly described as the view that there is no such thing as practical reason at all. According to Jean Hampton, for instance, Hume rejects the idea that the instrumental norm has authority over us (J Hampton, 'Does Hume have an Instrumental Conception of Practical Reason?' (1995) XXI *Hume Studies* 57). And Hume's general scepticism about practical reason is also what supports Elijah Millgram's claim that Hume is not a Humean (E Millgram, 'Was Hume a Humean?' (1995) XXI *Hume Studies* 75). The target of Korsgaard's argument is not this general scepticism. Korsgaard opposes the Humeans, or as she describes them, the 'empiricists who endorse the view that reason plays only an instrumental role in action' and who 'commonly claim Hume as the founding father of their view' (Korsgaard, n 29 above, 222).

then the instrumental principle has to go like this: 'if you are *going* to pursue an end, then you have a reason to take the means to that end'.[37]

Note that this latter formulation recalls the boot-strapping problem as a version of the 'ought derived from is' fallacy. Therefore, Korsgaard's own account of instrumental rationality can be interpreted as a way to avoid boot-strapping, although she does not present it in these words herself. Boot-strapping is avoided if one chooses, as Korsgaard does, the first formulation of the instrumental principle and makes the reason to take the means dependent on the reason to pursue the end, so that the instrumental principle derives a 'should' from another 'should'. This means that on Korsgaard's account, for the instrumental principle to provide an agent with a reason to take the means to an end, he must have a reason for that end to begin with. Korsgaard gives a constructivist account of reasons for ends according to which reasons for ends do not rely on the recognition of the independent value of the end. Korsgaard in other words opposes value realism which says that there are values or reasons out there in reality to be discovered by us. In her constructivist view, values and practical reasons are constructed by the agent himself. It is by willing an end that one gives a normative status to the end. In order to do so, the willing has to happen in accordance with normative principles – one cannot *will* anything in the Kantian terminology. One can *desire* anything, but willing something is a normative stance.[38] Given the scope of this chapter, I cannot go in great detail into Korsgaard's Kantian construction of normativity as generated by the will. But because Korsgaard's account of the normativity of the instrumental principle can only be understood within the Kantian framework, I shall have to say a few more words about the will according to Kant.

In the Kantian view, a desire is an inclination in the face of which we are passive. By reflecting on the inclination and deciding to act upon it, we become active and the desire becomes a volition. Desires or inclinations have no normative force. Only when we endorse a desire or adopt it as a maxim, the desire becomes an end, something that we *will*. The normativity of the instrumental principle is self-evident, on this Kantian picture, because what else can 'willing an end' mean but 'willing to realise the end'? As Korsgaard points out:

[37] Korsgaard, n 29 above, 223.

[38] Korsgaard believes that to mark the distinction between desiring and intending we need extra normative principles which bestow normative force to our ends, but there is an unwarranted assumption underlying this belief: that one could not make a distinction between desire and end without appeal to a normative principle. Wallace has criticised Korsgaard for this assumption, because he does not understand why mere *acceptance* of a desire as mine, rather than an endorsement on normative grounds, would not suffice to turn it into an end of mine. Against Korsgaard he maintains: 'Endorsement of normative principles will turn out not to be among the conditions for the possibility of willing anything at all' (RJ Wallace, 'Constructing Normativity' (2004) 32 *Philosophical Topics* 451, 459). Peter Railton summarises the conflict between Korsgaard and Wallace when he writes that whether it is possible to avoid Kantianism 'depends on the possibility of distinguishing between possession of ends from the making of judgments that certain ends are good' (P Railton, 'On the Hypothetical and the Non-Hypothetical in Reasoning about Action' in G Cullity and B Gaut (eds), *Ethics and Practical Reason* (Oxford, Oxford University Press, 1997) 53–79 at 65). Such internal discussions are not the subject of this chapter, but it is good to realise that each of the presented accounts raises questions of its own, apart from the question whether it can be used by Shapiro to complete his theory.

> To will an end just is to will to cause or realize the end, hence to will to take the means to the end. This is the sense in which the instrumental principle is analytic. The instrumental principle is *constitutive* of an act of the will. If you do not follow it, you are not willing the end at all.[39]

If an agent does not conform to the instrumental principle, and is always derailed from the pursuit of his ends, he does not really *will* an end, at most he desires it. The act of willing conforms to the instrumental principle by its very nature, because it is constituted by it. That is how Korsgaard explains the requirement to take the means to one's ends: following this principle is constitutive of willing.

But the instrumental principle cannot do the constitutive work on its own, Korsgaard adds. Her objection against the Humeans in 'The Normativity of Instrumental Reason' holds that the instrumental principle cannot exist without something which gives normative status to our ends. Here is another way to explain this idea:

> If I am to will an end, to be and to remain committed to it even in the face of desires that would distract and weaknesses that would dissuade me, it looks as if I must have something to *say to myself* about why I am doing that – something better, moreover, than the fact that this is what I wanted yesterday.[40]

Before the instrumental principle can 'kick in', the agent needs to rely on another normative consideration that helps him to turn a mere desire into an end. And so, Korsgaard concludes:

> If there is a principle of practical reason which requires us to take the means to our ends, then those ends must be, not merely ones that we happen to have in view, but ones that we have some reason to keep in view. There must be unconditional reasons for having certain ends, and, it seems, unconditional principles from which those reasons are derived.[41]

Hence, Humeanism, understood as the view that all practical reasons are instrumental reasons derived from the ends that we desire, is incoherent for Korsgaard.

So far, we know that the instrumental principle must be supplemented by further principles that make our willing an end normative. But which extra normative principles is Korsgaard referring to? At the end of 'The Normativity of Instrumental Reason' Korsgaard points towards the things that she has not talked about in the chapter: 'I have shown nothing so far about the *content* of those principles [the unconditional principles of practical reason]. As far as the argument of this essay goes, they could be principles of prudence, or moral principles or something else'.[42] From Korsgaard's other works, we know that she holds not only the instrumental principle but also the moral law to be a constitutive norm of

[39] Korsgaard, n 29 above, 244.
[40] ibid 250.
[41] ibid 252.
[42] ibid 252–53.

autonomous acts of the will.[43] Of course, Korsgaard has to give an argument for the equation of constitutive norms of autonomy with the substantive requirements of morality, but this is something we do not need to survey in this chapter.[44] All we need to know is that in Korsgaard's conception of the instrumental principle, it needs to be supplemented by other normative principles, such as moral requirements, to have normative force.

So Korsgaard concludes her analysis of the normativity of the instrumental principle by noting that 'the view that all practical reason is instrumental is incoherent, for the instrumental principle cannot stand alone'.[45] At first sight, this conclusion need not pose any problems for Shapiro's planning theory of law. After all, Shapiro never claims that the instrumental principle is the only normative requirement left in the practical domain. But a problem, or at least an indication of a lacuna in Shapiro's account, does appear if Korsgaard reformulates her conclusion as: 'Unless there are normative principles directing us to the adoption of certain ends, there can be no requirement to take the means to our ends'.[46] If Korsgaard is right, Shapiro has not gained any ground by focusing exclusively on the instrumental principle as the foundation of legal normativity. Because, if Korsgaard is right, a reference to the instrumental principle alone does nothing to undergird law's normativity. To activate the instrumental principle, other principles of practical reason must first confer value to the end intended.

It is unlikely that Shapiro would accept Korsgaard's conceptual connection of the instrumental principle with the other principles of practical reason. His positivist ambitions drive him towards an account of legal authority that avoids an appeal to moral legitimacy. That is why he puts his hopes on the instrumental principle. If this principle were to depend on other principles such as the moral one, his positivist project would fail. Korsgaard challenges what Shapiro calls the 'uncontroversially true' view that the existence and content of a plan never depend on moral facts. For Korsgaard, holding an end, which is arguably extensible to adopting a plan, is not as factual or a-normative as it seems. For Korsgaard, having an end always implies having reasons for this end, otherwise there would be no difference between desires and intentions. Therefore intending – or willing – cannot come about in a realm where all normativity is derived from the instrumental principle. Acts of the will, like adopting a plan, are bound by the principles of reason, including more substantive principles like moral ones. Korsgaard's objection against Humeanism thus problematises plan positivism and, indirectly, also legal positivism as it is conceived by Shapiro. Fortunately, her moralising interpretation of IP is not the only theory in the field. The planning theory of law asks for another conception of the instrumental principle than Korsgaard's. And

[43] See Korsgaard, *The Sources of Normativity*, n 1 above, especially the chapter entitled 'The Authority of Reflection', 89–130.

[44] She develops a comprehensive argument in *Self-constitution: Agency, Identity, and Integrity* (Oxford, Oxford University Press, 2009).

[45] Korsgaard, n 29 above, 251.

[46] ibid 220.

it is plausible that it can be found in the camp of Korsgaard's critics, most notably the contemporary Humeans attacked by her. Let us have a look at how Humeans defend themselves against the charges.

V STEPHEN FINLAY'S VIEW OF THE INSTRUMENTAL PRINCIPLE AS A LAW OF LOGIC

The Humean philosopher Stephen Finlay has recently developed a conception of the instrumental principle in response to the Kantian criticism. Finlay accepts Korsgaard's critique, but instead of surrendering he chooses radicalisation. He goes back to the original Hume and claims that the instrumental principle is *not* a norm of practical reason. He writes:

> There is no desire-independent normative principle commanded by reason (or anything else) that we ought to take the means to our ends, and all the intuitions and phenomena that seem to lend the idea credence are explicable in other, Humean ways.[47]

Even more, in order to save the desire-dependence theory of normativity from inconsistency, Finlay argues that one should deny the existence of *any* norm of practical reason. We will confine ourselves to his account of IP alone.

Finlay does not regard IP as a genuine normative command of reason, or in other words, a rational norm, because it cannot satisfy a basic criterion for rational norms which Finlay calls 'the violation criterion': if a principle is to be normative and to counsel, guide or command an agent, it must be possible for the agent to act otherwise than directed by the principle. The instrumental principle cannot be violated because it is analytic – and thus necessarily true – in Finlay's eyes. Remember that Kant also called the principle 'analytic', but he meant to create room for violations by adding a caveat: whoever wills the end wills the necessary means *insofar as he is rational*. Depression, or rage, or addiction, or passion could break the means–end connection because they equal states of irrationality. But Finlay doubts whether these cases, exemplified in 'the modern paradigm of instrumental irrationality, the addicted smoker', are genuine cases of violation of the instrumental norm. 'For that to be the case, they [the agents in these cases] must both be aware of the necessity of the means, and continue to will the end'.[48] Finlay finds this implausible. Imagine someone who resolved to quit smoking but succumbs to addiction and has another cigarette. In order to see akratic actions as violations of the instrumental principle, the Kantian philosopher has to interpret the smoker's attitudes as follows: the smoker resolves never to smoke another cigarette again, he knows that lighting up one more cigarette is incompatible with this end, yet he succumbs to temptation *while still intending* never to smoke again – and thereby exhibits irrationality. This does not strike Finlay as a plausible analysis. It

[47] S Finlay, 'Against All Reason? Scepticism about the Instrumental Norm' in CR Pigden (ed), *Hume on Motivation and Virtue: New Essays* (Basingstoke, Palgrave Macmillan, 2009) 155–78 at 156.

[48] ibid 165.

is much more likely that, at the moment of giving in to temptation, the smoker abandons his end never to smoke again and, for instance, changes it into a wish never to smoke again or makes it his new end never to smoke again starting from tomorrow. Finlay's analysis does not undo the akratic character of the example: the agent still is weak-willed, namely by being over-ready to revise his intentions in the face of temptation.[49] But the analysis gives support to Finlay's belief in the analyticity, or inviolability, of the instrumental principle: an agent cannot but intend what he believes to be the necessary means to his intended ends, and this even applies to irrational agents. Apparent counter-examples to this principle are really examples of where an agent changes his ends, and takes the means to this newly created end.

There is a lot going on in Finlay's argument on a fundamental level, not least because his conception of agency is thoroughly different from Kantian conceptions. We do not need to get deeply involved in the metaphysics of the story. We are interested to see how Finlay makes sense of IP. After he has shown that it is a metaphysical 'must', rather than a rational requirement, he cannot just leave it at that. He cannot ignore that common sense makes use of instrumental criticism. We feel the force of IP and we use it to decide about our own actions as well as to evaluate other people's behaviour. But if the instrumental principle is not a command of reason, what is wrong with an agent who intends to see the Mona Lisa, believes that in order to see the Mona Lisa in real life it is necessary to go to Paris, yet does not think that he should go to Paris? Why should he take the means to his end if it does not matter to reason? What can be said to the sceptic about the normativity of IP? Finlay must either have an alternative explanation of the normative force that is exerted by the instrumental principle, or give an error theory, that is, a theory that explains why we are all collectively mistaken in believing that there is something criticisable about the sceptic.

Finlay does not give an error theory. He is positive that there exists an instrumental 'ought' but his point is that it does not express a command of reason. Distinguishing rationality from normativity, he writes:

> Instrumental oughts and rational oughts fall into separate categories of normative propositions. The desire-dependence thesis makes room for instrumental normativity and rational criticism but not for criticism of instrumental rationality.[50]

If not a rational requirement, what is the instrumental 'ought' then on Finlay's view? And in what sense is Finlay entitled to an instrumental 'ought', especially

[49] Richard Holton's distinction between weakness of will and akrasia is illuminating at this point. He reserves the term akrasia for action against one's better judgement, but points out that when ordinary people speak of weakness of will, they have in mind a failure to stick to one's plans. The weak-willed agent changes his judgements so that he can give in to temptation without acting against this better judgement. R Holton, 'Intention and Weakness of Will' (1999) 96 *Journal of Philosophy* 241.

[50] Finlay, n 47 above, 173. As we will see below, Broome's scepticism about the instrumental principle is formulated in exactly the opposite way: Broome accepts that the instrumental principle is a rational requirement, but wonders whether that makes it also a normative requirement – whether it provides reasons.

given his postulation of the possible violation criterion? That we ought to will the ends that we believe are necessary to our ends, is not a command of reason but a law of logic, or a metaphysical 'must', says Finlay. But the world cannot violate the laws of logic, which implies that we cannot fail to comply with the instrumental principle. How, then, can Finlay speak about an instrumental *ought*?

The instrumental ought is what Finlay calls an 'end-relational ought': it 'presupposes some particular end as framing a normative perspective, and recommends a course of action from that particular point of view as serving that end'.[51] The instrumental principle is, as it were, a normative requirement *from the perspective of the intended end.* It does not matter to rationality whether an agent fails to fulfil his desires; it matters to the intention or the desire itself. As Finlay remarks: 'It is from the perspective of the desire for y that we judge *we ought to do z* when we believe doing z to be the means to y'.[52] The instrumental norm is transformed by Finlay to the principle that says: If an agent desires y and z is the means to y, then he ought to do z.

On this principle, even if the agent does not know that doing z was the means to y, he ought to do z because it remains true from the desire's perspective that he ought to realise it. From the agent's perspective, the instrumental norm can be violated. As it is evident that 'Ignorance, false belief, and confusion can lead us to neglect required means', it follows that the violation criterion is satisfied and that 'there is indeed room for an instrumental "ought"'.[53]

Apart from the fact that the ascription of a perspective to a desire feels a little uncomfortable (what does it mean that 'failure to satisfy a desire always *matters* to the desire'?)[54] Finlay's solution for the normativity of the instrumental principle is of no use to Shapiro. Shapiro wants to say more than 'from the perspective of the plan, the means should be taken'. He wants to speak about the agent's perspective, and about the authority that governs the agent because the agent places himself under the plan's authority. A plan indicates something that matters to the agent, something that he sets forward as an end – like cooperation, for instance. But that is different from saying that it matters to the plan that the end is realised. It is important *to the agent.* Therefore, Finlay's interpretation of the instrumental 'ought' cannot be reconciled with the general ambition of the planning theory of law and is in this sense of no use to Shapiro. He needs yet another explanation of the normativity of IP. Which alternatives are left?

Debates on practical reasons and practical rationality are often framed dualistically: Kantian approaches, on the one hand, Humean theories, on the other. This way of carving up the field leaves out an important player, namely the normative realist. According to the realist, reasons are not derived from what

[51] ibid 171.

[52] ibid 173. Note that Finlay opens the instrumental norm not only for intentions but also for desires; and not only for necessary means but for any means that could serve the desire. Since he interprets the norm from the perspective of the end, he is no longer constrained by what is required from the perspective of rationality.

[53] ibid 172.

[54] ibid 173.

constitutes rational agency, nor do they depend on the contingent desires of an agent. For him, reasons are facts that count in favour of doing something and their normativity is an independent, irreducible property of reality. Realism invites another way of thinking about IP. Very influential is John Broome's idea to distinguish reasons from rational requirements and to interpret IP as a rational requirement, avoiding the theoretical possibility that it boot-straps reasons out of nothing. Maybe Shapiro could appeal to this solution, if the Humean and Kantian views fall out of his reach. Before we look into the implications of Broome's account of IP for the planning theory of law, we need an analysis of Broome's own view, which has changed significantly over the years.

VI JOHN BROOME AND THE INSTRUMENTAL PRINCIPLE AS A WIDE-SCOPE REQUIREMENT

Like Korsgaard, John Broome wants to explain the normativity of the instrumental principle without boot-strapping. He believes that the solution consists in making appropriate distinctions of scope. Some 'oughts' govern combinations of attitudes, others are attached to one attitude as such. This distinction between wide-scope and narrow-scope requirements demands that we give up the identification of normativity with reasons that was pointed out at the outset of this chapter. Broome explicitly opposes Raz when the latter says 'The normativity of all that is normative consists in the way it is, or provides, or is otherwise related to reasons'.[55] According to Broome, reasons do not exhaust the field of normativity; there are other important features of normativity that are most aptly captured in what Broome calls 'normative requirements'. Normative requirements differ from reasons in that they are wide-scope. Wide-scope requirements are the solution to boot-strapping because they make it possible to explain the normative relation between intending an end and intending a means without boot-strapping reasons into existence. Let us have a closer look at how this works.

Imagine someone who intends to drink a beer and believes that drinking a beer can only be achieved by going to the bar. From this a rational requirement can be derived that says the agent should intend to go to the bar. The requirement can be expressed in two ways. One could say: 'an agent ought to intend M, if he intends an end E and believes that M-ing is the only means to E-ing'. But this formulation creates the boot-strapping problem – for imagine that the agent really should go home instead of having another drink; is it true then that he should intend to go to the bar? Broome thinks we should deploy a wide-scope operator and formulate the instrumental requirement as follows: 'an agent ought (to intend M if he intends E and he believes that M-ing is the only means to E-ing)'.The brackets are crucial; they mark the difference between normative

[55] Raz, n 2 above, 67; J Broome, 'Reasons' in J Wallace, M Smith, S Scheffler and P Pettit (eds), *Reason and Value: Themes from the Moral Philosophy of Joseph Raz* (Oxford, Oxford University Press, 2004) 28–55, reprinted in J Dancy (ed), *Normativity* (Oxford, Blackwell, 2000) 78–99.

requirements and reasons. The 'ought' in this latter example cannot be detached from the conditional, it cannot be attached to one part of the conditional: it just is not true that if an agent intends E and he believes that M is a necessary means to E, he ought to intend M. Replacing E by 'killing the crying baby next door' and M by 'sharpening the kitchen knife' makes that immediately clear. Intending an end is not normatively insignificant, but neither does it give rise to reasons. Intending an end *normatively requires* an agent to intend whatever he believes is a necessary means to it. Intending an end does not provide an agent with *a reason* to intend whatever he believes is a necessary means to it. In the words of Broome:

> If you ought not to intend the end, it may well be false that you ought to intend whatever you believe is a necessary means to it. Still, intending the end normatively requires you to intend whatever you believe is a necessary means to it.[56]

The difference between reasons and normative requirements is not one of kinds, but of scope. So there is only one sense of 'ought' at work in Broome's theory, but there are different scopes. Normative requirements govern over a combination of attitudes, reasons over one separate attitude. Another way to put this is that the instrumental requirement ranges over a conditional, not its consequent alone.[57] From 'you ought (to intend M if you intend E and believe that M is only means to E)' we cannot derive the detached conclusion that you ought to intend M, if you intend E and believe that M is the only means to E. Normative requirements do no permit this sort of detachment. That the instrumental requirement ranges over a conditional does not turn it into a conditional requirement. The requirement applies always, independent of the circumstances. It is more accurate to say that it is an unconditional requirement to fulfil a conditional. A very important implication of the wide-scope formulation of the instrumental requirement is that it allows for two ways to make the conditional true: by intending M or by ceasing to intend E.[58] An agent ought to satisfy a disjunction (either give up attitude A or take up attitude B), but he is not required to satisfy it one way rather than the other. He cannot know, on the basis of the instrumental requirement, which of the two options he should pursue: intending M or ceasing to intend E. This implication of Broome's account creates a problem for the application of the instrumental principle in the legal context, or at least it heavily circumscribes its use.

If Broome's interpretation of the instrumental principle as a wide-scope requirement is correct, then a legal theory that rests on the instrumental principle

[56] Broome, n 55 above, 29.

[57] Normative requirements are not confined to the practical domain of instrumentality. The fact that you believe proposition p is not a reason for you to believe what p entails. For instance, of an agent who believes that the world was created in six days, we do not want to say that he has a reason to believe that the world was created in less than a week. The restriction is better captured in a wide-scope requirement which says: you ought (to believe that world was created in less than a week, if you believe that world was created in six days). See Broome, n 55 above, 51.

[58] Mark Schroeder adds a third way: by acting to eliminate the efficacy of the means so that one can stop believing that M is a necessary means to E. M Schroeder, 'The Scope of Instrumental Reason' (2004) 18 *Philosophical Perspectives* 337, 339.

is built upon a disjunction: the agent ought (either to take the means he believes necessary, or give up the end). This might not be the foundation we hoped for. In the end we want a theory that explains why we have a reason to obey the legal system, not a theory that only provides us with the normative requirement that we ought (either to accept the legal system or give up on the end that the legal system is believed to be a means to). When Shapiro calls the instrumental principle the normative bedrock of the legal system, I assume he wants it to provide reasons to adopt law – as a plan. But Broome's interpretation of IP only gives him a normative requirement, an 'ought' that cannot be detached from a conditional: you ought (to adopt law if you intend cooperation and believe that adopting law as a social planning mechanism is a necessary means to cooperate). As far as the requirement goes, giving up the end of cooperation is just as good as adopting the law. But from the perspective of a legal theory, these two alternatives cannot be judged equally worthy. The interpretation of IP as a wide-scope requirement does not give Shapiro what his planning theory of law needs.

Moreover, Broome came to realise that the wide-scope reading of IP did not give him what he had thought either. Since his article from 2005 'Does Rationality Give Us Reasons?',[59] he has stopped calling the requirement 'you ought (to intend M if you intend E and believe that M is only means to E)' a *normative* requirement. All he claims is that it is a *rational* requirement. By calling it thus, it remains an open question whether rational requirements are normative. Broome joins Joseph Raz and Niko Kolodny in their defence of the so-called 'myth theory'.[60] The underlying thought of the myth theory is that for each source of requirements we can ask whether that source is normative. Broome, Raz and Kolodny believe that rationality is no exception to this rule. They raise the normative question with regard to rationality: do we have reason to do as rationality requires? This might sound a crazy question, but they can explain why their scepticism makes sense. The puzzle is that rationality requires things of us that we have no reason to do. The instrumental principle, which is only one of the many requirements of practical rationality, perfectly illustrates this puzzle by raising what we have called 'the boot-strapping problem'. Broome, at first, thought that he had found a solution to this problem by making distinctions of scope. But critics pointed out the defects of the wide-scope reading of IP, claiming that it did not avoid boot-strapping at all. I will summarise the criticism as it was formulated by Kieran Setiya. Afterwards we will see how the undermining of Broome's first solution leads to myth theory.

So Broome formulates the instrumental principle as 'you should (if you intend to E and believe that M-ing is a necessary means to E, intend to M)'. According to Broome one should make true this conditional, which can be done either by intending to M or by stopping to intend E. Imagine, writes Setiya, that there is nothing I can do to change my intention to, say, smoke. 'It follows that the only way in which I can conform to the conditional [if I intend to smoke and believe

[59] J Broome, 'Does Rationality Give Us Reasons?' (2005) 15 *Philosophical Issues* 321.

[60] See Raz, n 30 above and N Kolodny, 'Why be Rational?' (2005) 114 *Mind* 509.

buying cigarettes is a necessary means to smoking, then I intend to buy cigarettes] is by intending to buy cigarettes'.[61] So in this case, Setiya argues, Broome's principle says that I should intend to buy cigarettes all things considered. But this need not be so; it may still be that I should not intend to smoke even if I cannot change this intention, and this would make it false that I should intend to buy cigarettes. Boot-strapping is not vindicated by the fact that the agent cannot modify the intention to E. Setiya concludes that boot-strapping remains illicit in a way that Broome's wide-scope formulation of the instrumental principle cannot explain. The problem is that Broome's account does not constrain the means by which one makes the conditional true.[62]

Acknowledging the force of this and other objections against his wide-scope approach to normative requirements, Broome opts for another solution to the boot-strapping problem. He joins Kolodny and Raz in depriving the instrumental requirement of any normative force.[63] If IP has no normative authority, it cannot boot-strap reasons into existence. In this sceptical interpretation, IP retains its character as a rational principle, but it lacks normative authority: agents have no reason to obey IP, that is to say, no reason that is not derived from the reasons we have to reach valuable ends which we could realise through complying with IP. Because we have reasons to be rational agents and because there are many good things that we can achieve through complying with IP, the instrumental principle often has derivative or instrumental normative significance. But the idea that it has distinctive, non-instrumental normative significance is a myth. Kolodny and Raz defend a radical version of this myth theory, Broome is a little more cautious. He calls himself agnostic: he does not know whether there is a reason to do as rationality requires. He feels drawn towards the conclusion that rationality is normative in its own right, but admits that he has no good arguments for that conclusion. He writes: 'I think it is an open question whether the requirements of rationality are normative . . . whether, necessarily, if rationality requires us to F, we have reasons to F'.[64] The lesson is that we should not conclude too much from the wide-scope reading of IP. Even if it is a rational requirement, and it governs combinations of attitudes, it cannot be understood as a normative requirement that has independent authority as long as there is no definite answer to the question 'why be rational?'.

For reasons of systematicity, I covered the myth theory of instrumental reason. But it is immediately obvious that, for the planning theory of law, no help should be expected from this approach. If IP is merely a rational requirement and there

[61] Setiya, n 33 above, 660.

[62] As we will see below, Michael Bratman believes that the wide-scope account can be rescued from Setiya's objection by excluding compulsive behaviour as not relevant to a principle about rationality and thus not a problem for wide-scope reasons.

[63] Myth theory is not the only available solution. Setiya himself, for instance, does not turn to myth theory after he showed the deficit of the wide-scope reading of IP. His solution is cognitivism, as we will see in the next section.

[64] J Broome, 'Have We Reason to Do as Rationality Requires? A Comment on Raz' (2005) 1 *Journal of Ethics and Social Philosophy* 1, 3.

are no reasons to obey rational requirements, the integration of the instrumental principle in a theory of law does not add anything interesting in terms of normativity. To the contrary, if the myth theory is the correct view of instrumental normativity, the consequences for the planning theory are devastating. Shapiro has every reason to resist Raz's, Broome's and Kolodny's myth theory of the instrumental norm. After abandoning Korsgaard's moralising account, Finlay's understanding of IP as a law of logic, Broome's proposal in terms of distinct scopes and the subsequent myth theory with regard to instrumental normativity, what else is left? What other theories about the normativity of IP are there to evaluate? There is one distinct approach that we should look into, because it arises from a worry about Korsgaard's theory that suggests an affinity with Shapiro's positivist outlook. This approach is taken by R Jay Wallace and Kieran Setiya and it explains the normativity of IP, avoiding boot-strapping, explaining 'cleverness', while endorsing IP's independence of morality. Especially this latter part of their theory is likely to arouse interest from Shapiro.

VII R JAY WALLACE AND KIERAN SETIYA ON THE INSTRUMENTAL PRINCIPLE AS A REQUIREMENT OF THEORETICAL REASON

In search of a foundation for practical reasons, some philosophers have argued that differences between practical and theoretical rationality are not as significant as they appear. According to David Velleman, for instance, all the demands of practical rationality can be explained in terms of the requirements of theoretical rationality.[65] This view of practical rationality has been dubbed 'cognitivism'.[66] A less global form of cognitivism than the one defended by Velleman can be found in Wallace and Setiya. Their local cognitivism holds that certain requirements of practical rationality, most importantly the instrumental norm, can be explained in terms of the requirements of theoretical rationality. In this approach the instrumental 'ought' is really a theoretical or epistemic 'ought' because it expresses constraints on the cognitive elements of practical thought. It turns the requirement to take the means to our ends into an application of the belief-closure requirement. This is in general terms how Wallace and Setiya trace the normative force of the instrumental principle to the authority of theoretical rationality.

Looking into cognitivism in more detail, it is important to know that Wallace introduces cognitivism as an alternative to what he calls 'a moralizing tendency in reflection about instrumental reason' as it is exemplified in Christine Korsgaard's account.[67] Wallace interprets Korsgaard's account as an attempt to avoid the

[65] Velleman's view is 'that practical reasoning is a kind of theoretical reasoning, and that practical conclusions, or intentions, are the corresponding theoretical conclusions, or beliefs'. See D Velleman, *Practical Reflection* (Princeton, NJ, Princeton University Press, 1989) 15.

[66] Michael Bratman was the first to use the label in this context; see M Bratman, 'Cognitivism about Practical Reason' (1991) 102 *Ethics* 117, reprinted in M Bratman, *Faces of Intention: Selected Essays on Intention and Agency* (Cambridge, Cambridge University Press, 1999) 250–64.

[67] Wallace, 'Normativity, Commitment and Instrumental Reason', n 32 above, 1.

dubious hypothesis that the instrumental principle applies indifferently to any end that agents happen to pursue. But by constraining the application of the instrumental requirement to the ends that are actively endorsed by the agent, Korsgaard's proposal goes too far in the opposite direction, Wallace claims. It conflicts with far too common examples of akratic actions where an agent displays 'cleverness' in pursuing an end he does not believe to be worthwhile. Wallace's disagreement with Korsgaard goes beyond the issue of instrumental rationality. As a realist he resists her constructivist approach to normativity in general, and he explains in detail what is wrong with the interpretation of 'willing' as a normative stance. A survey of these arguments would take us into the deep waters of meta-ethics as well as theory of action. What is relevant within the limits of this chapter is the non-moralising account of the normativity of the instrumental principle developed by Wallace.

Wallace's goal is to show 'how we can explain the normative force of the instrumental principle without supposing that the ends to which the principle applies need be endorsed by the agent, as good or worthy of pursuit'.[68] He looks for an articulation of the requirement represented by the instrumental principle which poses constraints on the attitudes of agents (i) without entailing they have reason to take the means (that would be boot-strapping), and (ii) independent of the agent's normative judgements about the ends (that would be moralising and ignoring the phenomenon of 'cleverness'). To satisfy (i) Wallace adopts Broome's view of the instrumental principle as 'a constraint on combinations of attitudes that does not license detached normative judgements to the effect that we have reason to take the necessary means to our ends'.[69] With regard to (ii), Wallace starts out by observing that since the instrumental principle applies to intentions not to desires, 'there must be something about the attitude of intending that goes beyond the attitude of desiring in a way that brings a rational requirement into play'.[70] Korsgaard is right to define intending an end as a commitment to realising it, but she is wrong in identifying a volitional commitment with a normative endorsement. All we need to accept in order to defend the normativity of the instrumental principle with regard to an agent's end, is this:

> One specific respect in which these attitudes [desiring and intending] differ is that the commitment to realize an end is constrained by one's beliefs about the possibility of realizing the end, whereas desires are not similarly constrained.[71]

Unlike the desire for E, the commitment to realise E requires the belief that it is possible to realise the end. This requirement is constitutive, since Wallace understands it in the sense that 'agents who believe that they cannot do x should not even be described as intending to do x in the first place'.[72] Note that there are

[68] ibid 2.
[69] ibid 17.
[70] ibid 18.
[71] ibid 20.
[72] ibid 20.

other cognitivists who think that the belief implied by the intention to do x is more than just the belief that *it is possible to do x*, according to them it requires the belief that *one will do x*. Wallace believes he has enough by making the belief that it is possible to do x a constitutive ingredient of the intention to do x. Combining (ii) with (i), Wallace has cleared the path for rational constraints on certain combinations of attitudes, namely attitudes of believing. The attitudes that are governed by the wide scope instrumental requirement in Wallace's view are beliefs. The failure to take the means that one believes necessary to achieve an end is of the same kind as the failure to believe q if one believes that p and that if p, then q. Even more, not taking the means necessary to one's ends is a failure because it implies an incoherent set of beliefs. Wallace sums up his position as follows: 'the normative force of the instrumental principle can be traced to independent rational constraints on your beliefs – in particular, to constraints on certain combinations of beliefs'.[73]

Setiya is a cognitivist about instrumental rationality like Wallace, denying that the instrumental principle is a principle of *practical* reason. Rather, he writes, 'the "should" of instrumental reason flows from epistemic requirements on the beliefs that figure in our intentions. It is the "should" of theoretical reason'.[74] The deference to an epistemological 'should' covers (ii). But for (i) Setiya needs another solution than Wallace because he is critical of Broome's view, as we saw above. Whereas Wallace tries to avoid boot-strapping by distinguishing between narrow-scope and wide-scope requirements, Setiya relies on the distinction between practical and epistemic 'oughts'. If the instrumental requirement expresses an epistemic 'should', it can never create reasons for action, regardless of whether the end is morally justifiable or not. The boot-strapping problem is a problem about practical reasons for action and does not arise in Setiya's cognitivist view of instrumental rationality. In his view, an agent's reasons to take the means he believes necessary to his end are epistemic not practical.

Cognitivism conceives the instrumental principle as the application of requirements of theoretical rationality to the beliefs that figure in our intentions. An attractive feature of this theory is that it benefits from the uncontested normativity of epistemic requirements.[75] Whether one can accept the cognitivist explanation of the normative force of the instrumental principle largely depends on whether one shares the metaphysical conception of intentions that is implied. It is, however, not obvious to think of intentions as a species of belief, as Setiya does, nor to think of an intention to do x as necessarily involving the belief that it is possible that one does x. Michael Bratman explains why, as we will see in the next section. Whether the planning theory can be amended by the cognitivist explanation of IP

[73] ibid 21.

[74] Setiya, n 33 above, 650–51.

[75] It may seem easier to explain the normative force of theoretical demands – of coherence and consistency between beliefs – than to explain the normative force of demands on intentions. But some philosophers, arguably including the myth theorists Raz and Kolodny, are sceptical about the distinctive (irreducible)significance of norms of theoretical rationality too. It is therefore far from clear whether cognitivism succeeds in refuting the myth theory about the norms of practical rationality.

depends on Shapiro's metaphysical view of plans: does he think that adopting a plan necessarily involves holding certain beliefs? Or does he consider the attitude of planning as irreducible and unconnected to the stance of believing? Given his strong dependence on the planning theory of intentions developed by Michael Bratman, it is plausible to assume that Shapiro would reject cognitivism, just like Bratman. But while Shapiro acknowledges his debt to Bratman in general terms, it is not clear what features of Bratman's theory are exactly adopted by Shapiro, besides the obvious use of the concept of 'a plan' as central to his theory. In order to evaluate the significance of cognitivism for the planning theory of law, let us first look at Bratman's objections against it. He explicitly refuses to reduce intentions to a kind of beliefs. His explanation of the instrumental requirement invokes a specific understanding of intentions as mental states *sui generis*, on a par with beliefs and desires. If Shapiro adopts Bratman's conception of what an intention is, he will arguably also accept Bratman's theory of what gives these intentions normative force, such that they give an agent reasons to take the means that realise the intended end. The decisive question, at the end of our explorative study of contemporary theories about IP, will be: can Bratman's planning theory of intention fill in the empty spot in – or underneath – Shapiro's planning theory of law?

VIII MICHAEL BRATMAN AND THE INSTRUMENTAL PRINCIPLE AS AN IRREDUCIBLE PRACTICAL NORM

Bratman understands intentions as 'elements of larger and typically partial plans whose primary roles in our lives are ones of coordination and organisation, both cross-temporal and social'.[76] Associated with these roles are certain norms that put rational pressure on intentions. Bratman distinguishes between a norm of rationality stability over time, and the norms of coherence (between means and ends) and consistency (between ends) at a time. Though strictly speaking IP does not fully coincide with what Bratman calls the requirement of means–end coherence, these subtleties do not matter for our purposes and I shall regard Bratman's theory about the norm of coherence as transferable to the instrumental principle.[77] As planning agents, we are subject to the norm of means–end coherence. But why exactly should we care about this norm? What is its normative significance?

In developing an answer to the normative question, Bratman sets himself the aim to steer a path between cognitivism and myth theory. Against cognitivists, he argues that instrumental rationality demands more than consistency between beliefs. On the cognitivist reading of the instrumental principle, it only orders an

[76] M Bratman, 'Intention, Belief, Practical, Theoretical' in S Robertson (ed), *Spheres of Reason: New Essays on the Philosophy of Normativity* (Oxford, Oxford University Press, 2009) 29–61 at 29.

[77] Bratman explains the difference himself in 'Intention, Belief, and Instrumental Rationality' in D Sobel and S Wall (eds), *Reasons for Action* (Cambridge, Cambridge University Press, 2009) 13–36 at 13 n 2.

agent to form the belief that he intends y, rather than to actually form the intention to y. The problem with this lies in the apparent possibility of false beliefs about one's own intentions. According to Bratman, it is possible that an agent believes that he intends certain means, yet does not in fact so intend. If such a case is possible, then it satisfies the demand of coherence with regard to the relevant beliefs, but it does not satisfy the demand for means–end coherence because the agent does not in fact intend the means that he believes to be necessary.[78] Cognitivism leads to the false conclusion that the agent in this case is instrumentally rational.

In addition to this criticism of the cognitivist argument, Bratman also finds it problematic to accept the supposition central to cognitivism: that there is a tight connection between intention and belief. In the weaker version, defended by Wallace, this means that the intention to x is connected to the belief that it is possible that one will x. In the stronger version, which can be found in Gilbert Harman's and Setiya's work, intention to x involves or is even identical to the belief that one will x. The weaker version cannot make true its own ambitions, according to Bratman. It is perfectly fine for an agent to believe that E is possible and to believe that M is possible, while believing that it is not possible both that E and M. After all, 'a conjunction of beliefs about the possibility of different actions need not ensure a belief that the conjunction is possible'.[79] If an agent who intends E (and thus believes that E is possible) and judges intending M to be necessary (and thus believes, at least, that M is possible) does not need to hold the belief that the conjunction of E and M is possible, he does not contradict his own beliefs by intending E and failing to intend M. If cognitivism wants to succeed in showing that intentions need to be coherent because of requirements on the associated beliefs, it must associate the intention to E with a stronger belief than the belief that it is possible to E. But the stronger version of cognitivism is implausible for external reasons: Bratman believes that it is possible that one intends to x while retaining some doubt about whether one will remember when the time comes. He describes the example of someone who intends to stop at the bookstore on the way home. Yet, this person knows that he is very forgetful and that there is a chance he will forget to stop at the bookstore. According to Bratman it is accurate to say that in this case the agent intends to stop at the bookstore, yet does not believe that he will stop.[80] Even if one is not convinced of the possibility of these counter-examples (my own intuitions, for instance, are not crystal clear: would we say that an agent intends to x, when at the same time he admits that he does not hold the belief that he will x?) one can still prefer Bratman's theory over cognitivism. His planning theory of intention does not rest on the assumption that intending involves a belief that one will so act but it is nevertheless consistent with it. And after all, Bratman emphasises: 'The basic claim is not about the *word* "intend" but about how best to make sense of the characteristic norms of intentions and

[78] M Bratman, 'Intention Rationality' (2009) 12 *Philosophical Explorations* 227, 230.
[79] Bratman, 'Intention, Belief, Practical, Theoretical', n 76 above, 34.
[80] ibid 21.

plans. The planning theory, in contrast with cognitivism, sees these norms as fundamentally practical'.[81] Bratman interprets intentions as mental states to be distinguished from beliefs and desires. And like beliefs, they are constituted by certain norms and 'aims'. The demand of coherence on belief is often explained by tying it to the nature of belief because it is widely agreed upon that belief aims at truth. Bratman transfers this way of thinking to intentions. In the same way as, but irreducible to, the demands on belief, the demand of coherence on intention is tied to the nature of intention. According to Bratman, intention is constituted by the aim for coordinated and effective control of action. This interpretation of intention allows him to introduce IP as an essential demand on intentions, constitutive of this specific type of attitudes that are central to a specific kind of agency, namely planning agency. Modelling intentions after beliefs, without reducing the one to the other and regarding both as distinct mental states defined by distinct characteristics, Bratman can explain the normativity of IP by making use of the idea that intentions are characterised by constitutive norms. He rounds up:

> There can be agents who are not planning agents . . . But if you are, as we are, a planning agent, your intentions and plans have . . . characteristic aims, aims associated with norms of consistency and means-end rationality. And this does not require cognitivism about [IP].[82]

Against myth theorists, Bratman defends the genuine and distinctive normativity of the instrumental principle. The only normativity that myth theorists can ascribe to coherence is derived from something that is served by coherent behaviour and has independent value. Raz, for instance, grants that there is much to be said in favour of being a rational agent and having certain habits of mind associated with rationality. And Kolodny grants that on most occasions the agent will have reasons for her specific ends that transmit to instrumental reasons to take the means to the end. But it is a myth, according to them, to attribute non-instrumental, distinctive normative significance to the norm of means–end coherence. Coherence only has instrumental normative significance. Bratman believes that myth theory is in tension with commonsense understanding of practical rationality:

> When we think of ourselves as inconsistent or incoherent in our intentions in a particular case, we normally think of ourselves as failing to satisfy, in that very case, basic demands of reason. We think this whether or not conformity to those demands would have been instrumentally useful in the pursuit of other things.[83]

As akratic actions illustrate, one can intend an end without believing there is a reason for that end, but such intentions still engage the norms of coherence and consistency. In short, according to Bratman, myth theory fails to appreciate and explain the phenomenon of cleverness.

[81] ibid 49.
[82] ibid 26.
[83] Bratman, 'Intention Rationality', n 78 above, 229.

Bratman's alternative to myth theory consists in tracing the reasons for means–end coherence back to reasons for self-governance. Self-governance, for Bratman, consists in 'the guidance of practical thought and action by practical attitudes that speak for the agent and constitute, as Frankfurt puts it, "where . . . the person stands himself".'[84] Planning structures help to constitute forms of psychological and agential unity that enable self-governance. When an agent intends E but does not intend what he believes to be a necessary means to E, there is no clear place where the agent stands with respect to E. But self-governance requires one practical standpoint whose guidance constitutes the agent's governance. So, it follows that 'Means–end coherence of relevant intentions of a planning agent is a necessary constitutive element in her having a relevant standpoint, and so a necessary constitutive element of her self-governance with respect to an end E'.[85] So this is Bratman's explanation for the normativity of IP: to the extent that there is some reason for governing one's own life – which is plausible enough – there is a reason for means–end coherence of the relevant intentions, because means–end coherence is constitutive for self-governance.

The claim that there is a general reason for means–end coherence should not be confused with the claim that there is in any particular case an independent reason to intend the means to one's ends. In fact, for Bratman, the requirement of means–end coherence has wide scope: one cannot arrive at a reason to intend the means by detaching it from the requirement that governs the combination of one's attitudes. This wide-scope reading of IP allows Bratman to explain why there is a distinctive, non-instrumental practical reason for conformity to the norm of means–end coherence, even in the case of an akratic end intention. He can, in other words, explain cleverness without validating boot-strapping. He explains: 'In such a case [of an akratic, but non-compulsive end intention], our Broome-inspired rejection of factual detachment of a reason blocks a deductive inference to a reason in favour of necessary means'.[86]

An advantage of Bratman's view is that it has the resources to counter Setiya's objection to wide-scope accounts of the instrumental principle. Setiya invoked the case of a compulsive smoker: someone who cannot modify the intention in favour of the end and had only one way to meet the instrumental requirement, namely, by intending to take the means. In this case, the reason for means–end coherence can be detached and the agent has a reason to M, but then we wind up conceding that intentions provide reasons in general. Bratman can block this threat by appeal to his account of the reason for means–end coherence. This reason derives from the reason for self-governance. But if self-governance is not possible, the conditions that are necessary to achieve it no longer matter. The agent in Setiya's example lacks the power to modify her intentions in the light of reflection, and therefore is not self-governing. It follows that the norms of coherence are no longer relevant for this agent. If self-governance is impossible to achieve, there is no

[84] ibid 236.
[85] ibid 236.
[86] ibid 238.

sense in obeying the demands that are normative because they support self-governance. Thus, on Bratman's view, the reasons for self-governance induce a reason for means–end coherence of the relevant intentions, *only if self-governance is possible.* Means–end coherence has no normative significance in compulsive behaviour, so Setiya's example of the compulsive smoker leaves the wide-scope interpretation of means–end coherence intact.

In Bratman's view, demand for coherence is of an irreducibly practical nature. It is an internal norm for planning agents. Conformity to the norm of coherence is an essential element of planning agency. And planning agency is a capacity that we should cherish and esteem highly because it enables us to achieve complicated ends and enriches our lives. Against myth theory, the planning theory of intention entails that consistency and coherence have a non-instrumental normative significance. Against cognitivism, it interprets this normative significance as irreducible to the normative significance of epistemic requirements.

If there are good reasons for the agent to govern himself, there are, arguably, good reasons for societies to govern themselves. If Bratman is right, these reasons induce reasons for the community to be means–end coherent. So, if self-governance is possible and members of a community set themselves an end – like cooperation – they should conform to IP. But, remember, Bratman conceives of IP as a wide-scope requirement. It offers no more than a requirement to fulfil a conditional. Applied to the planning theory of law, the instrumental principle's normativity consists in requiring us either to adopt the means to our plans (thus to fill out the legal system), or to drop the end of cooperation. At the end of the paragraph on Broome, I already wondered whether Shapiro could be satisfied with the wide-scope requirement as the normative bedrock of the legal system.

Another incongruity between Bratman's planning theory and Shapiro's, is their use of the word 'plan'. For Bratman, intentions are elements in bigger plans that enable agents to achieve complicated ends. In Bratman's use of the word 'intention', it is possible that an agent is mistaken about the intentions he has. This already sounds a little counter-intuitive. How much more so if we extrapolate this idea to the word 'plan'? How could one be mistaken about one's plans? It seems far-fetched to suppose that an agent could have a plan without knowing it, or think that he has a plan without having it. As Shapiro writes: 'Plans are "positive" entities – they are created via adoption and sustained through acceptance'.[87] In Shapiro's conceptual framework, one cannot have a plan without adopting it. And adopting a plan seems to be something which is done consciously. This implies that one cannot have a plan passively or unconsciously. For Shapiro, plans are the objects of intention, which suggests that Shapiro does not think of intentions as something an agent can have without knowing. At least the intentions central to his theory, namely, to pursue social cooperation and to install a legal system in support of it, cannot be unconscious. This difference in Bratman and Shapiro's deployment of the word 'plan', and the subsequent different

[87] Shapiro, n 4 above, p 25.

conception of 'intention' that I suspect, does not make Bratman's explanation of the instrumental principle deeply incompatible with the planning theory of law. After all, Bratman's explanation is consistent with the cognitivist assumption that intending involves a belief that one will so act. But it does remove *a* reason in favour of Bratman's theory, and gives Shapiro *a* reason to have a second look at the cognitivist explanation of the instrumental norm. Despite the obvious affiliation between both views, Bratman's planning theory of intention might not be the best candidate to take up the empty space underneath Shapiro's planning theory of law.

IX CONCLUSION

This chapter focuses on a problem for the planning theory of law that is generated by the lack of an undisputed, fully satisfying account of the instrumental principle. It starts from the acceptance of Shapiro's claim that the authority and existence of law goes back on instrumental rationality, and then questions the strength of this foundation. It assumes that Shapiro considers it to be a major advantage of his theory that, in contrast to non-positivist or natural law theories, it relies on a relatively uncontroversial notion of normativity, namely, the normativity of the instrumental principle. However, as this chapter purports to show, the uncontroversiality is only prima facie.

Shapiro might dismiss all the foregoing, by insisting that the discussion about the normativity of the instrumental principle does not concern him. His aim, he could say, is not to explain normativity but to answer the metaphysical question how legal obligations come about. And it is true, after all, that Shapiro's theory does not handle the normative question explicitly; it does not start out as an attempt to show that citizens should obey the law. The following summary is probably closer to the initial aspiration of his exposition: by starting from individual actions and adding layers of planning, Shapiro builds a legal system from the ground up which secures the existence of legal authority without generating circles or regresses. So Shapiro could say that he uses the instrumental principle only in the metaphysical enterprise of explaining how law comes about, not in the normative project of explaining why we should obey the law. Anticipating this criticism, first, I find it hard to believe that if the instrumental principle underlies the legal system as part of the metaphysical theory, it would not play any role in justifying this system's normativity. I find it even harder to believe that the prospect of an explanation of legal normativity did not also play a role in Shapiro's development of the planning theory. It is revealing that Shapiro does not write about how to explain *the origins* of law, but about how to explain *the foundation* of law, which has a normative dimension. Shapiro is not interested in describing the historical causes of any particular legal system, rather he wants to give a theory that gives authority to legal systems in general. This aspiration comes close to answering the normative question as I defined it at the beginning of this chapter.

But secondly, even if this first point is due to my limited understanding of Shapiro's project, and Shapiro really does not count on the instrumental principle to play any role in the explanation of law's *normativity* – as opposed to the explanation of law's *existence* – then the upshot of this chapter still points towards a problem for the planning theory of law understood as a metaphysical quest. Arguably, the metaphysical question – how law comes about – precedes the normative question – why we should obey the law. This means that the planning theory of law runs into trouble even at an earlier stage of theory formation. If the instrumental principle lacks normative force, it cannot be 'the normative bedrock of the legal system' that Shapiro takes it to be. Though the normativity of the law might fall outside the ambit of the planning theory of law, Shapiro cannot leave it an open question whether the instrumental principle is normative. So before Shapiro helps himself to the instrumental principle in his metaphysical theory of law, he should have a story about the normativity of this principle. After all, if one wants to build a legal system upon an external, independent requirement, one better make sure it is a sound and firm basis.

II

Law, Normativity and Conventions

5

The Conventional Foundations of Law

ANDREI MARMOR

ONE OF HLA Hart's most lasting and influential contributions to legal philosophy consists in the thesis that in every developed legal system there are certain *rules of recognition* that determine what counts as law in that society. Such rules determine (to use a more recent term) the *sources of law*; they determine how law is created, modified or abolished in the relevant legal order. In the existence of these rules of recognition Hart saw (as he put it) 'the germ of the idea of legal validity'.[1] The idea that there must be some norms that determine what counts as law in any given legal system did not originate with Hart. Hans Kelsen, one of the most influential legal positivists of the twentieth century, had argued that a legal order can only make sense if one presupposes its *basic norm*, the norm that grants validity to the entire system.[2] Hart's rules of recognition, however, are not presuppositions. They are social rules, and it is this social reality of the rules of recognition that is supposed to ground the idea, central to the legal positivist tradition in jurisprudence, that law has social foundations. As Leslie Green noted, however, a satisfactory account of these rules of recognition has proved surprisingly difficult.[3]

Why is that? To fully account for all the difficulties, one would need to tell a rather long story about the history of this idea, an account that I will not try to provide here. Suffice it to say that Hart's original formulation of the nature of the rules of recognition, as customary social rules that are 'accepted' by the relevant population, rested on some general observations he had offered about the nature of social rules. These observations, which have been labelled 'the practice theory of rules', turned out to be unsatisfactory, for various reasons that need not detain us here.[4]

[1] HLA Hart, *The Concept of Law*, 1st edn (Oxford, Oxford University Press, 1961) 93.

[2] See eg H Kelsen, *Pure Theory of Law*, 2nd edn (M Knight (trans), Berkeley, CA, University of California Press, 1967) and his *General Theory of Law and State*, (A Wedberg (trans), New York, Russell & Russell, 1961). For a more detailed account of Kelsen's views, see my *Philosophy of, Law*, Princeton Foundations of Contemporary Philosophy Series (S Soames (ed), Princeton, NJ, Princeton University Press, 2011) ch 1.

[3] See L Green, 'Positivism and Conventionalism' (1999) 12 *Canadian Journal of Law and Jurisprudence* 35.

[4] I have elaborated on this theory and its difficulties in my *Positive Law and Objective Values* (Oxford, Oxford University Press, 2001) 2–7. See also my *Philosophy of Law*, n 2 above, ch 2.

When David Lewis' theory of conventions came to be known, however, some legal philosophers realised that in this highly sophisticated theory they could anchor Hart's insights about the rules of recognition.[5] Thus, a conventionalist account of the rules of recognition has emerged, and one that Hart himself, years later, seems to have endorsed in his postscript to *The Concept of Law*.[6]

Many contemporary philosophers of law, however, think that this conventionalist turn was a turn for the worse. Ronald Dworkin, for one, argues that there are no rules of recognition at all. Others, more sympathetic to Hart's legal positivist conception of law, argue that a conventionalist understanding of the rules of recognition is fraught with difficulties, and that such a view generates more problems than it solves.

Thus, the question I would like to address here is whether the conventional account of the rules of recognition is sound or not. I will argue that it is, with two important modifications. First, I will try to show that the rules of recognition are constitutive conventions, and not, as commentators generally assumed, coordination conventions. Second, I will try to show that the distinction between deep and surface conventions can be employed to solve some of the puzzles about the nature of the rules of recognition. With these two important modifications in mind, I believe that we will have the tools to respond to the objections that have been raised against the conventionalist account of the foundations of law.

The first step in the argument is to explain why we need a normative foundation to account for the idea of legal validity. The second step is to examine the nature of those norms, and see whether it makes sense to assume that they are social conventions. I will try to show that most of the difficulties with the conventionalist construal of the rules of recognition stem from the mistaken assumption that those rules are coordination conventions. Finally, I will present the idea that between the general reasons for having law in our societies, and the surface conventions of recognition that constitute what counts as law in a given legal system, there are some deep conventions of law.[7]

[5] See eg G Postema, 'Coordination and Convention at the Foundations of Law' (1982) 11 *Journal of Legal Studies* 165; C Gans, 'The Normativity of Law and its Co-ordinative Function' (1981) 16 *Israel Law Review* 333; J Finnis, *Natural Law and Natural Rights* (Oxford, Oxford University Press, 1980); and E Lagerspetz, *The Opposite Mirrors: An Essay on the Conventionalist Theory of Institutions* (Boston, MA, Kluwer Academic Publishers, 1995). J Coleman has also espoused this view, though he no longer does; see his *The Practice of Principle* (Oxford, Oxford University Press, 2001) 93–94.

[6] See the 2nd edition of *The Concept of Law* (J Raz and P Bulloch (eds), Oxford, Oxford University Press, 1994) 256. Whether Hart's remarks in the postscript really amount to an endorsement of conventionalism is somewhat controversial; see eg J Dickson, 'Is the Rule of Recognition Really a Conventional Rule?' (2007) 27 *Oxford Journal of Legal Studies* 373.

[7] I suggested the idea that there are some deep conventions of law in my 'How Law is Like Chess?' (2006) 12 *Legal Theory* 347. I now realise that there were some errors in that article that I hope to have corrected here.

I THE NORMATIVE FOUNDATION OF LEGAL VALIDITY

Consider the following sequence of propositions:

(1) According to the law in a legal system S (at time t), it is the law that N.[8]
(2) (1) is true because N had been enacted (prior to t) by P.[9]

Now (2) clearly presupposes something like (3):

(3) If P enacts a norm of type N in S, N is legally valid in S.
(4) (3) is true in S because it is generally the case that X.

There is a logical sequence here: if there is a doubt about the truth of a statement of type (1), we would normally expect it to be resolved by an account of type (2).[10] And if there is a doubt about (2), we would expect it to be resolved by an account of type (3). And then we need an explanation of what generally makes (3) true, and so we get to (4). This much, I take it, is common ground. But now a question that needs to be answered is this: why is it the case that (4) has to be grounded in pointing to *norms*. Why could it not be something else? Kelsen had a detailed answer to this question.[11] The law, Kelsen rightly observed, is first and foremost a system of norms. Norms are 'ought' statements, prescribing certain modes of conduct. Unlike moral norms, however, Kelsen maintained that legal norms are created by acts of will. They are products of deliberate human action. For instance, some people gather in a hall, speak, raise their hands, count them and promulgate a string of words. These are actions and events taking place at a specific time and space. To say that what we have described here is the *enactment of a law* is to *interpret* these actions and events by ascribing a normative significance to them. Kelsen, however, firmly believed in Hume's distinction between 'is' and 'ought', and in the impossibility of deriving 'ought' conclusions from factual premises alone. Thus, Kelsen believed that the law, which is comprised of norms or 'ought' statements, cannot be reduced to those natural actions and events that give rise to it. The gathering, the speaking and the raising of hands, in itself, is not the law; legal norms are essentially 'ought' statements and, as such, they cannot be deduced from factual premises alone.

How is it possible, then, to ascribe an 'ought' to those actions and events that purport to create legal norms? Kelsen's reply is enchantingly simple: we ascribe a legal ought to such norm-creating acts by, ultimately, *presupposing* it. Because

[8] N stands here for a particular legal norm, of any kind.

[9] Assume that P stands here for any institution that is legally authorised to enact laws or legal regulations.

[10] Dworkin famously denies that this is the only type of answer to the question of what makes statements of type (1) true (see R Dworkin, 'The Model of Rules I' in his *Taking Rights Seriously* (London, Duckworth, 1977) 14–45. But even Dworkin does not deny that a statement of type (2) can be, and often is, a perfectly adequate answer to the question of what makes (1) true.

[11] See n 2 above.

'ought' cannot be derived from 'is', and legal norms are essentially 'ought' statements, there must be some kind of an 'ought' presupposition at the background, rendering the normativity of law intelligible.

Thus, an act can create law (Kelsen argues) if it is in accord with another, 'higher' legal norm that authorises its creation in that way. And the 'higher' legal norm, in turn, is legally valid only if it has been created in accordance with yet another, even 'higher' legal norm that authorises its enactment. Ultimately (Kelsen argues) one must reach a point where the authorising norm is no longer the product of an act of will, but is simply presupposed, and this is what Kelsen called the basic norm.[12]

According to Kelsen, then, it is necessarily the case that an explanation of type (4) must point to a *master norm* that makes it the case that certain acts of will create law and others don't. Without presupposing such a norm, the normativity of the entire legal order remains unexplained. But of course, the problem is that not much is explained by Kelsen's idea of a presupposition, either. Instead of telling us something about the foundations of the basic norm, Kelsen simply invites us to stop asking. In fact, the problem is even worse. As I have explained in more detail elsewhere, Kelsen's idea of the basic norm fails on its own terms. The idea that the basic norm is a kind of conceptual presupposition was meant to block a reduction of legal normativity to social facts. But in order to know *what* the basic norm in any particular legal system is, as Kelsen explicitly admits, one must look at the practice of various agents in that system, mostly judges and other officials, and observe what is the basic norm that they follow. The basic norms of, say, the US legal system, and that of the United Kingdom, differ precisely because judges and other officials actually apply different criteria in determining what the laws in their respective legal systems are. The *content* of the basic norm is entirely practice-dependent.[13]

This leads us to Hart's solution: Hart seems to have concurred with Kelsen that the idea of legal validity must reside in some normative framework, one that rests on some norms determining what counts as a valid source of law in a given society. The relevant norm, however, is not a presupposition, as Kelsen would have it, but a social norm, a social rule that people – mostly judges and other officials – actually follow. This is what the rule of recognition is: the social rule that a community follows, the rule that grounds the answer to the question of what makes statements of type (3) true or false in that particular society.[14]

But now, if you take Kelsen's question seriously, you should be puzzled by this. How can a social fact – that people actually follow a certain rule and regard it as binding – be a relevant answer to Kelsen's question of what makes it the case that certain acts of will create the law and others don't? Crudely put, if you start with

[12] More concretely, Kelsen maintained that in tracing back such a chain of validity, one would reach a point where a first historical constitution is the basic authorising norm of the rest of the legal system, and the basic norm is the presupposition of the validity of that first constitution.

[13] I explain this in greater detail in my *Philosophy of Law*, n 2 above, ch 1.

[14] Hart, *The Concept of Law*, n 1 above, ch 5.

the question of how a set of 'is' statements can generate an 'ought' conclusion, you cannot expect an answer to it by pointing to another 'is'. Has Hart failed to see this? Not quite. Consider the game of chess. The rules of the game prescribe, for instance, that the bishop can only be moved diagonally. Thus, when players move the bishop, they follow a rule. The rule, undoubtedly, prescribes an 'ought'; it prescribes permissible and impermissible moves in the game. What is it, then, that determines this 'ought' about rules of chess? Is it not simply the fact that this is how the game is played? The game is constituted by rules or conventions. Those rules are, in a clear sense, social rules that people follow in playing this particular game. The rules of chess have a dual function: they constitute what the game is, and they prescribe norms that players ought to follow. Similarly, Hart has claimed, the rules of recognition define or constitute what law in a certain society is, and they prescribe – that is, authorise – modes of creating/modifying law in that society. Social rules can determine their ought, as it were, by being followed, ie regarded as binding, by a certain community, just as the rules of chess determine their 'ought' within the game that is actually followed by the relevant community.[15]

This cannot be so simple, however. The obvious difficulty with the chess analogy is that the rules of the game are 'ought' statements, in the sense of giving reasons for action, only for those who actually decide to play this particular game. As I noted elsewhere,[16] the normative aspect to the rules of chess is a *conditional* one: *if* you want to play *chess*, these are the rules that you ought to follow. But of course, you don't have to play at all, nor do you have to play this particular game. So it seems that by modifying Kelsen's account and replacing the presupposition of the basic norm with the idea of social rules, we have not made sufficient progress. The normativity of these social rules still remains unexplained.

Hart was very much aware of this difficulty. He first tried to solve it by offering a general account of social rules, one that purported to explain the normativity of such rules by the idea of 'acceptance'; acceptance is a complex attitude shared by the relevant participants that is manifest in their reliance on the rules as guiding their activities, as a basis for criticising those who deviate from them, and as grounds for exerting social pressure on others to comply. As I mentioned earlier, however, the main aspects of this 'practice theory of rules' turned out to be very unsatisfactory. Hart himself seems to have conceded the difficulties, and years later, when he wrote the postscript to *The Concept of Law*, he seems to have endorsed the conventionalist account of the rules of recognition. As he put it, the rule of recognition 'is in effect a form of judicial customary rule existing only if it is accepted and practised in the law-identifying and law-applying operations of the courts'.[17] And at the following page he says: 'certainly the rule of recognition is

[15] ibid 98–99.

[16] A Marmor, *Social Conventions: From Language to Law* (Princeton, NJ, Princeton University Press, 2009), especially ch 6.

[17] Hart, *The Concept of Law*, 2nd edn, n 6 above, postscript, 256.

treated in my book as resting on a conventional form of judicial consensus'.[18] Whether this conventional understanding of the rule of recognition is an improvement or not, we need to examine carefully.

II ARE THE RULES OF RECOGNITION CONVENTIONS?

Before we try to answer the question of this section, let me say a few words in response to a more fundamental objection to Hart's account, raised by Ronald Dworkin. He denies that the criteria employed by judges and other officials in determining what counts as law are rule governed, and thus he denies that there are any rules of recognition at all. But as far as I can see, Dworkin's argument is based on a single point, which is rather implausible. He argues that it cannot be the case that in identifying the law judges follow rules, because judges often disagree about the criteria of legality in their legal systems, so much so, that it makes no sense to suggest that there are any rules of recognition at all; or else, the rules become so abstract that it becomes pointless to insist that they are rules.[19]

The problem is this: to show that there are no rules of recognition, Dworkin would have had to show that the disagreements judges have about the criteria of legality in their jurisdiction are not just at the margins; that they go all the way down to the core. But this is just not plausible. Is there any judge in the United States who seriously doubts that Acts of Congress make law? Or that the US Constitution prevails over federal and state legislation? More importantly (as Hart himself mentioned in a slightly different context),[20] there is an inherent limit to how much disagreement about criteria of legality it makes sense to attribute to judges, because the judges' own role as institutional players is constituted by those same rules that they allegedly disagree about. The role and authority of certain persons qua judges is determined by the rules of recognition. Before judges can come to disagree about any legal issue, they must first be able to see themselves as *institutional* players, playing, as it were, a fairly structured role in an elaborate practice. Judges can only see themselves as such on the basis of the rules and conventions that establish their role and authority as judges, namely, the rules of recognition. In short, pointing to the fact that judges often have certain disagreements about the content of the rules of recognition simply cannot prove that there are no such rules. On the contrary, we can only make sense of such disagreements on the basis of the assumption that there are rules of recognition that constitute, inter alia, the court system and the legal authority of judges.

[18] ibid 266.

[19] See especially R Dworkin *Law's Empire* (London, Fontana, 1986) ch 1. The same idea is basically reiterated in his recent book, *Justice in Robes* (Cambridge, MA, Harvard University Press, 2006) 164, 190–96. This should not be confused with a different, and much more interesting, claim that Dworkin also makes, namely, that even if there are rules of recognition, they do not settle the question of legal validity. Norms can be legally valid, Dworkin argues, even if they do not derive their validity from the rules of recognition; see Dworkin, 'The Model of Rules I', n 10 above. This is a large topic that I will not address here.

[20] Hart, *The Concept of Law*, n 1 above, 133.

So let us make the plausible assumption that there are some rules, mostly followed by judges and other legal officials, determining what counts as law in the relevant legal system. Are these rules conventions? Let us go through the motions here; in order to show that the rules of recognition of a given legal system, say RR, are conventions, we would have to show that the following conditions obtain:

(1) There is a group of people, a population P, that normally follow RR in circumstances C.
(2) There is a set of reasons, call it A, for members of P to follow RR in circumstances C.
(3) There is at least one other potential set of rules, SR, that if members of P had actually followed in circumstances C, then A would have been a sufficient reason for members of P to follow SR instead of RR in circumstances C, and at least partly because SR is the set of rules generally followed instead of RR. The rules RR and SR are such that it is impossible, or pointless, to comply with both of them concomitantly in circumstances C.[21]

As we just saw, Dworkin's objection to the rules of recognition basically denies the truth of premise (1). But we also saw that this objections fails, so let us assume that (1) is true. Given the truth of (1), it would be extremely unlikely that (2) is false. If judges and other officials follow certain rules that determine what law is, surely they follow them for reasons. What those reasons, generally speaking are, however, turns out to be somewhat difficult to answer. In his original account of the rules of recognition, Hart suggested that the rationale of these rules consists in the need for certainty: In a developed legal system (Hart argued) people would need to be able *to identify* what types or norms are legally valid. In fact, he presented this advantage of the rules of recognition in providing certainty about the valid sources of law as the main distinguishing factor between 'primitive', pre-legal normative systems, and a developed legal order.[22] Later, in his postscript to *The Concept of Law*, Hart seems to have added another kind of reason for having rules of recognition, basically of a coordinative nature:

> Certainly the rule of recognition is treated in my book as resting on a conventional form of judicial custom. That it does so rest seems quite clear at least in English and American law for surely an English judge's reason for treating Parliament's legislation (or an American judge's reason for treating the Constitution) as a source of law having supremacy over other sources includes the fact that his judicial colleagues concur in this as their predecessors have done.[23]

I have some doubts about both of these explanations. That the rules of recognition contribute to our certainty about what counts as law in our society is surely true. But is it the main reason for having such rules? This I doubt. It is like suggesting that there are some rules or conventions about what constitutes opera so

[21] The details of this definition are defended in chapter 1 of my *Social Conventions*, n 16 above.
[22] Ibid ch 5.
[23] Hart, The Concept of Law, 2nd edn, n 6 above, postscript, 267.

as to enable us to identify the operatic genre as distinguished from other, similar artistic performances. Surely, if there are some rules or conventions that constitute an operatic genre, it is because there are some artistic reasons for having this kind of genre in the first place. Similarly, I would suggest, if there are reasons to have rules of recognition, those reasons must be very intimately linked to the reasons for having law in the first place. Certainty about what the law is cannot be the main reason for having law. There must be some reasons for having law first, and then it might also be important to have a certain level of certainty about it. It cannot be the other way around. To be sure, I am not suggesting that the reasons for having rules of recognition are the same as the reasons for having law in a society. My claim is that the reasons for having rules of recognition are closely tied to the reasons for having law, and in some ways (yet to be specified) they instantiate those reasons.

The coordinative rationale of the rules of recognition is even more suspect, and for reasons that are quite explicit in Hart's own writings. It is true, of course, that judges and other legal agents, acting in their official capacities, need a great deal of coordination in various respects. In particular, they would need to follow basically those same rules that other officials in their legal system follow in identifying the relevant sources of law in their legal system. That the rules of recognition enable this basic kind of coordination in the various actions of legal officials is not disputable. But again, it makes little sense to suggest that this is the main rationale of the rules of recognition. As we mentioned above, for judges to have any coordination problem that might need a solution, first we must be able to identify them *as judges*; we first need a set of rules that constitute their specific institutional roles. In short, and more generally, first we need the institutions of law, then we may also have some coordination problems that may require a normative solution. The basic role of the rules of recognition is to constitute the relevant institutions. The fundamental rules of recognition of a legal system are constitutive rules (or conventions, as we shall see) and their coordination functions are secondary, at best.

I have to say that there is a rather striking confusion in some of the literature on the conventionality of the rules of recognition that connects these two points. Because the standard understanding of conventions has been the one offered by Lewis, which consists of the idea that conventions are normative solutions to coordination problems, commentators have been drawn to the idea that if the rules of recognition are conventions, their basic rationale must be a coordinative one. But commentators have also realised that the rationale of the rules of recognition must be closely tied to the reasons for having law in the first place. And the combination of these two points has led many to assume that the main rationale *of law itself* – the main reasons for having law in society – are also coordinative in nature.[24]

[24] See eg Lagerspetz, n 5 above, and G den Hartogh, *Mutual Expectations: A Conventionalist Theory of Law* (New York, Kluwer Academic Publishers, 2002). Dworkin's interpretation of what he calls legal conventionalism relies on a very similar idea. See his *Law's Empire*, n 19 above, ch 7.

This has rendered legal conventionalism, as this view came to be called, rather implausible. The idea that law's main functions in society can be reduced to solution of coordination problems is all too easy to refute. Solving coordination problems, as complex and intricate as they may be, is only one of the main functions of law in society, and probably not the most important one.

I mention this confusion here because Leslie Green's critique of legal conventionalism, often cited as a main argument against a conventionalist construal of the rules of recognition, is based on it. Green is absolutely right to claim that the authority of law, and its main moral-political rationale, cannot be explained in terms of law's function in solving coordination problems.[25] But he is wrong to conclude that this undermines a conventionalist account of the rules of recognition. Neither the main functions of law in society, nor the main rationale of the rules of recognition, has much to do with solving coordination problems.

We have yet to show, of course, that the rules of recognition are conventions. The conventionality of the rules of recognition crucially depends on the third condition, namely, on the question of whether the rules are arbitrary (and compliance dependent) in the requisite sense. So let us turn to examine this aspect of the rules of recognition. On the face of it, the arbitrariness of the rules of recognition is strongly supported by the following two observations: First, we know that different legal systems, even ones that are very similar in all other respects, have different rules or recognition. Second, there is very clear sense in which the reasons for following the rules of recognition are compliance-dependent in the relevant sense. This is one of the points that Hart has rightly emphasised in the postscript, namely, that the reasons judges and other officials have for following certain norms about the identification of the sources of law in their legal systems are closely tied to the fact that other officials follow those same norms.

Now, I don't think that either one of these observations that supports the conventionality of the rules of recognition is really controversial. The reasons critics have for doubting the conventionality of the rules of recognition pertain to the normative aspect of the rules. Again, Green was one of those who observed this difficulty in the conventional account of the rule of recognition. As he put it, '[Hart's] view that the fundamental rules [of recognition] are "mere conventions" continues to sit uneasily with any notion of obligation',[26] and thus with the intuition that the rules of recognition point to the sources of law that 'judges are legally bound to apply'.[27] So the problem seems to be this: if the rules of recognition are *arbitrary* in the requisite sense, how can we explain the fact that they are supposed to obligate judges and other legal officials to follow them?

I think that by now we have all the tools we need to answer this question. First, even if Green had been right to assume that the main conventionalist rationale of the rules of recognition is basically a coordinative one, the puzzle he raises about

[25] See his 'Positivism and Conventionalism', n 3 above, 43–49.
[26] L Green, 'The Concept of Law Revisited' (1996) 94 *Michigan Law Review* 1687, 1697.
[27] ibid 1679.

their potential normativity is easily answered. As I argued elsewhere,[28] some coordination problems are such that there is an obligation to solve them. If a conventional solution has emerged, the relevant agents may well have an obligation to follow the conventional solution. However, since I do not think that the rules of recognition are coordination conventions, I will not avail myself of this simple answer. The main answer to Green's puzzle resides in the distinction between the legal obligation to follow the rules of recognition, and the separate question about a moral obligation, if there is one, to follow those rules.

The rules of recognition, like the rules of chess, determine what the practice is. They constitute the rules of the game, so to speak. Like other constitutive rules, they have a dual function: they both determine what constitutes the practice, and prescribe modes of conduct within it. The *legal* obligation to follow the rules of recognition is just like the chess players' obligation to, say, move the bishop diagonally. Both are prescribed by the rules of the game. What such rules cannot prescribe, however, is an 'ought' about playing the game to begin with. As I noted elsewhere,[29] the normativity of constitutive conventions is always conditional. Conventional practices create reasons for action only if the relevant agent has a reason to participate in the practice to begin with. And that is true of the law as well. If there is an 'ought to play the game', so to speak, then this ought cannot be expected to come from the rules of recognition. The obligation to play by the rules, that is, to follow the law, if there is one, must come from moral and political considerations. The reasons for obeying the law cannot be derived from the norms that determine what the law is.

Let me summarise and add a few observations. My main response to Green's worries about the normativity of the rules of recognition is this: once we realise that the rules of recognition are constitutive and not coordinative conventions, we can see that there is really nothing unique or particularly puzzling about the concept of legal normativity, or legal obligation. The sense in which a judge is obliged to follow the rules of recognition is exactly like the obligation of an umpire in a cricket game to follow the rules of cricket. Both obligations are basically conditional. If, and to the extent that, the judge, or the umpire, has reasons to play the game, they have reasons to play it by the rules, and the rules determine what their obligations in the game are. In both cases, however, we cannot expect the rules of the game to constitute the reason to play it. In other words, the internal, legal, obligation is determined by the rules themselves; the rules that constitute the game also prescribe modes of conduct within it. The external obligation to play the game (if there is one) is a different matter, one that cannot be expected to be determined on the basis of the normativity of the rules of the game. Whether judges, or anybody else, would have an obligation to play the game, as it were, is always a separate question, one that needs to be determined on moral- political grounds.

[28] Marmor, *Social Conventions*, n 16 above, especially ch 6.
[29] ibid.

Now of course, all this assumes that the rules of recognition are indeed constitutive conventions, and not coordination conventions, as has been generally assumed. Therefore, let me complete the argument by noting some further, important difficulties with the idea that the rules of recognition are coordination conventions. Since old habits die hard, it may be worth adding a few nails to the coffin.

There are three main problems with the view that the rules of recognition are coordination conventions. First, this view misses the constitutive function of the rules of recognition; it misses the point that these conventions constitute, to a considerable extent, what law is. Second, the idea that the rules of recognition are coordination conventions is not easy to reconcile with the apparent political importance of these rules. Finally, the coordination conventions account blurs the distinction between the question of what law is, and what counts as law in a particular legal order. Let me explain these problems.

The rules of recognition determine how law in a particular legal system is created, modified and abolished, thus also making it possible to identify what the law in the relevant community is. Notice that it is a rather complex function that the rules of recognition have; in determining the criteria of legality in a particular system, the rules basically constitute what counts as law in that system, and in this they also enable us to identify the legal domain as such. Very much like the constitutive rules of games, such rules determine what counts as the relevant type of activity. Hart's repeated reference to examples of games would clearly suggest that he himself was very much aware of this constitutive function of the rules of recognition. What critics seem to have missed is the fact that coordination conventions do not tend to have such a constitutive function. If there is a recurrent coordination problem and a social norm evolves to solve it, in this the rule has basically exhausted its function. Constitutive conventions, as I claimed elsewhere,[30] are much more complex. Conventions constitute a type of activity when they form a whole system of interlocking norms, both constituting a social practice and regulating certain activities within it. To be sure, I do not want to deny that some of the functions served by the rules of recognition are coordinative in nature. But the need to coordinate the actions of various officials is only one aspect of the rules of recognition. First, we must recognise them *as legal officials*, and this is only made possible by the constitutive function of the rules of recognition. Before any coordination problem between officials arises, we must know who counts as an official, or a player in this game if you like, and this is precisely what the rules of recognition do – they constitute the rules of the game and the various roles played in it.

And this brings me to the second point. Realising that constitutive conventions tend to emerge as responses to complex social and human needs, and not just coordination problems, should make it much easier to understand why the specific conventions we happen to have may matter to us, sometimes a great deal. And the rules of recognition do matter, morally, politically, and otherwise. After all, it does matter to us who makes the law in our society, and how it is done. The

[30] ibid, especially ch 2.

rules of recognition of legal systems are often politically important. Consider, for example, one of the most fundamental rules of recognition in the United States, namely, the rule that determines the supremacy of the US Constitution. It should be easy to recognise that this is no trivial matter; it is something that most Americans feel strongly about, to say the least.[31] There are political and moral values associated with rules of recognition, values that it would be much less rational to attribute to rules that are there to solve a coordination problem. There are, of course, many coordination problems that it is very important to solve; but it is usually not very important how exactly we solve them, as long as the solution is reasonably efficient.

Finally, the coordination account of the rules of recognition makes it very unclear how these conventions of recognition relate to the concept of law. Consider chess, again: without the conventions that constitute this game, there is no game of chess nor, consequently, a concept of chess. The rules of chess have a crucial constitutive role to play in constituting our concept of chess. On the other hand, if we think about a standard coordination convention, the picture is quite different: consider, for example, a convention that determines on which side of the road to drive, or how to spell a word correctly in English. In these cases we normally have the concept of the relevant activity irrespective of the conventions. In fact, this is typically so, since the whole point of coordination conventions is to solve a problem that had been there before the convention emerged, so it must be the case that we have a concept of the relevant activity irrespective of the conventions that have evolved to regulate it. Once again, it seems that law is more like chess than the coordination cases; without the social conventions that constitute ways of making law and recognising it as such, it is difficult to imagine what kind of concept of law we could possibly have.

III THE DEEP CONVENTIONS OF LAW

There are some reasons for having law, reasons that reflect the main functions of law in our society. For example, the reasons to have some authoritative rules of conduct, the need to resolve conflicts in society, to create public goods, to solve collective action problems, and so forth. And then there are, as we have seen, social conventions that determine what counts as law in a given community, namely, the rules of recognition. I want to argue that between the general reasons for having law, and the local conventions that determine what counts as law in particular legal system, there is an intermediary layer of *deep conventions*, conventions that constitute the main building blocks of the relevant legal system. The deep conventions of law are typically manifest in the surface conventions of recognition that are specific to any given society, or legal system.

[31] It is possible, of course, that people tend to project greater importance onto the rules of recognition than is morally or politically warranted. However, even if the precise content of these rules is less important than people tend to presume, I think it is safe to maintain that they are not entirely mistaken.

A quick reminder of how deep conventions differ from surface conventions might be in place. As I argued elsewhere:[32]

(1) Deep conventions emerge as normative responses to basic social and psychological needs. They serve relatively basic functions in our social world.
(2) Deep conventions typically enable a set of surface conventions to emerge, and many types of surface conventions are only made possible as instantiations of deep conventions.
(3) Under normal circumstances, deep conventions are actually practised by following their corresponding surface conventions.
(4) Compared with surface conventions, deep conventions are typically much more durable and less amenable to change.
(5) Surface conventions often get to be codified and thus replaced by institutional rules. Deep conventions typically resist codification of this kind.

Let us now return to law. The thesis I want to suggest here is this: the rules of recognition, of the kind Hart had in mind, are surface conventions. They determine what counts as law in a particular legal system, in a particular community. These surface conventions of recognition are instantiations of deep conventions about what kind of legal system the relevant community has. There is a wide range of reasons for having law and legal institutions in our society. Law serves an array of functions in every society in which it exists. These functions constitute the basic reasons for having law in our societies. But these reasons, universal as they may be, can be instantiated by different sets of deep conventions.

What would be the deep conventions of law? For lawyers who are familiar with different types of legal systems, the answer would be very clear: over the centuries different types of legal systems have evolved in different parts of the world. Some of these types of legal system, like the common law and the continental law traditions, are still with us, and in many respects, strikingly different from each other. Other, older traditions, like the feudal system, or the Roman law tradition, have ceased to exist. Now, what we call traditions, or sometimes families of legal systems, basically instantiate deep conventions of law. Let's take the paradigms of common law and continental law as our main example.[33] First, notice that the conventions that constitute each one of these traditions are not practised by following the conventions constituting the tradition; deep conventions are practised by following the surface conventions that instantiate them, namely, in this case, the rules of recognition of each particular legal system. In other words, American judges follow the rules of recognition of the US legal system, English judges follow the rules of recognition of the UK system, and so forth, and not directly (as it were) the deep conventions of common law. Similarly, German and French judges follow the rules of recognition of their respective legal systems, not the general, deep conventions of the continental system.

[32] Marmor, *Social Conventions*, n 16 above, especially ch 3.

[33] Other examples would be religious legal systems, like Jewish law or Islamic Shari'a, and presumably (though I know very little about it) legal systems in Southeast Asia, etc.

Now, if you think about the differences between common law and continental law, reflecting, as they do, very different conceptions of organising a legal order, you will immediately notice that though these two traditions are very different, they definitely respond to the same basic needs and functions that prevail in all the societies that have them. The basic needs to have law and a legal system, and the particular functions law has in these societies, are fundamentally the same. In other words, in spite of the considerable differences between the common law and continental law traditions, the societies in which these systems exist are very similar. Law serves in common law systems, like the United States, England and Canada, basically the same functions that it serves in the continental systems like the ones in Germany, France and Belgium. Nevertheless, the conventional solutions to the problems law is there to solve that have evolved in these two legal cultures are rather different. I am not an expert in comparative law, and therefore I will not attempt to give an accurate summary of these differences, just note some of them. Common law, for example, assigns a much greater role to judges in developing the law and adapting it to changing circumstances; continental law seeks to restrict the role of judges in this respect, and allows them much less flexibility in changing the law. Legislation in the continental systems is very structured, typically seeking to codify entire areas of law in a very systematic way; common law legislation is much less structured, typically avoiding codification of entire areas of law. In the procedural area, common law is committed to an adversarial system, whereby litigants argue their case in front of an impartial jury or judge; continental law is 'inquisitorial', not adversarial, allowing judges an investigatory role far beyond anything that would be acceptable in common law. And so on and so forth.

Let me summarise these points. In comparing the common law and the continental law traditions, we can see the following. First, they manifest very different forms of structuring a legal system. Second, in spite of the considerable differences between them, the two traditions basically respond to the same needs and serve the same basic functions in their respective societies. Finally, the conventions that are actually being followed by judges and other legal officials are not the deep conventions of the respective legal traditions, but their manifestation in the surface conventions of recognition that are unique to the particular legal systems in play.

Admittedly, I have not yet shown that the underlying differences between these two legal traditions, the common law and continental law, are really differences in deep conventions. But what else could they be? The fact, well known and undeniable, that these two legal traditions have evolved as a result of various political events, and to a large extent still reflect different political conceptions of law, does not necessarily undermine their conventionality. As we noted earlier, the conventionality of the rules of recognition is easily reconcilable with their moral-political importance. Conventional practices of various kinds often evolve in response to historical contingencies, and their constitutive norms tend to reflect the normative convictions that were involved in the historical events that have brought about their existence. Conventions, as we have seen all along, are always supported by reasons. What makes norms conventional consists in the fact that those reasons underdetermine the content of the norms. But the reasons are still there, and there is nothing in the nature of those reasons that precludes the possibility that they reflect moral-political convictions.[34]

Let me sum up: the conventional foundation of law consists of two layers. There are deep conventions that determine ways of organising a legal order, its main building blocks, as it were, and those deep conventions are instantiated by the surface conventions of recognition that are specific to particular legal systems. The concept of law is constituted by both layers of conventions. Our concept of law partly depends on the deep conventions that determine the basic organisation of a legal order, and partly on the specific institutions we have in our community – those that are determined by the rules of recognition. Both are conventional – and in this general insight, I think that Hart was quite right.

[34] Remember that even conventions of fashion reflect some aesthetic reasons or preferences, but that does not undermine their conventionality; and conventions of artistic genres reflect artistic reasons, conventions of games reflect reasons that we have for playing games, etc.

6

Multilayered Legal Conventionalism and the Normativity of Law

MARCO GOLDONI*

I INTRODUCTION

EVERY STREAM OF thought has its own fundamental concepts. In the last decades, the word 'convention' has become certainly one of the most evocative for those engaged in the field of legal positivism. Conventionalist approaches are now so widespread in the relevant literature that they are almost indicative of what has been defined, in recent years, as a 'conventionalist turn'.[1] The work of Andrei Marmor belongs certainly to this tradition and his contribution, one of the most elaborated and challenging in the conventionalist realm, represents a complete accomplishment in this stream of thought. Indeed, Marmor's conventionalist world is a much more accurate and nuanced representation of the legal and social realm than any of the conventionalist accounts currently on offer. By introducing a distinction between three different levels of conventions,[2] Marmor's theory aims at rescuing a conventionalist interpretation of legal positivism from two familiar objections. On the one hand, he intends to avoid the failures of a specific conventionalist position (based, as we shall see below, on coordinative conventions);[3] on the other hand, he intends to refute the project of those who try to provide a natural law theory as a realist account of the meaning of 'law'. Indeed, an analysis of the concept of law should not refer to 'a real or natural kind of entity whose essence and constitution do not consist of social conventions'.[4] Moreover, by putting forward a multilayered conception of conventionalism, Marmor hopes to give a correct interpretation of the Hartian idea of the rule of recognition and, at the same time, to secure the conventional foundations of law.

* I would like to thank George Pavlakos and Stefano Bertea for their helpful comments on an earlier draft of this chapter. This work is part of a five-year research project entitled 'The Constitution of Globalisation' which is generously funded by an Odysseus Research Grant of the Research Foundation Flanders (FWO).

[1] L Green, 'Positivism and Conventionalism' (1999) 12 *Canadian Journal of Law and Jurisprudence* 35.

[2] See, specifically, A Marmor, Chapter 5 of this volume.

[3] D Lewis, *Conventions: A Philosophical Study* (Oxford, Blackwell, 1969).

[4] A Marmor, 'Deep Conventions' (2007) LXXIV *Philosophy and Phenomenological Research* 65.

This chapter proceeds in the following way. In the first section, I will briefly illustrate how and why Marmor, in order to overcome certain theoretical hurdles which affected previous versions of legal conventionalism, has introduced multiple layers of conventionality. It will be noted that this move is not safe from certain criticisms. In the second section, I will focus on the essential elements of the so-called conventionality thesis and its self-avowed limited capacity to account for the normativity of law.[5] The focus will be in particular on the price Marmor has to pay to stick to his 'descriptive legal positivism':[6] His account of involuntary membership, when applied to law, turns out to be substantially reductive. The focus in the third section will be on the link between exclusive legal positivism and legal conventionalism. In particular, it will be remarked how complicated it is to respect fully the sources thesis (endorsed by Marmor) once deep conventions are brought into the picture as the foundational layer of conventionality. The analysis of these arguments will lead to the conclusion that the conventionalist approach, deep as it may be, can explain the social aspect of law, but not its normativity.[7] This is not surprising, to a certain extent, because it is part of the project of legal conventionalism to concentrate mainly on the social aspect of law and to downplay its normative dimension.[8]

II THE EMERGENCE OF CONVENTIONAL LAYERS

The aim of Marmor's ambitious project to ground the foundations of law on a conventionalist philosophy can be understood only when put in the appropriate context. As known, the first wave of legal conventionalist scholarship emerged after the publication of David Lewis' *Conventions*. According to Lewis, conventions are triggered by the need of securing some form of uniformity of action where such uniformity is in the best interest of the parties involved. This is a functionalist understanding of conventions and it is framed in the language of game theory.[9] It has some merits, as we shall see in a moment, but when translated into the legal domain it fails to explain certain basic features of the concept of law.

[5] A Marmor, *Positive Law and Objective Values* (Oxford, Oxford University Press, 2001).

[6] Marmor clarifies his position in the positivist field in 'Legal Positivism: Still Descriptive and Morally Neutral' (2006) 26 *Oxford Journal of Legal Studies* 683. According to him, legal positivism is best understood not as a normative, but as a descriptive and morally neutral theory. Normative (or ethical) positivism argues mainly for a moral or political stance that requires a certain vision of law. In short, 'ethical positivism is a political theory, not a theory about the nature of law', while descriptive positivism is focused on the topic of what counts as law.

[7] S Bertea, 'The Master Rule, Normativity and the Institutional Theory of Law', in E Fossum and A Menéndez (eds), *The Post-Sovereign Constellation: Law and Democracy in Neil McCormick's Legal and Political Theory* (Dordrecht, Springer, 2011) 69.

[8] To be fair, Marmor has also emphasised the limits of conventionalism: 'Conventionalism is a significant doctrine only it if is not maintained across the board. It is significant precisely because not everything is a matter of social conventions': Marmor, *Positive Law and Objective Values*, n 5 above, 23.

[9] See also T Schelling, *The Strategy of Conflict* (New York, Oxford University Press, 1963). In legal philosophy, see the works of K Lagerspetz, *The Opposite Mirrors: An Essay on the Conventionalist Theory of Institutions* (Boston, Kluwer, 1995) and G den Hartogh, *Mutual Expectations: A Conventionalist Theory of Law* (New York, Kluwer, 2002).

A paradigmatic example of a practice which is coordinative in its essence is traffic regulation. The rule that establishes on which side of the road people should drive is clearly a conventional rule. Driving on the right side of the road is just a matter of choosing a solution for coordinating those who are driving. It is, indeed, a functional solution because the chosen side of the street would not be valuable for those affected, save for the existence of the convention. In these cases, it is important to note that 'the reasons for the emergence of the convention and the reasons for complying with the convention in each and every instance, are basically the same: to solve the relevant coordination problem'.[10] Lewis' account carries with it two merits. First, it underlines the arbitrary nature of conventional rules. If a rule is conventional, there might have been, in principle, another alternative rule that the people could have followed to achieve the same purpose. Second, Lewis' conventionalism vindicates the widespread intuition that among the reasons for following a rule must be counted the fact that others follow it too. In this way, by following conventional rules we secure conformity and therefore predictablity of future behaviours. One has one more reason to follow a certain rule when one believes that the others will do the same. From this viewpoint, as believed by some authors, this conventionalist approach would have been adopted by HLA Hart, in the postscript of his *opus magnum*, for explaining the idea of the rule of recognition.[11] Despite the fact that this understanding of conventions provides a good explanation of certain conventional rules, difficulties arise when this paradigm is used to explain other features of legal orders. In particular, Marmor believes that a coordinative approach is helpless when it comes to the idea of the rule of recognition because the latter does not 'seem like a solution to recurrent coordination problems at all'.[12] In fact, if one looks at the rules of recognition of a legal system one will always find that they are valued by the relevant population.

A classic example illustrates perfectly how conventions work outside the framework of coordination. The rules of chess (to stick to Marmor's favourite example) have not been created and then codified because they had to solve already existing coordinative problems. In other words, the point of playing chess is not to solve the coordination problem that may arise during the game. Indeed, it works the other way round: coordination problems arise because we engage in the game. The basic conventions of chess create the game while at the same time providing for some of the basic rules which discipline players' behaviours. In light of these remarks, it is understandable that Marmor proposes to overcome the limits of a coordinative account of conventions by introducing another layer, that of consti-

[10] A Marmor, *Social Conventions: From Language to Law* (Princeton, Princeton University Press, 2009) 24.

[11] HLA Hart, *The Concept of Law* (Oxford, Oxford University Press, 1994) 256: 'certainly the rule of recognition is treated in my book as resting on a conventional form of judicial consensus'. Gerald Postema believes that according to Hart 'the authority of criteria of validity ultimately rests not on the justice, correctness, or truth of the criteria as a matter of critical morality, but rather on convention': G Postema, 'Coordination and Convention at the Foundations of Law' (1982) 11 *Journal of Legal Studies* 171. *cf* J Coleman, *The Practice of Principle* (Oxford, Oxford University Press, 2001) 93–94.

[12] Marmor, *Positive Law and Objective Values*, n 5 above, 9.

tutive conventions. This layer of conventionality is characterised by five features. First of all, constitutive conventions come usually in the form of a cluster of rules and never as a single solution to a specific problem. This is due to the fact that they establish (or partly concur to establish) a social practice. In fact, they have to regulate the basics of the relevant practice. Second, conventions are always related to basic human concerns. This aspect, known as 'radical underdetermination', makes them partially autonomous because there could be several different practices which could instantiate the same human concerns. A convention is something arbitrarily chosen between different but equally valuable options. Therefore, according to Marmor, 'in each social practice constituted by conventions, there is a mixture of general concerns these practices are there to serve or instantiate, and values associated with the practice in ways which are constituted by the conventions constituting the practice itself'.[13]

The third feature of constitutive conventions is that they are prone to change. Since they are less dependent on circumstances than coordinative conventions are, and more on evaluative concerns, they may change once the point of a practice is affected by a shift in the evaluative perspective. The fourth feature of constitutive conventions is the rather partial knowledge people have of them. Coordinative conventions are there to fix recurrent problems. If those interested do not know the relevant convention, then this convention cannot be expected to solve the coordination problem. Constitutive conventions work in a completely different fashion. Those who are inside the practice created by these conventions are not required to know them properly. In the legal realm, this difference is at its most visible. Most of the time, participants in a legal system rely on the knowledge of legal practitioners. This is true even among lawyers. Some know better than others what the law is. The rules of recognition are the conventions of judges and of other legal officials that can have an impact on the content of the rules of recognition.[14] Finally, constitutive conventions need to be followed, otherwise they lose their point. Marmor calls this 'the condition of efficacy'.[15] Only when a convention is practised can we seriously talk of conventionality.

Nonetheless, the condition of efficacy or the need for uniformity does not explain why people engage in conventional practices. Participation in a conventional practice is usually triggered by primary reasons strictly related to the values inherent in the same practice. However, the existence of values, as we are reminded by Raz, is rarely purely conventional in the sense that nothing but the fact that people follow a certain practice makes it good. The existence of a value depends only in part on a sustaining practice. This means that in every

[13] ibid 15.

[14] One may ask whether following the expertise of judges and officials is a conventional practice. In this case, it could have been possible to think of another set of people (religious people, for example) whose knowledge of the law could have been considered as authoritative. But then the point of the practice of following those who have better knowledge of the law would have changed radically. At this stage, the question is: How conventional is the law? Is it possible to think of a rule of recognition which ignores completely the work of judges? Or is the latter an essential component of the law?

[15] Marmor, *Positive Law and Objective Values*, n 5 above, 18.

conventional good there are non-conventional aspects which are constitutive of its value.[16]

Marmor's early account of constitutive conventions was detailed and accurate, but it had become unsatisfying even in the eyes of its author, probably because of the constitutive conventions' inability to account for their own normativity. Interestingly enough, Marmor feels the need, in his latest book on social conventions, to ask how is it possible for these constitutive conventions to emerge at all. Where do they come from? Do they have a non-conventional origin? Marmor comes to the conclusion that constitutive conventions are instantiations of other conventions, which he defines as deep conventions. These conventions are characterised by five features, which distinguish them from (as Marmor calls them) surface conventions.[17] It is helpful to recapitulate them.[18] First, they are the closest conventions to the basic needs of human beings. This implies that the degree of their arbitrariness is lower: since they emerge as normative responses to social and psychological aspects of the world, they are bound to be closely related to reasons than surface conventions. Deep conventions enable (and this is the second feature) surface conventions to emerge. A word of clarification is needed here. There is an almost genetic link between the two levels, because deep conventions can rarely be practised without engaging in some surface conventions. To give an example, one cannot play theatre in abstract, but must play particular genres like comedy or tragedy. This is the third feature: deep conventions are normally instantiated by the fact that surface conventions are being followed. Moreover, compared with surface conventions, deep conventions are more durable and less prone to change. This fourth feature tells us that deep conventions, even though they are followed by practising the relevant surface conventions, do not change when the latter are modified. This implies that there are several conventional ways of instantiating a deep convention. The fifth feature is a direct consequence of the lasting character of deep conventions. The latter tend to resist codification and, even when they are institutionalised, they can rarely be changed by modifying the relevant rules or codes. Since they are deeply ingrained in fundamental aspects of human nature, they cannot be changed authoritatively, that is *ex alto*. In

[16] J Raz, *The Practice of Value* (Oxford, Oxford University Press, 2003) 26, where Raz gives an example to illustrate his thesis: 'Paradigmatically conventional goods, like the good of giving flowers as a mark of affection, have reasons other than the convention. The fragrance, colours, and shapes of flowers are appealing partly for independent reasons, and make them appropriate for their conventional role. Most commonly these independent grounds for valuing flowers are themselves culturally dependent; they are not, at least not entirely, a product of our biology. But the cultural dependence of our valuing of flowers because of their colours, shapes, and fragrance is not in itself of the right kind to make their value a conventional value. We would not value them had we not been imbued with culturally transmitted attitudes. But we do not think that the fact that others value them is a reason why lilies are beautiful'.

[17] If I understand correctly, surface conventions are comprised of two layers: constitutive and coordinative. The main difference with deep conventions, at least for what concerns the law, lies in the fact that surface conventions are always instantiations of a particular legal order. This is not the case for deep conventions, as we shall see below.

[18] See Marmor, *Positive Law and Objective Values*, n 5 above, 58–59.

fact, deep conventions evolve gradually, 'in a process of habituation and learning that takes considerable time and practice'.[19]

We have finally come to reconstruct the conventionalist realm as depicted by Marmor. It is a rather complex representation of the role played by conventions in the social realm. This conventionalist triptych – coordinative, constitutive, deep conventions – claims to possess three advantages compared to the monist (that is, only coordinative and functional) version of conventionalism. With regard to at least the first two claims, one may safely affirm that they seem to be solidly grounded. First, this kind of conventionalism claims to vindicate the meaning of social practices in a more accurate way. The point of a social practice is usually explained by a deeper level of conventionality, which links the value of the concerned practice to one or more basic human needs, and by constitutive conventions, which tell us how and when a conventional response to a social need became 'our' own practice. A second, related, merit of multilayered conventionalism is to be found in its rejection of functionalism in favour of historicism.[20] Indeed, both constitutive and deep conventions become intelligible only if seen not as a solution to a coordination problem, but through an historical explanation that can tell us why a particular convention was adopted and how and under which circumstances it was developed. As already remarked, this historicist reading of conventions is able to save the idea of the rule of recognition from some misunderstandings. An example of the efficacy of this historicist reading can be given by the way nations have dealt with the problem of the relation between churches and the state. The solutions adopted to solve this problem are different from state to state and they cut across several other conventions (for example, they are not intelligible through the distinction between civil and common law).[21] Now, it is perfectly legitimate to look at the problem of the role of churches in a state as a coordination problem: A state legal order needs to coordinate between the demands coming from different religious institutions. It is also possible to explain the agreements between churches and states as an equilibrium which delimits the respective roles in the most efficient way for the actors involved. However, as it should have become by now evident, this is an impoverished reading of the problem. The value of the conventions which settle the relation between churches and the state can be understood only in historical terms, as a development involving the nature of religions with which the state must relate and the history of the same state. Marmor proposes to interpret the rule of recognition as the outcome of an historical progression of events whose circumstances proved to be essential for the setting of a constitutive convention. In this respect, the shape and the content of the social practices we encounter are determined by historical contingencies. As we shall see below, this contingency entails that conventional norms are arbitrary and path-dependent.[22]

[19] ibid 77.

[20] Marmor, *Social Conventions*, n 10 above, 20.

[21] For a comparative introduction to this theme see T Koopmans, *Courts and Political Institutions* (Cambridge, Cambridge University Press, 2003) 204–10.

[22] Marmor, *Social Conventions*, n 10 above, 78. For a more detailed analysis of arbitrariness and path-dependency see below.

The third advantage of adopting Marmor's specific understanding of conventionalism is to be found in its capacity to avoid a consent-based and an intention-based understanding of the law. However, this advantage does not survive a closer scrutiny. Marmor believes that conventions do not need to have a consensual basis.[23] Quite the contrary, conventions come out 'precisely in those cases where an agreement is difficult or impossible to reach'.[24] This proposal echoes Hume's idea that even the whole government rests not on consent (or contract) but on human conventions.[25] This is especially true when it comes to large-scale coordination problems, where it is clearly impossible for a large number of people to agree on a common solution. In this respect, conventionalism represents an alternative to other social philosophies that try to establish the cooperative nature of social practices. This is the case, for example, of Michael Bratman's work on shared agency.[26] According to Bratman, social practices are necessarily cooperative; that is, their existence implies the intention of the agents to cooperate. However, Bratman does not adopt a collectivist stance on the issue of intentionality. Indeed, he refers to shared intentions as a complex interaction of individual intentions and common knowledge.[27] In a conventionalist account of a social practice the intentional aspect of the action does not need to be excluded *a priori*. A conventionalist approach doubts that every participant in a conventional practice 'must actually entertain some underlying cooperative intention'.[28] Reasons for taking part in a practice are of different kinds and they do not need to be the same for all the cooperants.[29] To avoid any misunderstanding, this does not imply the absolute irrelevance of intentions in the social realm, as Marmor's idea of legal interpretation also confirms.[30] It is simply the case that intentionality is not deemed to be an essential part of social practices. Furthermore, in the field of law, conventions do not need to rely on sanctions as other theories (law as command, for example) are prone to concede. The reason why we constantly follow conventions has to be found in their capacity to meet our preferences for a solution or in the values embedded in a particular social practice. Participation in the specific activity called law is usually not engendered by fear of sanctions, but by reasons to

[23] This is how Dworkin presents legal conventionalism in *Law's Empire* (Oxford, Hart, 1998) 114–50 and, more recently, in *Justice in Robes* (Cambridge, MA, Harvard University Press, 2006) 188–98.

[24] Marmor, *Positive Law and Objective Values*, n 5 above, 6.

[25] D Hume, *A Treatise of Human Nature* (Oxford, Oxford University Press, 1991) 490. *cf* J Raz, *Ethics in the Public Domain* (Oxford, Oxford University Press, 1994) 369.

[26] M Bratman, *Faces of Intention* (Cambridge, Cambridge University Press, 1999). For a transplant of Bratman's theory in the legal realm see Scott Shapiro, Chapter 1.

[27] ibid 130–41.

[28] Marmor, *Positive Law and Objective Values*, n 5 above, 53.

[29] This is why Marmor is also sceptical of Searle's idea of collective intentionality. Indeed, for Searle, collective intentions are a primitive phenomenon that cannot be defined in terms of an interlocking set of individual intentions. In any case, Searle's metaphysical presuppositions need not be discussed by legal conventionalists because they do not affect directly the main tenets of conventionalism. On the differences between Searle's account of collective intentionality and Marmor's conventionalism, see G Tuzet, 'The Social Reality of Law' (2007) *Analisi e diritto* 185.

[30] On the role of intention in legal interpretation Marmor has written extensively (and, in general, in a positive tone) in his *Interpretation and Legal Theory* (Oxford, Hart, 2006).

take part into it.[31] Moreover, only institutionalised legal systems can provide a mechanism for ensuring compliance with the rules. Typically, institutional practices involve an apparatus to administer the sanctions. They indeed have what Hart defines as secondary rules.[32] Conventional practices do not have sanction mechanisms or, at least, they do not need to have them in order to generate conventional rules. If there is a massive deviation from a certain conventional rule, then it is likely that this lasting and consistent phenomenon will bring about a new rule, substituting the old one.[33] As we shall see in the next section, legal conventions are rarely apt to describe how law works. Their capacity to explain legal orders without resorting to the classic idea of consent is undermined by their ontological impossibility to account for dissent or disagreement.[34]

Before moving on to discuss the thrust of Marmor's thesis (the nature of conventionality), one source of perplexity on the formulation of Marmor's argument needs to be outlined. It is in the logic of Marmor's argument to ask where the proliferation of layers of conventionality will lead in the end. If deep conventions are needed for the emergence of surface conventions, then one may start looking for another convention which makes it possible to form deep conventions. At this stage, one may also question that deep conventions are really deep, because they might also appear as surface conventions when compared to deeper conventions.

Therefore, when the level of deep conventionality as described by Marmor is reached, one may stipulate three further possible moves. The first one is simply a *regressio ad infinitum*. If deep conventions will not suffice to ground the conventionality aspects of the law, then it will be necessary and possible to dig deeper looking for another layer of conventionality. Nothing can stop us (nor does Marmor try to do so) from retrieving a 'deeper than deep' convention which actually grounds deep and surface conventions. Such a move would clearly be exposed to a *regressio* and would lack a stable and clear foundation.

Another possible move would consist in introducing a final trascendental argument for squaring the circle. This move would imply the introduction of a final *grund* convention. Given the assumptions on which Marmor's proposal is based, this solution seems also highly improbable. Legal conventionalism cannot be grounded on a normative hypothesis because it follows strictly the so-called social thesis. According to this thesis, law is a social phenomenon and therefore the nature of law is basically a matter of social facts. This is precisely the gist of Marmor's critique to Kelsenian

[31] Marmor seems to share Raz's view according to which coercion is not essential to what the law is. See the well-known example of a society of angels which would still need a legal system: J Raz, *Practical Reason and Norms* (Oxford, Oxford University Press, 1990) 159–60. The fact that provision of sanctions is not conceptually essential to the idea of law does not mean that it should pass unnoticed. To the contrary, Marmor believes that the ability to provide sanctions (the coercive element of law) is one of the most important functions served by law.

[32] Hart, n 11 above, ch 5.

[33] Marmor seems to underestimate the role of disagreement in the justification and explanation of the authority of the law. On this point, more will be said below. See generally S Besson, *The Morality of Conflict: Reasonable Disagreement and the Law* (Oxford, Hart, 2005).

[34] It is an ontological incapacity because the very idea of a conventional practice presupposes that there is no strong disagreement among the participants.

normativism. It represents one of the advantages of the conventionalist perspective to be able to offer a more accurate description of what makes something legal than the pure theory of law.[35] Moreover, even Kelsen was forced to recognise that in order to know what is the basic norm in a particular legal system, one must look at the practice of officials in that system. In this scheme, the basic norm turns out to be a social norm. If this reconstruction is correct, then a transcendental norm as the final norm is not available to Marmor because it would amount to a blatant contradiction affecting the core of his theory.[36]

The third move represents possibly the 'best reading' of multilayered conventionalism. The task of this doctrine is not to explain and justify all aspects of the legal universe. Multilayered legal conventionalism is an avowed limited doctrine that does not aim to explain or justify every legal aspect of the world. Marmor's claim is indeed explicitly circumscribed to the explanation of how an object can be considered legal. Therefore, we can interpret deep conventions as being the conventional layer which is the closest to the basic needs of human beings. This implies that these, so to say, 'archetypical' conventions stem unavoidably from some features of the nature of human beings. Of course, Marmor does not investigate the anthropological assumptions which underlie his theory, but it is possible to retrieve a sense that sociality leads necessarily to the emergence of different social and legal conventions. In other words, the first answer to the most basic needs of human beings is already conventional. This assumption postulates the existence of a sort of *homo conventionalis*[37] as the cornerstone of the whole theory. It is quite hard, for example, to imagine a world without competitive games. If it were the case, than the inhabitants of this world would be quite different from actual human beings.[38] Yet, to circumscribe the level of conventionality at this highness strikes one as arbitrary. One may wonder why one could not think of another layer of conventionality between anthropological needs and deep conventions.[39]

III THE CONVENTIONALITY THESIS AND THE AUTHORITY OF LAW

Central to Marmor's approach is the precise and meticulous way he understands conventionality. According to him, the nature of the law is fundamentally con-

[35] See the comments on Kelsen's conception of normativity in Marmor, n 2 above, 145–46.

[36] For an assessment of this transcendental move see Corrado Roversi, Chapter 12.

[37] There might be a sense that this feature of conventionality (particularly its deep layer) has to do with culture, at least in the meaning given to that concept in cultural anthropology. The examples proposed by Marmor are usually culturally rooted. But the examination of a cultural quality in legal conventionalism exceeds by far the purposes of this chapter.

[38] Marmor, *Social Conventions*, n 10 above, 73.

[39] This last objection is recognised and rejected, perhaps not convincingly, by Marmor. He insists that 'even if I am wrong about this, and the most we can say is that conventions come in layers, some deeper than others, my basic contention that there are deep conventions remains basically intact. Even if there are just layers of depths and shallowness, it can still be the case, as I argue here, that many shallow conventions instantiate deeper ones; and that without the relevant deeper layer, certain shallow conventions could not have emerged': ibid 66–67.

ventional. This does not mean that every aspect of the law is conventional. The content of certain laws is not and cannot be conventional. The rule that establishes an absolute prohibition of torture is not arbitrary because it is the only possible instantiation of the reasons behind it. In other words, there are no alternative rules that can account for the idea that torture is a practice that must be banned. Having said that, if we want to understand what is the law in a given context we should look at its conventional traits. Therefore, an analysis of multilayered legal conventionalism cannot avoid examining the idea of conventionality. Marmor provides a detailed definition of the conditions which make a rule conventional. For a more accurate understanding, it is appropriate to quote Marmor's definition in its entirety: a rule A is conventional if all the following conditions obtain:

(1) There is a group of people, a population P, that normally follow R, in circumstances C.
(2) There is a reason, or a combination of reasons, call it A, for members of P to follow R in circumstances C.
(3) There is at least one other potential rule, S, that if members of P had actually followed in circumstances C, then A would have been a sufficient reason for members of P to follow S instead of R in circumstances C, and at least partly because S is the rule generally followed instead of R. The rules R and S are such that it is impossible to comply with both of them concomitantly in circumstances C.[40]

The first condition is a restatement of the social nature of conventions. It emphasises the fact that conventional rules must be followed by a population. The use of the verb 'to follow' means that the rule needs to be regarded as binding by the relevant population.[41] It is also important to note that conventions have to be followed by a large number of people because, as remarked above, they emerge as an alternative to agreements. The second condition reminds us of two things. It is not necessary that the reason or the combination of reasons be always the same. People can participate in a social practice for different reasons. Therefore, it turns out that conventionality is opaque precisely because reasons for following a convention do not have to be transparent.[42] Marmor believes, also, that this opaqueness does not entail that people may not know at all that by practising a social rule they are following a convention. But there should always be a potential awareness that one is following a rule. Two features must be stressed about the third condition: conventional rules are arbitrary and they normally lose their point if they are not actually followed. It is hard to underestimate the relevance of these two features for legal conventionalism. They constitute the core of this doctrine. For this reason, their formulation calls for a clarification. As already remarked, arbitrariness does not

[40] ibid 2.

[41] Of course, there can also be non-conventional rules. But what characterises conventionality is the idea that 'at least upon reflection, people would say that they behave in a certain way because the relevant conduct is required by the convention': ibid 3.

[42] ibid 6.

imply indifference, but conveys the idea that there could have existed an alternative convention which could have been engendered by the same reasons. However, this assumption flies in the face of reality when applied to law because it underestimates the role of disagreement. It may be opportune to bear in mind here that legal conventionalism does not need to resort to the concept of agreement for explaining social practices. But as presented by Marmor, conventionalism does not take into account the relevance of disagreement.[43] To a certain extent, it is unavoidable that the theme of disagreement is not tackled directly within a conventional framework, for the simple reason that, according to the definition of conventionality, there cannot be disagreement on the content of a conventional rule. The latter is exhausted by the application of the convention. In Marmor's words:

> [c]onventions are what they are, because there is a practice of applying the rule to certain cases; it is the application of the rule which constitutes its very existence. Once it is not clear to the norm subjects whether the convention applies to a certain case or not, then there is no conventional solution to the matter, and at least as far as the convention is concerned, this is the end of it.[44]

It seems that in case of pervasive disagreement, conventions would let the issue be solved by another force or power.[45] Be that as it may, the idea of conventionality does not explain the fact that an authoritative law claims to be legitimate even when there is persistent disagreement from a consistent part of the relevant population. Obviously, Marmor is aware of this feature of the law. In *Positive Law and Objective Values* he tackles directly the central question of involuntary membership. He suggests that the need for reasons does not entail the actual possibility of choice, affirming that 'the fact that one needs a good reason to do A simply does not entail that avoiding A must be a feasible option'.[46] In fact, there may be several good explanations for supporting this view. One, at which Marmor himself hints, is that there is a cultural aspect in the process of coming to terms with conventional rules and this is partly engendered by the fact that people are born and raised into numerous conventional practices[47] which shape (one is entitled to suppose) reasons for accepting them. Moreover, a great many practices constituted by social conventions can be both authoritative and impose their authority on their subjects regardless of their consent. I take this to mean that being raised in a social authoritative convention affects the personal value of the option,[48] while it probably leaves unchanged the impersonal value. In other words, in this context

[43] The classic reference on this topic is J Waldron, *Law and Disagreement* (Oxford, Oxford University Press, 1999).

[44] Marmor, *Positive Law and Objective Values*, n 5 above, 58.

[45] It must be mentioned that by delimiting the scope of conventions in such a way, Marmor saves the relative autonomy of law from other domains like morality or politics. A legal solution to a collective problem is always conventional. This is not the case when the solution comes from common morality or politics. On the non-conventional character of morality see Marmor, *Social Conventions*, n 10 above, 132–54.

[46] Marmor, *Positive Law and Objective Values*, n 5 above, 37.

[47] See the examples of friendship and respect in Marmor, *Social Conventions*, n 10 above, 150–51.

[48] J Raz, *Engaging Reason* (Oxford, Oxford University Press, 1999) 244.

one develops an attachment to a particular social practice in virtue of taking part in it.[49] Clearly, this is the perspective of an individual. However, if one goes back to the level of the rule-following community one might find a contradiction in this way of reasoning. The conventional nature of the constitutive rule is indeed at stake. We saw that the rules one ought to follow must be arbitrary. As remarked, this means that a rule is arbitrary only if it has a conceivable alternative. Having followed this alternative would have been equal to being guided by the same reason(s). Recall the fact that 'conceivable' is tantamount to saying that one could have followed an alternative rule.[50] But this assumption runs against the explanation of normativity provided by Marmor (he explicitely states that it is not necessary to be able to actually follow another rule). In other words: explaining the validity of the conventionality thesis by affirming that one does not need to have a concrete alternative option to the rule one is required to follow cannot be compatible with the conventional character of the same social rule, which is based, among other things, upon the fact that it would have been possible to comply with the same reason for action by following another rule.

Nor can one expect to solve this riddle by resorting to the deeper level of conventionality, because, as we shall see below, this won't provide a solution. The point is that even deep conventions do not seem to improve the capacity of conventionalism to justify an authority.[51] Law is a conventional game, but contrary to what happens in other games, this is an authoritative and coercive one. The problem is that authority is supposed to be binding, while conventions are only 'conditionally binding'. As aptly remarked by Leslie Green, 'each should conform if and only if he expects the others to do the same'.[52] All of this strikes one as a counterintuitive description of how a legal system works. Participation in a legal system is never conditional. Law makes claims on us independently from our willing acceptance. The case of migrants illustrates perfectly how strong and harsh the law can be even on those who have not accepted it or taken part in the conventional practices which created it. In general, the impact of law on the life of its subjects is anything but conditional, and also it is much deeper and all encompassing than that of any game. The analogy is insidious precisely because it might be taken to suggest that the participants in the game of law are bound to follow the directives of law only on the condition of their being willing to do so. The problem is that contrary to any kind of game, it is not possible to step outside law, or at least it is not possible to do it as easily as one can do with a game. It is not up to oneself to decide individually whether or not one will comply with the law, whose prescriptions apply regardless of any reluctance anyone may have to come

[49] On the value of personal attachment see J Raz, *Value, Respect, Attachment* (Cambridge, Cambridge University Press, 2001) 10–40.

[50] This is, again, Marmor's formulation: 'A rule is conventional if and only if there is at least one other potential rule that the relevant community could have followed instead, achieving the same purpose, as it were': Marmor, *Social Conventions*, n 10 above, 12.

[51] This is so because they are not concerned with what makes something legal, but with the building blocks of a legal order.

[52] L Green, *The Authority of the State* (Oxford, Oxford University Press, 1998) 121.

under their scope.

It is not enough to add to this explanation of involuntary membership, as Marmor does, the recognition that there may be people that deliberately alienate themselves from the legal practice of their country because of a lack of feasible alternatives.[53] To think of dissensus in terms of alienation means to misconstrue the problem. A legal theory should be able to explain why 'alienated people' should have reason to comply with the directive of the authority even when they do not have primary reasons for participating in the legal activity. For structural reasons, multilayered legal conventionalism does not have the intellectual resources to overcome this hurdle. That involuntary or reluctant participation in legal practices is a critical point for conventionalists is indeed confirmed by their view that law is a normative social practice. What makes it normative is its authoritative nature. Marmor proposes to look at normativity by underlining that conventions are rules of conduct 'and they are normatively significant as such'.[54] But are conventions truly authoritative? Marmor seems to answer in the negative when he distinguishes between an explanatory and a justificatory aspect of conventionality:

> The explanatory task consists of an attempt to explain how rules or conventions can give rise to reasons for action, and what kinds of reasons are involved. The task of justification concerns the elucidation of the reasons people *should* have for acknowledging law's normative aspect; it is the attempt to explain the legitimacy of the authority of law . . . The reasons for acknowledging the authority of law cannot derive from social conventions.[55]

Yet, it seems that according to legal conventionalism law should be understood as a social practice which has developed its authoritative nature as a response to some human basic needs. Clearly, it is valuable to engage in legal practices because they provide certain reasons for action. But at its core, law is presented as a 'social game' whose point consists in following the authority. Since authority plays a mediating role – it serves its subjects by providing them exclusionary reasons[56] – it is valuable to follow its directives. If we accept to play the game, then the sources thesis will guide our behaviour. According to Marmor, it does not matter on the basis of which kind of primary reasons we deliberate to participate. Or at least, this is not important from the perspective of the legal theorist. The main focus of the latter should be put on the conventions which identify what is law.

As a theory of the sources of law, legal conventionalism is perfectly compatible with exclusive legal positivism. But a problem arises when it is remarked that participation in the practice is linked to a conditional ought. The obligation to behave

[53] 'Generally speaking, people can deliberately alienate themselves from various aspects of their lives even when those aspects are not choosable in any straightforward sense': Marmor, *Positive Law and Objective Values*, n 5 above, 39.

[54] ibid 15.

[55] ibid 32.

[56] Raz, n 31 above, 35–48. See also J Raz, *The Morality of Freedom* (Oxford, Clarendon Press, 1986) 38–69.

in accordance with the directives emanating from or validated by the rule of recognition depends on the acceptance to take part in the practice of law. But if this is the case, the legal ought arising under the rule does not differ in kind from the duties we incur by participating in other more circumscribed practices that we typically take part in on a voluntary basis. Obligations emerge only after the willing acceptance to participate in the practice. In the case of judges, or other legal officials, who are called to identify the rule of recognition with their judicial practice, one may separate two kinds of reasons because, as Marmor says, 'the rules of recognition cannot settle for the judge, or anyone else for that matter, whether they should play by the rules of law or not. They only tell judges what the law *is*'.[57]

Common judicial practice, a necessary constituent element of rules of recognition, does not supply judges (and other officials) with reasons to accept those rules as binding. One may conclude that to constitutive conventions applies the same distinction which Marmor endorses between underlying primary reasons for action, which are not created by the existence of a convention, but by something else, and auxiliary reasons for action, which are engendered by conventions.[58] The reasons why a judge ought to follow the rule of recognition, if the latter is understood in a conventionalist way, should derive also from the very fact that judges should not follow their own political convictions in recognising sources of law, but they should be guided by a common practice of recognising certain things as sources of law. This being so, it seems that the practice in common among judges of recognising certain objects as law is not primary reason-giving, but plays only an identifying role. In fact, Marmor points out that his brand of legal conventionalism is not directly concerned with the question of what underlying primary reasons judges and others should have for following the rule of recognition, because the concept of legal normativity does not depend on the kind of reasons people and practitioners have for participating. Judges may indeed follow it for a variety of different reasons, coming from, for example, morality, religious belief or self-interest.[59]

In other words, the rule of recognition sets up an obligation only for practitioners who already have, from the outset, a reason to be participants in the practice of law. The primary reasons for participating in the practice of law are created outside the realm of law. Therefore, the obligation to follow the law (and to identify it) comes not from the convention that constitutes what the law is but from

[57] Marmor, *Positive Law and Objective Values*, n 5 above, 22.

[58] J Dickson, 'Is the Rule of Recognition Really a Convention?' (2007) 27 *Oxford Journal of Legal Studies* 397. Marmor states the point with clarity: 'in both types of conventions, we should distinguish between the primary reasons for action, which are not, by themselves, created by the existence of the conventions, and the auxiliary reasons which are engendered by the conventional rules . . . In the case of constitutive conventions, the primary reasons are those which would render the participation in the relevant practice desirable, intelligible, etc. Generally speaking, conventions would have little bearing on answering such a question as "Why should I do it?". Conventions typically determine the ways in which something is done, answering the "how", rather than the "why" question'. Marmor, *Positive Law and Objective Values*, n 5 above, 26–27.

[59] ibid 32–33.

external facts whose nature is not necessarily conventional. In light of this discussion of constitutive conventions, Marmor stresses once again the conceptual continuity between games and law:

> [T]he rules of recognition, like any other type of constitutive conventions, only define what the practice is. They only tell us what counts as law in our society. As such, namely as constitutive rules, they also define the legal validity of norms; which is simply to say that they define the rules of the game. This leaves open the question of why people should practise the law of their country; of why they should play the game as it were. Yet as long as enough people, particularly practitioners, do play the game, for whatever reasons for doing so they may have, the practice will exist as a normative practice . . . Whether judges, other practitioners, or laymen, have any moral or other reasons to play the game or not, is a totally separate question . . . those reasons cannot be prescribed by the social conventions themselves.[60]

While theoretically plausible and coherent with the rejection of the idea of collective intentionality, the distinction between two reasons for participating is not always clear and leaves certain aspects of constitutive conventions unexplained. Once again, the main point seems to rotate around the idea that arbitrariness does not imply indifference. One conventional solution may not be regarded as exactly equal to another one. However, Marmor does not take this conclusion to its most logical consequences. Constitutive conventions are necessary for the emergence of a social practice. They partly represent the point of the practice. It is often difficult to imagine that the point of the practice is in the best case only a secondary reason to take part in the practice. There is a point in following an activity like theatre. This point is certainly instantiated by the different constitutive rules which shape different theatrical genres. But one would hardly go to the theatre in search of a religious experience. This would be a misunderstanding of the practice's meaning and, as Marmor himself recognises, it cannot be the case that a majority of people misunderstands the point of the convention: 'conventions are, essentially, what people take them to be'.[61] If the majority of people have as a primary reason for going to the theatre the cultivation of a religious life, then the point of the practice will hardly remain the same. The same logic can be applied to law, a field where a further, dramatic dilemma, may arise. There might be cases where primary reasons conflict in certain ways with secondary (conventional) reasons. Take the case of the US Constitution, which Marmor, among many others, considers the rule of recognition of the US legal order.[62] In the nineteenth century, reasons for participating in this constitutional game were deeply related to moral and political considerations concerning the legal status of slavery. Because of this, one of the main points of the practice of American constitutionalism was deeply contested, even though almost everybody deemed the Constitution

[60] ibid 33.
[61] ibid 60 n 15.
[62] On the US Constitution as a rule of recognition, see the recent collection of essays edited by M Adler and K Himma, *The Rule of Recognition and the US Constitution* (New York, Oxford University Press, 2009).

as the supreme law of the land. The attitude toward slavery affected not only the cleavage between northern and southern states, but also between members of the judiciary.[63] How would an abolitionist judge adjudicate in cases concerning the constitutionality of slavery? Should he resign, ignore the constitutional convention or follow the latter? Even if Marmor were right on the separation between primary and secondary reasons for participating, he would still have to provide some criteria to solve the potential conflict between the two levels of reasons.[64]

Despite these remarks, Marmor's project to keep together an exclusive legal positivist conception of authority and legal conventionalism sounds plausible. In the economy of the whole theory of multilayered conventionalism, the status of the third layer of conventionality looks more controversial and it does not seem to fit easily into the framework of the sources thesis. And it is on this point that we will focus our attention.

IV THE PLACE OF DEEP CONVENTIONS IN LEGAL REASONING

Of the three levels of conventions described by Marmor, the deepest one is probably the most problematic. Deep conventions represent the building blocks of legal systems because they are the expression of a range of reasons for having law in our societies. Nonetheless, the examples Marmor gives are striking for they do not seem to fit comfortably within an exclusive positivist framework. When he wants to indicate a case of what would be a deep convention, Marmor refers to the types of legal systems that have evolved in different parts of the world. So, among others, are listed the following types of legal traditions: common law and civil law, Jewish law, Islamic Shari'a law.[65] This is a very revealing reference because it represents the best way to understand how deep conventions work in daily practices. Let's focus on the case of civil and common law legal systems. These examples demonstrate that deep conventions cannot be authoritative in themselves, but they open a space for the development of surface conventions. As previously discussed, deep conventions are practised by following the surface conventions that instantiate them which, in this case, is the rule of recognition of each particular country. At this level, it is appropriate to ask what is the relation between deep and surface conventions and, in particular, whether, despite being practised only indirectly, deep conventions somehow affect the other conventions. After all, deep conventions represent the closest layer to basic human needs and they may have a substantial impact on surface conventions. The common law

[63] See especially R Cover, *Justice Accused* (New Haven, CT, Yale University Press, 1975).

[64] It is necessary to note that this is not the objection raised by Dworkin against the concept of the rule of recognition: Dworkin, *Justice in Robes*, n 23 above, 190–96. Dworkin believes that since judges disagree about the criteria of legality of their legal systems the idea of a rule of recognition makes no sense. The objection moved to Marmor is of a different kind: what happens when primary reasons for participating are in stark conflict with conventional norms?

[65] One wonders whether other transnational traditions of law, like international and European law, are considered, according to Marmor's classification, constitutive or deep conventions.

and civil law effectively constitute a way of organising legal reasoning in the respective traditions, serving the same functions. They can be defined as two rather different legal cultures:

> Common law, for example, assigns a much greater role to judges in developing the law and adapting it to changing circumstances; continental law seeks to restrict the role of judges in this respect, and allows them much less flexibility in changing the law. Legislation in the continental systems is very structured, typically seeking to codify entire areas of law in a very systematic way; common law legislation is much less structured, typically avoiding codification of entire areas of law.[66]

Both legal traditions have evolved through centuries and they are not the product of institutional decisions. However, they do not claim to have legitimate or de facto authority. Nobody is asked to follow the French Civil Code because it is part and parcel of the deeper convention of civil law, but because, as a legal conventionalist would put it, the code has been enacted by a legitimated and recognised French authority on the basis of a convention that establishes what counts as law in the concerned country. Nonetheless, this may imply that deep conventions cannot be considered exactly as law, authority being a necessary property of a legal system, but either as a precondition for the existence of law or as part and parcel of legal reasoning.[67]

The example of common and civil law reinforces the idea that deep conventions structure legal reasoning. This implies that rules belonging to the layer of deep conventionality should be part of legal reasoning. However, it is not clear which level of legal reasoning they are relevant for. This question matters when it comes to the determination of identifying what counts as law. In other words, despite their not being authoritative, are deep conventions directly involved in the identification of law? The impression is that Marmor has not yet dealt directly with this problem. For this reason, every attempt to give an answer must be considered as tentative. A good starting point may be represented by Joseph Raz's conception of legal reasoning, whose approach on this point Marmor may support. Raz maintains that from an exclusive legal positivist perspective there are two kinds of legal reasoning. One is 'reasoning about the law', whose function is to establish what law is in relation to a given subject; and 'reasoning according to law', whose function is to determine 'how, according to law, courts should decide cases'.[68] Raz states that reasoning about law is guided by the sources thesis, so it concerns the identification of what is considered law in complete autonomy with respect to moral reasoning. By contrast, reasoning according to law 'can be

[66] Marmor, n 2 above, 156.

[67] The case of religious law is quite different, in my view. Several forms of religious law purport to be authoritative. Therefore, it seems misleading to put together different legal traditions with religious laws.

[68] Raz, n 25 above, 220. It is necessary to clarify that Raz distinguishes between a narrow sources thesis and a wide sources thesis. In the first version, the sources thesis only concerns 'pure legal statements', that is to say, statements on the content of law regardless of any reference to specific facts. In the second version, it also concerns 'applied legal statements', that is to say, statements relating to how law has to be seen in relation to a concrete case. One may doubt the validity of this distinction, but I will use it for heuristic purposes.

heteronomous, when it is law itself, identified through the sources thesis, that attributes to judges the discretion to deviate from the norms if they believe that there are valid moral reasons for making this deviation'.[69] In theory, deep conventions should not be relevant for reasoning about the law, because this is part and parcel of the work of the rules of recognition. Following Marmor's line of reasoning, it can be inferred that reasoning about the law belongs to the level of constitutive conventions. Deep conventions, structuring the way legal orders are organised, should belong to the level of reasoning according to law. In practice, it is not clear whether these conventions would respect the sources thesis, since, as is the case in the common law or in religious laws, moral reasoning is available from the beginning and it enters into the process before or at the same time as the identification of the sources. This ambiguity is due both to the examples chosen by Marmor and to a lack of clarity about the relation between deep and constitutive conventions. In fact, it is not immediately clear what are the consequences of affirming that deep conventions are practised through their instantiating constitutive conventions. Take, once again, the case of competitive games. One practises the deep conventions of competitive games by playing one of them. But this does not imply that the relationship between the two levels of conventionality must be thought of as unidirectional. Certain essential traits of the deep conventions of the practice of 'playing a competitive game' may have permeated the relevant constitutive conventions. In other words, unless Marmor clarifies what is the relation among deep and constitutive conventions in legal reasoning, the risk is to end up introducing elements of an incorporationist stance[70] in a theory which is supposed to reject this kind of position. If deep conventions are able to influence significantly surface conventions, then it is not possible to exclude *a priori* that they violate the sources thesis.

V CONCLUSION

Multilayered conventionalism is one of the most interesting and challenging contemporary theories of the nature of social practices. There is much to learn from it. When it comes to law, it can accurately explain its social nature. However, as it stands now, it has to face at least two serious theoretical hurdles. At the level of constitutive conventions, it cannot explain their normative force. Indeed, it underplays, in particular, the fact that participation in legal practices is hardly voluntary. At the level of deep conventions, their emergence exposes the whole theory to two main risks: either degenerating into transcendentalist assumptions

[69] A Schiavello, 'Law, Interpretation and Authority' (2007) *Analisi e diritto* 220.

[70] J Raz, *Between Authority and Interpretation* (Oxford, Oxford University Press, 2009) 182–202. See also Raz, n 25 above, 226–30. On inclusive legal positivism see W Waluchow, *Inclusive Legal Positivism* (Oxford, Oxford University Press, 1994). Of course, Marmor may offer an alternative example which would show how deep conventions are perfectly compatible with exclusive legal positivism. He may also provide a different account of legal reasoning than that of Raz.

or contradicting the kind of legal positivism to which Marmor is committed. But, of course, this *in fieri* philosophical project has still the time and the resources to develop an additional account which would redeem the core intuitions of multi-layered legal conventionalism.

7

The Normativity of the Practice of Officials

A Philosophical Programme

DIMITRIOS KYRITSIS

I INTRODUCTION

IN THE LEGAL systems that we are familiar with, the administration of law is entrusted to legal officials. In fact, it is doubtful that there can ever be a legal system without officials running it. But whether the presence of legal officials is a necessary feature of all law or not, their importance where they are to be found is undeniable. Hence, it is no surprise that they have provided a point of focus for much of our thinking about the nature of law. In this chapter I intend to continue this tradition of theorising. My aim is to highlight certain aspects of the practice of legal officials and offer a philosophical framework that makes sense of them. This philosophical framework is distinctly anti-positivist.

The present chapter follows up on an earlier article, which defended a partial reconciliation between two jurisprudential traditions, legal conventionalism and natural law theory.[1] It did so by showing how some salient themes in contemporary legal conventionalist literature could be accommodated within a robust version of natural law theory – namely, a jurisprudential view, according to which morality is necessarily among the truth conditions of propositions of law. These themes comprise what I there called 'the conventionalist package', which I summarised in the following way: 'the conventionalist package contains the idea that law is a practice of interaction between participants occupying different roles within it (who may – and in some variants of legal conventionalism must – include citizens)'.[2] The main claim of the earlier article was that a robust version of natural law theory would have no problem embracing the conventionalist package; it would view the practice of interaction in terms of the moral reasons that participants have to take heed of each other's contributions.

I dubbed this claim reconciliatory because it identified some common ground between two views which in many other respects are antithetical. Thus,

[1] D Kyritsis, 'What is Good about Legal Conventionalism' (2008) 14 *Legal Theory* 135.
[2] ibid 144.

while the view I put forward is anti-positivist, legal conventionalism is commonly understood to be a variant of legal positivism. For conventionalists the law is essentially a conventional practice of legal officials. This conventional practice specifies criteria of legal validity, which legal officials are bound to follow at least in part by virtue of the fact that they participate in this practice. Such an account of law is positivistic in at least two senses: first, it ultimately anchors law in a social fact, namely the fact that legal officials happen to follow a certain practice for the identification of valid law; second, it maintains that, although moral conditions may figure among the criteria of legal validity, they need not.

Furthermore, the reason I claimed to be offering only a *partial* reconciliation is that the earlier article did not tackle the main source of disagreement between standard conventionalist accounts of law and natural law theory, namely, their respective views of the foundation of law's normativity. As mentioned above, conventionalist accounts of law aim for the most part to offer a positivistic view of legal obligation; they maintain that legal obligation does not necessarily depend on morality. By contrast, natural law theory, especially in its robust versions, contends that legal obligation has a moral foundation; we have a genuine legal obligation if and only if it is in the relevant sense morally appropriate that we do. The earlier article did not adjudicate between these two views. It took as given the natural law theory view of law's normativity and merely assessed whether someone holding this view could also accept the conventionalist package. The content of the conventionalist package was accordingly trimmed down.

However, the earlier article started, so to speak, *in medias res*. It presupposed the philosophical significance of accommodating the conventionalist package within one's theory of law. This presupposition, of course, is by no means obvious. This chapter aims to provide some theoretical support for it. To this effect, it sketches a philosophical programme, which the claim of the earlier article and the natural law framework it proposed may be said to advance. My hope is that, viewed against the background of that programme, the claim and the framework will become better motivated. The chapter then repeats and amplifies the main parameters of the framework. Finally, it defends that framework from a number of objections.

II A PHILOSOPHICAL PROGRAMME

The philosophical programme I wish to defend starts by identifying two common (though perhaps not universal) features of the practice of officials. The first feature is that the competence of legal officials is rarely, if ever, unlimited. Officials occupy certain institutional roles, which define with greater or lesser precision what they may do and how they should go about doing it. The second feature is that in any given legal system there are different categories of legal officials and to each category corresponds a different institutional role. I do not want to deny that there may be legal systems with only one institutional role, but this is not the type of legal system that we are familiar with. The legal systems that we are familiar with do not recognise 'jacks of all trades'. Notice that the limited nature and the plurality of institutional roles are echoed in the conventionalist package. We cannot make sense of someone occupying a certain institutional role and not another, unless institutional roles are defined – and therefore limited. And the existence of interaction between legal officials occupying different institutional roles presupposes their plurality.

To focus the ensuing discussion I shall assume a legal system with a legislature and courts, C-L legal system for short. About such a legal system I shall ask: What reason do judges have to act in the way that we commonly expect them to vis-à-vis the legislature? The reason I choose to focus on C-L legal systems is twofold. To begin with, C-L legal systems exemplify both of the features listed above. First, they comprise more than one institutional role. Second, these institutional roles are limited. As common wisdom has it, legislators are there to pass statutes and judges to decide cases. There is, of course, nothing prima facie incoherent, say, about expanding the role of the legislator to encompass the adjudication of private disputes. But the piece of common wisdom illustrates the limited nature of the institutional roles that legal officials perform, as well as their plurality. Adherents to the common wisdom believe that, as things stand, it is not the legislators' job to decide private disputes; we have a different kind of legal official to do that, whom we call judges.

In addition, I discuss C-L legal systems, because judges and legislators are usual suspects in contemporary theorising about the nature of law, and in this sense the jurisprudential analysis undertaken here is continuous with current jurisprudential trends. Judges, it is fair to say, have attracted the attention of legal theorists more frequently than legislators. Their attitudes, practices, duties and powers have provided a focal point for the extrapolation of more general philosophical lessons about the nature of law. But legislatures are never too far off the picture.

The *locus classicus* of this approach is the theory of HLA Hart. Hart claims that judicial practice furnished rules of recognition, change and adjudication (which he calls secondary rules) that identified the criteria for a standard's membership in law. In fact, Hart illustrates this approach by drawing on a C-L legal system, the British. British judges, he writes, have a conventional practice of accepting the rules that the Queen in Parliament has enacted as law, which is what makes them law.[3]

Similarly, Dworkin, who consistently draws his examples from judicial decisions, explains his recourse to the practice of courts in the following way:

> We will study formal legal argument from the judge's viewpoint, not because only judges are important or because we understand everything about them by noticing

[3] HLA Hart, *The Concept of Law*, 2nd edn (J Raz and P Bulloch (eds), Oxford, Oxford University Press, 1994) 105–07. For criticism see S Lakin, 'Debunking the Idea of Parliamentary Sovereignty: the Controlling Factor of Legality in the British Constitution' (2008) 28 *Oxford Journal of Legal Studies* 709.

> what they say, but because judicial argument about claims of law is a useful paradigm for exploring the central, propositional aspect of legal practice. Citizens and politicians and law teachers also worry and argue about what the law is, and I might have taken their arguments rather than the judge's. But the structure of judicial argument is typically more explicit, and judicial reasoning has an influence over other forms of legal discourse that is not fully reciprocal.[4]

And after he has spelt out the nature of law in terms of the interpretive attitude toward legal practice he notes:

> We studied that attitude mainly in appellate courts, where it is dressed for inspection, but it must be pervasive in our ordinary lives if it is to serve us well even in court . . . It is a protestant attitude that makes each citizen responsible for imagining what his society's public commitments to principle are, and what these commitments require in new circumstances.[5]

So, for Dworkin judicial reasoning exemplifies the philosophical test for the truth of a legal claim. This test is not peculiar to the reasoning of courts. It tells us something about the nature of law, whether we look at it from the viewpoint of the citizen or a state official. This test consists in interpreting legal practice in the light of a set of principles of political morality that explain and justify it. On this test, legislative decisions belong to the practice toward which the interpretive attitude is directed; they are part of the pre-interpretive material, which judicial theories ought to be able to explain and justify in light of the appropriate principles of political morality.

Equally, Joseph Raz has argued that the task of courts is, at least in part, to apply the standards by which the legal system guides the behaviour of individuals. Thus, studying judicial practice can help us identify the content of the law:[6]

> The official evaluation of behaviour by the primary organs [like courts] must of course coincide with the guidance given by the system to ordinary individuals. If the system judges an individual to be doing what he ought not to do this entails that its norms guide him not to do that act, and vice versa. Hence if the primary organs do not regard themselves as bound to apply a certain norm it does not belong to the system.[7]

For Raz, then, a C-L system would direct courts to evaluate the behaviour of ordinary individuals according to the rules issued by the legislature. Importantly, Raz also thinks that such rules are meant to operate in a similar way in the reasoning of judges and ordinary citizens. In both cases, they are intended to be equipped with exclusionary force.[8]

[4] R Dworkin, *Law's Empire* (Hart Publishing, Oxford 1998) 14–15.

[5] ibid 413.

[6] We ought to be careful, though, when undertaking this task. According to Raz, adjudication includes recourse to standards that are not part of the law.

[7] J Raz *Practical Reason and Norms,* 2nd edn with a new postscript (Oxford, Oxford University Press, 1990) 142.

[8] ibid 142–46.

The philosophical programme I am pursuing builds on this way of thinking. Still, it diverges from it in one important respect; or, to put it differently, it singles out and problematises an aspect of this way of thinking that is largely taken for granted. Although it talks about legal systems that have the kind of institution that we commonly refer to as legislature and courts, it does not assume that a legislature is essentially a rule-creating institution and a court is essentially a rule-applying one. This assumption is fairly common in much conventionalist literature. According to this assumption, the rules created by the legislature are legal rules, by virtue of the fact that courts in their rule-applying function have a conventional practice of treating the legislature as a source of valid law. It may, of course, be that courts also treat other institutions as sources of valid law. It may be that even the rules coming from the legislature must satisfy further criteria, perhaps moral criteria, in order to count as valid law. But that does not change the fact that the legislature is one of the bodies – perhaps the most important body – that legal officials have a conventional practice of treating as a source of valid law. Now, given this characterisation of the legislature, the courts and their relationship, the task for conventionalist accounts of C-L legal systems is to explain the normativity of the practice of treating the rules coming from the legislature as legal.

More generally, the assumption that legislatures create rules and courts apply them arguably lends support to a positivist theory of law. If it is granted that we can identify a set of rules that have been created by an institution that is treated by courts as a valid source of law, then the stage of moral evaluation of those rules envisaged by natural law theories appears largely redundant, a mere add-on to an already complete account of law. If anything, the further stage tells us that something is good law. But we need to know what the content of the law is before we can judge whether it is good or bad.[9]

This assumption, and its connection with positivism, is evinced in a recurring criticism of Dworkin's theory. Many theorists have protested that Dworkinian interpretation presupposes the identification of a set of rules at the pre-interpretive stage; at best, it merely fills in the gaps or adds a moral gloss over the extant law. If we assume that the job of the legislature is to create rules, then it is only natural to think that the pre-interpretive stage already includes rules; and if it is further supposed that rules thus created have a robust normative dimension, then the conclusion seems inescapable that legal positivism cannot be challenged – indeed it is confirmed – by interpretivism.

By contrast, on the present proposal, the proper characterisation of the legislature, the courts and their relationship is a moot point. Obviously, this does not preclude that the characterisation provided by standard conventionalist accounts of law is the true one. But it opens up the possibility that we can explain the phenomena commonly described as rule-creation and rule-application in a different way, more congenial to the natural law position. To do so, we start from more

[9] See also below 192–94.

general features of the relationship between courts and the legislature. I have already identified two. I have said that C-L legal systems manifest a plurality of institutional roles, which are limited in a variety of ways. We should add another one, perhaps more controversial, namely, that the two bodies are involved in a common institutional endeavour. I shall say more in defence of this feature in the next section. For the time being, I only wish to point out that, like plurality and the limited character of institutional roles, it, too, connects the philosophical programme put forward here with the conventionalist package. In fact, it makes reference to a significant strand of legal conventionalism, which takes its bearings from the theory of joint action proposed by Michael Bratman. According to this strand, legal officials are involved in a shared activity structured by attitudes of mutual responsiveness, commitment and support.

At a second stage, we examine the relationship between the two bodies under the auspices of the joint activity. We should expect that their relationship is structured in a way that serves the point of the joint activity; thus, that the constitutional rules that organise this relationship reflect its connection with the point of the joint activity. This gives us a yardstick for understanding the (limited) institutional roles they are assigned and the rights and duties they have vis-à-vis one another, at least to a significant extent.[10] Working within this framework we can approach more specific aspects of their relationship. In particular, we can attempt to reconcile what we might call the receptive aspect of the role of courts towards the legislature with the more active aspects of that role, say, in legal systems that follow a practice of constitutional review of legislation for its conformity with higher-order legal standards. Both aspects can be accounted for, if at all, in light of the point of the joint activity.

This philosophical programme can establish a connection between C-L legal systems and natural law theory in at least two ways. First, it can do so by casting the point of the joint activity in morally laden terms. Second, more strongly, it can show that moral principles pertaining to the point of the joint activity play an essential role in the determination of judicial or legislative duty,[11] and in this sense that moral considerations form a necessary part of the ground for propositions of law. To this effect, it must establish that the (value-laden) point of the joint activity necessarily has a bearing on the truth of propositions of law. Besides, since it does not invoke the notions of rule-creation and rule-application to characterise the roles of the two bodies, it helps us account for the relationship between courts and the legislature without the mediation of such positivist-sounding ideas.

If convincing, then, the philosophical programme presented here helps us more satisfactorily capture the difference between legal positivism and natural law theory and possibly also suggests a new battleground for the two sides, namely, the explanation of the relationship between courts and legislatures. Of course, it may

[10] We should not exclude the possibility that some of their rights and duties are unrelated to the joint activity. But it is unlikely that this will be the case with regard to the most important ones.

[11] Dworkin, n 4 above, 90–96.

be objected that both the programme and the theoretical recommendations that it might generate are parochial in the sense that they are applicable only to a subset of legal systems, namely C-L legal systems; but, presumably, they do not apply (at least not readily) to law in general, since according to many legal theorists there can be legal systems without legislatures.[12] In defence, two things should be noted. First, it is not enough to point out that there are legal systems that are different from C-L legal systems. Additionally, the objection must identify a philosophically relevant difference between the two types of legal system. Is it perhaps that, in that other type of legal system, legal institutions do not have a legally limited role? Why is this difference relevant for a theory of law? This is not an extravagant theoretical demand. Many theorists casually draw conclusions from the relationship between courts and the legislature based on the implicit assumption that, despite superficial differences, these conclusions hold in legal systems that depart from the paradigmatic type. It falls on those who challenge them to point out in what sense the feature identified has limited scope. Second, it may be that, even without further elaboration, the philosophical programme I have outlined yields critical gains, in the sense that it exposes the difficulties that one or the other side has explaining the relationship between courts and legislatures in C-L legal systems. In such a case, the philosophical merit of the view in question will be seriously undercut, however well it fares in explaining the working of legal systems that are unlike C-L legal systems.

III LOOKING OVER ONE'S SHOULDER

Having sketched the philosophical programme that provides the background philosophical motivation for my account of C-L legal systems, I now wish to present its main parameters. As I have said, this account builds on some of the ideas that legal conventionalism has brought to the fore but integrates them in a non-positivist theory of law. More specifically, it draws on the conventionalist view that official practice might be regarded as a joint activity on the template of the model of collective action offered by Michael Bratman. Bratman has suggested that, when a group of individuals act in a way that shows mutual responsiveness, mutual commitment to a goal, and mutual readiness to provide support, then this group can be said to participate in a shared cooperative activity. These characteristics, then, mark the difference between, say, simultaneously taking a walk side by side and taking a walk together.[13]

[12] A further sense in which it might be risky to draw any conclusions about the nature of law from my proposal is that, as I have set it out for the purposes of this chapter, it leaves out citizens. For philosophers like Hart who thought that the foundation of law is official practice this was not much of a problem. Hart thought that for a legal system to exist it is sufficient that citizens by and large obey the law; see Hart, n 3 above, 112–16. But obviously the intuitions of other philosophers might point in a different direction. I indicate a way in which citizens may be included in the philosophical programme sketched here in n 17 below.

[13] M Bratman, 'Shared Cooperative Activity' (1992) 101 *Philosophical Review* 327.

The legal theorists that follow Bratman's analysis argue that the practice of legal officials exhibits the characteristics of a shared cooperative activity and maintain that, in order to describe this practice we need not make any reference to morality.[14] They further contend that participation in this practice generates an obligation on the part of individual participants to 'mesh' their practice-related conduct with that of their fellow-participants. The existence of this obligation, it is claimed, is independent of its moral evaluation. The obligation attaches to the role of participant in the practice, even if its content goes against what we morally ought to do. The account proposed here differs markedly. Whereas it accepts that one's duty qua official is partly determined by facts about the practice, it insists that this is so only insofar as there is a moral reason for it. Thus, the obligations flowing from one's participation in the practice crucially depend on morality. On this view, then, the task of legal theory is to identify what it is about the practice that gives rise to such a reason and what kind of reason that is.

The account offered here faces a preliminary objection. It assumes that the legislature and courts are involved in a joint activity.[15] Do we have any reason to go along with this assumption? In fact, there seems to be good reason to reject it. The relationship between the two bodies in C-L legal systems is often antagonistic. Especially in cases of constitutional moment, courts and legislatures clash. One need only think of the constitutional and political impasse that was caused by the striking down of social legislation during the early years of the New Deal. Neither does it seem to be true that the acts of the two bodies are united by a common purpose. Legislators are more likely to be motivated by a political platform or by a desire to promote the interests of their constituents. Sometimes, judges themselves will be driven by partisan agendas, which may or may not coincide with those of the legislators.

According to the objection, this does not mean that judges and legislators will be indifferent to one another's actions and decisions. If they are interested in having their agenda passed, they must act in ways that anticipate those actions and decisions. In fact, the objection is compatible with the stronger view that judges and legislators may have a moral reason to take each other's actions into account.

[14] J Coleman, *The Practice of Principle: In Defence of a Pragmatist Approach to Legal Theory* (Oxford, Oxford University Press, 2001) 74–102; K Himma, 'Inclusive Legal Positivism' in J Coleman and S Shapiro (eds), *The Oxford Handbook of Jurisprudence and Legal Philosophy* (Oxford, Oxford University Press, 2001) 125–65; C Kutz, 'The Judicial Community' (2001) 11 *Philosophical Issues* 442; S Shapiro, Chapter 1 in this book. Shapiro and Kutz have argued that the practice of officials falls short of a fully cooperative joint activity in Bratman's sense and have offered thinned down versions of his model.

[15] Arguably, this objection does not sting mainstream legal conventionalist theories, for at least two reasons. First, some legal conventionalists such as Hart himself tend to view the practice upon which the legal system rests as a *judicial* practice; see Hart, n 3 above, 256. On this view, even though judges may have a practice of accepting rules enacted by the legislature as valid law, they do not have a duty under the practice to mesh their conduct with that of legislators. Second, even those mainstream legal conventionalist theories that include legislators among the participants in official practice may be said to avoid the objection mentioned in the text, because they adopt a parsimonious description of the point of that practice. If the point of official practice is the establishment of a unified set of criteria for identifying valid law, it may be argued that both legislators and officials are committed to it despite their (sometimes intense) disagreements.

Suppose that a legislator wants to remedy a grave social injustice but that his proposal is seen with distrust by the conservative judiciary. Clearly, he has a moral reason to adjust his strategy, in order to curb or bypass judicial resistance and achieve his morally worthwhile goal. But his moral reason has nothing to do with a putative commitment to a project that he shares with the judiciary. To put the same point in Bratman's terminology, he may be responsive to the acts of the other officials, but without being committed to a common goal or prepared to support other officials to perform their part in achieving it.

Whether the acts of officials are contributions to a joint plan or side-constraints of individual plans will, of course, depend on which description makes better sense of legal practice. I shall have more to say on this after I introduce the main tenets of my proposal. Still, insofar as the objection relies on the existence of dissonance in C-L legal systems to dismiss the former description, it is flawed in at least two respects. First, it ignores that joint activities do not require that the intentions of participants are identical through and through. It is sufficient that they are shared up to an appropriate point. Beyond that point, they may diverge or even conflict. Two people walking side by side are still taking a walk together, even if one is there because he enjoys the other's company and the other because he wants to ask a favour. The legislator may wield the political power to crush the judiciary, if it opposes his plans. But as long as he continues to intend to pursue his plans in a way that takes proper heed of the judiciary, he can be said to participate, at some level, in a joint activity with it.

Second, the objection overlooks that competition, disagreement and conflict are not necessarily incompatible with participation in a joint activity. In fact, such elements are sometimes seen as partly constitutive of the joint activity and conducive to the achievement of its point. A good illustration of this is provided by James Madison's classic exposition of the point of separation of powers in the US Constitution. Madison thought that 'ambition must be made to counteract ambition'.[16] He anticipated that agents of government would be driven by a desire for self-aggrandisement, but he believed that, if they were pitted against each other, their interests would cancel themselves out, or at least they would keep one another in check. The result would be less state interference with the lives of citizens, which for Madison was the recipe for better government.

The account of C-L legal systems proposed here elaborates the Madisonian insight. It contends that at the most general level the point of the relationship between courts and the legislature is separation of powers. But it relies on a richer notion of separation of powers than Madison and thus buttresses its status as a moral idea. As I shall be using it, separation of powers is a desideratum of institutional design that comprises two dimensions, a division-of-labour and a checks-and-balances dimension. The division-of-labour dimension evaluates institutional arrangements by the extent to which they assign a certain government power to

[16] J Madison, 'The Federalist No. 51' in JE Cooke (ed), *The Federalist* (Middletown, CT, Wesleyan University Press, 1961) 331. Of course, Madison was talking about the relationship between the Congress and the President, but his point can be generalised.

the institution, when it is morally appropriate to exercise it. The checks-and-balances dimension reflects the importance of putting in place institutional mechanisms that monitor the exercise of government power and can effectively prevent its abuse. Separation of powers, then, furnishes the point of the practice of officials in C-L legal systems in the sense that this practice goes well, just in case it is organised on the basis of a defensible division of labour and incorporates an adequate system of checks and balances.

In addition, separation of powers gives the practice a *moral* point, insofar as an institutional practice that adheres to separation of powers makes a *pro tanto* stronger claim to moral legitimacy. That separation of powers, in the sense defined above, is a morally attractive idea is most clearly evinced by its connection with checks-and-balances. Obviously, it is a morally good thing to have effective controls on the exercise of government power. We can accept this without having to subscribe to a grim picture of human psychology or politics, simply on the strength of the observation that we are fallible and that some of the mistakes that fallible creatures like us make can be corrected, if we have our decisions second-checked. Equally, the moral attractiveness of separation of powers can be brought out, if we consider that the abstract idea is further fleshed out by appeal to a range of more concrete considerations of political and institutional morality, such as democracy, institutional independence, expertise, efficiency, and the like. These considerations (call them considerations of institutional design) specify whether it is morally appropriate to assign this or that state institution a certain government function. By virtue of considerations of institutional design, the acts and decisions of one set of officials make a difference to the duty of another. Such considerations bestow on these acts and decisions normative significance within the joint activity of legal officials. In the paradigmatic case, these considerations distribute government power among different state institutions and ground a corresponding moral duty on officials to respect exercises of power that are in accordance with this distribution.[17]

So far, I have given a rough outline of the proposal, and I have explained in what sense it depicts legal officials as involved in a joint activity that serves a moral point. Let me now try to make the thrust of the proposal more conspicuous by focusing on judges. The proposal maintains that they ought to do x in their official capacity, in part by virtue of the considerations of institutional and political

[17] It is not necessary that this duty be *owed* from one state institution to another. Whether or not this is true depends on the nature of the moral reasons that support the joint activity. But it is quite unlikely that these reasons will give rise to such duties. It is much more natural to suppose that the duties are owed to citizens. Officials owe it to them to work together. Some jurisprudents take a different view. For instance, Ken Himma explains the obligation of participants in the practice of officials in terms of mutual reliance and expectation. Obviously such attitudes arise only between officials. See Himma, n 14 above, 134. This is a crucial difference, but I cannot discuss it in any detail here. Suffice it to say that it highlights the link between understanding law's foundation in terms of a 'closed' practice among officials and a positivist conception of law's normativity. It is easier to accept, though still controversial, that a group of bullies owe it to one another to harass their weaker fellow-students. But the existence of such a duty becomes dubious, if the practice whose normative content we are trying to identify includes the weaker students. I am grateful to the editors for suggesting this link.

morality that structure the joint activity of officials of which they are part and assign roles to each type of official. Being partners in such a joint activity, judges, when deciding a case cannot just ask themselves 'What does justice require in this case?'. Rather they should ask themselves 'What is in my power to do, given that I take part in a joint activity underpinned by considerations of institutional design?'. To put it differently, their duty is not determined solely by considerations of content, considerations relating to the morally relevant features of the case before them. Such considerations have to be balanced alongside the pertinent considerations of institutional design to yield the right *legal* answer to the case.

Note though that it is possible that in a specific case the interplay of considerations of content and institutional design prior to the judicial determination yields an indeterminate outcome: it is neither true nor false that one option is morally superior over another. In such a case, the interplay of the two types of consideration fixes the right legal answer in two ways. First, it dismisses certain options, with regard to which it is determinate that they are sub-optimal. Second, it assigns the power to choose between the other options to one body rather than another. In such a case, although it is correct to say that the interplay of considerations of content and institutional design yields the right legal answer and thus sets a normative standard that exists prior to and checks the judicial determination, it still does not fully determine the content of citizens' legal rights and duties prior to the judicial determination.

Equipped with this account we can resist the view that courts are rule-applying institutions, whereas legislatures are rule-creating institutions. We can say instead that the respect courts owe legislative decisions is a function of the structure of the joint activity they are involved in and the considerations of institutional design that underpin it. This understanding of the role of courts vis-à-vis the legislature accounts for the phenomena that are commonly treated as instances of rule-application: in a few words, courts have a receptive role vis-à-vis the legislature because it is appropriate that they do so by virtue of, for example, the democratic credentials of the legislature or its ability to secure coordination, on the one hand, and the fact that the court is well positioned to give effect to the decisions of the legislature in individual cases, on the other.

At the same time, this understanding allows us to recognise doctrinal differences across legal systems, when it comes to issues such as methods of statutory interpretation, the role and weight of legislators' intention, and the relationship between statute and judge-made law. Such doctrinal differences reflect different arrangements of the courts-legislature relationship, underlain by different combinations of principles of institutional design and content. On the contrary, the supposition that there exists a common concept of rule-application that unites all the instances of judicial reliance on legislative acts and decisions leads either to vacuity or parochialism. It leads to vacuity, if it blocks out questions, say, about the relevance of intention in interpretation as not pertaining to rule-application. It leads to parochialism, if it attempts to present one contingent type of judicial reliance on legislative acts and decisions as paradigmatic and then to squeeze all other types into this one mould.

In similar fashion, the understanding of the courts-legislature relationship presented here can explain doctrines of constitutional review of legislation. Separation of powers recommends that we keep the exercise of power by state agents in check, and courts are by virtue of their institutional independence well suited to perform this function as regards the legislature. Thus, constitutional review is not at odds with the view that courts and the legislature participate in a joint activity. The joint activity of officials in a C-L legal system goes well, as far as its point is concerned, if it includes a robust checks-and-balances element, and it can achieve this by having courts ensure that the legislature does its assigned job properly. Still, the reasons counting in favour of constitutional review are not overriding. They have to be balanced against other reasons of institutional design, such as efficiency and democracy and the need to avert abuse of power by the courts themselves. The interplay of these reasons will determine the extent of the courts' supervisory role. This exercise is unlikely to yield a one-size-fits-all scheme of judicial supervision. A lot will depend on contingent characteristics of specific legal systems.

One might object that, even if we accepted that officials have a duty to take each other's acts into account, it would not follow that they participate in a joint activity. Why should we think of this duty as related to a joint activity? Why can't we think of the acts and decisions of others merely as constraints on the pursuit of whatever agenda a given official wishes to pursue? If his agenda is a moral agenda, and it is better served by his deferring to some extent to the exercises of power of other officials, then he has a moral duty to defer. To evaluate this objection, we need to examine whether there is a special sense of success that is associated with participation in the practice of officials in a C-L legal system, which is distinct from one official making an individual impact subject to constraints imposed by the acts of other officials. We do much the same thing to determine the existence of other joint activities. What counts as a successful joint camping trip cannot be the same as the separate successful camping trips of two people who just happen to share the same camping plot.

Overall, the relationship between courts and the legislature is indeed one of mutual commitment, and in fact probably also mutual support. This is so, first and foremost, because it is not up to either institution individually to govern. Governing in a C-L legal system is a project that they share. Within that project they have distinct roles, which complement each other. Courts display an attitude of commitment to this joint project, when they defer to the legislature. But equally they display it when they disregard or even strike down a statute passed by the legislature – assuming, of course, that they have the power to do so. For, they have a duty to defer only to those legislative contributions to the joint project that are worthy of deference according to the division of labour in force in a given C-L legal system. Besides, as we have seen, a practice regulated by separation of powers goes well, so long as it incorporates checks-and-balances mechanisms. So, even though courts, in exercising their power of constitutional review, may occasionally clash with the legislature, this does not negate their commitment to the joint project. Their role under the project is not to stay out of the legislature's way, in the same manner that the role of a chess-player is not to avoid frustrating her opponent. Thus, a legislator that sees his plan for social reform curtailed by the judiciary in the name of, say, due process rights, may well have reason to feel defeated or angry, but, if the courts have acted within their constitutional role, there is something that she can set against this feeling, namely, the recognition that they have jointly achieved the goal of governing together. Besides, many aspects of the relationship between courts and the legislature can be seen as involving mutual support. For instance, a centralised legislature could not ensure that its decisions are being implemented without a network of courts that further them when adjudicating individual cases. More generally, the roles of the two institutions are based on mutual support in the sense that they have a duty not to interfere with the exercise of each other's power, as determined by the scheme of division of labour.

Why would a natural lawyer be interested in defending a value-laden explanation of the interaction among officials along the lines suggested in the previous paragraphs? Here I shall limit myself to a couple of suggestions. First, this explanation provides an illustration of how social facts may have an impact on the content of the law in a manner compatible with the main tenets of natural law theory.[18] It thus accounts for what has been called the dynamic nature of the law. As we have seen, social facts about what the legislature has said and done in the past are relevant to determining what the judge may or may not decide in the case before him. Consequently, these social facts are also relevant to determining the judicially enforceable rights and duties of citizens.[19] Importantly, however, their relevance is sensitive to certain principles of political morality. If such principles do not make them relevant, they play no role in determining our legal rights and duties.

A second and related point is that the account offered here explains the distance between what the law requires and what morality requires, independently of the law. This is because according to it legal duty is partly determined by considerations of institutional design. Considerations of this type make our legal duties sensitive to contingent facts about the institutional history of a specific legal system. In fact, they may dictate that a judge enforce a right or duty, despite the fact that enforcing it is sub-optimal from the point of view of content.

With the outline of the main thrust of the proposal at hand, we can now turn to assess more closely its natural law credentials. In the following two sections I shall examine two suggestions that might be taken to cast doubt on these credentials; they might be taken to support the view that the proposal is implicitly committed

[18] A different illustration is provided by John Finnis; see his *Natural Law and Natural Rights* (Oxford, Oxford University Press, 1980) 284–90.

[19] I want to leave it open that there may be a separate class of legal rights and duties that are not judicially enforceable; see below.

to a positivistic understanding of law and that its natural law character comes too late in the day. The first suggestion starts from an argument made by Andrei Marmor in support of his own brand of legal conventionalism. The second takes its lead from Mark Greenberg's recent claim that underlying much of contemporary legal theory is what he calls a 'standard picture' of law.

IV LEVELS OF POSITIVISM

Andrei Marmor is one of the leading contemporary philosophers writing in the legal conventionalist tradition. His version of legal conventionalism, though, does not defend the idea that the practice of officials can be understood in terms of Bratman's model of shared cooperative activity.[20] Instead, he elaborates the idea of constitutive convention and argues that such conventions lie at the foundation of legal systems. Here, I do not take issue with Marmor's version of conventionalism. Rather, I focus on his criticism of Dworkin's famous argument against legal conventionalism in *Taking Rights Seriously*.[21] This criticism (I claim) could be replicated to apply to the proposal offered here. Showing why it would fail not only strengthens the proposal but also locates the courts-legislature relationship in a broader constitutional landscape.

Dworkin argues that Hart's conventionalist explanation of law as based on a social rule binding on officials, which is made up of a pattern of convergent behaviour and an attitude of acceptance, cannot account for the existence of widespread and reasonable disagreement in law. Disagreement negates the existence of a social rule. And yet, when judges disagree in hard cases, they argue for their own view, irrespective of the fact that it is not shared. In addition, they claim that their view better captures the law on this issue. They do not make a proposal about how the law should be developed.

In countering Dworkin's challenge, Andrei Marmor suggests that at best it makes the point that the standards applied by judges are not conventional. But it leaves untouched the conventionalist explanation of the rules defining judicial role. Surely (the argument goes) we cannot run the challenge, unless we assume the existence of such rules, which determine what makes someone a judge and what is in general terms his or her role in the legal system, never mind how they decide hard cases. We first need to determine what makes it the case that they get to be the ones who decide hard cases. On this question, arguably, Dworkin's challenge remains silent.

As Marmor puts it:

> Before judges can come to disagree about any legal issue, they must first be able to see themselves as *institutional* players, playing, as it were, a fairly structured role in an elaborate practice. Judges can only see themselves as such on the basis of the rules and conventions

[20] See A Marmor, Chapter 5 in this book.

[21] R Dworkin, *Taking Rights Seriously* (London, Duckworth, 1978) chs 2 and 3.

> that establish their role and authority as judges, namely, the rules of recognition. In short, pointing to the fact that judges often have certain disagreements about the content of the rules of recognition simply cannot prove that there are no such rules. On the contrary, we can only make sense of such disagreements on the basis of the assumption that there are rules of recognition that constitute, inter alia, the courts system and the legal authority of judges.[22]

Can a similar objection be raised against the proposal offered here? I think it is one of the strengths of the proposal offered here that it represents a plausible natural law response to Marmor's challenge. It acknowledges that theories of law must account for the normative force of standards that distinguish the institutional role of judges from that of other officials. But it insists that their force need not be thought of as stemming from any convention. Rather, it can be fully explained in terms of the considerations of political and institutional morality that underscore the joint activity of officials. It is such considerations, and the value of separation of powers that encompasses them, that identify someone as an institutional player. On this view judges do what they do because they are assigned a role within the joint activity and this role is normatively binding, insofar as it is morally appropriate that they have this role.

It may be said (as Marmor does say) that the considerations of institutional and political morality of the kind I am invoking underdetermine the content of the institutional roles assigned to judges, legislators and other officials within any given legal system. But if that is so, then they cannot provide the full normative explanation of the standards defining those roles. They leave it open that some positivist-sounding idea like a convention has to be added in, at the very least for the purpose of specifying which of the morally eligible schemes of division of labour is the one that is legally binding around here.

To respond to this argument we need to bear in mind that the joint activity of law is one that spans over time. So, the partners whose contributions bear on the determination of the institutional duty of current officials are not just their contemporaries, but also past participants, including those who sought with their decisions to shape the division of labour for the future. Think of constitutional assemblies. Decisions like those made by constitutional assemblies may help more closely to determine the content of institutional roles where, absent those decisions, abstract considerations of political morality would have left the issue underdetermined. Judges of today have (if they do) the same kind of reason to heed those decisions that they have to heed any other contribution to the joint activity of law. To elaborate, the reason is not simply the social fact that, say, there is a convention that recognises the judicial role as having a certain general content. Rather, it is the law that the judicial role has that content by virtue of the *moral* fact that this requirement is supported by the proper combination of considerations of content and institutional design, given that those decisions of constitutional significance have been made in the past. In other words, considerations of

[22] See Marmor, n 20 above, 148.

institutional design, coupled with the relevant considerations of content, render it morally appropriate that those decisions determine the content of judicial role. It is this moral fact that grounds the legal obligation of courts to follow legislative decisions or to test their constitutionality, before they can give them effect, if they do have such an obligation.

This understanding of the determinants of the judicial role also has the resources to explain the changes that the content of the role undergoes over time. It does not need to stipulate the shift from one convention to the other to explain them. Instead, it can attribute such changes to the moral relevance of the passage of time. Quite plausibly, the requirement for a working division of labour that governs the practice of officials undercuts the moral weight of decisions made at a distant point in time, even if that point is the founding moment.

V THE STANDARD PICTURE OF THE PRACTICE OF OFFICIALS

In an as yet unpublished but widely circulated and discussed paper, Mark Greenberg has sought to identify and challenge what he considers to be a widespread jurisprudential assumption.[23] He calls it the *standard picture of law*. At the heart of the standard picture lies the *command paradigm*, whereby it is the law that p simply by virtue of the fact that an authoritative pronouncement with that content has been made. The standard picture is based on two assumptions about how social facts determine the content of the law, *explanatory directness* and *atomism*. According to the former assumption, the basis of legal norms is (nothing but) authoritative say-so.[24] As Greenberg argues, 'in the complete constitutive account of the obtaining of a given legal norm . . . there are no explanatory intermediaries between an authoritative pronouncement's being made and the norm's obtaining'.[25] Norms thus created then combine to determine the content of the law. Therefore, the content of the law is not explanatorily prior to the existence of individual norms, except in the sense that individual norms may draw their legal validity from prior rules that confer upon their source law-making power, namely, the power to create norms by say-so.[26] The priority of individual norms over the content of the law is what is meant by the assumption of atomism.

Greenberg thinks that, even when (especially when) the standard picture is not explicitly articulated but is casually taken for granted, it skews one's perception of the alternatives. The alternative that Greenberg is particularly interested in sin-

[23] M Greenberg, 'The Standard Picture and its Discontents' (MS version, June 2010), available at http://papers.ssrn.com/sol3/papers.cfm?abstract_id=1103569. This paper is forthcoming in (2011) 1 *Oxford Studies in the Philosophy of Law* 39.

[24] As Greenberg puts it, 'the command creates an obligation to do what is commanded. Similarly, the content of the legal norm is what was pronounced – what we can call *the content* of the pronouncement' (ibid 47). He nevertheless concedes that commitment to the standard picture does not preclude the belief that law may be created in other peripheral ways.

[25] ibid 44.

[26] ibid 50.

gling out and dissociating from the standard picture is what he calls the *dependence view*. The dependence view says that the content of the law is one part of the *moral profile* of a society, by which Greenberg means the sum of moral rights and duties that exist in that society. More specifically, it is the part of the moral profile that 'has come to obtain in certain characteristic ways, typically as a result of actions of legal institutions such as the enactment of legislation and the adjudication of cases'.[27] So, the dependence view does not deny the impact of such actions on the content of the law. But it denies the explanation of that impact in terms of explanatory directness and atomism. The fact that the legislature has enacted a statute may well affect our moral rights and duties – the moral profile of our society – but not because legislative say-so creates norms in the explanatorily direct way suggested by the standard picture. Rather the reason is that this fact has changed the morally relevant circumstances of our society. The moral rights and duties that obtain as a result of this change may coincide with what the statute says, but they need not. Whether they do depends on the moral significance of this change, which may go beyond or fall short of the content of the statute, or in fact be very different from it. Thus, the dependence view rejects explanatory directness. Equally, it rejects atomism, in that it maintains that 'the content of the law is holistically determined because the effect of a given action by a legal participant on the moral profile depends on all the other actions by legal participants'.[28]

The standard picture lurks in all kinds of unlikely places. Perhaps, then, the proposal offered here also presupposes it. Here is how the challenge might be put. I have contended that some decisions acquire normative significance for participants in official practice, at least in part, by virtue of their provenance from a certain source, in the present case the legislature. Granted, on this proposal their normative significance is weighted depending on the credentials of the source. But this is not to disavow the standard picture completely. At best, the qualification does away with explanatory directness. Nevertheless, it leaves atomism untouched, insofar as it presupposes that the content of the law does not change (at least in the paradigmatic case) unless some institution, which by virtue of its credentials has the power to create norms, has exercised this power.

The reason such a conclusion, if sound, would be an embarrassment for the proposal offered here is that it would question its status as a plausible *alternative* to legal positivism. Perhaps, it does not entail that the proposal is in fact a variant of legal positivism. As Greenberg observes, 'SP [the standard picture] is consistent with anti-positivism'.[29] Still, 'it biases the [positivism/anti-positivism] debate towards positivism or legal realism'.[30] Arguably, the bias stings in our case as well.

I do not dispute that the view of the practice of officials induced by the standard picture is compatible with the proposal offered here. The analysis so far may actually have encouraged the association. Admittedly, it has focused on the duty of

[27] ibid 57.
[28] ibid 60.
[29] ibid 65.
[30] ibid 65.

respect courts owe legislative decisions. But, this focus was chosen for purposes of illustration. The proposal works also without reference to legislative decisions. For one thing, considerations of institutional design determine judicial duty even in the absence of legislative decisions. Take the following example. Although it may be a good idea, morally speaking, that every citizen have a right to a minimum income, I think it is rather uncontroversial that it is not the business of the courts to enforce such a right.[31] And this is so on the basis of the position that courts occupy within the joint activity, especially vis-à-vis the political branches, rather than on legislative say-so.

But isn't this just the flipside of the standard picture? It would be the law that every person has a right to a minimum income if the legislature passed a law to this effect, but, until it does, it is the law that there is no such right. Again, this may be compatible with the proposal but it is not entailed by it. We can easily imagine a variant of the proposal that says that, although courts cannot of their own initiative enforce a right to a minimum income, they may still have the power to do other things in the name of equality – that is, on the strength of a pressing consideration of content – independently of legislative action. They may, for instance, have the power to quash a legislative decision that violates equality, or extend a benefit that the legislature has given a certain class of citizens to other classes that from the point of view of equality cannot be denied it, once it has been granted to one.

We can generalise this point. According to the view of the practice of officials defended here the impact of a legislative decision on the content of the law depends on its moral significance. Its moral significance varies across different actors. As far as courts are concerned, it is also partly determined by considerations of institutional design, considerations about the relative positions of the two institutions in their common endeavour governed by the value of separation of powers. These considerations (we might say) also contribute to the moral profile of society, at least in the sense that they form part of the moral basis for the claims of citizens to specific state institutions and for legitimate uses of state coercion by those institutions. In this picture, what determines, at least in part, moral rights and duties is the role of different state actors in the joint institutional endeavour that the relevant considerations of institutional design carve out. Equally, it is this role that makes legislative decisions relevant to the moral rights and duties of judges, to the extent that they are relevant. But it does not only make legislative decisions relevant. As was shown in the example of the previous paragraph, a number of parameters may bear on judicial duty, which qualify the relevance of legislative decisions or indeed generate duties even in the absence of such decisions. In this sense, then, the proposal is not committed to either explanatory directness or atomism. Hence, although it is true that the proposal does not offer an argument against legal positivism, it is nevertheless a genuine alternative to it.

[31] Larry Sager offers a thoughtful and sustained argument for such a limit to judicial power; see L Sager, *Justice in Plainclothes* (New Haven, CT, Yale University Press, 2004) chs 6–8.

VI CONCLUSION

It is a truism that the fact that we live under the law makes a difference to our rights and duties. Importantly, law also makes a difference to the rights and duties of officials. This chapter has sought to specify the latter kind of difference in a way consistent with the main tenets of robust versions of natural law. It has done so in the name of a philosophical programme that aims to recast the debate between natural law theory and positivism. To this effect, it has explicated the normative implications of the fact that, at least in some legal systems, officials participate in a joint activity, under the auspices of which they are assigned different roles. Its main thrust is that by participating in this activity officials have a duty to govern together. This is a moral duty, because and insofar as the joint activity is underlain by an important value of political morality – separation of powers.

III

Law, Normativity and Autonomy

8

Law and Obligation: Outlines of a Kantian Argument

STEFANO BERTEA*

I INTRODUCTION

IT IS COMMONPLACE, at least in mainstream jurisprudence, for the notion of obligation to play a central role within the law understood as an authoritative structure. Indeed, an essential component of what is ordinarily meant by having or claiming authority consists in having or claiming the legitimate power to modify the normative standing of those subject to the authority. This means that one of the ways (though certainly not the only way) in which a legal institution can affect the status of subjects under the law is, at least in certain cases, by creating obligations for them. This being the case, law and obligation are regarded as conceptually connected even by those legal theorists who, quite justifiably, refuse to reduce the law to a merely obligation-imposing device and instead opt for a conception under which the normativity of law encompasses more than just obligations, and legal systems do not simply give rise to duties but also confer powers, grant permissions and attribute immunities, just to name a few of the normative statuses distinct from obligation. For similar reasons, insofar as an important part of the legal domain has to do with rules prescribing certain courses of conduct, key legal statuses can only be expressed through the use of such notions as those of obligation and duty, along with their counterpart, the notion of a right. And these notions make it necessary to consider issues relative to the content and origin of obligation as it applies to law. Therefore, a theory of

* This chapter is part of a five-year project entitled 'The Constitution of Globalization', funded by an Odysseus research grant of the Research Foundation, Flanders (FWO). I wish to express my indebtedness to the participants at the workshop on 'Normativity in Law and Morality', 3–4 June 2009, Antwerp, for their comments on the paper from which this chapter originates. Also, this essay has benefited from the feedback received at the seminar organised by the Centre for the Study of Law in Society at the Law School of the University of Sheffield, 26 October 2009. In particular, I would like to express my gratitude to Tawhida Amhed, Richard Collins, Dimitrios Kyritsis and Mark Taylor for their insightful and constructive critical comments. A special thanks is owed to Robert Alexy, Sylvie Delacroix, Cristina Lafont, Filippo Valente and Marcus Willaschek for their helpful remarks on previous versions of this chapter. Needless to say, responsibility for the views expressed herein, as well as for any errors of form or content, rests solely with me.

obligation features as a central element of jurisprudence, especially when this is understood as the philosophical study of the concept of law and the other legal concepts that are taken to be fundamental and common to legal systems having a comparable degree of maturity and organisation.

Now, an integral part of any theory of obligation in law aspiring to achieve any degree of comprehensiveness will have to be an explanation of the source of the obligatory force of law, that is, an elucidation of what enables law to apply to us and hold us bound to do anything, and hence why legal statements should be taken to be binding.[1] In working toward such an explanation we will have to identify the grounds on which to endow law with an obligatory status, this by addressing questions such as 'Why ought one to do what the law requires?' or 'Whence does the obligatory force of legal demands derive?' or, again, 'What makes the law binding?', which involves showing how obligation makes its way into the practice of law, or showing what the obligation-imposing capacity of law rests on and where it comes from.

These questions only provide the background for this chapter and will not be dealt with in an exhaustive way. My aim here is thus very much scaled down with respect to such a broader architecture, for I will only discuss some preliminary notions that can profitably be used in setting up an argument on which basis to construct a foundation for the obligation-imposing capacity of law. The argument I have in mind is rooted in the Kantian tradition of practical philosophy, and it accordingly proceeds from the belief that if we are to adequately explain the connection between law and obligation, we will have to take up some contemporary discussions of Kant's conception of humanity as the source of the normativity of practical reason. This belief in turn rests on the view that law and legal obligation enter into a special relationship with practical reason and with the normativity of practical reason, respectively, which is to say that law is being constructed here as a special case of practical reason, and so the normativity of law – a central part of which is its obligation-imposing capacity – is consequently being constructed as a special case of the normativity of practical reason. This is the thesis of the conceptual continuity between law and practical reason, a thesis that makes it possible to regard the normativity of law and that of practical reason as having the same foundation. Indeed, as a subset of practical reason, law must naturally be conceived as having its own distinct substance, sphere of application, and structure, but by the same token it must also be conceived as having its source in practical reason, and that precisely as an instantiation of practical reason. The law may differ from the other areas of practical reason in a number of important ways, but

[1] This proposition reflects the belief that no study of obligation in law can be regarded as complete unless it includes an account of how legal obligation can be grounded. Yet this is hardly a matter of general acceptance among legal theorists, some of whom deny the importance of such a foundation and claim that obligation can exhaustively be explained without having to enter into foundational issues. This seems to me the position found in J Coleman, 'Conventionality and Normativity' in E Villanueva (ed), *Legal and Political Philosophy* (Amsterdam, Rodopi, 2002) 157–75 and J Raz, *The Practice of Value* (Oxford, Oxford University Press, 2003) 138–50.

it nevertheless belongs to the same genus with the other areas and so shares with them the same foundation. There is ultimately no distinction, then, that can be made between the source of the normativity of practical reason and the source of the normativity of law. Hence, if we are to properly account for the foundation of the bindingness of law – a bindingness making up one component in the overall normativity of law – we will have to do so accounting for the normativity of practical reason: the former account will have to draw on, in a way that makes it derivative from, the latter.

That gives the essential rationale for the discussion that follows, where I confine myself to laying the *groundwork* for a Kantian argument for the foundation of the obligatoriness of law. I will do so by fleshing out a notion of action derived from the notion of human agency, in turn understood, along the lines of Kant's own treatment, as the source of the normativity of practical reason. While in defending this foundation of the obligatoriness of law I hope to achieve something that is Kantian in spirit, I do not mean this to be simply a restatement of his view. And so this will not be a study on Kant, since I am more interested in a theoretical approach attentive and sympathetic to Kant's practical philosophy – and in particular to his treatment of obligation – than in an exegesis of his work. This in turn makes my interest in Kant's practical philosophy systematic, rather than hermeneutical or exegetical, the reason for it being that while I believe there are some deep insights in Kant's account of obligation, it is not an account we can use in its original version, since it comes bundled with a disputable metaphysics serving as the basis on which the connection is established between normativity and humanity. Instead of defending the metaphysical view, I will defend the connection by offering a pragmatic, or action-centred, reinterpretation of Kant's notion of humanity. The view resulting from this shift in perspective amounts to a kind of revisionary Kantian approach: Kantian because it preserves the key insights central to Kant's foundation of the normativity of practical reason; revisionary because it recasts in pragmatic terms the concept of humanity that Kant posits as the notion grounding practical normativity – we no longer have a metaphysical attempt to define the essence of humanity, but a pragmatic one to single out the conceptual features of human agency.

II A CONSTRUCTION OF HUMAN AGENCY

Kant devotes large tracts of his writing on practical philosophy to the systematic study of obligation, and for him any moral project must centrally be concerned with explaining the binding force of practical reason.[2] In his foundational works

[2] Indeed, in his *Enquiry concerning the Clarity of the Principles of Natural Theology and Ethics* (in GB Kerferd and DE Walford (eds), *Kant: Selected Pre-Critical Writings and Correspondence with Beck* (Manchester, Manchester University Press, 1968 (1763)), AK 2:298) Kant defined obligation as 'the primary concept' in ethics, and so it would remain from that point onward.

on practical philosophy,[3] Kant locates the source of the normativity of practical reason in humanity, which he understands to be one of three fundamental capacities, or 'original predispositions', of agents, the others being animality and personality.[4] Animality consists in the instincts and impulses by which animal beings preserve their existence, and personality consists in the ability to give oneself over to the moral law. Humanity instead singles out the rational capacities, a set of capacities enabling us to represent an end to ourselves fully consciously and to deliberate on how to achieve such an end. In humanity we have the ability to select not only the proper means to a given end but also the end itself, by comparing and systematising different ends, thus forming an overall idea of our well-being.[5] Humanity can thus be described as an all-purpose ability – a condition necessary to the pursuit of any aim regardless of what that may be – and this is the feature that makes it an end in itself, not subordinate but prior to other ends, and a capacity we cannot give up without impairing our very possibility of acting purposefully.[6]

This approach outlines a conception of humanity conceived as the source of the normative dimension of practical reason, a conception deeply ingrained in Kant's transcendental idealism and, in particular, in his questionable metaphysical distinction between appearances, or phenomena, and things-in-themselves, or noumena. The conceptual dependence of humanity on Kant's peculiar metaphysics is widely perceived as being at odds with what is now the accepted scientific and naturalistic worldview, and so it may be seen as a serious obstacle to an acceptance of Kant's overall account of the foundation of the normativity of practical reason. Yet this stumbling block should not be a reason to dismiss Kant's study altogether, for it contributes too importantly to advancing our understanding of the foundation of the normativity of practical reason. The core of this account can be rescued, provided that it goes through a revision, and this is going to take a twofold move. First, the normativity of practical reason will have to be grounded in a conception of humanity that, unlike Kant's conception, is unencumbered by disputable metaphysical assumptions and yet, like Kant's conception, is necessary and universally valuable, at least for all practical purposes; second, it should be clarified how a conception of humanity unburdened by Kant's metaphysics can endow practical reason with any obligatory force. In the rest of this essay I will focus exclusively on the first part of this two-pronged rescue strategy and leave the second part for a later occasion.

[3] The source of normativity is discussed principally in I Kant, *Groundwork of the Metaphysics of Morals* (Indianapolis, Bobbs-Merrill, 1959 (1785)) and in I Kant, *Critique of Practical Reason* (Indianapolis, IN, Bobbs-Merrill, 1956 (1788)). Further remarks are found in I Kant, *Religion within the Boundaries of Mere Reason* (New York, Harper, 1902 (1793–94)); I Kant, *Anthropology from a Pragmatic Point of View* (The Hague, Martinus Nijhoff, 1974 (1798)); and I Kant, *Metaphysics of Morals* (Cambridge, Cambridge University Press, 1996 (1797)).

[4] These three fundamental capacities are defined in Kant, *Religion within the Boundaries of Mere Reason*, n 3 above, AK 6:26–28. Further discussion is provided in A Wood, *Kant's Ethical Thought* (Cambridge, Cambridge University Press, 1999) 118–22.

[5] See Kant, *Anthropology from a Pragmatic Point of View*, n 3 above, AK 7:183–86.

[6] See Kant, *Groundwork of the Metaphysics of Morals*, n 3 above, AK 4:428–29.

In this effort – in grounding the normativity of practical reason in an idea independent of Kant's metaphysics – I will proceed by putting forward a pragmatic reinterpretation of Kant's concept of humanity. From a pragmatic perspective, the concept of humanity summarises the predicates someone must have, or must be attributed, in order to be deemed capable of action and hence to be recognised as an acting self.[7] The properties of humanity (on the pragmatic view of the idea being developed here) are thus capacities without which an individual would be incapable of action, such that to bracket them would be to deny one's distinctive status as an acting subject, as an individual having a specific existence in the practical sphere. These capacities can thus be understood as encapsulating a system of action-enabling conditions, a set of requirements absent which no action could take place.[8] This means that they mark out a pragmatic unit – the subject understood as a doer of deeds, or as an agent – and one that is independent of Kant's metaphysics and does not rely on the questionable notion of noumena.

From here on, the difference between Kant's own view of humanity and the pragmatic reading of that notion just introduced will be signalled by reserving 'humanity' for Kant's notion of humankind and calling 'human agency' the pragmatic unit by which I am proposing to revise Kant's original idea. Like humanity, human agency singles out a general capacity; but unlike humanity, which is grounded in the metaphysical views underpinning transcendental idealism, human agency is an action-centred notion compatible with different, though certainly not all, metaphysical views.[9]

The strategy I follow in working toward such a pragmatic understanding of human agency has its point of departure in action. I accordingly start out defining the human agent by the range of necessary capacities making for the possibility of action: a human agent is a person capable of action as framed by the relevant

[7] The word 'action' is being used here as a term of art to designate not just anything done generally, but a specific sort of conduct, as explained in the next section.

[8] The idea of human agency typically describes adult humans with no serious disabilities, impairments or dysfunctions. But the capacities this idea singles out as here discussed are not distinctive to the human species (they may well be found in non-humans, too, to a greater or lesser extent), nor, for that matter, are they necessary for someone to be regarded as a human being. Hence, nothing about this particular idea of human agency should be taken to imply that human beings *alone* are capable of action (in the strict sense of *action* shortly to be clarified) or that *all* human beings have this capacity. Human agency, therefore, does not distinguish humans from non-humans: the traits of human agency do have a necessary role, to be sure, but as essential preconditions for action in the practical sphere rather than as preconditions for someone to be considered for membership among humans.

[9] It must be pointed out in this respect, as Robert Alexy correctly notes in Chapter 9, in a critique of my earlier remarks (S Bertea, *The Normative Claim of Law* (Oxford, Hart, 2009) 171–224), that my pragmatic conception is not metaphysically neutral, for it takes up and is grounded in a number of metaphysical notions, such as freedom of choice and causality. Hence, the pragmatic unit described through the capacities enabling and defining action cannot be made to hold up independently of any metaphysical support and does not make sense without some metaphysics to go along with it. What I am proposing here, however, is not an anti-metaphysical stance. I am only recognising that the metaphysical assumptions grounding Kant's account of normativity are strong ones indeed and debatable; and from that recognition I take away the idea that we should strive for an account whose underlying metaphysics are thinner and hence more palatable, in such a way that one need not subscribe to Kant's transcendental idealism as a precondition for considering the argument and conclusions presented here.

enabling conditions. The reason why action suggests itself here as a natural starting point in constructing human agency has to do with the way I am approaching the whole question of the normativity of law, namely, as an instantiation of the normativity of practical reason: practical reason is reason as it applies to action, hence the strategy of constructing human agency as the outcome of an exercise that begins with an inquiry into action. Such an exercise is constructive, to be sure, but it is not arbitrary, since it proceeds under the constraints framed by the overall aim of the study within which it is carried out, this aim being that of establishing the foundation out of which arises the requiredness of the demands of practical reason. Because at least some of these demands – most typically the demands of critical rational morality – are widely acknowledged to be necessarily and universally binding, the defining properties of human agency must analogously hold universally and necessarily; that is, every agent must embody these properties or must otherwise be led to embody them by force of rational argument and so must acknowledge them, however much only implicitly. This in turn makes human agency a transcendental concept: the capacities constitutive of human agency are capacities having universal application among all acting selves.[10] Human agency will thus be constructed here as the outcome of *a set of capacities having a necessary role in the practical sphere*: these capacities can accordingly be described as essential in the practical sense that (i) they are independent of subjective dispositions, personal incentives and individual peculiarities, and (ii) without them we would not be able to carry out actions, and they must therefore be shared by anyone capable of acting.

A Action

It was just explained that action is being used here as the entry point for a pragmatic construction of human agency: this makes agency derivative from action, and action an idea consequently requiring further clarification. As a generic term, *action* is ordinarily taken to mean anything done: any deed, act, or conduct engaged in. In this generic sense, *action* is clearly a rather loose term that can be used in reference to any number of different things so long as they involve something being done. But the meaning of *action* I am interested in is technical and therefore more specific, referring as it does to a paradigmatic case of doing, a privileged class designating what may be considered conduct par excellence. This then brings up the question, how do we go about selecting this special class of deeds that involve our doing something in a paradigmatic way that makes it count as action proper? This question I propose to answer through a comparative strat-

[10] This comports with the transcendental approach, which consists in singling out features that can be argued to be necessary for thought and action, and in deriving therefrom the truth of other necessary features whose necessity is not immediately apparent. The resulting set should ideally capture features both necessary and distinctive, such as apply invariably across an entire group and exclusively to that group.

egy: precisely because action singles out a special class, I will briefly consider different kinds of conduct and compare their main features so as to finally arrive at full-fledged action.[11]

We work from the simplest case, the most elemental, to the paradigm case; and the most basic form of doing from which to start is what might be called *spontaneous conduct*, namely, uncontrolled conduct that is neither intentional nor driven by any purpose, examples being blushing, hiccupping and blinking. While such spontaneous movements do count as action in a broad sense – they involve someone doing something – they lack two fundamental characteristics of less elemental kinds of acting, these being purpose and control. Purposeless and uncontrolled acts tend to simply 'happen' or 'come about' in an event-like manner, in that the subject with whom they originate is playing a passive role. This gives only a vague idea of what an actor is. Spontaneous conduct therefore falls quite short of the paradigm for action.

For something that will more closely resemble full-fledged action, then, we have to at least introduce purpose and control into our doing. Purpose and control narrow our range down to a kind of conduct that might be called *reflexive*, namely, conduct dictated by our reflexes, as illustrated, for example, by my realising that my glasses are falling, thereupon swinging my arm out in an attempt to catch them before they hit the floor and break. In reflexive conduct, someone does something for a purpose and controls it, rather than being controlled by it or passively receiving it. As much as reflexive conduct may be active, however, in the sense of its requiring an active role on our part, it is not yet fully intentional. And, absent an intentional element, conduct can be said to *precede* our acceptance, knowledge or endorsement of what is done. True, the act is one we may end up appreciating in hindsight, with consequences we may end up welcoming and may even have willed had we only had foreknowledge of them at the time of the act, but at that time, neither the act nor its consequences could have been genuinely intended.

Reflexive conduct can thus be described as controlled and purposive yet unintentional, a characterisation that sets the stage for the next level, where we find a doing or any movement or gesture that is controlled and purposive as well as intended. In contrast to the kind of conduct just described as reflexive, this form of doing does come about as a result of a thinking, or a pondered moment of decision, and can therefore be described as not only purposely but also knowingly carried out, actually meaning to do whatever it was that we did. Conduct at this level I will therefore call *reactive*, since its mechanics are those of an intentional response to a certain state of affairs, a response driven by forces internal to us. These forces I will call incentives, a broad term which I take to include any number of pattern-like instinctive impulses, feelings, drives and desires. Reactive

[11] As this idea of full-fledged action suggests, the comparative strategy here adopted is not blind but is rather guided by a sort of benchmark, what was just referred to as a paradigmatic case of doing. This manner of proceeding is standard in action theory: see eg D Velleman, 'Replies to Discussion on *The Possibility of Practical Reason*' (2004) 121 *Philosophical Studies* 277, 281–83.

conduct can thus be understood as anything one does owing to an interaction between one's incentives and the environment. The environment functions as either an inducement or a deterrent, as the case may be, and correspondingly engages or disengages someone's incentives, with this person behaving in response to the stimuli coming from the environment (a response thus secured by the interaction between the environment and the incentives). Reactive conduct thus consists in an adaptive reaction to the conditions in the world around us, a doing guided by our perception of our surroundings.[12]

As much as control, purpose and intention may be central to our practical mode of existence, and may account for a large part of it, they do not account for the whole of it nor, for that matter, do they make up the core of what I consider to be action par excellence. In order to get there, we need a further, accreting element whose incorporation yields what I will call *principled conduct*, for it consists in conduct that depends essentially on our adopting general standards, rules, policies, guidelines, plans, and the like, which might cumulatively be referred to as principles, understood as models that we reflect on and choose to adopt. So described, a principle corresponds to a Kantian *maxim*, not to a Kantian *law*; that is, a principle is not necessarily an *objective* standard of conduct, one that any clear-thinking, rational person should acknowledge, but rather a standard that not everyone can be expected to embrace or find sensible: a principle is in this sense a *subjective* guideline. While the standards characterising a principled form of conduct are not meant to apply objectively and universally, they nonetheless function as general practical models, namely, as models protected from the pressure of the incentives: principles can withstand such pressure and so are not subject to incentivised readjusting, nor will they be sidestepped just because we have an incentive to do so when choosing a course of conduct. This makes principled conduct largely autonomous from the incentives, and hence not necessitated or essentially driven by them. In principled conduct, we do not simply react or adapt to a stimulus, situation or environment that engages a more or less instinctive or deep-seated drive: we instead proceed from an idea or model, and it is this idea or model (rather than an incentive) that informs and ultimately determines our decisions as to the conduct to be undertaken. Stated in slightly different terms, principled conduct is not subject to the immediacy and occasional nature of the incentives but is instead guided by a broader range of considerations. As much as principles may be subjective, they cannot be reduced to the incentives and are therefore independent of the contingent play of stimulus and response: the incentives are closely tied to stimuli in a way that makes them utterly contingent; standards-based conduct, by contrast, can chart its own course and stay true to it, and in this specific and limited sense it can be considered non-contingent, or not ultimately determined for us by the incentives we have when it comes time to

[12] Christine Korsgaard has expressed the same thought by noting that reactive conduct 'requires both an intentional movement and a representation or conception of the world' (C Korsgaard, *Self-Constitution* (Oxford, Oxford University Press, 2009) 98).

act.[13] Precisely for the same reason, principles can be said to define the kind of person one is, not just the kind of conduct one is led to have under the influence of some incentive: they are an element of personhood and character, constituents of one's practical identity.[14]

In summary, if instead of acting on the basis of whatever particular feeling or desire makes the strongest demand on us when the occasion arises or when a stimulus elicits that feeling or desire, we choose to act in view of the long-term and general consideration of what seems best all-around, in such a way that the extemporary pressure of an incentive can be recognised and overcome, or otherwise taken into account consistently with the general standard we are acting from, then we will have principled conduct. This can be described as that class of conduct which is determined not just by circumstance but also, and indeed primarily, by a reasoned principle, something that enables us to take into view the larger picture of what lies beyond this or that circumstance: this is conduct by action rather than by reaction.[15]

The difference between action and reaction is crucial to the entire discussion and so needs to be articulated further. Reactive conduct – though it may be controlled, purposive and intentional – is really contingent conduct, on account of two related dependencies which characterise it: the first of these is a dependence on the incentives, which at this level ultimately decide what we end up doing, and the second is a dependence on particular circumstances, meaning that the situation before us at the very moment of acting functions as a force in its own right in shaping our conduct. It is the influence of these two forces, one of them internal (incentive) and the other external (circumstance), that determines the resulting conduct. Not so in the case of principled conduct, which differs from reactive conduct in both of these respects. This is because, where principled conduct is concerned, action proceeds the way it does on the basis of an assessment of the situation at hand, an assessment made in light of general standards devised and adopted beforehand. And this feature breaks the tight bond between stimulus and response at work in reactive conduct. Once principles are incorporated into our conduct, such conduct will no longer be dependent on either incentive or circumstance: in

[13] The point of so limiting the non-contingency here is to avoid setting up absolutes, with any stark contrast between contingency and absolute necessity, or full independence from considerations based on the senses. Conduct is non-contingent insofar as it is driven by an element that possesses some degree of stability over time and stands above, as it were, the flow of changing incentives operating in different circumstances. A principle, in other words, is non-contingent in the sense that once we forge or select one and resolve to live by it, making it integral to our conduct, it will inform such conduct on every occasion where it applies, until we forsake the principle for another one or revise it in light of some broad-based considerations.

[14] This point is argued with great clarity in T van Willigenburg, 'Being Bound by Reasons: Practical Identity and the Authority of Self-Legislation' in M Sie *et al* (eds), *Reasons of One's Own* (Aldershot, Ashgate, 2004) 39–55 at 47–48.

[15] The same idea (of principled conduct) has been expressed by J Raz, *Engaging Reason* (Oxford, Oxford University Press, 1999) 38–42, through a distinction between control and guidance: principled conduct is not just controlled but guided, and we are said to *guide* our conduct when, in addition to *controlling* our incentives (which essentially amounts to a *constraint* on action, however effective it may be) we look beyond and impart a broader sense of *direction* to whatever it is that we decide to do.

the former sense, our conduct can be described as proactive rather than reactive; in the latter sense, we as acting persons can be said to play a guiding role, in that a standard is brought to bear in our assessment of the situation we are responding to, and this standard is independent of what that situation would otherwise suggest or encourage. And a standard is something that, on the one hand, we follow regardless of what our incentives impel us to do and, on the other, has usually been worked out and endorsed beforehand, that is, before the situation arises which calls those incentives into play. This is not to say that action proceeds independent of the incentives at the root of reactive conduct, or even bypasses such incentives, as no such thing can be achieved, short of our becoming automata or creatures devoid of the sensible component of human subjectivity. So, instead of bypassing this reactive component, principled conduct takes it into account and incorporates it as a necessary ingredient of human sensibility, but an ingredient that can be abstracted from and be fashioned into something other than raw impulse, in such a way as to enable us to act in accord with a standard. Principles, then, embody a kind of generality that makes them irreducible to the incentives, and in fact their point is often enough to counter the forces of incentive. This brings into the equation a mediating element that loosens the strict connection by which an external stimulus prompts in us a corresponding reaction by the engagement or disengagement of a certain incentive. Unlike reactive conduct, then, action – its principled counterpart – is adaptive by mediation rather than by mere reaction. And while agents engaged in action do respond to incentive, this reactive component does not have the upper hand, for it can be outweighed or displaced by general standards, which in this sense function as the driving force, thus making this kind of conduct something that, relying once more on a Kantian vocabulary, we can describe more as 'willed' than as 'wished', more as standard-driven than as responsive to incentive and bound by circumstance.

So described, principled conduct differs from reactive conduct by bringing into play a further element – a principle or general standard – that mediates between stimulus and response, and gives a fuller measure of character, if nothing else because it opens up a space in which we can choose to act differently from the way in which occasional incentives might dictate given the situation at hand. And it is this further element that introduces the paradigmatic form which I am calling action. The distinguishing trait in this respect is that principled conduct, or action, by virtue of its incorporating general standards which actively guide conduct, is not just something we *attribute* to someone but something this person *performs*: attribution is an external relation; performance, by contrast, is an internal relation enabling us to generate action properly so called, whose distinction from all other sorts of conduct lies in its being essentially rooted in a standard or principle that (a) we actively choose and (b) guides us in the practical sphere. What drives action is not an incentive but a principle, and though in either case the conduct in question can be said to spring from within, only in the latter case does it require a conscious effort to reason about what we are doing and to act accordingly (and only in this latter case can we be said to be performers of action rather than receptacles for whatever stimuli might come our way and whatever conduct that can result in).

To sum up, I have argued in this section that we have a general sense of doing (conduct at large) and a specific sense of doing (principled conduct), the latter delimiting a form I call action proper, in which we act with intent and in such a way as to be responsive to and guided by standards we devise depending on how we represent to ourselves our own inner drives and the environment. This makes action a proactive form of doing, meaning that the doing is responsive to the incentives and the environment in a mediated way. It is only in this stricter sense that the term *action* will be understood as relevant to the discussion that follows, and it will have to be so understood unless specified otherwise.

B Human Agency

On the pragmatic approach taken here, a human agent is anyone capable of action. This capacity for action we have as human agents (which really is a complex of capacities) is such that we can do more than just react to stimuli and the environment: we can engage in conduct framed in light of general standards providing guidance; which is to say that we have an ability to act in ways not dictated by incentive or circumstance, and hence an ability to give ourselves a sense of possibility and direction that would not otherwise be available to us. Such principled conduct is conduct we perform (precisely on account of its requiring on our part that we act on the basis of principles), and it is the complex of capacities making it possible for us to so act that defines and structures human agency as an action-centred notion.[16] Human agency is thus an ability to perform action, such that if we can perform action, we owe it to our possessing certain dispositional capacities (dispositional in the sense that, except for any interfering factors, they come into play whenever the relevant occasion arises). These dispositional capacities function as prerequisites or preconditions for action, and in this sense they are constitutive of human agency (understood as a pragmatic notion), in that no action, and hence no acting person, would be possible without them. Let us see, then, how human agency can be characterised through these necessary enabling capacities.

The first of these basic capacities can be invoked by considering that general standards – the distinctive traits of action as just defined – cannot be worked out by a reliance on perception alone, that is, on an ability to receive sensory data from the environment and identify them as being of one sort or another. If we are to frame practical principles or devise plans of action, indeed if we are to base our

[16] It should emerge from this formulation that human agency is a *capacity* for action rather than the action itself, the done deed, a conduct performed. This is consistent with our sometimes acting by mere reaction to whatever stimulus excites an incentive. In fact, what is essential to human agency is the ability to act from a principle or standard, and hence the ability break the bond between stimulus and reaction that seems to assert itself as the default mode of conduct.

conduct on any sort of general standard we set for ourselves, we need to be able to have a representation of the world more articulated than that which mere perception makes possible, meaning that it will not suffice to process external stimuli and respond to them in a reactive or spontaneous way: it will also be necessary to reflect on these stimuli. Hence the first precondition of action – a capacity for reflection, or *reflectivity*.

Reflectivity is the general capacity to think before we act and so to take a critical standpoint from which to assess a situation. Reflectivity provides a mediating element by which we are enabled to step back and have a perspective on the situation before us, in such a way that we are not boxed into the blind mechanism of stimulus and reaction. Our reflective capacity enables us to respond to the promptings of the environment not simply by yielding to our likings and desires but by taking into account standards we endorse. As Connie Rosati puts it, a reflecting self 'comes to dissociate herself from some of her desires, motivations, and traits, while identifying with others. This capacity to step back, to engage in self-reflection, gives persons a kind of freedom from identity with their immediate activities or their immediate motivational tendencies'.[17] It is these standards that offer the standpoint making it possible to evaluate – to reflect on – all the forces, both internal and external, which make a claim on us here and now. So, instead of doing what seems most appealing (because most likely to satisfy an instant incentive) or most natural (because the situation makes it seem that way), we can make it so that these forces are not necessarily constraining; that is, we can bring to bear a standpoint in light of which other practical possibilities for action become apparent that we can choose to follow.

But it takes more than reflectivity to account for the whole of what enables us to engage in action, and so for what is distinctive about human agency. In fact, reflectivity links up conceptually with other capacities that derive from reflectivity itself (or from some aspects thereof). This is because reflectivity, in enabling us to reflect on our conduct, gives us as well an ability to reflect on our *selves*. In turn, self-reflection gives us *self-consciousness*, a turning inward on oneself and one's inner states. And self-consciousness takes two connected but conceptually independent forms of awareness: on the one hand, an *awareness of one's self as composite*, as made up of mutually irreducible components; on the other hand, an *awareness of the self as an individuality*, existing as such in distinction to other persons or selves. We should therefore want to take a closer look at self-consciousness in both of its components.[18]

Self-consciousness enables each of us to see that even though the self functions as a whole, in unity, it does not form a single, undifferentiated substance but is rather compound, its components being our different incentives (the instincts,

[17] C Rosati, 'Naturalism, Normativity, and the Open Question Argument' (1995) 29 *Nous* 46, 61.

[18] Self-consciousness is considered a distinctive element of human agents in Korsgaard, n 12 above, 109–32, where the subject is treated extensively, and my own treatment of it here owes much to Korsgaard's philosophical account of the self and the idea of self-constitution. But this should not be taken to suggest that Korsgaard would endorse my reading of her texts.

impulses, desires, drives, and so on). And through this discovery we come to appreciate that the unity of the self consists not in a state given to us but in a construction, in a composition and synthesis by which we work together our multiple elements. These elements exert on us forces that drive our conduct in different directions not necessarily compatible or coherent with one another. Hence the synthesis needed to achieve continuity of action: we will not have any coherent conduct unless we can reduce to unity (or at least to a working whole) the forces operating within our selves.[19] Unity is something to achieve which we must prioritise, and prioritise consciously, establishing among the elements of the self a ranking on which basis to determine what course of conduct we should take on any given occasion.[20] This effort in turn requires reasoning and deliberation. For in order to prioritise the constituents of the self, we must take into account not only our raw instinctual powers but also the resulting course of conduct and what it leads to – the advantages and disadvantages it carries – thus taking the larger picture into view. This requires some kind of reasoning, a weighing of the reasons for and against conducting ourselves in this or that way.[21]

Human agents thus have a capacity for reasoned conduct. But while this capacity can ultimately be said to originate in reflectivity, it moves beyond that point. To wit, as much as the capacity for reasoned conduct essentially requires the self-consciousness by which we can reflect on the components of the self, it cannot thereby be reduced to such reflectivity. Reflectivity, in other words, may well enable us to reflect on the pull of the incentives, but with the capacity for reasoned conduct we can go further and remake those incentives into reasons. This further capacity I will call *rationality as spontaneity*, using a terminology – spontaneity – introduced by Kant, and I accordingly mean by *spontaneity* a responsiveness to reasons:[22] this makes rationality as spontaneity our ability to heed, grasp and respond to reasons by working with, processing and acting from them. Spontaneity enables us to recognise general standards and take them into account as determinants of conduct by building them into our general framework of action and accordingly giving them the proper practical weight. It is therefore through rationality as spontaneity that some of the forces bearing on action are endowed with

[19] On this requirement, calling for unity of action, see Korsgaard, n 12 above, 18–26.

[20] On the need to prioritise, see Korsgaard, n 12 above, 107–08.

[21] On this need to reason and deliberate, see ibid 120–21.

[22] ‘Rationality’ is a term too abstract to be informative in its own right; hence the need to narrow down its meaning and content with the qualifier ‘as spontaneity’. But what this is also meant to do, as before, is to underscore the Kantian roots of my account. For Kant, spontaneity is the broad capacity to determine (or resolve) to act on the basis of general principles, be they subjective maxims or objective laws; and that differs from autonomy, which instead is the more specific capacity to determine one’s will independently of standards informed by the senses: autonomy involves the *moral* use of reason, while spontaneity involves moral as well as prudential considerations. In Kantian spontaneity, in other words, action is *underdetermined* by the senses, in that these affect but do not fully determine action: they are not a necessitating force with respect to action. Only by removing their force altogether do you get autonomy, correspondingly understood by Kant as full independence from the senses, whose role in autonomy is reduced to nothing: not only do they not *determine* action, they do not in any way *factor* into it, either. For an insightful treatment of Kant’s notions of autonomy vis-à-vis spontaneity, see H Allison, *Idealism and Freedom* (Cambridge, Cambridge University Press, 1996) 129–42.

specific force or a distinctive significance and are prioritised over other influences. Thus, although spontaneity cannot stay the forces of incentive, and so cannot deny either our receptivity to the senses or our being affected by them, for these forces still operate within the self and can therefore tilt action this way or that, it does free us from a strict dependence on such forces, by giving us the power not to take them with pre-assigned weights, and so ultimately the power to choose whether or not to be guided by the incentives. The pressure exerted on us by our incentives is not to be equated with an effective cause compelling us to act as the incentives themselves indicate: the relation at play is not one of causation but is rather akin to a proposal for action, one that we can filter and fashion into principle by synthesising and unifying the medley of items making up the proposal. In this way, spontaneity makes it possible to understand general standards as the genuine ultimate basis of action, and we can be described as the source of our own conduct in such a way that *we* – rather than our incentives – ultimately determine what we do, by making choices and hence determining the kinds of persons we end up being.[23]

In summary, spontaneity is the capacity that enables us to incorporate and appropriate the incentives in such a way as to turn them into reasons for action. This means that the incentives will not properly *determine* conduct for someone having a capacity for spontaneity but will rather function as ingredients in a complex out of which a standard will be forged.[24] Sense-driven forces can in this sense be said only to *influence* conduct (without determining it outright), and it is rational spontaneity that makes it possible to so temper these forces: for all that we may always fall subject to our incentives, as spontaneous agents we can equally well achieve an independence from them, meaning that we need not and do not come under any causal necessity deterministically shaping our conduct based on what our incentives dictate. This is to say that we as spontaneous agents can respond non-reactively to the immediate promptings of circumstance and incentive (the environment and the senses), and can do so because we can bring into play standards in light of which to critically assess the situation framed by such promptings. In other words, we have an ability to act in a reasoned way – we can act from reasons ultimately grounded in standards, rather than from reasons plainly reduced to incentives – and this capacity (spontaneity) I account to be a distinctive property of action, and so an essential part of human agency.

The second form of self-consciousness is that by which we gain an awareness of our own individuality, that is, of our distinct existence as individuals apart from other individuals. This awareness enables us to distinguish our own determinants

[23] As C Korsgaard, *The Sources of Normativity* (Cambridge, Cambridge University Press, 1996) 93, puts it, 'I perceive, and I find myself with a powerful impulse to believe. But I back up and bring that impulse into view and then I have a certain distance. Now the impulse doesn't dominate me'. For further elaborations on this theme, see Korsgaard, *Self-Constitution*, n 12 above, 109–32.

[24] This thesis parallels, on a pragmatic level, the metaphysical stance that Henry Allison calls the incorporation thesis. See especially H Allison, *Kant's Theory of Freedom* (Cambridge, Cambridge University Press, 1990) 35–41 and H Allison, *Idealism and Freedom* (Cambridge, Cambridge University Press, 1996) 109–14.

of action from those we might call heteronomous, the former being the kind issuing from our own choice, and the latter the kind that gets imposed on us, not only by the combined work of the incentives and the environment but also by other agents. Whenever a course of conduct gets imposed on us, we can regard ourselves as means to that conduct rather than as its authors. But if we can override such heteronomous imposition, we can to that extent regard ourselves as the authors of our own actions, and so as genuine agents. Such authoredness is something we owe to an ability to act from principle and to choose the principles from which to act, in such a way that responsibility for our actions ultimately rests with us. Stated in the negative, we cannot be described as self-guided, or as the authors of our own conduct, if we cannot filter out the heteronomous determinants of conduct. Only to the extent that our conduct is not forced on us from the outside can we be considered the authors of our own action; that is, we can be so considered only to the extent that we act based on principles which guide us in such a way as to overcome the heteronomous forces of determination forming the raw input of conduct.

This capacity for self-determination I will call *autonomy*: it is essentially the capacity for self-governance, or self-legislation, enabling us to establish for ourselves a practical principle that we choose to live by.[25] There are two interconnected dimensions to autonomy so described, one in the negative and the other in the positive: we are autonomous in the negative insofar as we are not bound by any external authority, and in the positive insofar as we can give ourselves a practical standard, in that we have a capacity to choose or work out principles by which to govern our conduct. Autonomy thus designates, in the negative, our independence from standards imposed from the outside, and in the positive our capacity to select or devise standards of conduct that count as authoritative, a capacity through which we can plan and organise and thus manage our own action and lives.[26] We are in this sense autonomous when we can make and carry out practical decisions without unwanted interference from others, or when we can use our judgement to develop on our own a rule or plan and commit to it.[27]

[25] Autonomy as I understand it here is thinly construed, meaning that as much as our action may ultimately be our own – insofar as we ultimately determine what we do, in the reasoned and principled way just described – the principles *we* act from need not be principles chosen independently of the input we get from the senses. Such an additional requirement would take us to the level of Kantian autonomy (see Kant, *Critique of Practical Reason*, n 3 above, AK 5:3–35, and Kant, *Groundwork of the Metaphysics of Morals*, n 3 above, AK 4:431–36, among other places), where in order for practical reason to count as the reason ascribable to an autonomous agent, it must have nothing to do with the incentives (which must be completely out of the picture). Autonomy thinly construed is less exacting than that, for it more simply describes our capacity to determine to act on the basis of self-imposed principles, which need not be rational, and whose independence from the incentives is not absolute but is rather an inflected independence, where the incentives influence conduct without so much as determining it. Autonomy thinly construed is in this sense in keeping with rationality as spontaneity as earlier discussed at n 22 and accompanying text. On these points, see also K Ameriks, *Interpreting Kant's Critiques* (Oxford, Oxford University Press, 2003) 212–25.

[26] This point is clearly stated in van Willigenburg, n 14 above, 46, among other places.

[27] This emphasis on planning shows that the thin idea of autonomy as here developed overlaps in significant ways with Michael Bratman's idea of planning agency. For a defence and clarification of this

Autonomy accordingly also enables us to set our own ends, rather than having ends imposed on us by others: these are ends that *we* judge (rather than other people judge) worthy of pursuit, and that we accordingly pursue based on reasons of our own choosing.[28] And the same attributes therefore also apply to the resulting conduct: autonomous conduct is self-directed conduct engaged in for reasons we formulate ourselves.

So conceived, autonomy is a precondition of action: no conduct is principled unless it is on the whole dictated by a standard that we choose for ourselves. And any lack of autonomy makes our conduct correspondingly unprincipled: it defeats the idea of principled conduct by turning into extemporary external forces the very standards on account of which our conduct can be described as principled. This entails that there is a specific way in which principles are constitutive of action: action is something we can be said to have performed not just by virtue of our rising above the contingent interplay of incentives and stimuli, achieving the level of generality proper to principles, but by virtue of our identifying with such principles, at least in the elemental and preliminary sense that we have chosen them ourselves. If general standards can play a role in shaping our identity, it is precisely insofar as they have not been imposed on us but have instead been selected by us, or at least we have accepted to take them up. They can be described in this sense as standards for our self-government, defining who we are not only by way of their content but also by virtue of their having been autonomously worked out. Autonomy so characterised makes it an essential and defining trait of human agency.[29]

With these points made, we have the groundwork on which to build the case for human agency as a pragmatic concept. The argument so far has been that action is not only controlled, purposeful and intentional but also principled; that principled conduct is made possible by a capacity for reflection, or reflectivity (which agents are consequently capable of); that reflectivity produces self-consciousness; that self-consciousness makes an agent aware of both the internal components of the self (the incentives) and the heteronomous determinants of action (the environment); and that this awareness – enabling agents to lead an existence distinct from that compelled by the contingent forces internal to their selves and from the heteronomous determinants of action – brings with it two further capacities: rationality as spontaneity (owed to an agent's independence

idea, see M Bratman, *Intention, Plans and Practical Reason* (Cambridge, MA, Harvard University Press, 1987), among other places. See also W Nelson, 'Kant's Formula of Humanity' (2008) 117 *Mind* 85, 92–97, bringing out the connection between Bratman's planning agency and autonomous agency, especially when autonomy is interpreted in a thin, or weak, sense.

[28] To use a formulation found in Korsgaard, n 12 above, 110, autonomous agents have the capacity to choose the principles of their doing, and so it is up to them to decide what they will do and for the sake of what.

[29] This property of autonomy can be further appreciated by bearing in mind that what gives us autonomy is our awareness of our individuality, separateness and independence. And this awareness in turn we get from our self-consciousness, which figures as a distinguishing feature of agents, what makes agents different from non-agents.

from the internal components of the self) and autonomy (or independence from the heteronomous determinants of action). In brief, reflectivity goes through self-consciousness to accomplish spontaneity and autonomy. Although both of these originate in reflectivity, they importantly elaborate on it. In fact, spontaneity and autonomy do not simply function as variants on the capacity to *reflect* on action but also entail the capacity to *act on reasons* and to *independently determine* what these reasons should be, or what standards should form the *grounds of action*. Thus, whereas reflectivity, spontaneity and autonomy all connect conceptually to one another, none can be reduced to the others, because each encapsulates a different aspect of human agency. This means that spontaneity and autonomy come into play alongside reflectivity in making up the foundation of human agency and providing its most basic content; from which follows an understanding of human agency as the capacity to make decisions independent from internal extemporary forces and external interferences, establishing in this way not only what conduct to have but also the reasons on which to base such conduct. Stated otherwise, human agency is the capacity to act on models established by reflective, spontaneous and autonomous choice; and human agents are agents capable of acting on self-imposed reasons, reasons they have worked out for themselves exercising their capacity for reflection.

III CONCLUDING REMARKS

The overall aim of this chapter was to lay the groundwork from which to proceed in seeking to adequately explain the ability of law to create obligations. The central unifying element in this entire background construction was an account of human agency with which to explain the normativity of practical reason. The account is based on Kant's practical philosophy, but that does not yet tell us how human agency relates to law and how it might figure in an account of the binding force of law. This relation (between human agency and legal obligation) is framed by two basic tenets underlying my discussion: that of legal obligation as a special case of the normativity of law, and that of practical reason as a unity, a single activity that develops in different ways according to the area it applies to, each such area being an instance of this single activity. One of these areas is law, whence it follows that the normativity of law shares the same foundation with the normativity of practical reason: it does so by virtue of its being a specific case of the normativity of practical reason (under the second tenet, the unity of practical reason), and legal obligation (the obligation-creating capacity of law) fits into this scheme as a specific case (in its own turn) of the normativity of law (under the first basic tenet). Once this overall foundation is worked out, then, it can also be used to ground the bindingness of law.

My discussion of human agency thus forms part of a broader strategy designed to answer the question as to what it is that grounds the obligatory force of law. The discussion is therefore only a start and does not amount to any exhaustive

Kantian argument for the foundation of the bindingness of law. In fact, even granting all that has been argued so far, we are left with a construction, human agency, which has not yet been shown to ground the normativity of practical reason, not to mention the obligatory force of law. The argument needs to be made complete by further explaining how its components connect: it must be clarified in greater detail (a) how human agency connects with the normativity of practical reason, and then (b) how the normativity of practical reason connects with legal obligation. But since this would take up more space than this contribution is allotted in this book, I will confine myself to laying out the direction I think such an investigation should go, thereby showing what I take to be the significance and interest that my construction of human agency has for law and jurisprudence.

(a) Human agency can be explained as the source of the normativity of practical reason by following and expanding on Kant's own view that the normativity of practical reason rests with *us* rather than with the world.[30] From this perspective, what makes something normative (and so also what makes it binding, or obligatory) is not an inherent property but its having been so constituted by us, and so it is located *within* human agents and their constitution (rather than occurring outside the human agent). Normativity does not come to an agent as a result of a pre-existing state of the world, nor is it the outcome of a search for something that is already out there, but is rather intrinsic in features of human agents themselves. This inherence of normativity in human agency can be explained by pointing out the conceptual connection that binds normativity to reasons. Normativity is reason-centred, in the sense that normativity will not arise except through the use of reasons: reasons *for* something and reasons *against* something; reasons why something ought to be done and reasons why it ought not to be done – reasons that in either case lend special force to the idea that this something ought to or ought not to be done. And reasons appeal and make sense only to human agents, who alone, among all living beings, are responsive to reasons.[31] On this view, it is the capacity to recognise something as a reason and respond to it in some appropriate way – it is the capacity to consider and give reasons – that endows with normativity a world of practices otherwise normatively inert. This capacity to use reasons I have described as a distinguishing feature of human agency, and this

[30] *cf* Korsgaard, *The Sources of Normativity*, n 23 above, 44–47. What follows is specifically framed to apply to normativity understood as a practical concept and not also as an epistemological concept: my account is specifically concerned with the normativity of practical reason rather than with normativity at large, by which is meant the 'characteristic common to everything that appears on the "ought" side of the distinction between what is and what ought to be' (J Dancy, 'Editor's Introduction' in J Dancy (ed), *Normativity* (London, Blackwell, 2000) vii–xv at vii). This is a wide class of things inclusive of deontic statements, evaluative considerations,and rules originating out of social practices, such as language and etiquette; and it also includes, alongside the *practical* oughts, having direct implications for conduct, *theoretical* oughts such as are established by science. So, instead of taking into account the entire spectrum of what counts as an 'ought', I am only considering that portion of it delimited by the practical uses of reason.

[31] This point finds a clear statement in Raz, *Engaging Reason*, n 15 above, 67, who observes that 'aspects of the world are normative inasmuch as they or their existence constitute reasons for persons, that is, grounds which make certain beliefs, moods, emotions, intentions, or actions appropriate or inappropriate'.

makes it so that human agency not only enters into a conceptual connection with normativity (in that reasons are central to both) but also imparts normativity to the world, by conferring value on some of its parts and attaching reasons to what would otherwise be normatively inert. It is therefore through the essential capacity to offer, appreciate and respond to reasons that human agency can legitimately be viewed as the source of normativity.

Importantly, the connection obtaining between normativity and human agency holds true in general, independently of the specific characteristics and subjective dispositions of single human agents. Stated otherwise, the normativity of practical reason does not depend on an agent's contingent desires or inclinations, since an agent's desiring a certain state of affairs or inclining to do something cannot in itself become normative or make a situation normative. The normativity of practical reason instead ultimately lies in an agent's responsiveness to reasons – or spontaneity – and this responsiveness, being rooted in the general capacity for self-reflection, describes *any* human agent: it is a distinctive property of human agency ascribable to all human agents indistinctively. Stated otherwise, normativity is not imprinted into the world by the fact of an agent's choice – since such a choice may well be arbitrary or random – but rather derives from features that, on a pragmatic and transcendental account, can be shown to be constitutive of human agency.[32]

(b) Finally, how does grounding the normativity of practical reason bear on legal obligation? This grounding relation can be clarified by taking into account the thesis that the binding force of law is a specific instantiation of the normativity of law, which in turn figures as a special case of the normativity of practical reason. It follows from this that the specific normativity of law – including its obligation-creating capacity – is rooted in the same foundation as the general normativity of practical reason. Once this overall foundation is identified, we can thereby also rest on it the obligatory force of law. An inquiry into the grounds of the normativity of practical reason therefore bears directly on our understanding of the connection between law and obligation. In other words, the main components of normativity previously discussed make it possible to see an unbroken line running from human agency to practical reason, a line showing how practical

[32] Of course, these remarks only scratch the surface when it comes to the idea of human agency as the source of the normativity of practical reason. A fuller appreciation of this idea would require considering the role that human agency plays through its defining features, those framing an agent's broadest and most basic self-conception, the one we must necessarily have of ourselves as human agents. Now, while this is a much more involved discussion than can be taken up here, one basic idea can be mentioned: it can be found in Korsgaard, *The Sources of Normativity*, n 23 above, 120–22, whose argument is, in outline, that agents must necessarily commit to and be governed by some conception of their practical identity because they would otherwise lose their compass and be unable to make reasoned choices between different options. This is a practical necessity (we cannot really choose not to have a conception of ourselves that we live by), but it is also importantly a general necessity, in that the conception involved (this sense of identity) is understood as something by which to distinguish ourselves not from other agents but from non-agents: it is that on account of which we view ourselves as members of humankind, rather than as unique individuals. If we cannot acknowledge a generic practical identity originating in human agency, we will not be able to act in accord with any self-conception. Hence the need to have a broad conception of ourselves as human agents.

reason ultimately borrows its normativity from human agency, which instantiates a model without which we would have no guidance in the practical sphere, and this is precisely the guidance involved in practical reason. This conceptual chain (from human agency to the guidance which comes with practical reason) is such that whatever normativity is found in human agency – as a model making it possible for us to engage in action – carries over to any practice, framework or institution informed by practical reason. One of these practices is law, and if we can qualify law as a special case of practical reason, we have a basis on which to make the normativity of practical reason relevant to law: the essential features of the normativity of law, as well as of its obligatory force, can be arrived at by considering the normativity of the activity of which law is a special case, namely, practical reason. This is to say that, just as the normativity of practical reason is grounded in human agency, so is the normativity of law, and hence its obligatory force.

To conclude, in providing an account of the source of the normativity of practical reason, the foregoing discussion of human agency pursues a strategy ultimately aimed at also grounding legal obligation. The final port of call for the argument initiated here is thus the thesis that if law can hold us under any obligation, that is owed to the way law connects to human agency, such that law can obligate insofar as it operates in forms compatible with the features constitutive of human agency: what is legal owes its obligatory force to its connection with the regulative idea of human agency. Stated otherwise, it is from human agency that law and the other institutions shaped by practical reason derive their obligatory force, and this force can only come about insofar as the relative institutions in some way reflect or support the defining capacities of human agency. The capacities of human agency (its defining features) thus act as the measure of the ability of law to set out for us requirements we are bound to commit to: the bindingness of law can be specified through the functionality of law in supporting, or at least not counteracting, the reflectivity, spontaneity and autonomy of its addressees.

9

Normativity, Metaphysics and Decision

ROBERT ALEXY*

I THE THESIS

IN HIS BOOK *The Normative Claim of Law* Stefano Bertea presents a 'modified Kantian approach' to normativity.[1] The modification consists in an attempt to eliminate metaphysics. Bertea claims that it is possible to develop a conception of normativity that follows Kantian lines but 'apart from any metaphysics'.[2] He contends that the elimination of metaphysics can be achieved by substituting for Kant's metaphysical notion of humanity a concept of human agency that refers to a 'pragmatic unit'[3] defined by a set of capacities related to action and agents. I will contest this claim and try to defend the thesis that normativity necessarily presupposes metaphysics.

Notwithstanding metaphysical abstinence, Bertea's 'pragmatic, or action-centred'[4] approach leads to very strong conclusions. He argues that his conception carries 'normative force, defining a model that no agent can afford to ignore without thereby falling outside the boundaries of human agency and so contravening the organising principle expressive of the subject in the practical sphere'.[5] To be sure, this can be interpreted in various different ways. In any case, however, it expresses a certain necessity, namely, that moral requirements must be complied with. Bertea puts the points as follows: 'there is no option but to comply with the demands of practical reason'.[6] This, too, I will contest. Bertea's assumption of necessity underestimates the practical nature of normativity, which is essentially connected with the concept of decision. My argument, therefore, is twofold: normativity is not possible without metaphysics on the one hand, and not possible without decision on the other.

* I should like to thank Stanley L Paulson for suggestions and advice on matters of English style.

[1] S Bertea, *The Normative Claim of Law* (Oxford, Hart Publishing, 2009) 189.

[2] ibid.

[3] ibid.

[4] ibid.

[5] ibid 209.

[6] ibid 210.

II THREE LEVELS OF NORMATIVITY

This twofold argument is based on a concept of normativity that comprises three levels or dimensions: semantic, justificatory and motivational levels. At the semantic level, normativity is a part of the meaning of a normative statement or of the content of a normative thought. 'Jones ought to tell the truth' is an example, and so is 'Jones ought not to tell the truth'. If A gives expression to the first sentence, and B to the second, both are uttering normative statements notwithstanding the fact that both statements cannot be correct or true. This shows that normativity at the semantic level is not, as such, connected with correctness, truth, assertability, objectivity, rationality, validity, or the like. This becomes very clear when we insert the 'ought' into a question: 'Ought Jones to tell the truth?'. The question shows that the speaker is trying to move toward stronger forms of normativity.

At the second, justificatory level, the normative meaning-content is backed by arguments that establish its correctness, truth, assertability, objectivity, rationality or validity. The question of which kinds of arguments can accomplish this will be left open here. The variety of argument employed in history and in our own time is great. It reaches from revelation, intuition, tradition and custom and authority, to maximisation of individual and collective utility, up to transcendental explications along Kantian lines. The only point of interest here is that the normative meaning-content now acquires validity. The reasons lying behind the normative thought transform merely potential reason for action at the semantic level into an actual reason for action, now at the justificatory level.

One might well assume that this is the end of the story. But that would be a mistake. A glance at Kant's distinction between *principium diiudicationis* and *principium executionis* may help to explain why.[7] In Kant's 'Moralphilosophie Collins', a student's transcription of his *Lecture on Ethics* held in the winter semester of 1784–85, one reads:

> Here we have, first, to look at two elements, 1) at the principium of the dijudication of the committment, and 2) at the principium of the execution or performance of the commitment. Guideline and motive have to be distinguished here . . . If the question is: what is or is not morally good, this is the principium of the dijudication, according to which I judge the goodness and badness of actions. If, however, the question is, what motivates me to live according to this law? This, then, is the principium of the motive. The approval of the action is the objective reason, but not yet the subjective reason.[8]

[7] See G Patzig, '"Principium diiudicationis" und "Principium executionis"' in G Patzig, *Gesammelte Schriften* (Göttingen, Wallstein, 1994) vol I, 258–60.

[8] I Kant, 'Moralphilosophie Collins' in *Kant's gesammelte Schriften* (Göttingen Academy of Sciences (ed)), vol 27.1 (Berlin, Walter de Gruyter, 1974) 274 (author's translation). As far as I can see, Kant does not use the expressions '*principium diiudicationis*' and '*principium executionis*' in works published by himself. But there are utterances in his published work that come rather close to the text quoted above. For example 'All legislation (whether it prescribes internal or external actions, and whether it is prescribed a priori through simple reason or through another person's will) consist of two elements: first, a *law* represents *objectively* the action that is to be done as necessary, that is, that makes the action into a duty; second, a

In this text, which stems from the period after which the *Groundwork of the Metaphysic of Morals* from 1785 had already been conceived, Kant stresses with greatest emphasis the thesis that it is one thing to consider a moral principle as well-grounded or justified, and in this sense valid, and quite another thing for one to be willing to act accordantly. Many people, for example, agree that there is an obligation to pay taxes, but they are, nevertheless, not willing to do so, and they try, often successfully, to avoid this obligation. To be sure, Kant not only separates justification and motivation, he also attempts, with the greatest force, to reconnect them, particularly in his theory of 'respect for the law'.[9] But the fact that some things have to be connected is no argument at all against their conceptual separation. If they were not to be distinguished, it would make no sense to connect them. For that reason the motivational level has to be added to the semantic and the justificatory levels as a third level.

III BERTEA'S MODIFIED KANTIAN APPROACH

A The Concept of Full-Fledged Action

The key concept of Bertea's modified Kantian approach, which is deeply influenced by Christine M Korsgaard, is the concept of human agency. Human agency is defined as 'a practical concept summarising the essential capacities . . . without which we would not be able to carry out action, and which are therefore shared by all beings capable of acting'.[10] With this, the concept of action acquires a central role. Bertea distinguishes different kinds of behaviour or action.[11] Only his concept of 'full-fledged action'[12] is of interest here. A full-fledged action is, first, '*deliberative* and therefore proceeds the way it does on the basis of a reasoned assessment of the situation at hand'.[13] Full-fledged action or '*action* proper'[14] thus has a discursive nature. In this way, the concept of action is intrinsically connected with the concept of argument. This connection is said to break 'the tight bond between stimulus and response at work in reactive behaviour. Thus, in the first place, action breaks the dependency of conduct on the inclinations'.[15] Therefore the second feature of action proper is that reasons can determine the action even against countervailing inclinations, that is, can determine it in a non-natural way.

motive that *subjectively* links the ground determining will to this action with the representation of the law'. I Kant, *Metaphysical Elements of Justice*, 2nd edn (J Ladd (trans), Indianapolis, IN, Hackett, 1999 (1797)) 22.

[9] I Kant, *Critique of Practical Reason* (1788) in I Kant, *Practical Philosophy* (MJ Gregor (ed and trans), Cambridge, Cambridge University Press, 1996) 201.

[10] Bertea, n 1 above, 191.

[11] ibid 191–94.

[12] ibid 195.

[13] ibid.

[14] ibid 196.

[15] ibid 195.

To this, a third property is to be added. Action proper is said to be 'principled conduct', based on 'one or more principles'.[16] The content of these 'principles' or 'standards'[17] has, again, something to do with human agency. Choices 'posing an obstacle to our flourishing as human agents' are ruled out.[18] The principled conduct, therefore, is conduct oriented to the idea of universalisability. The Categorical Imperative in all three of its variants enters the picture.

B Three Enabling Capacities

This rather strong concept of action, defined by deliberation, non-natural determination and universalisability, presupposes, according to Bertea, three 'necessary enabling capacities'.[19] The first is reflectivity.[20] Reflectivity is said to be 'the general capacity to think before we act'.[21] But reflectivity is more than mere thinking. Reflectivity is said to make it possible that '*we* cause our own conduct instead of our impulses causing us'.[22] Reflectivity is said to 'link[s] up conceptually'[23] to rationality, the second enabling capacity. Rationality is defined as the 'ability to grasp, work with and process reasons'.[24] This 'capacity for reasoned conduct' is said to enable us 'to transform the pull of our inclinations into *reasons*'.[25] Now, reasons can drive the action in different directions. Therefore, rationality requires the weighing of reasons in order to give them 'the proper practical weight'.[26] In this process of weighing or prioritising, principles, with reference here to Korsgaard, are said to 'become the ultimate basis of action'.[27] The third enabling capacity, finally, is autonomy, which is defined as the 'capacity for self-determination' and as 'self-governance'.[28] This capacity, again, is conceptually connected with the first and second capacities,[29] that is, with reflectivity and rationality.

C Human Agency and Normativity

At this point, Bertea erects the bridge between human agency and normativity. Normativity is aptly described as the concern with the category of the 'ought', in

[16] ibid 196–97.
[17] ibid 201.
[18] ibid 210.
[19] ibid 197.
[20] ibid.
[21] ibid.
[22] ibid 198.
[23] ibid.
[24] ibid 199.
[25] ibid.
[26] ibid.
[27] ibid.
[28] ibid 200.
[29] ibid 202.

contrast with the category of the 'is',[30] and the 'ought', alluding to Raz,[31] is associated with the concept of reasons: 'reasons why something *ought* to be done and reasons why it *ought not* to be done'.[32] In this way, the semantic and the justificatory level of normativity are adequately connected. It is not difficult for Bertea to argue that only agents possessing the 'capacity to offer, appreciate and respond to reasons'[33] are capable of normativity. Normativity is, indeed, intrinsically connected with the concept of the reasoning or discursive creature. Without discursive creatures, normativity would not be possible.

Up to this point, capacities or competences have been at the centre of our enquiry. Having a capacity, however, is something different from using it. Why should we make use of the capacities that define human agency? Bertea's answer is that we must use these capacities if we do not want to fall 'outside the boundaries of human agency'.[34] Reflectivity, rationality and autonomy describe what he calls the '*minimally necessary self-conception*',[35] and to give them up would expose us to what Korsgaard calls the 'threat of a loss of identity'.[36] We would be assimilating ourselves 'to non-human agents, that is, to subjects incapable of action'.[37] For this reason, there is, for human agents, 'no option but to comply with the demands of practical reason'.[38]

These demands of practical reason not only comprise the more or less procedural capacities of reflectivity, rationality and autonomy, they also include substantial moral demands that are, according to Bertea, implied by the minimally necessary self-conception, which, again, is defined by reflectivity, rationality and autonomy. In this way, the minimally necessary self-conception is said to 'compel certain practical choices, those tending to preserve and advance the basic capacities of human agency, and rule out certain others, those that run in quite the opposite direction, posing an obstacle to our flourishing as human agents or even to our acting in a way consistent with human agency'.[39] The word 'our' in this quotation indicates that this requirement has an universalistic character, and the demand not to pose obstacles to the flourishing of human agents, but rather to preserve and advance their basic capacities, can be understood as a reformulation of the postulate to respect each person as a purpose in itself. With this, Bertea's argument has arrived at something like the first and second, and perhaps even the third form of Kant's Categorical Imperative. The question is whether this argument is sound. As already noted, only two issues are of interest here: metaphysics and decision.

[30] ibid 203.

[31] J Raz, 'Explaining Normativity: On Rationality and the Justification of Reason' in J Dancy (ed), *Normativity* (Oxford, Blackwell, 2000) 34.

[32] Bertea, n 1 above, 205.

[33] ibid.

[34] ibid 209.

[35] ibid 206.

[36] CM Korsgaard, *The Sources of Normativity* (Cambridge, Cambridge University Press, 1996) 102.

[37] Bertea, n 1 above, 210.

[38] ibid.

[39] ibid 209–10.

IV METAPHYSICS

The concept of metaphysics is, as Anthony Quinton aptly remarked, 'large, controversial and, in consequence, somewhat indeterminate in outline'.[40] Relatively simple is a negative determination. It says that metaphysics is whatever cannot be drawn from experience. This idea is well expressed by Aristotle's question of whether we must 'say that sensible substances alone exist, or that there are others besides these',[41] as well as by Kant's thesis that metaphysical cognition is cognition 'lying beyond experience'.[42] A positive determination is not so easy, for the range of possibilities lying beyond perception or experience can be understood in very different ways. Fortunately, it is not necessary to take up this matter here. For my argument, the negative concept of metaphysics will suffice.

Bertea never tires of stressing that his approach does not intend 'to single out the psychological, and much less the physical, characteristics that make it possible for us to engage in action'.[43] He claims not to be concerned with 'factual or empirical traits'.[44] This is a clear rejection of naturalistic approaches. But what is the character of the approach he has chosen in place of naturalism? Bertea describes the non-naturalistic character of his approach in different ways. Three of these descriptions are of special interest.

The first is the classification of his approach as 'pragmatic'.[45] The predicate 'pragmatic' is used in philosophy in a variety of different ways. There seems, however, to exist a common element. All pragmatic approaches refer to a practice, constituted by basic assumptions, rules and intentions. Here this practice is the practice of action in general and the practice of reasoning, as connected with it. By this means, however, metaphysics is not ruled out at all. The basic assumptions might be metaphysical assumptions, and both the rules of the practice and the intentions at play in it may be pointless without certain metaphysical presuppositions. The question of whether this is the case is a question of the substantive analysis of the practice.

The second description Bertea offers of his approach is its characterisation as a 'conceptual approach'.[46] Bertea, indeed, presents a highly complex conceptual framework that attempts to explain the relationship between human agency and normativity. But to work at a conceptual level is not to say that one is not working at a metaphysical level. The decisive question is, first, whether one is assuming that the things to which the concepts refer really exist, and, second, whether these things, if they exist, are metaphysical entities. There are formulations that could

[40] A Quinton, *The Nature of Things* (London, Routledge & Kegan Paul, 1973) 235.

[41] Aristotle, *Metaphysics*, B 2, 997a, 34–35, quoted from *The Complete Works of Aristotle: the Revised Oxford Translation* (J Barnes (ed), Princeton, NJ, Princeton University Press, 1984) vol II, 1575–76.

[42] I Kant, *Prolegomena to Any Future Metaphysics* (G Hatfield (trans), Cambridge, Cambridge University Press, 1997 (1783)) 15.

[43] Bertea, n 1 above, 203.

[44] ibid.

[45] ibid 206, see further 176, 189, 204.

[46] ibid 203.

perhaps be read as saying that the things to which the concepts refer do not really exist. This is the case when Bertea says that his account might be interpreted as a '"creation myth"', or as a 'narrative'.[47] Myths and narratives need not refer to things that really exist. But such formulations as these are only of passing interest. The bulk of the text seems to express that the things to which it refers really exist. The 'subject understood as a doer of deeds',[48] 'beings capable of responding to the environment',[49] or 'agents, that is, authors of our own conduct'[50] seem to be not only mere fictions, constructions or ideas, but entities that actually exist. Again, the question is whether metaphysics is not being presupposed in assuming the existence of such entities.

Bertea's third description of his approach is its characterisation as a 'transcendental account'.[51] With this he refers to the constitutive character or the necessity of his three enabling capacities – that is, reflectivity, rationality and autonomy – for human agency.[52] Being transcendental in the sense of being a necessary condition of the possibility of something else, however, by no means excludes its having a metaphysical character. Precisely the opposite is the case in Kant's philosophy.

Bertea's three self-descriptions of his approach, therefore, do not exclude its metaphysical character at all. In order to decide whether in fact, contrary to his claim, he is making metaphysical assumptions, several of his central concepts will be considered.

Of special importance is the concept of 'free choice',[53] which is an indispensible element of his concept of autonomy as 'self-governance'.[54] The question of whether we are really free, at least in some cases – at the very least one case – is, however, a question that cannot be decided by experience or self-perception. It is the paradigm of a metaphysical question. This implies that the idea of freedom makes sense only if a rational metaphysics is possible.[55] The same applies to all the other fundamental concepts used by Bertea. Of special importance is the idea that '*we* cause our own conduct instead of our impulses causing us'.[56] This causality is a causality of reasons that we have judged to be correct. The question of whether judgements, in contrast to inclinations, can cause our actions is, again, a metaphysical question.

The concepts of freedom of choice and of causality of reasons are, as Kant puts it, 'reciprocal concepts'.[57] Now, there is far more reciprocity in Bertea's system.

[47] ibid.
[48] ibid 189.
[49] ibid 196.
[50] ibid 200.
[51] ibid 206.
[52] ibid 206–07.
[53] ibid 200.
[54] ibid.
[55] See on this R Alexy, 'Menschenrechte ohne Metaphysik?' (2004) 52 *Deutsche Zeitschrift für Philosophie* 23–24.
[56] Bertea, n 1 above, 198.
[57] I Kant, *Groundwork of the Metaphysic of Morals* (HJ Paton (trans), New York, Harper & Row, 1964 (1785)) 118.

Only one further point is of interest here. It is the concept of 'a rational person . . . as one who can understand, respond to and act from reasons'.[58] The concept of a person seems, again, to be – as a concept standing in reciprocity to the concepts of freedom and causality of reason – a metaphysical concept. Bertea, however, attempts to distinguish, as he puts it, the concept of a 'subject understood as a doer of deeds, or as an agent' from 'a metaphysical entity, a being'.[59] Is a 'doer of deeds' not a being? Does being exclude acting? Perhaps Bertea's argument is directed against Kant's idea that the moral subject has to be conceived as 'a member of the intelligible world'.[60] But this membership stands in opposition to something like a pure being. It expresses itself in precisely those terms that Berta deems to be crucial: by moral action. Thus, being and acting are two sides of the same coin. In sum, and as brief as possible: Bertea's argument is filled with metaphysics, and this is no accident. It is required by the nature of normativity.

V DECISION

At this point, one might think that normativity is exclusively a matter of metaphysics. This, however, would be a fundamental error. As already mentioned, normativity presupposes, besides metaphysics, decision. This is the second point in my critique.

In Bertea's approach, decision has no systematically relevant place. According to Bertea, human agents have 'no option but to comply with the demands of practical reason'.[61] The demands of practical reason comprise an universalistic morality as expressed by Kant's Categorical Imperative. To be sure, Bertea does not claim that our 'ability to act for reasons' has the effect of '*stay*[*ing*] the forces of instinct, for these still operate within the self and can therefore tilt action this way or that'.[62] But the ability to act for reasons gives 'us the power to *choose* whether or not to be guided by inclinations'.[63] This choice, however, is not a choice with options. Human agents, as already remarked, are said to have 'no option but to comply with the demands of practical reason'.[64] Kant's question: 'But why should I subject myself to this principle . . .?'[65] would make little sense if one were prepared to follow Bertea here.

To be sure, Bertea's argument can be constructed in a way that renders it indubitably sound. If one defines action as full-fledged action, and if one includes acting on moral reasons as a necessary element in the concept of full-fledged action, then one will have to conclude that a person who does not act on moral reasons is

[58] Bertea, n 1 above, 199.
[59] ibid 189.
[60] Kant, *Groundwork of the Metaphysic of Morals*, n 57 above, 122.
[61] Bertea, n 1 above, 210.
[62] ibid 199.
[63] ibid.
[64] ibid 210.
[65] Kant, *Groundwork of the Metaphysic of Morals*, n 57 above, 116–17.

not performing a full-fledged action and, therefore, *per definition*, is not acting. This, again, implies that a person that decides always to pursue only its inclinations and never to follow moral reasons, has decided to give up acting.

The weakness of this argument is that it proceeds from too strong a premise. The concept of action, as such, does not include moral elements. A person who follows only hypothetical imperatives in order to maximise individual utility can well be described as an agent. To be sure, such a person is not making use of all its capacities. But this is not a question of whether this person is able to act or not. The concept of action or agency, therefore, cannot open the way to a *principium executionis*.

More interesting in this respect is the concept of identity. In chapter III of the *Groundwork of the Metaphysic of Morals* Kant makes his well-known distinction between two standpoints:

> [A] rational being . . . therefore [has] two points of view from which he can regard himself and from which he can know laws governing the employment of his powers and consequently governing all his actions. He can consider himself *first* – so far as he belongs to the sensible world – to be under laws of nature (heteronomy); and *secondly* – so far as he belongs to the intelligible world – to be under laws which, being independent of nature, are not empirical but have their ground in reason alone.[66]

One might call the first point the natural point of view and the second point the moral point of view. The mere distinction between these points of view says, however, nothing about the priority of the moral point of view. For this priority Kant offers an ontological argument resting on his thesis that '*the intelligible world contains the ground of the sensible world*',[67] an argument that is, in this context, highly contestable. But he also presents elements of another argument, one that has an existential character. Kant argues that 'even the most hardened scoundrel' would 'wish' to be a moral person provided that this would not impose costs for the satisfaction of his inclinations, for he could 'expect', in taking up the moral point of view, 'a greater inner worth of his own person'.[68] At another place, Kant speaks, instead of the 'greater inner worth', of the 'highest vocation'.[69]

Having a vocation, even a highest one, does not mean, however, that it is necessarily followed. There may be countervailing motives. At exactly this point the idea of decision comes into play. The moral law, or the moral point of view, can acquire the status of a *principium executionis* only if we decide so. Indeed, elements of this argument of decision are to be found in Kant. In his *Religion within the Bounds of Pure Reason* he speaks of a 'single unchangeable decision' by which a 'bad man'

[66] ibid 120.

[67] ibid 121.

[68] ibid 122.

[69] Kant, *Critique of Practical Reason*, n 9 above, 210. On a somewhat more elaborated interpretation of this argument see R Alexy, 'Kants Begriff des praktischen Gesetzes' in O Behrends (ed), *Der biblische Gesetzesbegriff* (2006) 278 *Abhandlungen der Akademie der Wissenschaften zu Göttingen, Philologisch-Historische Klasse, Dritte Folge* 209.

acquires a 'new man',[70] and of one's 'own *free* choice'.[71] This free choice between the natural and the moral point of view, which reappears in Kierkegaard's choice between an aesthetical and an ethical way of life,[72] is an existential decision. But can a decision be a *principium executionis*?

This would not be the case if the decision were a pure decision, a decision from nowhere or from somewhere. Our considerations with respect to metaphysics show that the opposite is the case. The moral point of view has been established as a necessary possibility rooted in our practice of acting and arguing. The existential argument adds nothing to this. It says no more, and no less, than that our possibilities stand in need of confirmation in order to acquire reality. Thus, metaphysics and decision are not opposites. Rather, they are necessary constituents of an adequate conception of normativity.

[70] I Kant, 'Die Religion innerhalb der Grenzen der bloßen Vernunft' in *Kant's gesammelte Schriften* (Royal Prussian Academy of Sciences (ed)), vol 6 (Berlin, Georg Reimer, 1907) 47–48 (author's translation).

[71] Ibid 182 (author's translation).

[72] S Kierkegaard, *Either/Or* (HV Hong and E Hong (trans), Princeton, Princeton University Press, 1987 (1843)), vol II, 166–67.

10

Law, Normativity and Legitimacy: Can Moral Constructivism be Fruitful for Legal Theory?

CRISTINA LAFONT

ONE OF THE most attractive features of Kantian constructivism in moral theory is its promise to illuminate the internal connection between the autonomy of agents and the validity of norms. The underlying idea behind this view is that the validity of norms depends on the reasonable agreement of those to whom the norms apply. This idea captures two correlative aspects of the notion of autonomy, namely, that forcing anyone to act against her own reason is wrong and thus that the rightness of norms cannot lie beyond the possible reasonable agreement of those who are subject to them. The centrality of the notion of free and reasonable agreement makes Kantian constructivism seem particularly apt for an extension from moral into legal contexts, because one and the same notion appears to be able to account for two dimensions of the validity of legal norms: their justice (or substantive correctness) on the one hand, and the legitimacy of their enforcement, on the other. Moreover, regarding the latter, it seems natural to assume that a criterion of *democratic* legitimacy can be straightforwardly extracted from constructivism, since the distinctive feature of democracy is precisely that it is based on the 'consent of the governed'. In fact, in recent years several versions of a principle of democratic legitimacy along constructivist lines have been offered by authors like Rawls, Cohen or Habermas.[1]

However, a closer look at the notion of agreement operative in Kantian constructivist approaches cast doubt on its ability to account for the legitimacy of democratic decision-making procedures. The main problem is that any appeal to agreement as the source of the validity of norms must include some normative constraints in order to be plausible. At the very least, agreements must be *voluntary* (ie not reached under coercion, deception or duress) and *rational* (ie based on

[1] *cf* J Rawls, *Political Liberalism, 1st edn* (New York, Columbia University Press, 1993) 137; J Cohen, 'Deliberation and Democratic Legitimacy' in A Hamlin and P Pettit (eds), *The Good Polity* (Oxford, Blackwell, 1989) 17–34 at 22; J Habermas, *Between Facts and Norms* (W. Rehg (trans), Cambridge, MA, MIT Press, 1996) 110.

suitable reasons) in order to lend any validity to the norms agreed upon. Different constructivist approaches offer different accounts of the specific content of these constraints, but they all share the assumption that only agreements under suitably ideal conditions can confer validity on those norms that are agreed upon. This in turn suggests that the normative notion operative in constructivist approaches is merely a notion of *hypothetical agreement* and not a notion of *actual consent.*

It is often pointed out that traditional social contract theories like those of Hobbes, Locke and Rousseau crucially relied on the notion of consent, whereas in Kant hypothetical agreement becomes the central notion. This remains the case for contemporary Kantian constructivist approaches, like those of Rawls or Scanlon.[2] The key element to the notion of hypothetical agreement is, obviously, not the act of consenting, but the soundness of reasons that could lead everyone to an *agreement in judgment* as to the correctness of any given norm. In that sense, to claim that a norm 'could be agreed to' means that it has no features that would make it impossible for any reasonable person to endorse it. To the extent that this notion of hypothetical agreement is supposed to track the soundness of reasons that can lend validity to collective norms, it may indeed prove fruitful in terms of accounting for the justice or substantive correctness of such norms.[3]

However, appealing to a notion of hypothetical agreement in order to account for the legitimacy of the enforcement of legal norms can lead to problematic conclusions. On the one hand, such an appeal may suggest that to the extent that the suitably ideal conditions can never be met in real social contexts, the actual agreements reached by democratic procedures cannot confer genuine legitimacy on collective political decisions. Since asymmetries of power and information are bound to be ineliminable from actual democratic decision-making procedures and unanimous agreement among citizens can hardly be expected for most political decisions, the actual agreements that can realistically be obtained through democratic procedures can hardly be ideally reasonable, and thus, cannot lend genuine validity to the collective norms or the political decisions agreed upon, according to the constructivist's own standards.[4] On the other hand, the appeal

[2] See especially J Waldron, *Liberal Rights: Collected Papers 1981–1991* (Cambridge, Cambridge University Press, 1993) 51, and F D'Agostino and G Gaus, 'Contemporary Approaches to the Social Contract' in EN Zalta (ed), *Stanford Encyclopedia of Philosophy* (September 2008) available at http://plato.stanford.edu/.

[3] Since my focus in this chapter is on the feasibility of following a constructivist strategy when trying to account for the legitimacy of the collective enforcement of legal norms in a political community, I leave aside the issue of whether a constructivist strategy can ultimately succeed in accounting for the substantive correctness of norms. I analyse some difficulties involved in a constructivist interpretation of discourse ethics in C Lafont, *The Linguistic Turn in Hermeneutic Philosophy* (Cambridge, MA, MIT Press, 1999); C Lafont, 'Realismus und Konstruktivismus in der Kantianischen Moralphilosophie: Das Beispiel der Diskursethik' (2002) 50 *Deutsche Zeitschrift für Philosophie* 39; C Lafont, 'Procedural Justice? Implications of the Rawls–Habermas Debate for Discourse Ethics' (2003) 29 *Philosophy and Social Criticism* 167; and in other contemporary versions of moral constructivism in C Lafont, 'Moral Objectivity and Reasonable Agreement: Can Realism be Reconciled with Kantian Constructivism?' (2004) 17 *Ratio Juris* 27.

[4] For an argument along these lines, although as part of a different overall argumentative strategy, see D Estlund, *Democratic Authority: A Philosophical Framework* (Princeton, NJ, Princeton University Press, 2008) 241.

to hypothetical agreement may also suggest that nothing else is needed for the legitimate enforcement of collective norms. So long as legal norms track the interests and views of reasonable persons, such that they could in principle agree to them, the enforcement of such norms would be considered legitimate, even in lieu of asking citizens (or their representatives) for their actual agreement through democratic decision-making procedures such as elections or referenda. One way or the other, the appeal to hypothetical agreement does not seem to lend any support to a defence of democracy. In fact, it can have pretty disquieting implications. By challenging the assumption that the actual consent of citizens can be a genuine source of validity for collective political decisions, it may actually undermine our confidence in the superior legitimacy of democracy, that is, of the *actual* collective authorisation of laws and policies by the people subject to them through democratic elections or referenda. If the only notion of consent that can be extracted from constructivism in order to account for the legitimacy of democracy is hypothetical consent – or, to put it the other way around, if actual consent, irrespective of the conditions under which it is procured, can never be ideal enough to lend validity to political decisions – it is then hard to see why we cling to the view that countries which lack democratic elections where citizens can actually consent to political decisions, or to the appointment of office-holders who make them, by vote are not democracies. Obviously, democracies as they actually exist involve numerous political decisions, often of great importance, that are (perhaps correctly) not determined by democratic means. But, it also seems obvious that a system of government in which political decisions are *at no point* subject to the *actual* consent of citizens through a democratic procedure (such as voting) cannot count as democratic political systems. However, if a government makes decisions that could indeed be met with the reasonable agreement of citizens – because these decisions track the best reasons – without even needing to ask after their actual consent, then why should this not be enough to count as democratic? Why shouldn't hypothetical agreement be enough for a form of government to qualify as democratic and, by implication, as legitimate?

I AGREEMENT AND CONSENT IN KANT

In some of his political writings, Kant indeed suggests that hypothetical agreement is a sufficient criterion for the legitimacy of law enforcement. In a passage of his essay *Theory and Practice*, the non-democratic nature of the notion of hypothetical agreement becomes explicit. After emphasising the fact that the notion of agreement operative in the idea of a social contract should not be understood as an act of consenting, but rather as an idea of reason, Kant explicitly argues that the lack of actual consent among citizens (even their actual dissent) by no means invalidates a government's decision that meets the conditions of hypothetical consent:

> [The original contract] is in fact merely an *idea* of reason, which nonetheless has undoubted practical reality; for it can oblige every legislator to frame his laws in such a way that they could have been produced by the united will of a whole nation, and to regard each subject, in so far as he can claim citizenship, as if he had consented within the general will. This is the test for the rightfulness of every public law. For if the law is such that a whole people could not *possibly* agree to it (for example, if it stated that a certain class of subjects must be privileged as a hereditary ruling class), it is unjust; but if it is at least *possible* that a people could agree to it, it is our duty to consider the law as just, even if the people is at present in such a position or attitude of mind that it would probably refuse its consent if it were consulted.[5]

With the last remark, Kant is pointing out something pretty obvious. Since the actual consent of citizens may be based on all kinds of unreasonable, unfair, uniformed or otherwise defective considerations, it cannot offer a valid criterion for the justice or substantive correctness of laws. Thus, it is the hypothetical agreement in judgment among reasonable people, and not the actual consent of citizens, that can confer validity on collective norms and, in doing so, also serve as a guide to legislators.

Now, if one looks at some contemporary proposals of a principle of democratic legitimacy built along constructivist lines from this (Kantian) perspective, the hypothetical reading of the notion of agreement employed seems straightforward. For example, Joshua Cohen's principle of democratic legitimacy states that 'outcomes are democratically legitimate if and only if they *could* be the object of a free and reasoned agreement among equals'.[6] Interpreted in terms of 'hypothetical agreement', this principle imposes an obligation to frame laws in such a way that they could be endorsed by reasonable people as the necessary and sufficient condition for their legitimacy. As Kant argued, this obligation is not empty, since it imposes some constraints on the legislator, but this is certainly not the same as imposing a democratic obligation to win citizens' consent to political decisions by submitting them to democratic procedures as a condition of legitimacy. Thus, as a criterion of democratic legitimacy in particular, the hypothetical interpretation of the principle should be alarming, since it would imply that a political system would count as democratic even without the actual participation of citizens in political decision-making.

Cohen himself, however, does not seem to endorse a purely hypothetical interpretation of the principle, since he claims that the sense of this principle is captured by an ideal deliberative procedure that provides a model that actual democratic institutions should mirror. According to him, the ideal deliberative procedure aims at reaching a unanimous consensus among citizens, but 'even under ideal conditions there is no promise that consensual reasons will be forthcoming. If they are not, then deliberations conclude with voting, subject to some

[5] I Kant, *On the Common Saying: 'This May be True in Theory, but It Does not Apply in Practice'* in HS Reiss (ed), *Kant: Political Writings* (Cambridge, Cambridge University Press, 1970 (1793)) AK 8:297.

[6] Cohen, n 1 above, 22.

form of majority rule'.[7] This clearly indicates that, in order to mirror the ideal deliberative procedure, institutions must include actual democratic decision-making procedures such as voting, so that their outcomes reflect the actual consent of citizens in particular and not just the hypothetical agreement of reasonable persons. But if, according to the hypothetical interpretation of Cohen's principle, what makes outcomes legitimate is just that they could be agreed upon by reasonable persons, it is unclear why democratic decisions reached by majority rule should be considered particularly apt – let alone required – to meet such a criterion of legitimacy.[8]

The widely shared assumption that democratic legitimacy requires obtaining citizens' actual consent to (some) political decisions through their votes can hardly be justified solely on the basis of a general requirement to reach reasonable outcomes, ie outcomes that track the hypothetical agreement of reasonable persons. At best, it seems an open, empirical question as to which decision procedures may be best equipped to reach that goal. At worst, it may seem doubtful that democratic, majoritarian decisions in particular could ever be singled out among all possible alternatives as the best equipped to reach substantively correct outcomes. The democratic requirement suggests that there is something independently valuable in the notion of actual consent that cannot be captured by hypothetical agreement. Unless a constructivist strategy can incorporate and give some plausible account of the former and not just the latter, its ability to account for the legitimacy of democracy seems highly dubious.

Interestingly enough, in the *Doctrine of Right*, the first part of *The Metaphysics of Morals*, Kant appeals to a notion of actual consent that seems clearly irreducible to the notion of hypothetical agreement. Precisely in the context of justifying 'consent by the governed' as the only source of governmental legitimacy, he appeals to the Roman maxim *volenti non fit iniuria* in order to highlight the internal connection between justice and voluntary consent. He argues that whenever someone decides in the name of someone else it is always possible to wrong those for whom one decides, whereas this is not possible if they decide for themselves. Thus, consent

[7] ibid 23.

[8] The very same difficulty can be found in the case of Rawls. On the one hand, his liberal principle of legitimacy seems open to a hypothetical reading of agreement: 'our exercise of political power is fully proper only when it is exercised in accordance with a constitution the essentials of which all citizens as free and equal *may reasonably be expected to endorse* in the light of principles and ideals acceptable to their common human reason' (emphasis added); see Rawls, n 1 above, 137. On the other hand, it is hard to see how, when starting with a purely hypothetical reading of this principle, one could derive a specific principle of *democratic* legitimacy that requires actual consent to the outcome of majoritarian decisions, under the constraints of public reason, as Rawls unequivocally does, when he claims: '[W]hen, on a constitutional essential or matter of basic justice, all appropriate government officials act from and follow public reason, and when all reasonable citizens think of themselves ideally as if they were legislators following public reason, the legal enactment expressing the opinion of the majority is *legitimate* law. It may not be thought the most reasonable, or the most appropriate, by each, but it is politically (morally) binding on him or her as a citizen and is to be accepted as such. Each thinks that all have spoken and voted at least reasonably, and therefore all have followed public reason and honored their duty of civility' (emphasis added); J Rawls, 'The Idea of Public Reason Revisited' in S Freeman (ed), *John Rawls: Collected Papers* (Cambridge, MA, Harvard University Press, 1999) 573–615 at 578.

by the governed simply wins by default as the only *guaranteed* legitimate option among its alternatives:

> The legislative authority can belong only to the united will of the people. For since all right is to proceed from it, it *cannot* do anyone wrong by its law. Now when someone makes arrangements about *another*, it is always possible for him to do the other wrong; but he can never do wrong in what he decides upon with regard to himself (for *volenti non fit iniuria*). Therefore only the concurring and united will of all, insofar as each decides the same thing for all and all for each, and so only the general united will of the people, can be legislative.[9]

Here it is important to notice that, according to Kant, 'consenting' does not lend validity to a decision merely because or to the extent that it is consent to the right decision. Kant's claim is not that individuals infallibly know what is best for them and that therefore their consent has the epistemic virtue of tracking substantively correct decisions, ie those that would be agreed upon by ideally reasonable persons. Kant recognises that *volenti* confers validity independently of whether the decision ends up being substantively correct or not. This becomes clear in another passage of *Theory and Practice*, where Kant appeals again to the argument from *volenti* in order to justify his requirement that the will of an entire people must be included when deciding public laws. In that context, Kant indicates that, since disagreements are bound to occur among the people, all citizens must unanimously consent to making decisions by majority rule:

> [A] public law which defines for everyone that which is permitted and prohibited by right, is the act of a public will, from which all right proceeds and which must not therefore itself be able to do an injustice to any one. And this requires no less that the will of the entire people (since all men decide for all men and each decides for himself). For only towards oneself can one never act unjustly … An entire people cannot, however, be expected to reach unanimity, but only to show a majority of votes . . . Thus the actual principle of being content with majority decisions must be accepted unanimously and embodied in a contract; and this itself must be the ultimate basis on which a constitution is established.[10]

Here Kant argues that a way in which a law may fail to be valid, ie it may wrong or do injustice to some, is if any of those who are subject to it are excluded from the process of decision-making. This is not an argument about any substantive characteristics that the law must have such that it could be acceptable to reasonable persons. In fact, it is not an argument about the content of the law at all, but about the scope of inclusion in decision-making that can confer validity to its enforcement. If Kant's argument is plausible, the requirement of consent expressed by the 'volenti' principle implies that all citizens must have decision-making status; ie all citizens must be included in the collective act of binding their will to a procedure for determining legislation and thus such a decision must be

[9] I Kant, *The Metaphysics of Morals* in *Immanuel Kant: Practical Philosophy* (MJ Gregor (ed and trans), Cambridge, Cambridge University Press, 1996 (1797)) AK 6:313–14.

[10] Kant, *On the Common Saying*, n 5 above, AK 8:294–96.

unanimous. It is this requirement of political *inclusion* that singles out majority rule as the appropriate decision-making procedure in cases of disagreement – instead of, say, letting a single ruler or a minority of experts decide. Now, in claiming that citizens must bind their will to the procedure of majority rule in particular the inevitability of disagreements among them regarding the substantive correctness of decided-upon laws is already recognised, and with it the inevitability that some legislative decisions will be considered substantively wrong by some citizens. This strongly indicates that the notion operative here is a genuine notion of voluntary consent. More specifically, *the act of consenting under the relevant, suitable conditions* authorises and thus lends validity to the enforcement of the laws at issue, even if citizens disagree about their substantive correctness.

The notion of consent expressed in the *volenti* principle that Kant uses here is thus not the notion of a (hypothetical) *agreement in judgements* among citizens, but the notion of a *voluntary authorisation to be bound by the outcome of a collective decision.* Kant's argument suggests that laws can acquire some kind of validity in virtue of the normative power citizens have to bind themselves when they consent to their enforcement (under specific conditions) regardless of whether or not they agree on their substantive correctness. It is because this validity can only be guaranteed by inclusion in political decision-making that the foreseeable lack of agreement in judgements among them singles out democratic majority rule as the right procedure. Seen from this perspective, the interpretation of Kant's approach as relying on a purely rationalistic account of the notion of autonomy seems at least questionable.[11]

However, beyond an exegesis of Kant, the difficulties that we have seen so far suggest that a constructivist approach which exclusively relies on one element of the notion of autonomy forces a choice between a purely rationalistic or a purely voluntaristic account of political legitimacy and neither of these choices can plausibly account for the two dimensions of the validity of legal norms. A constructivist approach that appeals to a single notion of ideal rational agreement in order to account for both dimensions of the validity of legal norms is bound to give a distorted view of one or the other dimension. What is needed is a strategy that can accommodate both elements of the notion of political autonomy without reducing one to the other.

In my view, among contemporary constructivist approaches, Habermas' discourse theory seems to be the best candidate for providing such a comprehensive account of political autonomy. The formal-pragmatic interpretation of the notion of rational agreement involved in the discourse approach means that it can account for the different senses in which the *reasonableness of an agreement* and the *voluntariness of consenting* to such an agreement matter for the validity of social norms. The set of formal-pragmatic conditions that the discourse approach singles out as necessary for rational agreement simultaneously meet the cognitive requirements for rational

[11] J Simmons, 'Justification and Legitimacy' (1999) 109 *Ethics* 740–71, offers such a rationalistic interpretation of Kant's approach as based exclusively on the notion of hypothetical agreement, although he does so in the quite different context of discussing the legitimacy of the state rather than the legitimacy of specific laws or policies.

opinion-formation and the conative requirements for autonomous will-formation. In virtue of this lucky overlap, discourse theory does not need to face the highly problematic choice between reason and the will and can thus provide a unified account of the necessary conditions for forming a reasonable collective will. To that extent, the discourse approach to deliberative democracy provides a plausible model that institutions can mirror in order to meet the dual demands of substantive correctness and legitimate enforcement of laws. However, this interpretation of discourse theory requires recognition of the fact that the two dimensions of the validity of norms are logically independent of one another. As a result, such an interpretation is incompatible with a constructivist account that explains both dimensions of the validity of norms in terms of a single notion of discursive agreement. As I will try to show in what follows, the notion of discursive agreement that can be extracted from discourse theory can indeed provide a plausible account of democratic legitimacy and thus serve as an ideal that democratic institutions should mirror only if it is not overburdened with the task of providing a constructivist account of justice at the same time.

II AGREEMENT AND CONSENT IN DISCOURSE THEORY

According to the discourse approach, reasons and arguments are rationally justified if they could be accepted as convincing by everyone under the conditions of an ideal speech situation. The latter term refers to pragmatic features of the process of argumentation such as symmetry among participants, equal opportunity of participation, lack of coercion and deception, openness to criticism, etc. The discursive interpretation of the notion of rational acceptability, when applied specifically to a discussion about the validity of norms, results in the discourse principle:

(D) Just those action norms are valid to which all possibly affected persons could agree as participants in rational discourses.[12]

It is important to notice that the notion of validity contained in the discourse principle is purely procedural, since it does not refer to any conditions that action norms should satisfy other than that they be the outcome of a rational discourse, that is, of an argumentation process under discursively ideal conditions. Thus, the specific contribution of discourse conditions to the validity of outcomes is not itself clarified by the discourse principle. Merely on the basis of the discourse principle we do not yet know whether discourse conditions bear on the justice, or substantive correctness, of norms, on the legitimacy of their enforcement, or on both. In order to offer such a specification, Habermas introduces two further principles. He adds a requirement of impartiality to the discourse principle in order to provide a rule of argumentation for moral discourses which are specifically concerned with the justice of norms. As Habermas explains in *Between Facts and Norms*: 'The moral principle first results when one specifies the general discourse principle for

[12] J Habermas, *Between Facts and Norms*, n 1 above, 107.

those norms that can be justified if and *only* if equal consideration is given to the interests of all those who are possibly involved'.[13] The moral principle that results is the so-called principle of universalisation (U), according to which:

> (U) Only those action norms are valid to which all possibly affected persons can accept the consequences and the side-effects that their general observance can be anticipated to have for the satisfaction of everyone's interests.[14]

Since this principle aims to capture the substantive correctness – ie justice – of action norms, it requires an *agreement in judgement* among all possibly affected persons as to which norms are valid, ie just. Discursive conditions bear on the process of reaching such an agreement to the extent that they lead it to track the best reasons available to all possibly affected persons. Thus, the moral principle captures the specifically cognitive impact that discourse conditions have on the substantive validity of its outcomes. A separate question is whether discourse conditions may also have a normatively significant impact on the process of deciding which legal norms to enforce in a particular political community. As an answer to this question, Habermas introduces in *Between Facts and Norms* a 'principle of democracy',[15] according to which:

[13] ibid 108.

[14] Habermas's moral principle can be seen as a reformulation of Kant's categorical imperative in intersubjectivist terms. As McCarthy explains it, 'Rather than ascribing as valid to all others any maxim that I can will to be a universal law, I must submit my maxim to all others for purposes of discursively testing its claim to universality. The emphasis shifts from what each can will without contradiction to be a general law, to what all can will in agreement to be a universal norm.' (T McCarthy, *The Critical Theory of J. Habermas,* Cambridge, MA, MIT Press, 1978) 326. This reformulation aims to capture two important moral intuitions that are absent in other attempts to model impartiality on a principle of universalisation such as Kant's categorical imperative or Rawls's original position. First, it captures the importance of real argumentation among those possibly affected in the process of determining the validity of norms that are supposed to bind them in order to solve their moral conflicts. This insight is lost whenever moral reasoning is modelled as a monological, hypothetical process of deliberation occurring in the individual mind. Second, this reformulation captures the importance of empathy and reciprocal role-taking in the process of determining the validity of moral norms. By modelling impartiality on a process of argumentation that includes all those possibly affected by a norm, it forces discourse participants to put themselves in the shoes of all of those possibly affected, that is, to offer arguments from the perspective of what things would be like if they were in any of the circumstances to which the norm applies. This is, of course, crucial for ensuring that those who, by chance, may already know that they will never be in the position of some of those affected by a particular norm nonetheless base their agreement on whether they could accept the consequences of the norm, if they were in *any* of the relevant circumstances to which the norm applies, that is, if they were *any of those possibly affected* by it. The inclusion of all those 'possibly affected' in Habermas's moral principle is thus the functional equivalent of the 'veil of ignorance' in Rawls's original position. However, in contradistinction to the latter, this feature of the moral principle makes it possible to model impartiality not on the detached, neutral, third person perspective of an ideal spectator or deliberator, but rather on the engaged perspective of participants in moral argumentation who must be able to adopt the perspective of all those possibly affected by the norm at issue. For Habermas's detailed explanations of the similarities and differences between the discourse approach and the approaches used by Kant and Rawls see J Habermas, *Moral Consciousness and Communicative Action* (C Lenhardt and S Nicholsen (trans), Cambridge, MA, MIT Press, 1990) 63–68.

[15] The logical independence between the democratic and moral principles is explained by Habermas as follows: 'The principle of democracy results from a corresponding specification [of the general discourse principle] for those action norms that appear in legal form. Such norms can be justified by calling on pragmatic, ethical-political, and moral reasons – here justification is not restricted to moral reasons alone'. Habermas, *Between Facts and Norms*, n 1 above, 108.

(L) Only those statutes may claim legitimacy that *can* meet with the assent of all citizens in a discursive process of legislation that in turn has been legally constituted.

In contradistinction to Cohen's principle of democratic legitimacy, it is hard to interpret Habermas' principle as appealing merely to a hypothetical agreement among reasonable persons. In its most natural interpretation, this principle does seem to impose a democratic obligation to win the consent of all citizens for political decisions by way of submitting them to democratic procedures that meet discursive conditions as a condition of legitimacy. As Habermas explains in *Between Facts and Norms*:

> This principle [the democratic principle] explains *the performative meaning of the practice of self-determination* on the part of legal consociates who recognize one another as free and equal members of an association they have joined voluntarily. Thus the principle of democracy lies at another level than the moral principle (emphasis added).[16]

Only if it is interpreted as expressing the normative power of citizens to bind themselves by consenting to the enforcement of norms, is it then plausible to claim that, according to the democratic principle, rational opinion and will formation must be institutionalised 'through a system of rights that secures for each person an equal participation in a process of legislation'[17] and also that these political rights 'must guarantee participation in all deliberative and *decisional processes relevant to legislation*'(emphasis added).[18] Now, whether or not this interpretation of the democratic principle is defensible within the discourse approach depends on how the notion of discursive agreement contained in the discourse principle is itself interpreted. But the answer to this question in turn depends on which notion of discursive agreement is actually needed for defending a constructivist interpretation of the moral principle.

III THREE POSSIBLE INTERPRETATIONS OF DISCOURSE THEORY

A Constructivist Interpretation

According to the constructivist interpretation of the moral principle that Habermas favours, discursive agreement among all those possibly affected by a norm is not just the most reliable indicator of the justice or moral rightness of a norm. Instead, this is what the moral rightness of a norm consists in.[19] Such agree-

[16] ibid 110.
[17] Habermas, *Between Facts and Norms*, n 1 above, 110.
[18] ibid 127.
[19] This view is widely shared among contemporary defenders of moral constructivism. See J Habermas, 'Rightness versus Truth: On the Sense of Normative Validity in Moral Judgments and Norms' in *Truth and Justification* (B Fultner (trans), Cambridge, MA, MIT Press, 2003) 237–77 at 258–59; T Scanlon, 'Contractualism and Utilitarianism' in A Sen and B Williams (eds), *Utilitarianism and Beyond* (Cambridge, Cambridge University Press, 1982) 103–28 at 110, 119; T Scanlon, *What We Owe to Each*

ment is thus a *sufficient* condition for moral rightness. As Habermas explains in *Truth and Justification*: 'An agreement about norms or actions that is reached discursively under ideal conditions has more than merely authorizing power; it *warrants* the rightness of moral judgments'(emphasis added).[20]

Now, to the extent that discursive agreement is supposed to warrant the moral rightness of norms it must be a universally valid agreement, that is, an agreement that could be accepted by *everyone*. This further requirement can only be met by adding to the strictly *procedural* conditions of an ideal practical discourse (such as symmetry, equal opportunity of participation, lack of coercion and deception, etc) the further, *cognitive* condition that discourse participants base their agreement on the same substantive reasons. According to this interpretation, the notion of discursive agreement expressed by the discourse principle (D) is the notion of an agreement in judgments among all those possibly affected (under discursively ideal conditions) as to the substantive correctness of the norm at issue.

This interpretation strongly indicates that the notion of agreement in the sense of voluntary consent from distinct individuals carries no independent weight when determining the justice of norms. The more reasons there are to expect that under such conditions everyone would reach the same conclusion, the less plausible it seems to assume that the consent of distinct individuals matters. The hypothetical agreement of judgments among all participants is a function of the soundness of their reasons, rather than of hypothetical consent. In other words, 'consent on the basis of good reasons' is consent without a choice, since dissenting in spite of the goodness of reasons is ruled out as irrational. Thus 'consent' and 'good reasons' are not two logically independent constraints in the context of moral discourses since they cannot come apart or, if they do, the later trumps the former.

The inclusion of substantive agreement among the 'discursively ideal conditions' contained in the discourse principle (D) is indeed unavoidably required by a constructivist interpretation of the moral principle, but this inclusion also forecloses a plausible interpretation of the democratic principle. Interpreting the democratic principle (L) in light of such a notion of 'discursive agreement', it would then seem to be the case that the outcome of a discursive process of legislation could only be legitimate if it were based on unanimous consensus among all citizens regarding its substantive correctness. Thus, democratic decisions made under conditions of reasonable disagreement would be *ipso facto* illegitimate. If unanimous agreement on the substantive reasons that justify the validity of a certain norm is a necessary condition for the legitimacy of its implementation, then majority decisions in pluralistic societies, which are needed precisely because of a lack of substantive consensus, cannot be considered legitimate. It seems obvious that the discourse approach could hardly have an impact on a theory of democracy if it could not

Other (Cambridge, MA, Harvard University Press, 1998) 1–5; B Barry, *Theories of Justice* (Berkeley, CA, California University Press, 1989) 268, 292; R Milo, 'Contractarian Constructivism' (1995) 92 *Journal of Philosophy* 181, 184–85, 190.

[20] Habermas, 'Rightness versus Truth', n 19 above, 258.

distinguish legitimate from illegitimate ways of reaching agreement, even for those cases in which participants in processes of democratic deliberation disagree on the substantive reasons that justify the specific outcomes of such processes.[21]

Under conditions of reasonable disagreement, a principle of democracy that appeals to *hypothetical* unanimous agreement in judgements among citizens as a condition of legitimacy could certainly not capture the *performative meaning of the practice of self-determination* among legal consociates – a meaning that Habermas rightly identifies as the distinctive feature of democratic legitimacy. The principle of democracy can only capture the normative power of citizens to bind themselves if the discursive agreement that it entails refers to the actual 'assent of all citizens in a discursive process of legislation'. Only if it could be reasonable for citizens deliberating under discursively ideal conditions to freely consent to the enforcement of a norm despite substantive disagreement between their respective judgements, could then the claim that the notion of voluntary consent (under such conditions) plays a distinctive role in explaining a dimension of the validity of norms, be justified.

B Antirealist Interpretation

However, if we try to solve this difficulty by interpreting the notion of 'discursive agreement' entailed by the discourse principle (D) as the notion of an 'actual agreement under discursively ideal conditions' required by the democratic principle we immediately run into problems when trying to defend the constructivist interpretation of the moral principle (U). For, according to this interpretation, the actual agreement of citizens under discursively ideal conditions not only authorises the legitimate enforcement of norms but it also *warrants* their moral rightness. The fact that the enforcement of a legal norm has been authorised by the voluntary consent of all affected parties under discursively ideal conditions *is* what makes the norm just or morally right. This decisionistic interpretation of the moral principle would directly undermine the moral universalism of discourse ethics. Beyond this problematic consequence, it would also have a very negative impact on the discourse theory of democracy. For, as a consequence of reducing substantive correctness to discursive correctness, the claim that a norm may be unjust in spite of the procedural legitimacy of the discursive process that brought about its implementation no longer makes any sense. This in turn would imply that the validity of norms agreed upon under discursively ideal conditions could not be undermined no matter how blatantly unjust the (unforeseeable) consequences of such norms turned out to be.

[21] As I will try to show later, I do think that the discourse approach has the resources to explain that crucial distinction. The distinctive contribution of the discourse approach to democratic theory consists precisely in the claim that, under conditions of reasonable disagreement among citizens, the legitimacy of their political decisions is a function of the discursive quality of their deliberation.

It seems that collapsing the distinction between substantive and discursive correctness in order to defend a constructivist account of moral rightness has equally devastating consequences for both the moral and the democratic principle. Including substantive correctness among the conditions of procedural correctness leads to the (potentially anti-democratic view) that all it takes for the enforcement of a norm to be legitimate is that the norm be morally right (ie (L) is reducible to (U)), whereas interpreting substantive correctness as a mere function of procedural correctness leads to the relativistic view that what makes a norm just is simply the fact that its enforcement has been authorised by the voluntary consent of all affected parties under discursive conditions (ie (U) is reducible to (L)). In view of these difficulties, it seems more promising for the discourse approach to accept the logical independence between procedural and substantive correctness and abandon the constructivist interpretation of the moral principle.

C Non-reductive Interpretation

According to the non-reductive interpretation of the discourse approach,[22] the role that discursive agreement plays in the moral principle is evidentiary rather than constitutive of moral rightness. In other words, discursive agreement *entitles* us to assume that a norm is morally right, but it is not what its moral rightness *consists* in. Discursive agreement among all those possibly affected is necessary for us to tell whether a norm is morally right, but the moral rightness of the norm depends in turn on whether the norm is in fact equally in everyone's interest. Our discursive agreement cannot make a norm any more or less just than it actually is, whereas it can certainly be the most rational procedure for us to evaluate *here and now* whether or not a specific norm is just. This is one sense, in fact a *cognitive* sense, in which discursive agreement matters for the validity of social norms. However, the logical gap between agreement and moral rightness opens up the possibility that reasonable people might fail to converge in their judgements in cases of difficult moral conflicts. Given this possibility and the need to reach some decision as to which norm to implement in order to avoid those conflicts, a further distinction is needed for evaluating the validity of social norms. One aspect of the validity of norms is their substantive correctness. Another aspect is the legitimacy of their enforcement. With regard to the latter, the actual consent of citizens reached under discursive conditions of deliberation matters for their validity not in the cognitive sense mentioned before but in a quite different sense, namely, in a *volitive* sense.

[22] For a detailed account of this interpretation of discourse ethics see C Lafont, 'Pluralism and Universalism in Discourse Ethics' in A Nascimento (ed), *A Matter of Discourse: Community and Communication in Contemporary Philosophies* (London, Avebury Press, 1998) 55–78; Lafont, *The Linguistic Turn*, n 3 above; Lafont, 'Realismus und Konstruktivismus', n 3 above; and Lafont, 'Procedural Justice?', n 3 above. Habermas' objections to this interpretation can be found in J Habermas, *On the Pragmatics of Communication* (Cambridge, MA, MIT Press, 1998) 381 n 55 and Habermas 'Rightness versus Truth', n 19 above, 237–77.

According to the democratic conception of legitimacy, collectively enforced norms are valid to the extent that those who are subject to them can see themselves as *authors* of them. In order to meet this requirement, participants in political deliberation must be able to convince one another of the putative correctness of their proposals with reasons that all can accept. This in turn requires that political deliberation takes place under conditions in which it is possible to tell how genuinely convincing the arguments and reasons are, ie under non-coercive, non-deceptive, non-exclusionary discursive conditions. However, in tracking the mutual justifiability of political proposals, political deliberation is not simply tracking their substantive correctness, as it would in moral discourses, but more importantly such deliberation is at the same time tracking the extent to which they can in fact attain *the reasoned assent of those who must comply with them.*[23] Taking into account this intrinsic value of the process of public *deliberation* as such, it is possible to see what is wrong with a constructivist interpretation that assimilates the democratic to the moral principle. It is not simply because discursive agreement may be the best indicator of substantive correctness that participants in political deliberation must justify their views with reasons that others can accept, as in any other discourses, moral or scientific. It is because citizens are under the democratic obligation of *securing each other's free and reasoned assent* before making collective decisions to which all must comply that they must seek discursive agreement.

Seen from this perspective, the main problem with the constructivist interpretation is that it leads to the view that discursive agreement among citizens of a political community matters just in the same way that it does in the context of moral discourses, namely, insofar as it offers the best epistemic means for the goal of reaching substantively correct decisions. It is not surprising that, as we saw before, this line of argument can lead to anti-democratic conclusions, since it makes the validity of democratic decision-making procedures contingent on whether or not they are indeed the best means for the goal of reaching substantively correct outcomes. What this view ignores is the fact that, in the political

[23] In recent writings Habermas does underline the importance of the volitive aspect of the notion of a citizen's consent for democratic legitimacy: 'When collectively binding decisions are at issue, the requirement of deliberative quality needs to be integrated with the inclusion of all possibly affected persons into the deliberative *and decision* processes. After all, knowing about the "yes" and "no" of each potentially affected is already important in practical discourses for epistemic reasons . . . A person cannot let herself be represented by others when controversial interpretations of needs are at stake that affect her self-understanding and world-view . . . But democratic procedures require the equal inclusion of all the affected *not only* because of such epistemological reasons. Otherwise, we could not understand the intuition we connect with the inclusive participation in the political practice of self-determination. Equal participation is just as important as clarifying deliberation because the will of each individual participant has to enter into the "common", collectively binding will. Democratic opinion- and will-formation is targeted at a common will that is not merely rational in the sense of being an adequate solution to a given problem which might just as well be found by experts alone. The common will has to prove at the same time "rational" in the volitional sense that each individual must be able to recognize her or his own individual will in it (even if only on the reflexive level of a procedural consensus)' (author's translation); J Habermas, 'Kommunikative Rationalität und grenzüberschreitende Politik: eine Replik' in P Niesen and B Herborth (eds), *Anarchie der kommunikative Freiheit* (Frankfurt, Suhrkamp, 2007) 406–59 at 433–44).

context of enforcing social norms, an intrinsic element of our goals is to reach mutually justifiable decisions and not just putatively correct ones. Taking into account both goals, the intrinsic contribution of citizens' discursive agreement to the validity of norms does not turn on whether it is the most reliable indicator of substantive correctness, but on whether it is the most reliable indicator of substantive correctness *among the reliable indicators of mutual justifiability*.

The non-reductive interpretation of the discourse approach can offer an affirmative answer to that question by showing how democratic deliberation under discursive conditions, through tracking the force of the better argument, can contribute to determining *where the burdens of proof lie* in the deliberative process.[24] If deliberative democracy is understood as an ongoing process of public deliberation punctuated by elections, majoritarian post-deliberative views can be interpreted as indicators of where the onus of argumentation lies at a particular moment of the deliberative process. This is a genuinely epistemic feature that must be present in any discourse geared to reaching substantively correct outcomes. For if tracking the force of the better argument through deliberation is possible at all, determining where the balance of argument lies at a given time must also be possible in order for the process to have any sort of orientation. However, given the specificities of the commitment to public justifiability that underlies democratic political deliberation in particular, this common epistemic feature – intrinsic to any discourse – becomes democratically significant. For tracking which side of the argument failed to provide convincing arguments in support of a particular decision at a specific time also tracks who failed to meet the democratic commitment of public justifiability at the time a decision had to be made.

Recognising this deliberative failure can thus provide a reason for the minority to give their voluntary consent to the majoritarian outcome of the deliberation process. This recognition is internal to the deliberative process and does not depend on renouncing one's own judgement regarding the substantive correctness of a decision, as the decisionist interpretation of the discourse approach would suggest. It offers a genuine deliberative explanation of why what the majority finds more convincing after deliberation under discursive conditions can[25] lend legitimacy to its implementation, even by the minority's own lights. According to this view, the minority can give its voluntary assent to enforcing the outcome of the collective decision neither because they think it is substantively correct (*per hypothesis* this is not the case), nor because the post-deliberative views of the majority are more likely to be correct (although they may well be, as many epistemic

[24] For a detailed analysis of the account of deliberative democracy that follows from the non-reductive interpretation of discourse theory proposed here see C Lafont, 'Is the Ideal of a Deliberative Democracy Coherent?' in S Besson and JL Martí (eds), *Deliberative Democracy and its Discontents* (Aldershot, Ashgate, 2006) 3–26.

[25] Obviously, whether it does in any given case is, according to discourse theory, a function of whether the deliberative process is genuine, ie whether it actually takes place under discursively ideal conditions such as the inclusion of all available views and arguments, equal opportunities of participation, lack of coercion or deception, responsiveness to the force of the better argument, etc.

democrats claim).[26] Instead, such assent is given because (and to the extent that) the post-deliberative majoritarian views are more likely to reflect the force of the better argument available at a given time. Of course, even if they do, this does not indicate that the minority is wrong from a substantive point of view. But it does indicate that the onus of argumentation is on them to more effectively satisfy the requirement of public justifiability.

Now, recognising that public justifiability can fall short of substantive correctness, as the non-reductive interpretation of the discourse approach does, implies recognising that the conditional agreement of the minority by no means makes the political decision any more or less substantively correct than it actually is. Thus, the minority's success at a future time in finding convincing arguments to show the specific way in which the norm is actually incorrect (unjust, inefficient, etc) would in principle undermine the prior, majoritarian agreement, even by the majority's own lights. This indicates that the commitment to mutual justifiability requires an additional commitment to deliberative contestability, that is, to the permanent possibility of effective deliberative contestation of collective decisions.

This requirement is justified for reasons related to both dimensions of the validity of social norms, their substantive correctness and their democratic legitimacy. A commitment to deliberative contestability guarantees the permanent inclusion of all relevant considerations (evidence, arguments, objections, etc) available at any given time. In so doing, it helps to secure the best possible outcomes from the point of view of their substantive correctness. At the same time, a commitment to deliberative contestability serves the democratic goal of securing the free and reasoned assent of all citizens. It surely does so by guaranteeing the fair value of equal opportunities for participation in the deliberative decision-making process.

However, this is not its only contribution. By ensuring that responsiveness to the quality of reasons is a *permanent* feature of the deliberative decision-making procedure, it also gives necessary assurance to citizens that their consent will not require them to sacrifice substantive correctness for the sake of democratic legitimacy, or vice versa. To the extent that this is so, they can reflectively endorse the ideal of a deliberative democracy as articulated by discourse theory. For, in virtue of the fact that it can track the mutual justifiability of political decisions, democratic deliberation under discursively ideal conditions can promise to secure the substantively best outcomes among those that can attain the free and reasoned assent of citizens.

[26] For epistemic accounts of voting and majority rule see J Coleman and J Ferejohn, 'Democracy and Social Choice' (1986) 97 *Ethics* 6; D Estlund, 'Beyond Fairness and Deliberation: the Epistemic Dimension of Democratic Authority' in J Bohman and W Rehg (eds), *Deliberative Democracy* (Cambridge, MA, MIT Press, 1997) 173–204. For purely epistemic justifications of majority rule as reflecting the best supported views, ie those most likely to be correct, see S Benhabib, 'Toward a Deliberative Model of Democratic Legitimacy' in S Benhabib (ed), *Democracy and Difference* (Princeton, NJ, Princeton University Press, 1996) 72; B Manin, 'On Legitimacy and Political Deliberation' (1987) 15 *Political Theory* 338, 359. In *Between Facts and Norms* (n 1 above), Habermas seems to support this purely epistemic view of majority rule; see eg 306. However, in recent writings he has explicitly rejected it in favour of a view of the kind I am defending here; see Habermas, 'Kommunikative Rationalität und grenzüberschreitende Politik', n 23 above, 434.

Before concluding, let me briefly indicate how this interpretation of the discourse approach to deliberative democracy can resolve the potential conflict between reason and the will – between actual consent and reasonable agreement – and in doing so provide a unified account of the normative conditions necessary for forming a reasonable collective will, as I announced at the beginning. In a nutshell, the conflict can be expressed as follows. On the one hand, the democratic commitment to attain the actual consent of citizens for the enforcement of norms to which they are subject requires granting all citizens decision-making status, that is, equal opportunity to influence the outcome of democratic decision-making procedures in which they participate. On the other hand, the commitment to reach substantively correct decisions requires that the views supported by the best reasons are given greater influence over the outcome – something that is clearly incompatible with giving equal consideration to everyone's views.

The discourse approach to deliberative democracy offers a way out of this potential conflict between epistemic quality and political equality by adding a requirement of democratic deliberation, under discursively ideal conditions, prior to collective decisions as a condition for the legitimacy of its outcomes. Democratic deliberation grants citizens equal opportunities of participation in the deliberative process of shaping or contesting the public justifiability of laws or policies before reaching a collective decision. However, to the extent that such deliberation tracks public justifiability, it can grant better reasons greater influence over the outcome, as reflected in the post-deliberative majority decision, while preserving equal voting rights.

11

Law, Normativity and the Model of Norms

GEORGE PAVLAKOS*

I OUTLINE

THERE EXISTS A widespread consensus amongst contemporary jurisprudents, positivists and non-positivists alike, that the meaning of 'obligation' should not radically shift from law to morality, or any of the other domains of practical reason. Yet there is limited effort in contemporary discussions of legal obligation to engage with the metaphysics of normativity with an eye to a well-founded account of those elements that deliver its non-conditional character.

On a recent occasion I discussed the shortcomings of a prominent positivist account of legal obligation, that of Jules Coleman.[1] In this chapter I turn to a prominent non-positivist account, the model of principle,[2] and argue that, even though it identifies key elements or conditions of normativity *simpliciter*, it stops short of delivering a conclusive account of unconditional legal obligation, an account that would place legal obligation in the same continuum with all other types of obligation. Taking up from where the model of principle halts, I propose a complementary – if more fundamental – account of normativity *simpliciter*, which I dub the *model of norms*. I make a case for it, by looking into universal conditions of normativity and, in conclusion, offer some more specific remarks about the advantages of the model of norms over other competing models.

The first part of the chapter looks into the account of legal obligation tendered by the model of principle. According to it, law is an instance of action-directing action or action that purports to get other agents to comply with the ends it sets out to attain. The idea here is that the very logic of action-direction draws moral

* The paper is part of a five-year research project on 'The Constitution of Globalisation', which is funded by the Research Foundation-Flanders (FWO). I received many a valuable comment from those present at the conference 'The Normative Dimension of Law', which was held in Antwerp in June 2009. I am especially grateful to Ralph Wedgwood and Jules Coleman for saving me from a number of philosophical blunders. Finally, the text has benefited throughout from the detailed comments of Triantafyllos Gouvas.

[1] See my 'Practice, Reasons and the Agent's Point of View' (2009) 22 *Ratio Juris* 74.

[2] I take the model of principle to comprise the host of non-positivist legal theories that is more commonly referred to as interpretivism and whose main exponent is Ronald Dworkin (for the most comprehensive statement of interpretivism's key ideas to this date, see R Dworkin *Law's Empire* (Cambridge, MA, Harvard University Press, 1986), especially chs 2, 7 and 9).

reasons – principles – into the picture of legal obligation, as the one item that can explain how and whether the facts of a social practice, which purports to direct action, come to acquire the status of reasons for action for the subjects of law. Subsequently, this model is contrasted with an alternative model of obligation that takes facts of authority to constitute reasons of action in virtue solely of their structure. In conclusion it is argued that, in contrast to the second model, the model of principle manages to capture what is distinctive about action-directing action in the domain of law – that is, the special normative significance of the possibility to coerce others under a scheme of public institutions.

The third part opens by pointing to a more widespread worry that needs to be addressed before the model of principle can be deemed fit for the role in which it is employed: the worry relates to the ability of principles to constitute genuine reasons for action. In particular, the enquiry investigates the nature of principles and their ability to avoid certain flaws that might pertain to reasons for action in general. In taking up this line of enquiry, the chapter looks into the more general debate on normativity with a view to specifying requirements that anything which purports to be a reason ought to meet. I employ a rationalist analysis of normativity, which brings the idea that intentional thought is normative to bear on the analysis of the meaning of normative terms, such as 'ought', 'obligation', 'duty'. In conclusion, I argue that the content of normativity consists in normative facts, ie norms, which purport to model the content of ideal (or counterfactual) states of the will. Such norms give exhaustively the content of normativity.

In light of the above, the final part advances a two-layered *model of norms*, with the higher level being populated by *norms simpliciter*, and the lower by *norms in a domain*. When considered jointly, the two layers ground the possibility of non-conditional obligation without evoking moral realism and the concomitant suspicion of scepticism. Some key advantages of the model of norms, on the face of it, are discussed over the two other models of legal obligation, that of principle and that of authority. On the one hand, norms resist the 'talking past each other objection' which is commonly levelled against principles. On the other, norms are much better suited to account for the moral limits of action-directing action than either principles or facts of authority, for they illustrate cogently that the grounds of any reason for action already include a concern for others' autonomy.

II THE NATURE OF LEGAL OBLIGATION

Next I turn to two central arguments, which are put forward by exponents of the model of principle. The first is metaphysical and purports to elucidate the interplay between facts and reasons as the two key determinants of legal obligation. The second is normative, aiming to illustrate that legal institutional facts are instances of action-directing action that give rise to an obligation to justification. Both arguments arrive from a different route at the conclusion that law gives rise to obligations *simpliciter*. Subsequently, the model of principle is contrasted with another influential explanation of legal obligation, the model of authority, which explains legal obligation in a contextualist or perspectival manner. Finally, the conclusions drawn from the comparison between the two models serve the purpose of introducing the key themes of the discussion of normativity that follow in the third part.

A The Model of Principle I: Rational Determination

The point of departure of the first argument is that, when looking into the grounds of legal obligation, we ought to assert the priority of reasons over institutional facts. This thesis is recast as the rational determination condition (RDC), which Mark Greenberg has proposed in a recent paper.[3] According to RDC, in order for the facts of any legal practice to determine the content of the relevant legal norms, more than a relation of supervenience is required – all that supervenience can deliver is metaphysical determination, or the condition that the facts of a particular legal practice (LP) determine *factually* a legal norm (LN) across possible worlds. However, more is required in order to establish the *normative* relevance of social facts to the content of any legal norm. Rational determination captures this requirement in pointing to normative entities (for simplicity *reasons*)[4] that make the social facts of the practice relevant to the content of legal norms. More specifically, Greenberg proposes a two-stage model for cashing out rational determination: in the first stage what determines the truth of legal propositions are models, or sets of rules, that make (rational and non-opaque) connections between the factual components of the practice and the content of legal norms. In a second step, models must be validated by reasons. On pain of failing to provide for rational determination, reasons must be conceived of as being external or independent of either the facts of the practice or the legal norms they purport to connect. Finally, Greenberg proposes to understand reasons not merely as rational but also as evaluative standards – value facts; value facts are, in his words, 'all-things-considered truth(s) about the applicable considerations – the Truth, for short'.[5]

The particulars of Greenberg's proposal aside, the crucial point he makes is that the connection between the factual components of legal practice and the content of legal norms must be one that is *normative*, along the lines of RDC. Thus, a great deal of the success of any account of law's normativity will turn on how we

[3] M Greenberg, 'How Facts Make Law' (2004) 10 *Legal Theory* 157, reprinted in S Hershovitz (ed), *Exploring Law's Empire: the Jurisprudence of Ronald Dworkin* (Oxford, Oxford University Press, 2006) 225–64.

[4] Since I am discussing the model of principle, it would be more appropriate to use 'principles' instead of 'reasons'. However, I prefer to stick to 'reasons' for the reason that it captures a wider range of normative items that purport to guide action. In any event, principles are but one kind of reason: they are public reasons of political morality.

[5] See Greenberg, n 3 above, 189. Interestingly, Dworkin argues that Greenberg connects values only indirectly with legal propositions for, actually, in his theory values are only standards for the evaluation of theories (models), not legal propositions themselves. See Dworkin's 'Response' in S Hershovitz, *Exploring Law's Empire*, n 3 above, 291–311 at 310–11.

conceive of the reasons that validate our model of rational determination. Amongst the conditions reasons ought to respect, with an eye to normativity, count those requirements that contribute to a unified point of view of agency.[6] This shows precisely that RDC is not self-standing – it can only cash out law's normativity if it stays in line with the conditions for a unified point of view of agency. For the search for such a point of view concerns as much legal reasons as does those extra-legal reasons that purport to satisfy RDC. In other words, it is more than just the content of the law that needs to be in line with whatever counts as the unified point of view of agency – also, the reasons which ground the rational determination of the law in connecting the facts of the practice with the legal norms must agree with it. Depending on one's understanding of the point of view of agency and the type of reasons this authorises, the project of rational determination will be more or less successful. To that extent, it is simply not enough to ask with Mark Greenberg 'how facts make the law?'. One ought also to ask 'how reasons make the law?'. The first question merely postpones the normative question to the 'meta-level' of rational determination. But it is the answer to the latter question, the one about reasons, which will determine the success of the rational determination of legal norms.

This last question addresses the problem of normativity – that is, the concern that for something to be normative it should be normative for the agent themselves. Let me turn now to an additional suggestion for establishing the internal link between agency and reasons for action.

B The Model of Principle II: the Morality of Action-directing Action

The rational determination condition explains why we need to structurally close the gap between the indeterminacy of the facts of the practice and some normative understanding thereof. However, it still lacks a clear answer about how this gap is to be bridged. What is really that which directs us to the 'correct' principles in whose light the facts of the practice will make normative sense, giving rise to determinate legal obligations?

One way to look at this problem is to think of the facts of the legal practice as having a moral impact;[7] that is to say, that the facts of the legal practice will have a moral effect, will invoke a moral evaluation, in whose light they will acquire normative significance and the power to lay down obligations. In virtue of what do the institutional components of the practice invoke the moral dimension that gives shape to legal obligations?

The answer to this question involves the notion of coercion: institutional interaction has a moral impact because it always involves the *possibility* of coercion. No

[6] I cannot deal at present with this point in more detail. For the complete argument, see my 'Practice, Reasons and the Agent's Point of View', n 1 above; and the discussion below.

[7] My reconstruction of the model of principle is heavily indebted to Nicos Stavropoulos; see his 'The Relevance of Coercion: Some Preliminaries' (2009) 22 *Ratio Juris* 339.

sooner, however, has coercion been drawn into the picture than an evaluative dimension is invoked. Here is how: coercion is not a neutral concept but, instead, can be deemed legitimate or illegitimate. Hence the determinants of legitimacy or the absence thereof can be invoked with an eye to reasons – principles – in whose light the relevant facts of the coercive institutional practice produce legal obligations. However, one should be more fine-grained with respect to coercion. It is not the case that government and its officials need to actually invoke coercion in order for it to become relevant to law. Coercion is already relevant to law in virtue of the fact that the law impacts on the network of the normative relations that obtain between those whom it addresses. How so?

Coercion is always on the cards when it comes to law, because institutional facts are action-directing in an inherent or intrinsic manner. They interfere with the reasons agents have antecedently to institutions by rearranging those reasons in one or the other way. This rearrangement, however, is (normatively speaking) not indifferent, at least not to the extent that we take action-direction to be action-direction of autonomous agents who already respond to reasons and who are likely to be already embedded in a network of reasons at the moment when an institutional act impacts on their lives. Hence, action-direction is not morally neutral: in fact, it acquires the morality of those reasons – principles – that already apply to agents who are capable of handling reasons for action. But if so, then the morality of action-directing action points the way forward in establishing the content of legal obligation: institutional facts amount to legal obligations to the extent and in the manner that they fit into the overall scheme of reasons on which they impact.[8] You see now how coercion is always on the cards: proper action-directing action entails legitimate coercion while flawed action gives rise to illegitimate coercion and, by the same token, to an instance of injustice that ought to be blocked.[9] But, then, all institutional intervention counts as action-direction action. Hence, it can be deemed one of either only: legitimate or illegitimate, *tertium non datur*.

A few more remarks on the logic, and morality, of action-direction are due. Action-directing reasons are reasons that purport to get other agents to act in ways that converge with one's purposes, usually against the background of joint projects or activities. To that extent action-direction is a special mode of normativity that usually pertains to contexts of joint endeavours. Given that such contexts require coordination, action-directing reasons, if successful, can underpin the task of coordination. Thus, if A is engaged in a joint project with B and R is a valid action-directing reason, then A is entitled to appeal to it for guiding B's behaviour. More specifically, if the joint project is one that encapsulates elements

[8] See ibid 343–44, where he builds upon ideas of Thomas Scanlon on the grounding of promissory obligations; see T Scanlon, 'Reasons: A Puzzling Duality?' in RJ Wallace, P Pettit, S Scheffler and M Smith (eds), *Reasons and Value: Themes from the Moral Philosophy of Joseph Raz* (Oxford, Oxford University Press, 2004) 231–46.

[9] AJ Julius, 'Getting People to Do Things' (unpublished manuscript, April 2009, on file with the author) 7–9.

that are typical of a basic structure of a political community, then action-directing reasons can be legally enforced with an eye to coordination.

But when is an action-directing reason a valid source of obligation? It is when it meets the negative constraint of not amounting to illegitimate coercion. Although this negative constraint does not point directly at any grounds that positively shape the content of action-directing reasons, it does so indirectly. Before elaborating further on this point, let me spell out the negative constraint for action-directing action:

(1): A should not (do y, believe that her y'ing will lead B to x and that this fact is a reason to y and fail to believe with justification that A's y'ing will facilitate B's coming to x on the basis of her recognition of reasons to x that she has independently of A's y'ing).[10]

(1) says that leading B to x on grounds that B does not share as leading to x independently of A's action-directing action would constitute an instance of – illegitimate – coercion.[11] Clearly this stipulation does not directly spell out which among such independent grounds are involved; it does so indirectly, however. In recognising the authority of any agent as a negative constraint for coercion, it implicitly takes the same authority to be capable of specifying positively the content of such grounds that would constitute appropriate action-directing reasons. Thus, (1) tells us that action-directing reasons may be only such items that can be authorised by the reason-giving or deliberative capacities of agents *and* do not violate (1). But notice this: (1) is not an extra filter or sieve that comes later to contain or purify items that have been designated as reasons for action antecedently of (1). Rather, (1) is the starting point for grounding action-directing precepts in a manner that is agent-relative, if not relativistic – in fact, as I will argue later, (1) assumes something like a unified normative point of view, one that can ground reasons for action *simpliciter*.

In light of the above, it becomes easier to appreciate how the structure of action-directing action furthers the model of principle: in the model of principle action-directing reasons amount from the impact institutional arrangements have on the scheme of reasons, qua principles, that underpins the interaction of agents in a political community. Those principles comprise substantive principles of jus-

[10] I copy with minor alterations from Julius, ibid 1. I am aware that at the time of writing Julius was elaborating further his thoughts on the matter. To that extent I am not claiming that the quoted formulation captures exhaustively or uniquely the content that Julius confers to action-directing action. That said, it suffices for my purpose here.

[11] Further intricacies of action-direction arising from (1) include: (a) the thesis that an independent reason that applies to my doing x, should also apply to all antecedent actions that lead me to x; (b) in the absence of any reason to the contrary, the same structure should be expanded to interpersonal relations – I ought not to lead you to do x without considering the reasons you have for x-ing as applying also to my own acts that purport to lead you to x; (c) finally, (a) and (b) yield the thesis that coercion, when it serves to coordinate joint action, is justified under the condition that it is legitimate from the first-person point of view before it is addressed to others; for, if coercion facilitates someone's response to a joint requirement, then this person can rely on the fact that the threat of coercion will facilitate everyone else pursuing the same joint requirement, without wronging them in any way; see Julius, n 9 above.

tice plus a procedural principle of equal treatment for all, which is addressed to everyone – and the government – and which, as it were, activates an obligation to establish coherence among the other substantive principles of justice, with an eye to identifying each time the 'moral footprint' of any novel institutional fact, and the legal obligation this may give rise to.

C The Model of Authority

The model of principle, as a source of action-directing reasons for action, can be readily contrasted with the model of authority.[12] The model of authority, prominently defended by Joseph Raz,[13] also purports to generate action-directing reasons with reference to a background network of reasons that apply to agents antecedently of legal institutions.

However, the main difference between the two models lies therein: while the model of principle aims to ground legal obligation on those reasons that apply anyway to agents, by including them in the determinants of legal obligation, the model of authority severs legal obligation from any background normative considerations.

The main reason for doing that is that the model of authority takes a very narrow view on what constitutes an action-directing reason, when it comes to legal obligations. It takes the view that action-directing action is exhausted by the content of the edicts which are uttered as institutional facts within a legal practice. This view stems from the claim, itself almost a stipulation, that for something to be capable of directing action it must be self-contained in its directing powers, which is to say, it must make a practical difference to the reasons of an agent directly, that is without any reference to its impact on any of the other normative circumstances of the agent.

It is not difficult, of course, to see why coercion comes too late in this picture. As we saw earlier, when discussing the structure of action-directing action, the role of coercion was to invoke, as a negative constraint, the whole palette of reasons against which agents operate in virtue of their capacity to reason. However, under the stipulation of action-direction as edict, which the model of authority submits, any such reference to external or indirect determinants of action would deprive legal edicts of their action-directing force. In that case, by conforming to coercion agents would be following a totally separate reason from the reason the edict is pressing – hence, on the authority model, coercion is at most 'a philosophical distraction'.[14]

[12] In the presentation of the model of authority I follow Stavropoulos, n 7 above, 346–49.

[13] J Raz, *The Morality of Freedom* (Oxford, Oxford University Press, 1986); 'The Problem of Authority: Revisiting the Service Conception' (2006) 90 *Minnesota Law Review* 1003, reprinted in J Raz, *Between Authority and Interpretation: On the Theory of Law and Practical Reason* (Oxford, Oxford University Press, 2009) 126–65.

[14] Stavropoulos, n 7 above, 347.

Hence, in preventing coercion from having an impact on legal obligation the model of authority also drives out the conditions for legitimate action-direction from the determinants of legal obligation; and yet no stipulation of authority can change the fact that any action-directing action that fails on the count of legitimacy[15] becomes coercive in an illegitimate sense. However, this may point to a shortcoming of the authority view, rather than the irrelevance of coercion: on the contrary, when action-direction is in play, coercion is always on the cards!

A further undesirable consequence of the authority model is that it fails to live up to the needs of coordination. On the edict view, the coordination capacity of the law is limited, for law is allowed (conceptually) to direct action only up to the point that other directing items take over. If law is in the edicts then it can only trigger off a practice of joint action, but later it is that practice itself that does the work and law drops out of the picture.[16] Conversely, coordination presupposes that the prospect of coercion of others gives a reason for action against the background of a scheme of reasons of which all reasonable agents can partake – in this case, joint requirements.[17]

One last remark is due: it might be far-fetched to claim that the model of authority is straightforwardly guilty of illegitimate coercion. But it is not far-fetched to say that it might be conducive to illegitimate coercion, for it circumscribes the structure of action-directing action and, hence, obliterates the normative requirements attached to it. What is more, the reduced role it assigns to coercion threatens to make the exercise of coercion rather oppressive: in the model of authority, coercion has persuasive force only on the basis of its impact as brute force, as in that case it provides a distinct – prudential – reason to subjects to conform with it, with an eye to avoiding suffering. This, however, would entail, in light of the frequency of actual government coercion, a dangerous impoverishment: by severing coercive action from its reasonable requirements, we would be rendering the state immune from the obligation to legitimise its actions in all those cases (and they are many) where coercive enforcement has taken over the task of coordination from the edicts of officials.

Thus, on the model of authority it is a contingent fact whether legal obligation qua edict is actually in line with the antecedent background reasons of subjects. Of course, one should hope that this is so more frequently than not. However, whether it is or is not has no impact on the existence of legal obligation – or at least it becomes relevant only *ex post facto*, that is, only after the legal obligation has been identified independently of background reasons. In other words, it is not the case that the existence of a legal obligation depends on the background reasons that support the edict of the authority. Such reasons may effect an *ex post* annulment of the duty to obey the relevant edict (conditions of success) but do not affect

[15] Such failure equals to a failure to satisfy formula (1).

[16] See Stavropoulos, n 7 above, 349.

[17] However, for it to work we need to take on board the action-directing structure of coordination: the prospect of coercion can coordinate only if it is deemed legitimate from a first personal point of view (*cf* n 11 above).

the constitution of the legal duty qua edict (content and grounds).[18] For in the model of authority the say-so of the authority bears by itself and without further ado the normative force of a reason that purports to make a practical difference in the overall balance of reasons. To that extent, one may say that legal obligation under the model of authority is always action-directing in a contextual or perspectival sense, from the point of view of the law, and less frequently so in an unconditional manner, as obligation *simpliciter*. Accordingly, the existence of any obligation precedes its capacity to be action-directing; or, what is perhaps a more accurate formulation, its ability to be action-directing *simpliciter* depends on its existence within a context.

III THE DEMANDS OF NORMATIVITY

Rounding up the conclusions of the previous part, the model of principle has argued that for any facts of an institutional practice to make sense to its agents as normative items, the rational determination condition should apply: that is, there should exist normative reasons – principles – in whose light those facts become relevant for the determination of the grounds of legal obligation. Such principles cannot be replaced by authoritative norms because (and this is a further contribution by the model of principle) law is an instance of action-directing action, hence answerable to any moral reasons that ensure for legitimate coercion.

However, this line of reasoning needs refinement: it is imperative that one illustrate in virtue of what principles discharge their role of rational determination. This is a key question with far-reaching implications. It becomes urgent to know whether there is hope for a unified account of normativity or whether legal obligation must be deemed inherently distinct, an *aliud* vis-à-vis moral obligation. In the latter case we would end up with a form of strong contextualism whose disadvantages I have discussed elsewhere.[19] To steer clear of contextualism, however, we must make a convincing case for a unified account of normativity, one that goes beyond the account offered currently by the model of principle. For the latter, in invoking an obligation of government to treat everyone equally, takes a quietist stance and shuns the task of a more detailed explanation of the sources and nature of normativity, or so I will argue.

[18] Thus, the model of authority needs to introduce an artificial distinction between the content and grounds of legal obligation, on one side, and the conditions of success thereof, on the other. For a similar distinction see Stavropoulos, n 7 above, 341–42.

[19] Painting with a broad brush, contextualism is the semantic counterpart of a host of relativist and sceptical philosophies. Its main thesis argues that the content of a proposition varies with the context it is uttered in. The upshot of this view is that, insofar as every sentence takes its meaning from the proposition that pairs with it, it is possible to affirm and deny the same sentence without contradiction, provided it has been uttered in different contexts or from different 'points of view'. Despite its noble cause – that is, to account for apparent inconsistencies in speech and preserve the diversity of ordinary discourse – contextualism threatens with semantic confusion and the loss of communication and ought to be rejected (with some notable exceptions) for most domains of discourse. For a more detailed exposition of the relevant argument and a survey of the contemporary literature, see Pavlakos, 'Practice, Reasons and the Agent's Point of View', n 1 above.

In particular, we must look into conditions of normativity more generally, in a manner that would preclude a contextualist or relativist understanding of obligation. That is to say, it is not enough to merely discharge the obligation of grounding legal obligation by invoking normative principles of a more general order. One must also demonstrate how these principles succeed to be normative in the sense one needs them to be, if legal obligation were to be deemed one of the *simpliciter* type. In other words, one should seek to explain the nature and content of obligation *simpliciter* independently of law and other normative domains.

Such an account could take many forms. For present purposes I would like to focus on such key normative terms as 'ought' or 'obligation' and attempt through a discussion of their meaning or content to explore general conditions and insights about the nature of normativity as a whole. Let me spell out the rough steps of the argument and the main conclusions I seek to establish.

I shall argue that an adequate explanation of the normativity of anything that may serve as a reason for action requires adherence to some kind of internalist account; that is, an account that is capable of connecting the reason with the agent, in a manner that would preclude that x is a reason for an agent A and yet A can still ask 'ought I to follow x?'. At this juncture two options are available: first, to offer a psychological account, one that presents the will or some other mental state as the link between agents and reasons. As a synecdoche for a large host of such accounts I will use the term 'mentalism': mentalism reduces normativity to motivational force and also the question 'what should I do?' to 'what shall I do?'.[20]

The model of authority,[21] when it serves as an account of legal obligation, replicates some of the characteristics of mentalism, albeit in a somewhat covert form. Its mentalism is manifested by the claim that for any legal norm to be given any authoritative content, it must be imputed to the expression of the will (a mental state) of someone (authority) from which point onwards it is assumed to be binding for the will of every other member of the political community.[22] As I shall argue later in more detail, similar mentalist explanations of reasons are forced into a semantic picture which threatens with radical forms of relativism and scepticism.[23] In collapsing the content of any normative proposition into the mental state some agent is in, such accounts pay a high price, for they invert the standard picture of semantic content.

On the standard picture, propositions are semantic items which can be communicated between agents and serve as public standards for determining the content of the sentences we utter and the mental states we are in. Conversely, the

[20] D Parfit, 'Normativity' in R Shaffer-Landau (ed), *Oxford Studies in Metaethics* (Oxford, Oxford University Press, 2006) vol I, 325–80 at 332–33.

[21] See above section II C.

[22] The relation of imputation brings the model of authority very close to the semantic picture inherited from expressivism, which I discuss below. For the discussion in this and the next paragraph, I owe a considerable debt to Ralph Wedgwood for pressing several critical objections during the conference and to Nicos Stavropoulos for valuable discussion on the semantics of reasons.

[23] See below section III B.

mentalist model inverts that picture by suggesting that propositions, and derivatively sentences, be individuated on the grounds of speakers' mental states. Rendering mental items the grounds of semantic content, however, is bound to lead to confusion and, on occasion, even to the suspension of communication. Although more needs to be said in order to establish a clear link between the model of authority and the mentalist conception of reasons, there exists enough evidence that the two may share the same semantic premises. If so, the model of authority would have to struggle hard to avoid the sceptical conclusions that are associated with those premises, with an eye to rescuing the publicity of meaning, as a requisite for accounting for the coordinating role of authoritative directives.

Conversely – and this brings me to the second option – the account I shall advance proposes replacing mentalism and its contextualist results with an account of normativity *simpliciter*. The main requirement for such an account is to switch from mental states to objective grounds of reasons. This shift will take us away from an explanation of normativity qua motivational force. What is more, it will inverse the order of explanation between normativity and motivation: on this view for something to be motivationally efficacious, it ought to be normative first.

The level of objectivity required here should be specified carefully in order to avoid other undesirable results. In working out the level of objective articulation of normative reasons I invoke the tenet of *content-* or *judgement-internalism* (JI).[24] JI is a view about intentional content that applies to a wider context than the realm of practical reason. It is the view that all content must be linked to thinkers in a manner that would preclude that, if p is a proposition about, say, cars, then a thinker judging 'that p' could still be asking: 'is p about cars?'. With this move, normative content, expressed by normative language, requires insertion into the wider picture of intentional content *tout court*: in it content ought to make sense to thinkers in a manner that is objective or invariable – as opposed to contextual – by avoiding being identified with mental states, without, at the same time, making appeal to any brute fact that escapes the possibility of articulation in propositional language.[25]

Interestingly, JI requires a deeper sense of normativity: this is the normativity of thought/content, or the idea that the components of thought are rule-like items which 'obligate' thinkers to certain (intentional) moves on pain of losing their identity as normative beings. This deep sense of normativity further comprises the idea of a fundamental practice – call it the *practice of predication* – whose key characteristic is its non-conventionality.[26]

To round up these intervening remarks, the view I propose holds that the problem of action-guidance is less a problem for motivation (or the distinction between

[24] This is inspired by Ralph Wedgwood's idea of normative judgment internalism; see R Wedgwood, *The Nature of Normativity* (Oxford, Oxford University Press, 2007) ch 1, 23–28. For present purposes I confine judgement-internalism to the normativity of the intentional. An alternative, albeit less elegant, term would be *content-normativism*.

[25] This requirement is formulated as the condition of reason-dependence below section III E.

[26] For a more detailed exposition of this idea see G Pavlakos, *Our Knowledge of the Law: Objectivity and Practice in Legal Theory* (Oxford, Hart Publishing, 2007) ch 4 and my 'Practice, Reasons and the Agent's Point of View', n 1 above.

theoretical and practical reason) and more one of normativity in a broad sense,[27] that is, the sense of linking propositional content to thinkers in an objective manner, as a matter of following a rule. This general way of capturing normativity is, furthermore, most basic. It requires us to think of propositional content as normative and of thinkers/agents as normative, or reflective, beings. Falling below this threshold would obliterate not just practical normativity but also meaning and content in general.[28] On the other hand, once below the threshold it won't help to appeal to psychological states or, what is equivalent, to brute fact for restoring meaning and content.[29]

A Setting the Stage

The argument will unfold in two steps. First, I shall explore a set of ideas that seem to be fundamental to normativity. In exploring those I shall try to spell out conditions of adequacy for any account of normativity. In this sense those ideas will be assumed (somewhat axiomatically) to spell out elements that are intrinsic to normativity, at least on some reflective understanding of our normative practices and the use of normative vocabulary when judging in evaluative contexts.

I shall identify three ideas that are going to function as such conditions of adequacy for any account of normativity:

(i) *Action-guidance*: for something to be a reason for action it is required that there be an internal connection between the reason and the agent. This requirement, which has frequently been labelled 'the normative question',[30] aims to show that normativity requires that something acquires the status of a reason for action by remaining relevant to the practical problem of the agent. When taken seriously, the normative question points to some form of normative internalism. There are two ways to understand normative internalism: first as requiring that there exist a psychological connection between reasons and agents' mental states; alternatively, as merely requiring that reasons stand in an internal relation vis-à-vis the agent, to the extent that, if x is a reason for an agent A, A may not ask 'ought I to follow x?'. On the former understanding, internalism amounts to a number of problems, mainly associated with

[27] In this I concur with the view that there exists something like an autonomous question of 'normativity' over and above the domains in which more specific normative questions arise. This view seems to be gaining in popularity amongst contemporary analytical philosophers. See Wedgwood, n 24 above; T Cuneo, *The Normative Web: An Argument for Moral Realism* (Oxford, Oxford University Press, 2007); and the most illuminating A Gibbard, 'Normative Properties' in T Horgan and M Timmons (eds), *Metaethics after Moore* (Clarendon, Oxford, 2006) 319–37.

[28] As Ralph Wedgwood argues, the two kinds of normativity are (to avail myself of a fanciful expression) equiprimordial; see Wedgwood, n 24 above, chs 1 and 4, and especially 7.

[29] See J McDowell, 'Wittgenstein on Following a Rule' (1984) 58 Synthese 325, reprinted in AW Moore (ed), *Meaning and Reference* (Oxford, Oxford University Press, 1993) 257–93; also reprinted in A Miller and C Wright (eds), *Rule-Following and Meaning* (Durham, Acumen Publishing, 2002) 45–80.

[30] See especially C Korsgaard, *The Sources of Normativity* (Cambridge, Cambridge University Press, 1996) ch 1.

one or another form of mind-dependence and concomitant ideas of mentalism.[31] These problems will pave the way to the second sense of internalism, which is compatible with mind-independence.

(ii) *Mind-independence* (qua independence from mental states): internalism, once purified from the shortcomings of mentalism, can supply valuable insights into normativity. For it to be purged from mentalism it needs to be linked to the objective level of thought. The latter becomes available only if – in one move – we presuppose that thinkers/agents are normative beings insofar as there are normative items that structure intentional content; that is, content that relates to what agents' mental states are about. Judgement internalism (JI) will supply the idea that drives home this intuition.

(iii) *Reason-dependence*: the third requirement can be summed up under the rubric 'semantic version of the open-question argument'. Although the starting point here is Moore's 'open-question', I am employing this idea in a much looser sense. This submits that normativity as a general property of reasons for action should not be 'fixed' in advance in any manner that would give rise to an instance of talking past each other. This, however, would be the case if normativity were to be identified with any substantive evaluative property, say, goodness as utility, or rightness as integrity or equality or distributive justice, etc. A clear instance of this problem occurs when we postulate a mind-independent reality[32] that is not merely independent of mental states, but also reason-independent; that is, independent from the normativity of intentional thought. In this case what is content-giving, with respect to propositions and their components, becomes by stipulation external to the normativity of thought. Yet, if normativity *means/denotes* what lies beyond agents in a radical manner, then it invites a dualism between the method of knowing and the object of knowledge, which is likely to lead to radical scepticism and the loss of meaning.[33]

In light of the three parameters of normativity we can now turn to an account of the normativity of reasons, an account that will prove adequate for an explication of the role of principles as justificatory items of action-directing action, and will further discharge the requirement of rational determination of the facts of a legal practice. Although I shall not delve into the specifics of such principles of action-directing action, the structural account that I will tender will be rich enough to draw some substantive conclusions with regard to the content of legal obligation and the principles of action-directing action that underpin it. In conclusion, I shall argue that some conception of norms, suitably defined, is better suited than that of principles to account (also for the realm of law) for reasons of action-directing action.

[31] See below section III B.

[32] I assume here that presupposing any such reality, not just an evaluative one, would give rise to the problems identified under this point.

[33] The point will be explored in more detail section III E i–ii below.

B Action-Guidance

Normative internalism, to put it in a nutshell, is the view that normative reasons must exercise a special pull to agents' actions, by being internally connected to them. Expressed in more precise terms it is the view that there should be no gap between someone's judging that 'x out to be done' and asking 'ought I to do x?'. As it happens, however, even a quick look at the relevant meta-ethical debates would readily reveal that it is a matter of great dispute how the nature of the required internality should be understood, if it were to bridge the gap between reason and action. There are two important issues that arise in this context, each of which may lead to radically different understandings of the internal connection between reasons and agency. The first concerns the fundamental question whether reasons admit of truth-values or not. Those who say 'no' usually identify reasons with psychological states, while those who say 'yes' hold reasons to be items capable of evaluation in terms of truth and falsity – that is, they ascribe to reasons propositional form. For brevity let me dub the first position 'mentalism' and the second 'factualism'. Investigating further into this distinction and the relevant consequences is the topic of this section.

There is a second issue of equal importance: irrespective of which of the two paths one chooses to walk, mentalism or factualism, there is a further question about the role of the will: is a connection with the will necessary for something to develop normative effects? If yes, does this confine our understanding of reasons within mentalism, in the sense that only mental states can be states of the will? Or is there room for conceiving the will, and the attendant question of motivation, in a manner that disengages it from the relevant mental items? The answer to this question will be postponed until addressed below. There, I shall offer the outline of an argument for arriving at a normative conception of the will, which would account seamlessly for motivation and normativity, as the two sides of the same coin, at the same time as it does away with motivational mental states.

On a popular view, internalism comprises two distinct theses: first, that reasons are mental states internal to the agent (call this 'psychologism'); second, that reasons are normative to the extent that they *are* motivational states.[34] Arguably one may assume that the first idea derives from the second: because motivation is taken to exhaust the meaning of normativity, mentality must be given precedence, for motivating states can only be mental items.

What does this tell us about the content of reasons for action? Basically, it forces upon one a subjectivist semantics whereby the meaning of a reason for action depends on the mental state the agent is in. To understand how this works we need to look in more detail into the semantics of what is probably the dominant form of psychologism, that is, expressivism, and take it to its logical conclusion.

[34] For these distinctions and the discussion that follows, I have benefited considerably from Parfit, n 20 above.

In contrast to standard semantic explanations, expressivism identifies semantic correctness conditions not as truth-conditions but as assertability conditions. This alternative semantic model, labelled by Mark Schroeder 'assertability expressivism' for obvious reasons,[35] submits that the content of any sentence is semantically associated with the condition that the speaker is in a mental state.[36] Take the sentence S: *pain ought to be avoided*. In a truth-conditional semantics, the meaning of this sentence would amount to the proposition *pain ought to be avoided* which subsequently would also determine the content of the mental state one is in. Not so in assertability expressivism! Here the content of S is still derived from the proposition 'pain ought to be avoided' and yet the latter is not the last instance for adjudicating on S's content. For *that* proposition is itself individuated according to the mental state (belief, desire or other) the speaker is in when uttering S, or quoting from Schroeder, 'As a shorthand, we can say that the sentence "expresses" this [mental state]'.[37] Thus, on this understanding, mental states are antecedent to propositions (and, by the same token, also to sentences) with regard to settling meaning and content. What are the consequences of this?

Assertability expressivism as a semantic view leads to a radical form of contextualism[38] and eventually subjectivism. If the proposition expressed by my uttering of any sentence x depends on my having or being in a particular mental state, then the same sentence uttered by different speakers could be corresponding to different propositions. If this were the case, however, it would lead to a devastating form of context-relativity, so much so that it would endanger meaning and communication.[39] This is a devastating objection that needs to be addressed; in fact, it is precisely the objection pressed by the model of principle when it tries to redeem legal obligation as obligation *simpliciter*.

The easiest way to steer clear of psychologism in the form of expressivist semantics is to turn to an understanding of normativity that does not identify it with motivational force; this is possible if one disentangles motivating reasons from motivational states and links them to a more objective level of thought. On this view, a motivating reason is not the fact that one is in the psychological state of, say, believing or desiring that x but, instead, simply, the fact 'that x'.[40] No sooner have we disentangled motivational reasons from motivational states, than we

[35] M Schroeder, *Being For: Evaluating the Semantic Program of Expressivism* (Oxford, Oxford University Press, 2008) 28–35.

[36] Given a postulate of consistency, what is the case for desires applies also to beliefs.

[37] Schroeder, n 35 above, 31.

[38] For the main tenets of semantic contextualism, *cf* n 19 above.

[39] See my 'Practice, Reasons and the Agent's Point of View', n 1 above. There are a number of other problems connected to the semantics of psychologistic internalism. Amongst them is the problem of *embeddedness*, or the objection that if normative sentences were the expressions of mental states then they would fail to embed in the various logical contexts: negation, conditionals, and so on. I shall leave those problems aside here, given that assertability semantics arguably purports to deal with them; see Schroeder, n 35 above, ch 2.

[40] See Parfit, n 20 above, 364–65. This corresponds, at the level of semantics, to what Mark Schroeder calls the standard semantic picture: in it propositions enjoy primacy over either mental states and sentences, in that they ensure that those are individuated uniformly, with an eye to sameness of content – 'same content account'; see Schroeder, n 35 above, 28–33.

realise that the same facts that function as motivational reasons are also our normative reasons.

As it happens, moving away from psychologism requires ascending from the level of mental states to that of – propositional – thought. This move is *in tandem* with a more fundamental distinction, which we must respect when drawing the realm of normative reasons: that between mental states and thoughts (henceforth, propositions). Propositions are items that come as objective as you want, for they can be communicated between agents independently of mental states, or particular sentences of a natural language, in virtue of their being truth-evaluable. They exist, to use Frege's language, at the level of 'senses', not of 'ideas'.[41] This understanding, more or less, underpins the picture of normativity that was earlier dubbed factualism.[42]

This picture amounts to a wholesale rejection of the psychologist version of internalism. However, another version of internalism might and ought to survive; one that satisfies the requirements of the normative question, without falling into the trap of contextualism. For this view to work it must be combined with an account of normativity at the level of objective thought. This I turn to next.

C Mind-Independence

There is a second, healthy, form of normative internalism, one that requires that there exist an internal relationship between reasons for action and agency, without allowing normative reasons to collapse into motivational force. For this type of normative internalism to work the normative significance of reasons should be reconstructed at the (objective) level of thought, in a manner that explains why it is the case that accounting for normativity in this fashion does not leave any residual task to account for motivation separately, which of course would anew require the reintroduction of motivational mental states. To recall an earlier idea, the

[41] Frege's classical distinction can be found in his 'Über Sinn und Bedeutung' (1892) 100 *Zeitschrift für Philosophie und philosophische Kritik* 25 in P Geach and M Black (eds and trans), *Translations from the Philosophical Writings of Gottlob Frege*, 3rd edn (Oxford, Blackwell, 1980) 56–78 and reprinted with minor revisions as 'On Sinn and Bedeutung' in M Beaney (ed), *The Frege Reader* (Oxford, Blackwell, 1997) 151–71 at 154 n D.

[42] With the passing from mentalism to factualism there is one more issue to be settled with regard to the role and importance of mental states: in mentalism desires play a prominent role for normativity, because normativity is conceived of as a non-cognitive affair and, naturally, desires are non-cognitive. Here, beliefs play a secondary role, remaining 'the slaves of passions'. Conversely, in factualism, given the truth-evaluative nature of propositions, beliefs, when compared to other non-cognitive mental states, appear far more apposite to capture the cognitive element involved. True enough, the same proposition (and the reason embedded in it) may become the object of a number of other, non-cognitive, mental states, including desires. However, because the shift from psychologism to factualism renders desires of secondary importance as determinants of normativity, it also 'demotes' their importance at the level of mental life. An attempt to combine the cognitive element of propositions with the motivational efficacy of motivational states is factual motivationalism; see ME Kalderon, *Moral Fictionalism* (Oxford, Oxford University Press, 2005) as mentioned by Wedgwood, n 24 above, 37. Even there, however, the rejection of psychologism yields that beliefs are important only as reflecting, at the level of the mental, the cognitive status of reasons, and by no means as constitutive of reasons.

point that needs to be made is that if reasons are propositions of the form 'that x' then 'that x' is both truth-evaluable and capable of motivating an agent, although it would be better in this case to talk of a motivating reason, than a motivating (mental) state. To put it differently: once normativity has been moved to the level of propositional thought, motivation must also make sense within the same context of objective thought. And it can do so only if motivation ceases to be a matter that is antecedent to normativity, and instead is interpreted in the light of the latter.

How to account for normativity at the (objective) level of thought? The easiest place to start from is the semantic content, or meaning, of reasons. Given that reasons are thoughts, we are looking into the semantic content of reasons qua thoughts – call these normative thoughts. Let me call this for short the meaning of 'being a reason', assuming that it stands for the meaning of 'ought' or 'ought'-like expressions. As we saw earlier, the first condition is that any reason has as its content a proposition and not a mental state:

R: 'that x ought to be done' *as opposed to* R: <my being in 'that x ought to be done'>

Before we proceed with the semantic analysis a few remarks are due with respect to the conception of the objectivity of thought defended at present. This is a normative conception of objectivity, which I have already referred to as judgement internalism (JI).[43] JI comprises two components: the thesis that thought encompasses normative entities, mind-independent, if not reason-independent; second, that agents are rule-followers who precisely respond to the normativity of thought.

The objective level of thought consists of items that reject reduction either to psychological states or to any other non-psychological brute facts of the environment, which would fail to guide thinkers conclusively.[44] Such items must remain cognitively significant[45] or accessible to thinkers – in other words be efficacious in guiding their thought – but also in a manner that does not rid them of objectivity. The best way to understand them is as rule-like entities. This has a couple of consequences: if thought contains rule-like elements, for them to be cognitively significant, we ought to postulate that agents are capable of, or disposed to, rule-following precisely in the manner that is required by those rule-like components of thought.[46] To put it figuratively, the requirement of normativity as (a guarantee of) objectivity is a basic idea that strikes one as true when one realises how little the sub-normative conceptions of the mental can deliver. Yet, no sooner has the requirement of normativity entered the stage than it becomes impossible to disentangle it from another basic idea: that of the normative disposition of thinkers/agents. It is not possible – and it doesn't make sense – to postulate normative

[43] See Wedgwood, n 24 above, 23–28.

[44] This point will be developed in more detail below, section III E.

[45] See Wedgwood, n 24 above, ch 7, for the two dimensions of sense and reference and the importance he bestows on reference.

[46] There is some instance of the circularity that is typically involved in a transcendental argument here.

entities without presupposing that thinkers are normative beings. And the other way round: to understand in what sense thinkers are normative beings we need to postulate an irreducible realm populated by normative entities.

The normativistic explanation of thought aptly demonstrates why mental states, and motivation, cannot be antecedent to normativity, but instead must follow suit from it. If thinkers/agents are normative beings, in the precise sense that they respond to a distinct normative level of thought, then their mental states must also be governed by those same rules, which regulate the content of what these states are about!

These are the main parameters of judgement internalism. However, a lot of flesh needs to be added to this outline. First, we need to spell out, if only briefly, the elements comprised by the normative structure of thought. As soon as this becomes transparent we can move on to explain the normativity of practical reasons.

I shall assume (alluding to Frege's context principle)[47] that the basic unit of the normativity of thought is that of the proposition. Propositions are structured entities that provide the background for interpreting concepts and other semantic items as normative items: only if those can be inserted into a proposition can they count as having discharged their normative role. Most significantly, it is the embedding within a proposition that further discharges the ontological function of such semantic items; thus, a name or a singular term would denote an object within a proposition that is deemed true, that is, depicting a fact.[48] It follows that facts are the ontological environment for objects and properties to flourish.

On the face of it, the structure of the proposition delineates a grammar of thought, which allows for the normative role of the components of thought to unfold.[49] Accordingly, one must refer to the capacity of propositions to function as rules for thought and reasoning and then locate, on the grounds of the normative role propositions play in thought, the specific normative content of any practical or evaluative term. In what follows, although I am simplifying considerably, I remain reasonably confident that I am not leaving out any important details.

[47] This, in few words, is the idea that the content of any linguistic term can only be retrieved within the context of the sentence in which the term occurs. The *locus classicus* is to be found in G Frege, *Grundgesetze der Arithmetik, 2 vols* (Jena, Verlag Hermann Pohle, 1893 and 1903 each vol respectively), translated as *The Foundations of Arithmetic* in M Beaney (ed), *The Frege Reader* (Oxford, Blackwell, 1997), especially paras 60–62. See also the discussion in M Dummett, *Frege: Philosophy of Mathematics* (London, Duckworth, 1991) chs 16 and 17.

[48] For a semantic explication of ontology, see the pioneering work of M Dummett and some of his most prominent students: Dummett, *Frege: Philosophy of Mathematics*, n 47 above; M Dummett, *Frege: Philosophy of Language*, 2nd edn (London, Duckworth, 1981); M Dummett, *Truth and Other Enigmas* (London, Duckworth, 1978); C Wright, *Frege's Conception of Numbers as Objects* (Aberdeen, Aberdeen University Press, 1983); and to a certain extent, despite his more realist undertone, J McDowell, *Mind and World* (Cambridge, MA, Harvard University Press, 1994). Critical of this project is Timothy Williamson, most recently in T Williamson, *The Philosophy of Philosophy* (Oxford, Blackwell 2007) 1–9.

[49] For extensive discussion in the context of legal theory, see Pavlakos, *Our Knowledge of the Law*, n 26 above. On a cautionary note, it should be mentioned that the grammar of propositions does not exhaust the grammar of thought, even though it constitutes an important component thereof. The grammar of thought includes a wider set of normative operations which are allowed between propositions (negation, conjunction, etc).

To make things clear, I shall say in advance that I take normative reasons for action to be normative facts (norms) which are depicted by true normative propositions.[50] Considering, however, that normative propositions constitute the environment within which normative terms discharge their normative function, we can begin by asking about the content of normative terms. In what I have elsewhere called a rationalist strategy,[51] I propose to reconstruct the normative content of normative terms through reflection on the role they play within the grammar of thought.[52] The inquiry is performed at the level of the cognitive significance of thought. Following Frege,[53] intentional content is assumed to be individuated on two levels: the level of sense, that is, the level at which terms have cognitive significance; and that of reference, which comprises all that is signified by true thoughts. On the face of it, the present account begins with concepts and propositions and only derivatively refers to facts and properties. Also for the sake of simplicity let me take 'ought' to stand as a synecdoche for all normative terms.

To put it in a nutshell, what is rationalist about this strategy is that, in subjecting practices to practice-immanent reflection, it arrives at rational principles that place the entire practice in a normative light. Although such principles are accessible only via some concrete practice, their scope extends beyond the particulars of any one practice; thus, it is possible to use these principles with an eye to correction, modification and criticism.[54] What makes the rationalist strategy available is a particular conception of normativity, which regards human agency as fundamentally reflective. On this view, the element of reflection is pivotal in distinguishing mere reflex moves from tokens of intentional behaviour that exemplify the idea of compliance to a rule.[55] More importantly, the idea of reflective rule-following, as the key feature of agency, is placed at the most fundamental level of intentionality, that is, the 'activity' or 'practice' of predication.[56]

Along these lines, the meaning of 'ought' in the most general sense would be given in a (normative) proposition which, if true, would depict a normative fact. How can we arrive at this most general normative proposition?

In order to retain the priority of the level of thought over that of reference, the enquiry should avoid helping itself to items that are thought-independent in a

[50] Some explanation of the advantages of this view will be added below, section IV.

[51] See Pavlakos, *Our Knowledge of the Law*, n 26 above; and 'Practice, Reasons and the Agent's Point of View', n 1 above.

[52] The entire enterprise resembles, methodologically speaking, a kind of conceptual analysis which is circular but informative. For a discussion of the requirements of an adequate conceptual analysis see Wedgwood, n 24 above, 68–76.

[53] See Frege, 'On Sinn and Bedeutung', n 41 above.

[54] See T Burge, 'Frege on Sense and Linguistic Meaning' in his *Truth, Thought, Reason: Essays on Frege* (Oxford, Oxford University Press, 2005) 242–69; S Schiffer, *The Things We Mean* (Oxford, Oxford University Press, 2003) especially chs 1 and 2.

[55] For the details of this view, which draws on ideas of Christine Korsgaard and other constructivist philosophers, and a thoroughgoing analysis of its implications for legal theory, see S Bertea, *The Normative Claim of Law* (Oxford, Hart Publishing, 2009).

[56] See for a more detailed analysis, Pavlakos, *Our Knowledge of the Law*, n 26 above and 'Practice, Reasons and the Agent's Point of View', n 1 above.

manner that deprives them of their cognitive significance.[57] On this condition the most general normative proposition can be understood as a definite description of the meaning of 'ought', which may be arrived at through some form of modest conceptual analysis.[58] Modest conceptual analysis of normative concepts is performed by focusing on one only out of the two dimensions of semantic content, that is, the dimension of intension. Typically, the intension of a concept maps a possible world to the class of referents that fall under the concept in that world.[59] What is most crucial with respect to the dimension of intension is that it does not fix the content of a term by pinning it down to its referent in the actual world, but allows for it to vary across possible worlds. What remains invariable, however, is the general sentence (qua definite description) that keeps us focused on the same concept across possible worlds.

Postponing more detailed argument for now, let me state that the description which would give the full meaning of the practical 'ought' in it most general form, would be some variation of the Kantian Categorical Imperative:

> Act only in accordance with that maxim through which you can at the same time will that it become a universal law.[60]

The proposition expressing the Categorical Imperative, or some variant thereof, gives the content of 'ought' in its more general form – *obligation simpliciter*. In addition, given that it is concluded from conceptual analysis, this fundamental proposition is to be *a priori* true. Thus, insofar as true propositions correspond to facts, the proposition that captures the meaning of ought can be assumed to denote a (normative) fact.[61] Cutting the long story short, the upshot of this line of reasoning is that *it is a priori true that there is a normative fact, a norm, which gives the role of the 'ought' in its most general form.*

At this juncture, we need to pause in order to ask in a more sustained manner about the suitability of any proposition, including the categorical imperative, to express the meaning of *normativity simpliciter*. Why, for instance, won't other forms of conceptual analysis do?

[57] Thought-independence would lead to a dualism between conceptual scheme and conceptual content, whose detrimental effects are well-known. Instead of others see the classic formulation: D Davidson, 'On the Very Idea of a Conceptual Scheme' (1974) 47 *Proceedings and Addresses of the American Philosophical Association* 5; reprinted in D Davidson, *Inquiries into Truth and Interpretation* (Oxford, Oxford University Press, 2001) 183–98.

[58] For the details of modest conceptual analysis see F Jackson, *From Metaphysics to Ethics: A Defence of Conceptual Analysis* (Oxford, Oxford University Press, 1998); TS Gendler and J Hawthorne (eds), *Conceivability and Possibility* (Oxford, Oxford University Press, 2002); M Garcia-Carpintero and J Macià (eds), *Two-Dimensional Semantics* (Oxford, Oxford University Press, 2006); D Chalmers, 'Two-Dimensional Semantics' in E Lepore and BC Smith (eds), *The Oxford Handbook of Philosophy of Language* (Oxford, Oxford University Press, 2006) 574–606.

[59] See Chalmers, n 58 above.

[60] I Kant, *Groundwork of the Metaphysics of Morals in Immanuel Kant: Practical Philosophy* (MJ Gregor (ed and trans), Cambridge, Cambridge University Press, 1996 (1785)) AK 4:421.

[61] For an exhaustive discussion of a semantic constitution of normative facts, which also serves as a model for the present discussion, see C Heidemann, *Die Norm als Tatsache: Zur Normentheorie Hans Kelsens*, Studien zur Rechtsphilosophie und Rechtstheorie, vol 13 (Baden-Baden, Nomos, 1997).

D Normativity and the Will

We need to take up the thread from where we left it section B above. There I argued that the normative question requires us to take up the issue of the relationship between practical reason and the will. The reason is that despite judgement internalism, something more needs to be added in order to answer fully the normative question. Until we have further clarified this issue, it will not be possible to 'fully fledge' the content of obligation *simpliciter*, as this is expressed from a unified point of view of agency.

True enough, if thought is normative then there exists already a proof that propositions are rules. However, while all propositions are rules with respect to intentional content, not all propositions are rules with regard to action – 'what should I do?'; only normative propositions are such rules. Let me unpack this a little bit: the idea of judgement internalism is that the normativity of thought offers the platform for explaining the meaning/content of the various terms we use. Along these lines, we can say that evaluative propositions – and derivatively, owing to the context principle, evaluative terms[62] – acquire their special practical meaning according to the normative use they are being put into, within the semantic structure of thought. Thus, one level of normativity, that of thought, reveals another, that of practical reason. Further, to the extent that we are rational in the sense of judgement internalism, that is, we are disposed to take up thoughts and their components as rules, we are looking out for the normative impact of evaluative propositions on us. But then (and this is the rub) we discover that evaluative propositions are rules that bind thought *as they purport* to regulate action.

This further aspect of the practical 'ought' must be made explicit. Making it explicit, although it presupposes judgement internalism, also requires some additional remarks. Before I attempt a demonstration of how the Categorical Imperative (or some equivalent formulation) may fulfil this task, let me briefly refer to an alternative proposal by Parfit. This exemplifies a standard move of practical realism, which incidentally yields a weaker understanding of judgement internalism;[63] realists say that it is an unanalysable property of normative reasons that they are about what one ought to do. The idea here is that there is no gap between any normative reason 'that p' and the respective motivating reason. How so? Because our motivating reason can be traced back to the same fact that is our normative reason, ie 'that p'. But this may by interpreted at least in two ways: one is to say that 'reason' refers to which action should be undertaken by the relevant agent, as in what the agent ought to be motivated to do;[64] or it might simply

[62] See, on the context principle, n 47 above.

[63] I mean that the realist move, by introducing thought-independent normative content, robs judgement-internalism of its inherent normative capacity. These problems are addressed below under reason independence.

[64] This could be developed further. I can only hint here at the form of an argument: an objective understanding of motivation would entail that mental states are normative states that need to be shaped according to model formulations of the will. Such model formulations of the will can take the form of norms – modal facts expressed in true modal propositions; see also below.

report, in the form of a descriptive proposition, what the contents of some possible action are without prescribing this content qua action. Let us assume for a moment that the latter is what Parfit suggests.[65] Would that be enough?

I think not. For the normative question (as expounded in sections A and B above) leaves a residual role for the will, which cannot be discharged by the role practical realism reserves for motivational reasons. As a result, the role of the will must be taken on board, if in a manner that is free from the predicaments of psychologism. Parfit resists this move, arguing that, by letting the will re-enter the stage, we cannot help but revert to psychologism. Parfit interprets any will-based test of normativity as requiring a test of rationality, whereupon we need to compare actual motives with those we would have after having reviewed all relevant (non-normative) facts.[66] If so, he observes, isn't it possible that we have reviewed the facts and find ourselves still to be compelled by some crazy impulse/motive? He is right, of course. But this, to be sure, is not the whole story.

A variant of the same argument is rehearsed when he dismisses Korsgaard's proposal of normative necessity qua motivational necessity as resting on some notion of psychological necessity, which Parfit takes to be non-normative.[67] In her Tanner lectures Korsgaard asks 'what compels me to do what I am rationally required to do?', and after rejecting the most common answers (Humeanism, voluntarism and practical realism) she proposes an alternative understanding of normative reasons that would answer the normative question.[68] On this, normative reasons should imply some kind of necessity that passes through the will of agents. For Korsgaard, this type of necessity requires that one cannot have a normative reason unless one has a compelling psychological reason – one that amounts to a test of Kantian reflective endorsement. Parfit disagrees. He argues that all psychological necessity is non-normative.[69] To buttress his argument he avails himself of an argument by Williams.[70] The latter contrasts a normative meaning of 'ought' as requirement with a non-normative meaning thereof as incapacity. Incapacity is understood as the psychological incapacity to bring oneself to perform, or even to think of performing, some action – some kind of psychological 'I can't help it!'. On Parfit's interpretation, not only the Kantian test of reflective endorsement, but also any other attempt to involve the will in an understanding of normative reasons would amount to a reduction of normativity to psychological incapacity. He adds characteristically: 'if kleptomaniacs could not act differently, that doesn't make their stealing morally or rationally necessary'.[71]

[65] This interpretation seems to be in line with the idea of practical realism that Parfit detects in Nagel's early work and endorses; there he argues that any reason-judgement 'that p' involves the belief 'that p' which, if not motivating by itself, would still be sufficient to explain our motivation; see Parfit, n 20 above, 340 *et seq*.

[66] ibid 354.

[67] For what follows, see ibid 374–76.

[68] See Korsgaard, n 30 above.

[69] Parfit formulates Korsgaard's view on reasons as follows: 'The reason why some act is *normatively necessary* is the agent's being, through an act of will, in a certain motivating state' (Parfit, n 20 above, 368).

[70] ibid 375–76.

[71] ibid 376.

But one ought to disagree with this understanding: as the displacement of action-guidance from motivation to normativity, effected by judgement internalism, has suggested, it should be possible to conceive of motivation – or the will – in a normative sense. In other words, when, under conditions of judgement internalism, we are 'compelled' to do x, then the meaning of 'compelled' no longer has anything to do with some actual motive of ours but with what would be commanded by what Kant calls a good will, that is, the will that is bound by a norm conceived as an objective normative fact. The content of this norm would be capable of being shared by every other agent. Let us dub the idea of the will as being bound by such a norm 'the normative conception of the will'.[72] The norm of the good will is a fact about what we ought to will given that we are rational. In slightly bolder terms: the norm of the good will tells us that there are some motives that are objective as a matter of knowledge, not of subjective will!

But why would Parfit insist on rejecting objectified will-contents? Presumably, Parfit thinks that there are two ways to capture what a reason for action is about, which are jointly exhaustive: either to say that every reason is the fact of one's being in the psychological state 'that p'; or simply to say that the reason is the fact 'that p'. In the former case we reside in the realm of mentalism, and we take reasons to be motivational states. In the latter we aspire to some form of factualism, assuming that reasons are the very propositions our mental states refer to. However, one must allow for a third possibility:[73] that there are prescriptive facts involving the will. On this view, a reason is the fact 'that I ought to will p'. Such facts can be explained as modal facts that purport to model agents' motivating sates, and admit of reconstruction as norms in a Kantian sense of the term, ie authorised by the reflective endorsement test of a Categorical Imperative.[74]

The normative conception of the will is not a curiosity of the Kantian camp. Others, even amongst those who profess realism, appear to assume some version of it in their accounts of normative reasons. To mention but two prominent examples: one version of realism takes, under conditions of rationality (or rule-responsiveness) the meaning of normativity to involve the disposition of the agent to act upon it.[75] A second view takes normative facts to be counterfactual facts about motivation: here what discharges normativity is not a fact about the actual motivational state of any agent but a fact about a motivational state that is counterfactually simulated under conditions of full rationality.[76] I don't think one would be missing the mark by far if one interpreted those proposals as presupposing, in different degrees of intensity, the involvement of the will in the content of normativity.

[72] I cannot say more here about this concept. However, I assume that an element of 'construction' is essential to it.

[73] Parfit alludes to other possibilities but without elaborating; see Parfit, n 20 above, 363.

[74] See Heidemann, n 61 above, for a reconstraction of norms as second-order modal facts, although this author offers a different grounding of normativity.

[75] See Wedgwood, n 24 above.

[76] See M Smith, 'Internal Reasons' in (1995) 55 *Philosophy and Phenomenological Research* 109, reprinted in M Smith, *Ethics and the A Priori: Selected Essays on Moral Psychology and Meta-Ethics* (Cambridge, Cambridge University Press, 2004) 17–42.

And why should it be otherwise? Once we have ascended from the level of psychology to that of thought, it is natural to assume that the will should also respond to the normativity of content in a manner that is intrinsically action-guiding. Accordingly, the normativity of content will involve action-guiding items that have propositional structure and are intrinsically will-involving. Such items will be normative propositions which, when true, will depict modal facts – norms – which will constitute practical reasons for the performance of action and its justification.

Having established the central elements of normativity *simpliciter*, one further question still remains: does the norm that grounds normativity *simpliciter* exhaust the whole range of practical normativity? The quick answer is that, most certainly, it does not. This, however, should not come as a surprise. Recall that the rationalist model of analysis puts forward a two-level understanding of normativity. While normativity *simpliciter* is given by the general norm of the Categorical Imperative, there are other norms in the various domains of action which actually flesh out the details of what ought to be done. I shall postpone their discussion until the final part.[77]

At present, there is a last point to be taken up before the rationalist account and its contribution to a unified normativity is rendered valid. This is the issue of reason-dependence, as it was announced in the stage-setting section, earlier on.[78] Even though the will can be conceived in normative terms, there is a sense in which it cannot become independent of the conditions that enable the normative conception of the will. To that extent, norms as propositions that model ideal states of the will cannot and ought not in principle to remain inaccessible from within deliberation and reasoning.[79] This reflects the requirement that reasons for action remain tied down to the normative structure of the grammar of thought, rather than 'being given' to us in virtue of some normative environment that is populated by evaluative substances.[80]

In addition, the requirement of reason-dependence as a condition of normativity will shed further light on the shortcomings of practical realism: in claiming thought-independence, practical realism is in danger of undermining the idea of rationality at the grass-roots level. If reasons can in principle be unfathomable, then we may lose our grip on the idea that agents are normative beings in the sense of being disposed to respond to rule-like items within their intentional environment.[81] Conversely, I shall argue that reasons remain always reason- or

[77] See below, section IV.

[78] See above, section III A.

[79] For similar ideas see Parfit, n 20 above, 362–63 and 366; see also Wedgwood, n 24 above, 253 *et seq*.

[80] This would, notoriously, evoke Mackie's objection from queerness; see JL Mackie, *Ethics: Inventing Right and Wrong* (Harmondsworth, Penguin, 1977) 38–42.

[81] It is crucial that the normativity of content be placed at the level of intentionality and not beyond it for the following reason: if non-thought related items are taken to be rules (such as unadulterated properties, facts, etc), then the question of freedom arises: on the plausible assumption that conceptual freedom is the starting point for moral freedom, only if we presuppose that there is a 'first cause' that is not causal itself it is possible to arrive at an understanding of ourselves as free/autonomous in a moral sense. This is exactly why facts/properties cannot be the rules of the practice of predication – as one that embodies conceptual freedom or spontaneity. If they were, then the normativity of thought would be

thought-dependent, if not mind- or psychology-dependent. Such dependence is not neutral vis-à-vis the issue of the will: no sooner have we established the dependence of reasons on thought, than we are supplied with a further reason to treat the idea of the involvement of the will as plausible.

E Reason Dependence

The discussion of the condition of mind-independence and the proposed rationalist strategy for the (re)construction of a unified normative point of view – that is, the point of view of *obligation simpliciter* – has insisted on remaining at the level of objective thought, or the level of cognitive significance, to use the Fregean jargon. Of course, this makes sense in the light of the requirement to get rid of psychologism and the contextualist semantics it fosters. However, there is at least another strategy that would be compatible with the rejection of psychologism: the one suggesting to take on board a strong externalist view which would detect the content of normative propositions in the referents of normative terms in a manner that would make semantic content dependent on the dimension of the reference rather than that of the sense of normative or evaluative terms.[82] Downplaying this second option needs some justification. This I turn to next under the heading of reason-dependence.

Within the short confines of this section, I shall try to touch upon three things: first, I will address a sceptical worry that would emanate from a strong externalist – call it realist – explication of reasons. Such an explication, I will argue, evokes something like the semantic version of Moore's open question, which leaves agents talking past each other. In discussing this worry I will be shedding light, in a retrospective manner, on the two-tier model of reasons and agency of the previous section. Second, I shall briefly claim that the sceptical worry can be traced back to the more general idea of a reason-independent reality, against which our various conceptual schemes are supposed to be measured up. This damaging idea, also known as the dualism of scheme and content, would always lead to a devastating loss of meaning and content. Finally, I will briefly touch upon the issue of truth, with a view to steer clear of the tensions arising from any dualist understanding of content. The three points will be discussed in order.

imposed from the outside, giving rise to a devastating dilemma: either content would be determined externally (as is submitted by the causal theory of reference and other forms of externalism), reducing our conceptual – and hence moral – freedom to a minimum; or there would exist an unbridgeable gap between rules of thinking and their applications, leading to scepticism and the loss of meaning. Assuming freedom, however, facts are not independent in this radical sense. As I have repeated throughout, they are mind-independent, but not reason-independent.

[82] This seems to be, despite some early remarks, the view that Ralph Wedgwood concludes with in his *The Nature of Normativity*, see n 24 above, especially chs 6 and 7. For the topic of normative externalism more generally, see the classic discussion of Bernard Williams in 'Internal and External Reasons' in R Harrison (ed), *Rational Action: Studies in Philosophy and Social Science* (Cambridge, Cambridge University Press, 1979) 17–28, reprinted in B Williams, *Moral Luck: Philosophical Papers 1973–1980* (Cambridge, Cambridge University Press, 1981) 101–13; see also Korsgaard, n 30 above; and Parfit, n 20 above.

(i) Semantic Open-Question

Succinctly put, this is the constraint that accounts of reasons ought not to lead to conceptual disagreement between the various parties to a dispute. Such disagreement occurs when an account attempts to fix essential properties of something's being a practical reason or a value.[83] This takes place when a substantive moral theory claims for itself metaphysical necessity, or the condition that normative properties remain stable across possible worlds. On a successful characterisation, this leads to something like the semantic version of Moore's open question argument:[84] if the properties 'being right', 'wrong', 'just', and so on are fixed according to any of the available substantive moral theories (utilitarianism, deontology, divine command theory, libertarianism, interpretivism, etc), then any disagreement about the meaning of the relevant normative concept will amount to conceptual disagreement, whereupon parties are *talking past each other*.[85] Jules Coleman brings this point to our attention vividly when he says:

> if an adequate account of law must make reference to the values . . . we are going to run into a number of familiar philosophical problems. For example, we will have a hell of a time explaining the possibility of meaningful disagreement using the same concept because there is some reason to think that a utilitarian and a libertarian are not using the same concept of law.[86]

This, of course, is highly undesirable and would lead to a fragmentation of agency, albeit from a different route than the one suggested earlier, with respect to the semantics of contextualism. If, conversely, we wish to ensure that parties in normative disagreement are still disagreeing about the same concept of normativity, then we need to specify quasi-descriptive sentences that state the point of view of agency, without fixing the substantive properties of particular reasons/values in any manner that would disable the possibility of substantive disagreement. Scanlon proposes:

> It might be that the parties to such disagreement are using the words 'morally wrong' to express different concepts. If this is so then they are simply 'talking past each other' when one says 'This action is wrong' and the other says 'No it is not'. But if they are using the words 'morally wrong' to express the same concept, such as 'must not be done' or 'violates standards we all have good reason to treat as authoritative' then there can still be disagreement between them. For one thing, they may disagree about what standards we have most reason to take as ultimate standards of action. More fundamentally, they may have conflicting views about which reasons suffice to justify ultimate standards of conduct.[87]

[83] Although the relation between reasons and values is far more complex, I shall assume considerable overlap for the sake of the discussion. Given the level of abstraction at present, this should not lead to any grave misunderstandings.

[84] T Scanlon, 'Wrongness and Reasons: A Re-examination' in R Shafer-Landau (ed), *Oxford Studies in Metaethics* (Oxford, Oxford University Press, 2007) vol II, 5–20 at 12–13.

[85] ibid 12–13.

[86] J Coleman, 'Beyond the Separability Thesis: Moral Semantics and the Methodology of Jurisprudence' (2007) 27 *Oxford Journal of Legal Studies* 581, 607.

[87] Scanlon, n 84 above, 13.

Such definitions allow us to accommodate the possibility of substantive disagreement about reasons without slipping into devastating conceptual disagreement. They are definite descriptions, amounting from modest conceptual analysis, and keep meaning constant across different contexts (and possible worlds); their great strength is that they leave room for picking out different substantive properties depending on the context or the practice on which we focus. This model is particularly apt for legal reasons, given the need to explain their content in line with their dependence on particular social practices.

(ii) The Scheme–Content Dualism and the Threat of Scepticism

The roots of the 'talking past each other' objection go deeper. Externalist explications of intentional content lead to what has been labelled the dualism of scheme and content. This is roughly the idea that there exists some uninterpreted reality, which functions as a common coordinate system for holding together multiple points of view of cognition. Accordingly, it is submitted that the postulated uninterpreted reality functions as a single, unifying *content* to the many possible *schemes* of cognition, one that secures understanding and, at the end of the day, communication. In setting up the realm of uninterpreted reality as antecedent to thought, however, such views undermine the claim of objectivity they purport to defend. For the idea of an unadulterated reality gives rise precisely to the sort of scepticism that is connected to the existence of multiple conceptual schemes. If there is no guarantee that our thoughts converge on grounds they themselves generate, but instead it is assumed that amongst their determinants count some thought-independent, uninterpreted items, then it becomes tempting to assume that there exist as many schemes of thought (that is, conceptual schemes) as exist thinkers. Yet, no sooner has the plurality of conceptual schemes been granted, than the sceptic can argue that any reason put forward to support an interpretation is merely a construct from a point of view, or *perspectival* construct. But then, if all we are left with are subjective interpretations, how can we remain confident that our reasons are genuine, let alone shared by others? Donald Davidson, in a passage that in the meantime has become one of the *loci classici* of contemporary philosophy, warns against this temptation. In its place he restores the objectivity of thought qua structure of grammar, which he calls 'language':

> In giving up dependence on the concept of an uninterpreted reality . . . we do not relinquish the notion of objective truth – quite the contrary. Given the dogma of a dualism of scheme and reality, we get conceptual relativity, and truth relative to a scheme. Without the dogma, this kind of relativity goes by the board. Of course truth of sentences remains relative to language, but that is as objective as can be. In giving up the dualism of scheme and world, we do not give up the world, but re-establish unmediated touch with the familiar objects whose antics make our sentences and opinions true or false.[88]

[88] Davidson, n 57 above, 198.

The problems of dualism and scepticism become the more intense when one introduces two conflicting rationales for the determination of the semantic content of normative expressions. In more jargon-related terms, this is the case when the gap is allowed to grow between, on the one hand, cognitive significance and, on the other, semantic value of sentences. This needs some explanation; for the purposes of this discussion, I shall remain within a broadly conceived Fregean framework[89]

Both aspects compete for the determination of semantic content (meaning); a sentence, according to Frege, like any other semantic unit, has two aspects: a sense and a reference. The sense of every sentence is a thought-proposition, or an abstract object that represents reality from a point of view; however, notice that this is the unified point of view of cognition, not a mentalistic point of view. Its reference is its truth-value. Thus, any sentence will derive its meaning from the combination of the thought it expresses (which is mostly a question of grammar), plus whatever makes it true. While cognitive significance already includes the various possibilities (informational states) that could make the sentence true, it cannot determine its truth-value. That is a matter that escapes the capacities of cognitive significance. It must be delegated to some evaluation of the thought in light of its truth-maker.

Without breaking any new ground, truth-makers of thoughts have, throughout this chapter, been conceived as facts. Facts are those entities that are denoted by true thoughts. But here a potential conflict comes to light, depending on the way facts are understood. If facts are conceived as thought-independent items, then the rationale of reference takes over from the rationale of cognitive significance with respect to the determination of content. Conversely, if cognitive significance retains its primacy, then the dimension of reference becomes dependent on the former. However, one cannot retain the primacy of both rationales, given that they both compete on the same level. We can see the reason when we ponder the effects of each strategy on the tenet of judgement internalism, which requires that content be normative for the agent.

If thoughts are normative in virtue of their reference (ie a fact, antecedently to their cognitive significance), then what actually guides the thought is the fact. On this model of cognition, facts impinge upon us in an unreflective, automatic manner: here the element of normativity is less important, for conceptual content derives from the environment, irrespective of any normative structure. This model of cognition corresponds to that with which Wittgenstein credits Augustine in the opening lines of the *Philsosophical Investigations*, with a view to taking issue with it later.[90]

[89] See n 41 above.

[90] L Wittgenstein, *Philosophical Investigations*, 3rd edn (GEM Anscombe (trans), Oxford, Blackwell, 2001) para 1; see also the very illuminating discussion in D Charles, 'Wittgenstein's Builders and Aristotle's Craftsmen' in D Charles and W Child (eds), *Wittgensteinian Themes: Essays in Honour of David Pears* (Oxford, Oxford University Press, 2001) 49–79.

Conversely, if thoughts are rules in virtue of their cognitive significance (ie as reasons for the thinker to employ them in a specific manner), then some element of normativity is rendered an antecedent condition of what counts as a property or a fact. In this second interpretation, normativity remains antecedent to factuality, as a condition of the latter.[91]

The latter model, which is the one I wish to abide by, views predication as the rule-guided activity of fact-construction. Facts are not pre-reflective ontological categories, but abstract objects which possess normative structure that is identical with the structure of a (true) proposition. This picture can still accommodate realist concerns about truth and objectivity.

If a proposition for which we claim truth is indeed true, it is so because it accurately refers to existing objects, or accurately represents actual states of affairs; albeit objects and states of affairs about which we can state facts only under descriptions that depend on our linguistic resources.[92] And on another elegant formulation, this time from John McDowell:

> [T]here is no ontological gap between the sort of thing one can mean, or generally the sort of thing one can think, and the sort of thing that can be the case. When one thinks truly, what one thinks *is* what is the case. So since the world is everything that is the case . . . there is no gap between thought, as such, and the world. Of course thought can be distanced from the world by being false, but there is no distance from the world implicit in the very idea of thought.[93]

It is at this basic level of predication that the reflective element of agency makes its first appearance. Owing to its fundamental character for any form of intentional activity, the level of predication imports reflectivity to all other instances of practice, be they of a lower or higher degree of complexity.

Any failure to appreciate the conflict between the two models, leading to placing both at the same level, would effect a breakdown of normativity by evoking something like Moore's open question with respect to the semantic content of intentional items, ie concepts, properties, propositions, and so on. If, in other words, normative propositions' content were to be individuated in a manner that is inaccessible to thought, then there would be no guarantee that thought would continue to track its determinants.

(iii) A Minimal Conception of Truth

One crucial constraint is not to conceive of those determinants as reason- or grammar-independent, for it would render them unintelligible or unfathomable

[91] Interestingly, John McDowell in his influential work *Mind and World* admits 'an alignment of minds with the realm of sense, not with the realm of reference . . . thought and reality meet in the realm of sense' (n 48 above, 179–80).

[92] See J Bohman and W Rehg, 'Jürgen Habermas' in EN Zalta (ed), *Stanford Encyclopedia of Philosophy* (Fall 2008 edn), available at http://plato.stanford.edu/archives/fall2008/entries/habermas/; *cf* Pavlakos, *Our Knowledge of the Law*, n 26 above, chs 1–4.

[93] McDowell, n 48 above, 27.

in principle. This requirement can be met through an appropriate conception of truth. Depending on how one understands truth, one determines the constitution of facts (recall that a fact is what is lined up with a true proposition); if truth is taken to amount to, or to be concluded from, a comparison between a thought and a thought-independent item, then, naturally, facts will remain antecedent to thoughts and the afore-mentioned problems will threaten to emerge. Conversely, if truth (as in *truth of a proposition*) becomes part of the *determinants* of what counts as a fact, then the primacy of the level of cognitive significance is preserved and the normativity of thought remains unscathed.

Although a more detailed account of an appropriate conception of truth must be postponed for another occasion, it is safe to say now that it should be sought amongst the minimalist theories of truth that are available in the philosophical market. Such theories take care to preserve the referential function of assertoric speech, yet without presupposing a robust notion of reference, a notion that would operate independently or antecedently to the semantic structures of thought. A minimal account of truth seeks to settle the question of reference by attending to the grammatical role played by the relevant semantic terms whose reference is at stake. Consequently, while minimalism of truth and reference leaves room for accounting for correct and mistaken uses of assertoric content, it eschews the danger of evoking a robust notion of reference, which threatens with scepticism.[94]

IV THE MODEL OF NORMS: AN OUTLINE

Having put in place the main parameters of the rationalist strategy, I can now flesh out the model of norms that I propose. As a general guideline to consider, this ought to be constructed in two moves. At the top level we have a set of general norms that are *a priori* true: call them *reasons simpliciter*. Reasons *simpliciter* are definite descriptions that specify the *meaning* of normative terms, such as 'ought', 'right', 'wrong', 'obligation', 'duty', and so on. Definite descriptions of the kind suggested are concluded via modest conceptual analysis of normative terms, when those are inserted into the normative structure of thought.[95] Admittedly, reasons *simpliciter* are meagre and can do little to guide action effectively. That said, they might still function as a reliable compass to rationally determine the extension of more concrete norms by 'projecting' their evaluative point upon the context of particular social practices. This brings us to the second level of norms.

The second level of our account of normativity consists in an account of substantive reasons that defers the content of reasons to the specifics of some relevant (social) practice. This account of reasons is rooted in the view that all value needs,

[94] To my knowledge, the most sophisticated instance of a minimal theory of truth (and reference) has been proposed by C Wright in his *Truth and Objectivity* (Cambridge, MA, Harvard University Press, 1992) especially chs 1 and 2.

[95] See above, section III C.

at some level, to be anchored, ontologically speaking, to some practice.[96] Here, in specifying reasons' content, we focus on the second dimension of semantic content, ie their extension. Reasons are given, in this context, by the normative facts that correspond to true normative propositions (call these, *reasons in a domain*). Reasons in a domain are *a posteriori* norms and amount to the projection of reasons *simpliciter* onto the particular facts of a practice. Reasons in a domain behave like propositions that contain proper names: they retain the same reference (for a particular configuration of practice) across possible worlds without, however, blocking the possibility of genuine substantive disagreement, as is the case with other practice-independent conceptions of value. Reasons in a domain are worked out against the various particular social, moral and legal practices which, nevertheless, are constituted in light of the agent's point of view as representing intentional normative activity. Here it is possible to have intelligible disagreements with other participants within the same practice in the light of the abstract formulations of reasons *simpliciter*: consequentialists, libertarians or virtue-ethicists may still engage in meaningful disagreement, provided they remain on the side of the agent's point of view. This comes very close to Jules Coleman's suggestion that it is possible to retain substantive disagreement over the content of the rules of a practice.[97] To the extent that we retain two levels of normativity, it is possible to keep meaning invariable without fully determining content, thus allowing disagreement about the correct configuration of (even) conventional rules. All this would work, of course, only on the caveat that all reasons have a practice-dependent component, for otherwise, if we assume that there existed fully fledged, practice independent *moral* reasons, then disagreement would fall prey to the 'talking past each other' objection.[98]

A related consequence of the two-layered model of norms is that no strict separation can be postulated between norms from different domains. For instance, legal reasons may be related to a particular 'legal' value, such as the value of *Rechtssicherheit*. And yet, to the extent that reasons become relevant from the agent's point of view, no strict separation between 'legal' and other values may be postulated: legal value will make sense only as justified value, and for justification to work, the involvement of reasons from other domains will be required. This means that there is no direct route leading from legal values to the agent's point of view. This route must be demonstrated in a manner that requires backing from all relevant reasons, those that originate in any other relevant domain: morality, ethics, and so on. This, however, should not obliterate the fact that legal reasons may occasionally be assigned equal or even higher weight than other (eg moral) norms. In this sense there is no fixed priority between legal and other reasons in a domain, as, perhaps, the vocabulary of natural lawyers and, occasionally, interpretivists might suggest. What bestows on a reason in a domain its particular weight is its

[96] J Raz, *The Practice of Value* (Oxford, Clarendon Press, 2003) lecture 1.

[97] J Coleman, *The Practice of Principle: In Defence of a Pragmatist Approach to Legal Theory* (Oxford, Oxford University Press, 2001) ch 7.

[98] For the content of this objection see above, section III E(i).

interaction with the level of normativity *simpliciter*, plus reasons from other domains, and should be determined ad hoc.[99]

So far, the account may evoke the impression that reasons *simpliciter* are weak in their regulatory capacity and that, in order for them to guide action, they ought to be combined with reasons in a domain. Notwithstanding their thin status, reasons *simpliciter* retain a direct regulatory impact when it comes to constituting certain kinds of reasons in a domain. This is particularly the case for reasons *simpliciter* that give expression to core ideas of agency, such as *reflection* and *justification*. An example of such a reason simpliciter is: 'there is a general obligation to justify actions'. This proposition, although falling short of fleshing out a full reason for action, would still be capable of preventing certain categories of normative propositions from acquiring the status of genuine reasons in a domain, eg any sentence imposing an obligation on the grounds that morality leads to the perpetuation of the human species. To that extent reasons *simpliciter* and reasons in a domain stand in a relation of synergy and mutual contribution to the agent's point of view.

A Some Advantages of the Model of Norms

I would like to conclude by pointing out some of the advantages of the model of norms over the two other models of legal obligation that were discussed earlier, that is, the model of principle and the model of authority.

I begin with the model of principle. The concept of the norm employed by the model of norms is normatively richer or conceptually antecedent to the concept of principle as employed in the model of principle. Norms in the sense of the model of norms are invoked to answer the normative question, which goes far deeper than the concerns addressed by the model of principle. They do so, not only with respect to the issue of the objectivity of the will, but also with regard to what was earlier referred to as the 'talking past each other' objection. I shall briefly recall both themes in what follows.

Main exponents of the model of principle seem to reject the idea that reasons for action are norms, insofar as norms are linked to the *conventional expression of a psychological state*. However, conventionality in this sense is not a necessary condition for being a norm, as the discussion above has shown. Let me address this point in more detail.

It has been submitted that norms cannot, strictly speaking, be reasons for action, for only facts can credibly perform this function.[100] In this case, the remedy for understanding norms as reasons would be to focus in each case on the relevant

[99] Yet, such ad hoc-ness is not devastating as it is already aligned with the content of the relevant reasons *simpliciter*.

[100] See J Broome, 'Reasons' in RJ Wallace, P Pettit, S Scheffler and M Smith (eds), *Reasons and Value: Themes from the Moral Philosophy of Joseph Raz* (Oxford, Oxford University Press, 2004) 28–55; see also D Parfit, 'On What Matters' (draft manuscript, January 2009), available at http://users.ox.ac.uk/~ball2568/parfit/bibliography.htm, chs 1–4.

(institutional) fact of norm creation. Focusing on such facts of creation, however, would give a head start to the model of authority in the explanation of legal obligation, given that the vehicle of normativity – ie norms – would always presuppose some moment of institutional expression of the content of someone's will. So, the implied conclusion goes, better do away with norms.[101] This is slightly misleading. As the discussion above has illustrated, there is a normative explication of the will which allows us to conceive of norms as modal facts that 'correspond' to true normative propositions, which involve the will in a manner that is non-psychological, hence, objective. Such propositions spell out standards for action which are binding not because they are expressions of the content of some actual state of the will, but because they model the content of an ideal (or counterfactual) state of the will.[102] Such counterfactual 'simulation' of a fully rational will ceases to be an institutional or psychological fact and is rendered normative in an absolute manner: propositions, we should not forget, are as absolute as we want. In the model of norms the objective dimension of the will comes into expression by the level of normativity *simpliciter*, while the various domains of action are left with the more modest task of generating more particular reasons in the light of norms *simpliciter*.

Finally, a few words on the 'talking past each other' objection. In contrast to principles, norms, conceived of as response to the normative question, can explain away the sceptical gap arising from assuming robust normative facts that are enshrined into the fabric of an un-interpreted reality. Given that facts of that sort are doomed to evoke some variant of the scheme–content dualism, with all the devastating consequences that follow for content and meaning, they ought to be expelled appropriately. While the model of principle remains silent on this topic, the model of norms employs the idea of judgement internalism and a minimalist conception of truth to prevent the dualist menace from leaving the ground.[103]

B Norms and the Justification of Action-Directing Action

The advantages of the model of norms are not limited to the model of principle, but extend to include the model of authority. As it was argued in Part II, the model of authority ignores the normative consequences of action-directing action, as a result of which it fails to give a plausible account of legal obligation as obligation *simpliciter*. The model of norms replaces authority by tackling the concerns raised by the model of principle, while improving on the latter's intuitions.

The model of norms brings to expression the internal link between action-directing action and institutional impact in the manner suggested by the model of principle, while doing away with some ambiguities pertaining to the latter. Despite

[101] Stavropoulos in 'The Relevance of Coercion', n 7 above, strikes me as reasoning along these lines.
[102] For a similar construction see Smith, 'Internal Reasons', n 76 above.
[103] See section III E above.

having brought to light the importance of coercion, as an intrinsic constraint of action-directing action, the model of principle faces a further difficulty: it remains open-ended as to the possibility of locating moral principles *inside* the process of action-directing action. Given the residual question 'what guides the will?' it always seems (as the model of authority assumes) that some institutionalised instance of the will – an authoritative will – ought to be imported to discharge the task of action-direction.

This ambiguity disappears in the model of norms: in taking on board normativity *simpliciter* as consisting in a Kantian Categorical Imperative, the model of norms buys into the familiar idea that the way we direct ourselves and (derivatively) others entails that action-direction is subject to a constraint: that of not subjecting anyone who is capable of reason-giving to coercive interaction. This constraint to action-direction is intrinsic to how we conceive of reasons, in a manner that introduces a substantive justificatory constraint to all action-guiding items. The pairing of the activity of action-direction with constraints imposed by practical reason, once in the model of norms, is enabled through the conceptual relation between two of the formulations of the Categorical Imperative in Kant: that of the *humanity formula* and that of the *means–ends formula*. Because (Kant tells us) the process of giving reasons to ourselves acquires the rational structure he describes, this is why action-directing actions are necessarily subjected to a constraint from coercion: a coercer is legitimate in directing the action of a coercee only if the latter has a reason to perform the action, a reason that he would in any case have independently of the coercer's ends, which are served by the action directed at the coercee.

This relation can be best brought into expression through the hierarchical relationship between the two-tier structure of normativity, envisaged by the model of norms. On the one hand, normativity *simpliciter* demarcates the nature and function of normativity and introduces an obligation to justify action-direction that is intrinsic to the nature of action-guidance. On the other, normativity in a domain provides for the terrain where substantive justificatory reasons are fully articulated, be it through institutionalised legal processes or other less formalised practices of practical reasoning.

In slightly different terms, the model of norms combines the two aspects of norm-based normativity: the fact that norms are directed at the will (cancelling the gap between knowing a norm, and being required to act according to it) with the idea that norms, in their basic mode of existence as action-directing reasons for one's own will, already contain the ideal aspect of obligation *simpliciter*, as one requiring that one should not get others to do things in an illegitimately coercive manner.[104]

Thus, it is an essential requirement of the model of norms that there exist a hierarchical relation between the various levels of normativity. This is not an unfamiliar idea in legal theory. Norms stand in inferential relationship, as Kelsen

[104] *cf* Julius, n 9 above; for the transition from the personal to the interpersonal level *cf* n 11 above.

has demonstrated and as the model of authority most likely assumes.[105] What the model of norms adds to this picture is a postulate to expand the hierarchical chain of norms beyond law, in a manner that satisfies the normative link between the two levels of normativity it introduces – normativity *simpliciter* and normativity in a domain. The outcome of this expansion is that for a legal norm to give rise to an obligation, it becomes a requirement that it be linked to a 'higher' justification of action-direction; or, in related terms, that amongst the determinants of the grounds of validity of any legal norm there exist an inferential link with some norm *simpliciter*.

This would also steer clear of the danger of a regress of norms to which Kelsen's edifice remains vulnerable. In the model of norms there can be no regress because there are, necessarily, two and only two levels of normative inquiry: the level of the Categorical Imperative, or reasons *simpliciter*, where the notion of normativity is first articulated, and the level of domain normativity, where reasons are ingrained in the various practices. No higher level would make sense, for the level of obligation *simpliciter* exhausts the meaning of normativity. Further, domain reasons are not insular between domains but instead are made to communicate via the level of reasons *simpliciter*, while remaining bound to the perspective of normativity.

[105] This hierarchical relationship between norms has recently been introduced with great force in the model of authority through the idea of the deep convention; see A Marmor, *Social Conventions: From Language to Law* (Princeton, NJ, Princeton University Press, 2009) ch 3.

12

On Constitutive Normativity

CORRADO ROVERSI

I INTRODUCTION

THERE HAS BEEN much discussion in philosophical literature in recent years about what has come to be known as 'constitutivism', or the 'constitutive strategy'.[1] The main ambition of this strategy is to find a solution to the so-called normative question, namely, the search for the ultimate grounds of moral obligations, by showing that these grounds are to be found in the constitution, or essential make-up, of human agents.[2] This solution is clearly and explicitly the offspring of a Kantian approach to normativity, based on an explanation of the inherent constitution of agency – of our ability to act – and on a series of transcendental arguments. Typically considered a champion of this view is Christine Korsgaard, who first argued for it in *The Sources of Normativity* and continues to do so in her recent book, *Self-constitution: Agency, Identity, and Integrity*.[3] David Velleman, too, has argued extensively for a constitutivist view, in *The Possibility of Practical Reason*[4] as well as in his recent *How We Get Along*.[5] It is also worth noting that the fundamental argument at the core of these views may be traced back to Alan Gewirth's 'argument from agency', expounded in *Reason and Morality*.[6] And recently, in *The Normative Claim of Law*,[7] the constitutivist view has been applied by Stefano Bertea to the problem of the normativity of law.

Oddly enough, many authors who in recent years have dealt with the constitutivist strategy seem to have overlooked the striking similarities it bears to another Kantian approach to moral normativity, namely, discourse ethics (*Diskursethik*). This is the view put forward over the last 40 years by Karl-Otto Apel and Jürgen

[1] The expression 'constitutivism' can be found in D Enoch, 'Agency, Shmagency: Why Normativity Won't Come from What is Constitutive of Action' (2006) 115 *Philosophical Review* 169, and in L Ferrero, 'Constitutivism and the Inescapability of Agency' in R Shafer-Landau (ed), *Oxford Studies in Metaethics* (Oxford, Oxford University Press, 2009) vol IV, 303–33. The expression 'constitutive strategy' can instead be found in S Bertea, *The Normative Claim of Law* (Oxford, Hart Publishing, 2009) 212.

[2] See C Korsgaard, *The Sources of Normativity* (Cambridge, Cambridge University Press, 1996) 7.

[3] C Korsgaard, *Self-constitution: Agency, Identity, and Integrity* (Oxford, Oxford University Press, 2009).

[4] JD Velleman, *The Possibility of Practical Reason* (Oxford, Oxford University Press, 2000).

[5] JD Velleman, *How We Get Along* (Cambridge, Cambridge University Press, 2009).

[6] A Gewirth, *Reason and Morality* (Chicago, IL, University of Chicago Press, 1978).

[7] Bertea, n 1 above.

Habermas, as in Apel's *Transformation der Philosophie*[8] and Habermas' *Moralbewußtsein und kommunikatives Handeln*,[9] and it is aimed at grounding moral normativity as constitutive of discursive rationality. This same view has been applied to the problem of law's normativity by Robert Alexy, for example in his *Theorie der juristischen Argumentation*[10] and in *Begriff und Geltung des Rechts*,[11] and by George Pavlakos in his recent *Our Knowledge of the Law*.[12]

In this chapter, Korsgaard's and Apel's work are discussed as paradigmatic of the two afore-mentioned approaches and are brought into comparison by underscoring how they complement each other.[13] The discussion is laid out as follows. In Section II, I explain how Korsgaard's constitutivist strategy and Apel's discourse ethics revolve around transcendental arguments, and in Sections III and IV I specifically take up their theories and bring out their similarities. In Sections V and VI, I discuss the sense in which these two approaches can be considered as a single approach, that is, I will show them to be interdependent, arguing in particular – in Section V – that a central challenge to discourse ethics can be answered by appealing to the constitutivist strategy, and that the converse is also true (Section VI). In Section VII, I outline a merged approach obtained by combining some basic tenets from the constitutivist strategy with some from discourse ethics. I draw my conclusions in Section VIII, pointing out that even though this merged approach has more explanatory punch than the two independent views from which it issues, it nonetheless falls short of answering some other crucial problems confronting those views.

II THE TRANSCENDENTAL STRUCTURE

In *The Grounds of Ethical Judgment*, Christian Illies discusses as two variants of the same transcendental approach to the moral foundation Alan Gewirth's derivation of the right to freedom from the constitution of human agency and Karl-Otto Apel's transcendental arguments for discourse ethics.[14] In this chapter, I will attempt a similar comparison between Korsgaard's constitutivist and Apel's discursive approach to normativity. For the sake of brevity, I will take up Illies' terminology and will call Korsgaard's central argument 'the argument from agency' and Apel's 'the argument from discourse'.

[8] KO Apel, *Transformation der Philosophie* (Frankfurt am Main, Suhrkamp, 1973).

[9] J Habermas, *Moralbewußtsein und kommunikatives Handeln* (Frankfurt am Main, Suhrkamp, 1983).

[10] R Alexy, *Theorie der juristischen Argumentation* (Frankfurt am Main, Suhrkamp, 1978).

[11] R Alexy, *Begriff und Geltung des Rechts* (Freiburg, Karl Alber, 1992).

[12] G Pavlakos, *Our Knowledge of the Law: Objectivity and Practice in Legal Theory* (Oxford, Hart Publishing, 2007).

[13] It is mainly for the sake of simplicity and clarity that I have chosen these two authors as paradigmatic. In fact, I believe that (with some adjustment) the arguments developed in this chapter can be extended to David Velleman and Stefano Bertea as regards the constitutivist strategy, and to George Pavlakos as regards the discursive approach. This is why I will draw on these other authors when that will prove necessary to elaborate on my points.

[14] See C Illies, *The Grounds of Ethical Judgment: New Transcendental Arguments in Moral Philosophy* (Oxford, Oxford University Press, 2003).

As was just mentioned, both Korsgaard's argument from agency and Apel's argument from discourse are aimed at finding an answer to the problem of the moral foundation, namely, the question of how moral reasons can ultimately be grounded: Why must I do what moral norms ask of me? Why should I follow them? Where does the normativity of moral reasons ultimately come from? These are all variants of what Korsgaard calls the 'normative question' and Apel the problem of the 'ultimate foundation of ethics'. Both Korsgaard and Apel think that this question cannot be solved through an appeal to direct experience, such as the experience we have of natural phenomena. Indeed, both authors describe in full detail how the materialistic conception stemming from the scientific revolution inevitably rules out the possibility of deriving values from any description of the world.[15] Hence, the normative question – the quest for the ultimate moral foundation – is not something we can hope to solve by looking at moral phenomena in the same way as we look at natural phenomena, because natural phenomena are morally neutral.

This does not mean, however, that the normative question is something we cannot find an answer to: Korsgaard and Apel both think it possible to answer the normative question by changing the observer's point of view. Natural phenomena are something we observe from the outside: we apply to them our rational capacities and formulate hypotheses about their structure and behaviour, possibly gaining significant confirmations or refutations. Not so with moral phenomena. As Hans Albert has famously argued, when the normativity of moral norms is analysed from the outside, it falls subject to the 'Münchausen Trilemma', whereby any moral justification must inevitably lapse into an infinite regress or into circularity or into *petitio principii*.[16]

This 'external' point of view is not, however, necessary. According to Apel, any attempt to ground moral normativity from this point of view is fated to fall into the Münchausen Trilemma, because that view necessarily compels us to answer the normative question by tracing normativity to a higher principle different from that around which we have framed the question, thus pushing the same question further along indefinitely. Further, the external point of view is not just unnecessary according to Korsgaard: it is also *insufficient* as a way to go about answering the normative question, because this question arises in 'the first-person position of the agent who demands a justification of the claims which morality makes upon him'.[17] As Korsgaard writes in another passage, '[v]alue, like freedom, is only directly accessible from the standpoint of reflective consciousness . . . Trying to actually see the value of humanity from the third-person perspective is like trying to see the colours someone sees by cracking open his skull'.[18]

[15] See eg KO Apel, 'Das Apriori der Kommunikationsgemeinschaft und die Grundlagen der Ethik: Zum Problem einer rationalen Begründung der Ethik im Zeitalter der Wissenschaft' in KO Apel, *Transformation der Philosophie* (Frankfurt am Main, Suhrkamp, 1973) vol II, 358–435, especially at 361–63; and Korsgaard, *The Sources of Normativity*, n 2 above, 1–5.

[16] See H Albert, *Traktat über kritische Vernunft* (Tubingen, Mohr, 1968) 11.

[17] Korsgaard, *The Sources of Normativity*, n 2 above, 16.

[18] ibid 124.

Moreover, aside from being neither necessary nor sufficient, the external point of view is even impossible in some cases. Korsgaard and Apel both agree that we cannot have such an external knowledge of everything – there are some things that we, as human and rational agents, cannot but view from within. Why? Because, in a sense, we *are* those things. Hence, if we could demonstrate that moral normativity inevitably stems from what we *are*, then we would manage to find the source of moral normativity – this time not from an external point of view but from an internal, or rather, a reflective one.

This project for the foundation of normativity revolves around a transcendental argument, meaning an argument that proceeds from two fundamental features: first, a starting point that we cannot but take for granted (here, reflective rationality); and second, the derivation of something inevitably linked to that starting point, something *constitutive* of that starting point. Korsgaard's and Apel's arguments differ significantly in the specific fleshing out of such an argument, but both can be traced to this common transcendental core.

Some authors have drawn a distinction between 'explorational' and 'retorsive' transcendental arguments.[19] Explorational transcendental arguments proceed from a given starting point assumed as necessary, and then derive conclusions inevitably linked thereto, conclusions typically constitutive of that starting point. The structure of these arguments is that of a *modus ponens*, with the second premise in contrapositive form:

'Necessarily A; if not necessarily B, then A is impossible; hence, necessarily B'.

Retorsive transcendental arguments instead have the typical structure of a *reductio ad absurdum* and are designed to show that calling something into doubt is absurd because such calling into doubt would necessarily presuppose that which is doubted. The structure of these arguments is therefore apagogic:

The sceptic says 'Not necessarily A'; if the sceptic says 'Not necessarily A', then necessarily A; the sceptic falls into contradiction; hence, necessarily A.

Korsgaard's argument from agency and Apel's argument from discourse can be recast as transcendental arguments differing by the distinction just mentioned. That is to say, Korsgaard could be said to use an explorational transcendental argument and Apel a retorsive one. These two arguments will briefly be reconstructed in Sections III and IV on the basis of this distinction, but I should point out from the start that the distinction is not to be taken too much at face value. Indeed, as will be made clear, Korsgaard clearly derives from her main explorational transcendental argument another retorsive argument inextricably bound up with the first. And, conversely, however much Apel prefers to cast his argument as a retorsive one, there are passages in which he reframes it in an explorational form.

[19] The terms 'explorational' and 'retorsive' I take up from Illies, n 14 above, 31, but the same distinction has been advanced in other contexts, too; see eg C Roversi, 'Constitutionalism and Transcendental Arguments' (2008) 59 *Northern Ireland Legal Quarterly* 109.

III KORSGAARD'S ARGUMENT FROM AGENCY

Korsgaard's argument for constitutivism has two variants, one discussed in her 1996 book *The Sources of Normativity* and the other in her recent *Self-constitution* of 2009.

The first variant of Korsgaard's argument proceeds from the premise that we, as human beings, are self-conscious beings. As such, we can distance ourselves from our perceptions and impulses and consider whether they are good reasons for the beliefs and actions we take up. It is this reflective scrutiny, essentially consisting in our seeking reasons, that raises the normative question.[20] In *The Sources of Normativity* – and this is indeed a central point of her view in general – Korsgaard argues at length that we could not discern what counts as a reason for us if we did not have what she calls a 'practical identity'. She writes in this regard:

> When you deliberate, it is as if there were something over and above all of your desires, something which is *you*, and which *chooses* which desire to act on. This means that the principle or law by which you determine your actions is one that you regards as being expressive of *yourself*.[21]

In Korsgaard's view, this practical identity is therefore the source of normativity for all our reasons: 'Your reasons express your identity, your nature; your obligations spring from what that identity forbids'.[22] And she further maintains that we cannot be governed by our practical identity without necessarily valuing our being human as a crucial part of that identity:

> *this* reason for conforming to your particular practical identities is not a reason that *springs from* one of those particular practical identities. It is a reason that springs from your humanity itself, from your identity simply as a *human being*, a reflective animal who needs reasons to act and to live.[23]

Hence (Korsgaard concludes) given that we act under reflective scrutiny, we must treat our practical identity as normative, and so must value our being human as a fundamental part of that identity. But this is not confined to *our* human nature. We cannot, in Korsgaard's view, value ourselves as human beings without valuing *other* human beings, too, this because these other beings can immediately elicit in us reasons for valuing them which are analogous to the reasons we have for valuing ourselves.[24] The conclusion is that human identity, both ours and that of other people, is for us a *normative* affair.

The second variant of Korsgaard's argument is not essentially different from the first. Indeed, Korsgaard describes it as having 'the same conclusion, but with

[20] See Korsgaard, *The Sources of Normativity*, n 2 above, 93.
[21] ibid 100.
[22] ibid 101.
[23] ibid 121.
[24] ibid 143–45.

a more direct focus on agency'.[25] Here, the argument starts with the consideration that we, as human beings, cannot choose not to be agents. As Korsgaard states from the outset in *Self-constitution*: 'Human beings are *condemned* to choice and action'.[26] Korsgaard argues here for a specific concept of action roughly equivalent to 'performing an act for the sake of an end', thus building into that concept an essential link between actions and reasons: 'An action is an essentially intelligible object that *embodies* a reason'.[27] As in *The Sources of Normativity*, Korsgaard proceeds here by maintaining that in order to be able to perform actions (in the sense of 'action' just specified) we must see them as expressions of our selves as unified agents. In *Self-constitution*, however, Korsgaard draws from this essential connection between practical deliberation and identity the new conclusion that to act is to constitute ourselves as unified agents: self-constitution through action is our essential function as rational agents.[28] She then argues at length that we could not conceive of ourselves as unified agents – as agents distinct from the impulses we find within us – if we did not universalise our reasons in accord with the categorical imperative; she thus concludes that the categorical imperative is a constitutive standard of rational unified agents, its normativity depending on this constitutive role.[29]

However, the passage from valuing my own reasons to valuing the reasons of others is obtained by Korsgaard in a slightly different way here than in *The Sources of Normativity*. She maintains that acting as a unified agent is equivalent to interacting with others in accordance with reasons which can be shared, this because 'acting is quite literally interacting with yourself', in such a way that 'constituting your own agency is a matter of choosing only those reasons you can share with yourself'.[30] Thus, when acting as a unified agent, you make choices in keeping with reasons you may share with your future self – which is the same as acting according to reasons that you may share with any other rational agent. Hence, 'respect for humanity is a necessary condition of effective action'.[31]

It should be clear that these two are indeed explorational transcendental arguments. They start from a premise which claims to be necessarily true, namely, that we are reflective creatures, or agents. And, as happens with transcendental arguments, this is not meant to be simply an empirical or scientific truth. Scientific truths are discovered from a third-person perspective, while a transcendental premise is something we should concede from our first-person perspective as agents, and as was just remarked, this latter perspective is the only one through which (according to Korsgaard) the normative question can be answered. Korsgaard's transcendental deduction is meant to show that there is something necessarily presupposed in this reflective nature of ours, and this something is

[25] Korsgaard, *Self-constitution*, n 3 above, 25.
[26] ibid 1.
[27] ibid 14.
[28] ibid 42.
[29] ibid 32–33, 72–76, 81.
[30] ibid 202.
[31] ibid 206.

precisely the conclusion we are looking for, namely, moral normativity. The normativity embedded in human identity stems from our constitution as reflective and rational agents. Given that we cannot escape our reflective and rational agency, and given that moral normativity is constitutively linked to that agency, 'moral identity is therefore inescapable'.[32]

Normativity is in this view unconditional because constitutive of a game we cannot avoid playing. In fact, it is odd to even call it a game, because we *are* that game. Korsgaard seems not to worry about the doubts that many authors have raised about the normative status of constitutive rules.[33] In her view, constitutive rules are standards, and as such are clearly normative, for otherwise we would not have a concept of defectiveness. Just as there is a conceptual distinction between a bad tool and a good one, and this distinction is owed to the normativity of the standards constitutive of a tool, so there is a distinction between good and bad human beings which is traceable to the constitutive standards of agency and humanity. That is to say, human beings *must* value humanity, as represented in themselves and in others, in the same sense of *must* involved in saying that a tool *must* serve its function. But Korsgaard does not stop here. Not only does she say that constitutive normativity is perfectly possible, she also says it is the *only* conceivable normativity which may claim to be unconditional:

> the *only* way to establish the authority of any purported normative principle is to establish that it is constitutive of something to which the person whom it governs is committed.[34]

Constitutive normativity is therefore not only unproblematic: from Korsgaard's perspective, it becomes the basic *paradigm* of normativity. This leads to a strong unified conception of normativity: moral normativity is conceived by Korsgaard as continuous with epistemic normativity. In *Self-constitution*, Korsgaard argues the categorical imperative to be normative in the same sense as the laws of logic, since both serve to unify the agent and are as such an instance of constitutive normativity:

> if George lacks logic, his mind will be a disunified jumble of unrelated atomistic premises, unable to function as a mind at all. It will be a *mere heap* of premises. And that is where the normativity comes in . . . The principles of practical reason, if they are to be normative, must be the principles of the *logic* of practical deliberation. They must be formal principles. For without such principles the will, like George's mind, will be a *mere heap*, not of ideas now, but of impulses to act.[35]

[32] ibid 129–30.

[33] The normative status of constitutive rules is problematic even for the philosopher who introduced the concept, JR Searle. As Joseph Raz has correctly pointed out, Searle himself wavers with regard to the normative status of constitutive rules: see J Raz, *Practical Reason and Norms*, revised edn with new postscript (Oxford, Oxford University Press, 1990) 110. On at least one occasion, however, Searle does explicitly state that constitutive rules have a normative status: see JR Searle, *The Construction of Social Reality* (London, Allen Lane/Penguin Press, 1995) 48.

[34] Korsgaard, *Self-constitution*, n 3 above, 32.

[35] ibid 67.

This constitutive role makes it so that, just as the laws of logic cannot figure as premises in a logical demonstration – because they are the conditions for the very possibility of logical reasoning – neither can the categorical imperative figure as a premise in *practical* reasoning, precisely because the categorical imperative is the fundamental law of practical deliberation. Practical reasoning presupposes from the outset the categorical imperative, and so it also consequently presupposes, in Korsgaard's view, the value of humanity.

This means that Korsgaard's argument can quite simply be reformulated as a retorsive transcendental argument. For if the sceptic asserts through reasoning that humanity should not be valued, then the sceptic (according to Korsgaard's argument from agency) is by that very measure presupposing the value of humanity and is falling into contradiction. In *The Sources of Normativity*, Korsgaard discusses this retorsive reformulation of her argument from agency by referring to the debate between communitarians and liberals.[36] According to a well-known communitarian critique, the liberal and universalistic conception of the person assumes an 'empty self' – in the communitarian view, persons must instead conceive themselves as essentially situated in a specific culture and community. However, as Korsgaard argues, this tenet, which forms part of the communitarians' practical identity, implies that they recognise human beings as having inherent value. In fact, if communitarians argue that cultural and communitarian bonds are to be valued for our development as human beings, they are thereby presupposing that human beings must be valued. As Korsgaard argues:

> Someone who is moved to urge the value of *having* particular ties and commitments has discovered that part of their normativity comes from the fact that human beings need to have them. He urges that our lives are meaningless without them. That is not a reason that *springs from* one of his own particular ties and commitments. It is a plea on behalf of all human beings, which he makes because he now identifies in a certain way with us all. And that means that he is no longer immersed in a normative world of particular ties and commitments.

Korsgaard concludes this argument with a vivid formula: 'Philosophical reflection does not leave everything just where it was'.[37] It may be worth noting that this same formula could perfectly serve as the motto of Apel's retorsive argument from discourse, the topic to which I will now turn in the next section.

IV APEL'S ARGUMENT FROM DISCOURSE

It becomes immediately apparent, as we look at Korsgaard's argument from agency in its retorsive form, how the argument traces back to Apel's well-known retorsive transcendental argument for the foundation of discourse ethics. In briefly presenting Apel's argument, I will mostly consider his seminal work of

[36] See Korsgaard, *The Sources of Normativity*, n 2 above, 118–19.
[37] ibid 119.

1973, entitled *Das Apriori der Kommunikationsgemeinschaft und die Grundlagen der Ethik.*[38] In fact, even though Apel has extensively discussed and developed his work over the last 30 years, I believe that the core of his argument for the foundation of ethics has not significantly changed with respect to that initial statement.

The argument proceeds as follows. Moral scepticism should be regarded not as an abstract thought existing *in vacuo*, but as an interlocutor's concrete assertion. This restatement of the sceptic challenge is rooted in Apel's thorough criticism of what he calls 'methodical solipsism' (*methodischer Solipsismus*), the view that 'the possibility and validity of judgements and of will-formation can in principle be understood . . . as a constitutive performance of individual consciousness'.[39] In Apel's view, which in this respect takes up many classic Wittgensteinian arguments within a rationalistic framework, thought is essentially linked to language, and language is in its own turn understood as an essentially interactive phenomenon. The validity of individual thinking therefore presupposes communication between thinkers: any assertion is essentially an argument advanced within a community.[40] This means that, according to Apel, a sceptic doubting the possibility of any moral foundation does nothing different from making an assertion, such as 'moral judgments cannot be grounded' or 'there is no moral reason that can be grounded'. But this pragmatic restatement of the sceptical doubt has some crucial consequences. In fact, sceptics asserting something as true are making a claim, namely, that they can defend their thesis against any possible interlocutor.[41] Hence, in advancing such a thesis, moral sceptics implicitly endow their potential interlocutors with rights, among which the right to advance reasonable objections; while at the same time implicitly taking on obligations and duties, among which the duty to reply pertinently: this because 'assertions are at least implicitly connected with *communicative actions* – actions making moral claims on all the members of the community of communication [*Kommunikationsgemeinschaft*]'.[42] In arguing against the possibility of any ethics, moral sceptics therefore implicitly presuppose some moral norms, namely, 'the basic moral norms [*die moralischen Grundnormen*] of a community of critical communication'.[43] These moral norms are described by Apel as follows:

> Whenever we make an argument, we implicitly recognise all the possible claims that any member of the community of communication can make which can be justified through rational arguments . . . and at the same time we commit ourselves to advancing arguments by which to justify all our claims to the other members. Further, the members of

[38] See n 15 above; it should be noted that Apel does not use the expression 'discourse ethics' (*Diskursethik*) in this essay. This is an expression originally used by Habermas in *Moralbewußtsein und kommunikatives Handeln* (n 9 above), an expression Apel later adopted himself: see, eg KO Apel, 'Diskursethik als Verantwortungsethik: Eine postmetaphysische Transformation der Ethik Kants' in G Schönrich and Y Kato (eds), *Kant in der Diskussion der Moderne* (Frankfurt am Main, Suhrkamp, 1996) 326.

[39] Apel, *Das Apriori*, n 15 above, 375 n 26 (author's translation).

[40] ibid 399–400.

[41] See ibid 401.

[42] ibid 401 (author's translation).

[43] ibid 415 (author's translation).

the community of communication (and so, implicitly, all thinking beings) are in my view obligated to take into account all virtual claims of any virtual member; that is, they must take into account all human 'needs', so long as these needs bring into being claims on others.[44]

In Apel's view, the normativity of these moral norms must be presupposed even in the face of the most radical doubt about moral normativity: such normativity is therefore grounded.

The link is clear between this argument and Korsgaard's argument retorsively reformulated: it is argued in either case that moral normativity is implicitly presupposed even when someone calls it into doubt. And if Apel's transcendental argument is reframed in an explorational form, the analogy emerges even more clearly. Indeed, according to Apel, those who doubt the possibility of moral normativity contradict themselves *because* moral normativity is constitutive of argumentation, and argumentation is constitutive of thought and action. Hence, the explorational variant of the argument from discourse starts out from the universality of argumentation as constitutive of reflective thinking:

Even de facto solitary thinkers can only explicate and verify their own argumentation to the extent that they can . . . internalise the dialogue of a potential argumentation community.[45]

It is important to note that this kind of reflective thinking is, for Apel, a condition for the possibility of an individual's self-comprehension (*Selbstverständniss*) and self-identification (*Selbstidentifikation*), something very much akin to Korsgaard's insistence on self-constitution and practical identity. Apel, though, seeks to replace Kant's transcendental starting point of the unity of self-consciousness with the 'intersubjective unity of interpretation', which 'must in principle be acquired in the unlimited argumentation community'.[46] Apel's next step is to show how, given that argumentation entails the moral norms of the community of critical communication:

whoever acts even only meaningfully – whoever, for example, has an alternative and takes a decision, claiming to understand himself or herself in doing so – implicitly presupposes the logical and moral conditions . . . of critical communication.[47]

The conclusion is that:

accepting a basic moral norm . . . is part of the conditions of possibility of any argumentation, and insofar as methodical solipsism can be said to have been refuted, such acceptance forms part of the conditions of possibility of any valid self-understanding.[48]

[44] ibid 424–25 (author's translation).
[45] ibid 399 (author's translation).
[46] ibid 411 (author's translation).
[47] ibid 414 (author's translation).
[48] ibid 416 (author's translation).

For Apel, as for Korsgaard, the starting point for this transcendental explorational argument – reflective thinking essentially conceived as argumentation – is justified by way of reflection:

> Whoever takes the obscurantist decision can nonetheless *understand* this decision only by presupposing that which he himself or herself is denying . . . and when he or she takes such a decision in a radical and principled sense, he or she thereby abandons the transcendental community of communication, and in so doing he or she forsakes the possibility of self-understanding and self-identification. (In speculative and theological terms, this point may be stated by saying that only through an act of self-destruction can the devil become independent from God.)[49]

According to Apel, this reflective, first-person perspective entails that we, as linguistic agents, cannot but ascertain what is inevitably implied by the pragmatics of our own language. This insistence on pragmatics as an object of philosophical reflection is the reason why Apel often calls his own argument a 'transcendental-pragmatic argument' for the ultimate foundation. And it is important to note that in Apel's view this is intended not only as an argument for moral foundation but also as a confutation of universal fallibilism in the theoretical domain. In his 1973 essay, as well as in many other essays, Apel argues at length that the principle of fallibilism as applied to all theoretical judgements is inconsistent, showing how argumentation must be taken for granted even by fallibilism.[50] This leads him to the same conclusion which Korsgaard later comes at, too, namely, that some truths can neither be logically demonstrated nor called into question, because they are presupposed by logical demonstration. Aristotle's famous elenctic argument, as presented in Book Gamma of *The Metaphysics*, is clearly the antecedent for such a view, and it is no accident that both Apel and Korsgaard make explicit reference to this argument as an antecedent of their own.[51]

V THE PROBLEMS OF FREEDOM AND OF AUTONOMY

It should emerge from the discussion in Sections III and IV that Apel's argument from discourse and Korsgaard's argument from agency are in many respects twin arguments. Both are aimed at grounding moral normativity, and both are transcendental arguments that can be framed in either a retorsive or an explorational form. Both start out from the unavoidability of rationality and agency, and both purport to show that moral normativity is constitutively linked to this starting point. The two arguments do also *differ* in several respects, however. Thus, Apel's

[49] ibid 414 (author's translation).

[50] See, among many others, KO Apel, 'Fallibilismus, Konsenstheorie der Wahrheit und Letztbegründung' in his *Auseinandersetzungen in Erprobung des transzendental-pragmatischen Ansatzes* (Frankfurt am Main, Suhrkamp, 1998) 149.

[51] See eg Apel's thorough discussion in 'Fallibilismus', n 50 above, 172; see also Korsgaard, *Self-constitution*, n 3 above, 79.

central concern is the rational structure of language as constitutive of thought, while Korsgaard's is reflective thinking and autonomous action; Apel insists on the pragmatic structure of argumentation as a transcendental language game, while Korsgaard focuses on the individual process of reason-giving; and on a broader note, it seems that while Apel is more interested in publicness, intersubjectivity and pragmatic questions, Korsgaard instead lays more emphasis on the autonomy of individuals along with their epistemic capacities.

In this section, I argue that rather than taking the argument from discourse and the argument from agency in different directions, these differences make them interdependent, or complementary. I will illustrate this complementarity by presenting two central objections to these two arguments and discussing how an adequate answer to them makes it necessary to tweak both arguments to the point of making them almost undistinguishable. Given that the argument from discourse and the argument from agency fold into each other in the face of these objections, it is in my view much more accurate to regard them as representing a single theoretical perspective.

According to the argument from discourse, moral norms are constitutively linked to the pragmatics of the transcendental language game of argumentation. This puts moral normativity on a par with the normativity typical of the rules constitutive of assertive speech acts, and in taking this path, the discursive approach risks collapsing moral normativity into semantic normativity. This tendency becomes apparent in the recent book by George Pavlakos entitled *Our Knowledge of the Law*, where the argument from discourse is recast in an original way, developing a conception Pavlakos calls 'pragmatic rationalism'. Like Apel, Pavlakos takes as his starting point the fundamental language game of assertion and argumentation, a game conceived as the practice of giving and asking for reasons: he calls this game 'the practice of grammar'.[52] Pavlakos conceives this practice as the common ground enabling both objectivity and normativity in linguistic rule-following – this because, in his view, all the questions about correctness in linguistic usage ultimately lead to the fundamental practice of assertion and justification. Hence, the practice of grammar is presupposed as a Wittgensteinian 'bedrock' where all rational agents stand *ab origine*: its status is prior to our conceptual operations and provides us with an ultimate and conventional ground for justification, thereby conferring a normative 'depth' on all linguistic practices. Pavlakos thus proceeds from the unavoidability of the practice of grammar by showing that this practice presupposes a weak notion of autonomy, conceived as 'something like the freedom to willingly abide by a normative standard' and consisting of 'choice, freedom, responsibility'[53] – the reason being that semantic content, as we have seen, is essentially connected here with justification. If (i) speaking a language means knowing how to make assertions and (ii) knowing how to make assertions is equivalent to knowing how to give reasons ((i) and

[52] Pavlakos, n 12 above, 114–15, 124–26, 136–41.
[53] ibid 143, 145.

(ii) being the two pillars of pragmatic rationalism), then, as the argument goes, speaking a language necessarily presupposes the autonomy of linguistic agents. The second step in the argument consists in showing that, just as autonomy conceived as our ability to follow rules is the necessary precondition of the normativity of grammar, so *moral* autonomy conceived as our ability to hold our will bound to rules is the precondition for the normativity specific to practical reason, a normativity that Pavlakos identifies with that of Kant's categorical imperative. Hence, from this perspective the value of moral autonomy is grounded in the normativity typical of practical reason, which in its own turn is grounded in the normativity of grammar.[54]

In grounding the normativity of fundamental moral values in the unavoidability of the normative linguistic practice of giving and asking for reasons, Pavlakos' pragmatic rationalism clearly proceeds in synchrony with the argument from discourse, and it takes that idea even further, arguing that argumentative rationality is linked to the normativity of meaning. However, Pavlakos' greater accuracy in arguing this point throws into even greater relief the problems connected with the approach. There are two distinct problems here, one which I will call the problem of freedom and the other the problem of autonomy.

Let us proceed in that order and start with the problem of freedom, which arises from the idea of normativity as constitutive of language. Consider this idea in light of the paradigmatic example of constitutive rules, that of the rules of chess: are we free with respect to the rules of chess? The answer to this question (it seems) is that we *are* free in a sense, but in another we are not. Clearly, we are free to choose whether to play or not. This, however, is freedom we have not with respect to the constitutive rules of chess – the freedom to choose whether or not to follow them – but with respect to the practice of *playing* in general. This freedom depends on a structural feature of the practice of playing, namely, that this practice essentially consists in our engaging in recreational activities and that in normal circumstances we can choose whether or not to participate. In this broader sense, then, we are free to choose whether or not to play chess. But if I do choose to play chess, I will then be bound by its rules: I will not be free to choose whether to follow its rules – I will not, in Pavlakos' words, have 'a range of choices as regards their application'.[55] The rules of chess are constitutive of the game, and this means that if we do not follow them, we are not properly playing *chess*. The moment we choose to play chess, the game's constitutive rules will tell us *how* that is to be done.

Let us now extend this simple observation to the matter of language. On the one hand, we are not free with respect to the rules of grammar, given that they are constitutive of this practice – we cannot choose for ourselves how to make assertions, judgements or inferences, and in this respect the rules of grammar can be compared to the rules of chess. But on the other hand, a radical difference separates the two:

[54] Pavlakos, n 12 above, 147–48.
[55] ibid 143.

there is a sense in which following the practice of grammar bears no relation to playing a game like chess, for as essentially linguistic agents, we cannot choose to speak a language in the same sense as we can choose to play a game. As Wittgenstein makes clear with his well-known considerations on the 'form of life' (*Lebensform*), we grow up *within* a language, and for this reason our conceptual structures are inevitably rooted in it.

When the argument from discourse looks to language as a necessary foundation for normativity, it clearly relies on these observations by Wittgenstein. Apel explicitly uses Wittgenstein's theory of language games, strengthening it to serve a foundational role, and Pavlakos does the same thing in discussing the practice of grammar. But if the practice of grammar cannot, as a transcendental condition of possibility, be avoided, how can we say we are free with respect to morality? And, if we want to retain moral freedom of choice, how can this constitutive normativity of language, which unavoidably constrains our conceptual operations, be the ground for moral normativity? It seems that the argument from discourse faces here a dilemma. On the one hand, the argument postulates language as an unavoidable, transcendental necessity, something without which we could not find an ultimate foundation for normativity. On the other hand, the argument seeks to derive moral normativity from the constitution of language, were it not that moral normativity is something with respect to which we must be conceived as free agents. So, the argument from discourse must either concede that agents are free with respect to language – but this would contradict the unavoidability of language as a starting point for the argument – or it must concede that agents are not free with regard to the moral norms constitutive of discourse, but then we are left with the question of how we could conceive these norms as moral.[56]

Quite interestingly, this same problem has previously been sensed by another crucial author in discourse ethics, Jürgen Habermas, who, unlike Pavlakos, maintains that the normativity of language, along with epistemic normativity, is not continuous with moral normativity. Habermas' point of view on normativity emerges clearly in an essay where he discusses the philosophy of Robert Brandom:

> Brandom misunderstands himself to a certain extent because he makes use of an overly inclusive conception of normativity and assimilates norms of rationality in the broadest sense – logical, conceptual and semantic rules as well as pragmatic ones – to norms of action . . . Being affected by reasons is, however, quite a different matter to being obliged by norms. Whereas norms of action *bind* the will of agents, norms of rationality – and conceptual norms in general – *direct* their minds.[57]

[56] One could object here that moral freedom is not touched by the constitutive nature of moral normativity, because this nature inevitably forces us to accept not specific moral norms but the game of moral justification. Such a solution, however, seems to imply that the principles whose normativity is justified on constitutive grounds are not, strictly speaking, moral principles in themselves – in Pavlakos' case, the solution implies that moral autonomy is not a moral value. I am not sure whether constitutivist theorists would accept a similar conclusion.

[57] J Habermas, 'From Kant to Hegel: On Robert Brandom's Pragmatic Philosophy of Language' (2000) 8 *European Journal of Philosophy* 328.

Habermas clearly connects this difference with the question of constitutive rules. In his view, constitutive rules and moral rules entail two entirely different sorts of obligation:

> There is no single 'deontological' sense of normative obligatoriness. The rules of logic, geometry, and arithmetic; the rules of measurement in physics; the rules of grammar and of linguistic pragmatics serve the production and syntactic order of symbolic objects – signs, figures, numbers, calculations, propositions, argumentations, etc. These rules, broadly understood as conceptual rules, are constitutive of their corresponding practices [*Praktiken*]. As long as these practices do not refer to anything outside their own praxis [*Praxis*], any infraction of the rules will have intrinsic consequences only . . . Nobody punishes us – not our conscience, not society, not nature. On the contrary, social action-norms [*Handlungsnormen*] have the 'deontological' sense of holding their addressees bound to follow the rules in question, and here the kind of sanction depends on the kind of rule (it depends on whether what we break or depart from are moral rules, legal rules, customs, conventions, or social roles).[58]

As a consequence, Habermas does not think that the moral norms of discourse are constitutive of discourse. In fact, if moral norms were to be conceived as rules constitutive of the transcendental language game of assertion and argumentation, then we could not, in Apel's words, make an assertion without necessarily 'taking into account all virtual claims of all virtual members' in the community of communication, and that conclusion would seem quite odd. As Habermas clearly states in his essay 'Diskursethik', of 1983, the moral norms of discourse need not be followed in order for an assertion to be successful: It suffices to this end that those participating in argumentation *assume* these norms to be effective, 'and it does not matter whether, and if so to what extent, this assumption in any given case is counterfactual'.[59] This is an important point, making it clear that the community of communication as represented in the argument from discourse – what Habermas calls the 'ideal speech situation' (*ideale Sprechsituation*) – is at least partly counterfactual, and so the moral rules of discourse cannot properly be conceived of as *constitutive* of discourse but only as *regulative* idealisations by which discourse is governed. Apel, too, often speaks of a dialectical tension between the idealised presuppositions of assertion and their factual concretisations.[60]

It follows from these considerations that we cannot, on the argument from discourse, conceive moral rules and values as constitutive in the same sense as the rules of grammar or of speech acts are said to be constitutive. The argument cannot be that a speaker must *follow* the moral rules of discourse in order to make an assertion, but rather that a speaker must *recognise* these rules as binding. The practice of discourse, then, is constituted not by our *meeting the conditions* set forth in the rules of discourse, but rather by these rules' *normativity* – by their bindingness

[58] J Habermas, *Wahrheit und Rechtfertigung: Philosophische Aufsätze* (Frankfurt am Main, Suhrkamp, 1999) 22–23 (author's translation).

[59] J Habermas, 'Diskursethik – Notizen zu einen Begründungsprogramm' in *Moralbewußtsein und kommunikatives Handeln*, n 9 above, 53–125 at 102.

[60] See eg Apel, *Das Apriori*, n 15 above, 426.

rather than their efficacy. Thus, if the moral norms and values grounded through the argument from discourse are not conceived as rules constitutive of the language game of assertion and argumentation, but rather as regulative rules binding the participants in that language game, then the constitutive normativity based on the argument from discourse is not necessarily incompatible with freedom of choice, and the problem of freedom is solved.

This clarification, however, does not succeed in defending the argument from discourse from the other previously mentioned problem, that of autonomy. How can the argument from discourse derive the autonomy of moral agents from the essential heteronomy of linguistic practices? If moral normativity stems from language, then it depends on something thrust upon us since birth: Wittgenstein's *Lebensform*, which the argument from discourse appeals to, does not come from within us but rather surrounds us 'from without'. Hence, from this perspective we are not, properly speaking, morally autonomous, because it seems that moral normativity is made here into the outcome of a contingent education within a given language. But, clearly, if we are not autonomous with regard to the sources of moral normativity, then it becomes difficult to understand how the argument from discourse can serve a foundational role for morality, for the question arises as to why we should abide by the moral constitution of something that has simply been imposed on us. There is no evident reason why we should recognise the inner morality of language as binding, given that we recognise language to be simply the outcome of education. From this perspective, constitutive normativity cannot provide an answer to the normative question, because that same question bears on the status of that which is constituted.

The reason why the argument from discourse risks incurring this problem lies in its peculiar insistence on the pragmatics of language. However, the problem can be avoided by framing the argument from discourse so as to link it more closely to Korsgaard's argument from agency. In Korsgaard's view, moral normativity stems not from a heteronomous source such as language but from our own constitution as agents. And if normativity stems from our own constitution, then that amounts to saying we are autonomous – our being autonomous becomes equivalent to recognising constitutive normativity as binding. According to Korsgaard, agency, unlike language, does not come 'from without' – we *are* agents in the first place. Thus, linking normativity to agency is tantamount to providing a strict definition of autonomy.

Given that the argument from discourse, unlike Korsgaard's argument from agency, is aimed at conceiving language as the source of normativity, the only way to avoid qualifying normativity as heteronomous is, from this perspective, to challenge the postulate that language comes 'from without', by maintaining that human agency is essentially and in the first place a *linguistic* agency. In such a view, the normativity stemming from the language game of assertion and argumentation would not stand on its own but it would be equivalent to the normativity of reason, which is rooted in human agency. Reasons would be conceived as essentially linguistic, and the deep structure of language would be nothing if not an image of the deep structure of rationality. This reframing of the matter, however, reverses the order of explication assumed by the argument from discourse: here, normativity results not from language but from autonomous and rational agency, which in its own turn is conceived as linguistic agency; and so the argument from discourse becomes an argument from linguistic agency. This argument will be sketched out in greater detail in Section VII.

VI THE PROBLEM OF THE NORMATIVE BRIDGE

Korsgaard's argument from agency explains in depth why agents must value humanity: they must do so because human identity is the necessary precondition for having a practical identity, and hence for being a unified agent. We cannot treat our *practical* identity as normative without thereby treating our *human* identity in the same way.

As Korsgaard knows full well, however, this conclusion is not in itself morally significant. Grounding moral normativity is not a matter of providing a good reason for valuing our *own* humanity but is rather a matter of giving us a reason for valuing the humanity of *others*. Why, then, ought we to value other human beings, given that normativity depends exclusively on our own humanity? In *The Sources of Normativity*, Korsgaard answers this question by appealing to the argument presented in Thomas Nagel's *The Possibility of Altruism*:[61]

> Suppose that we are strangers and that you are tormenting me, and suppose that I call upon you to *stop*. I say: 'How would you like it if someone did that to you?' And now you cannot proceed as you did before. Oh, you can proceed all right, but not just as you did before. For I have obligated you to stop. [H]ow does the obligation come about? Just the way Nagel says that it does. I invite you to consider how you would like it if someone did that to you. You realise that you would not merely dislike it, you would resent it. You would think that the other has a reason to stop, more, that he has an obligation to stop. And that obligation would spring from your own objection to what he does to you. You make yourself an end for others; you make yourself a law to them. But if you are a law to others in so far as you are just human . . . then the humanity of others is also a law to you.[62]

As Korsgaard makes clear, 'there is an appeal to consistency in this argument', an appeal that can be interpreted as follows. Given that, according to Korsgaard, normativity stems from the conditions for the possibility of our own agency, I can place value on something other than myself only if I am forced by reasons of consistency: I value X *insofar* as I value myself and X is like me. If this reading is correct, moral reasons stem from my giving reasons to myself, and moral normativity is a game that only revolves circularly within me as an agent.

But this account of moral normativity is quite implausible, for it implies that there are no moral agents apart from me. It presupposes an account of the first-person

[61] T Nagel, *The Possibility of Altruism* (Oxford, Clarendon Press, 1970).
[62] Korsgaard, *The Sources of Normativity*, n 2 above, 142–43.

perspective from which I, as a moral agent, find that other persons are capable of prompting in me instances of moral reasoning, but from which I also find that I am the only real source of these reasons. On this view, other persons are not considered moral agents who can put forward reasons, as I can: they are rather a sort of perceptual stimulus holding me to a test of consistency, and it is this internal test of mine that provides moral reasons.[63] And here, clearly, scepticism about rule-following can bear its full relevance. The sceptic could ask, for example, 'what assures me that my application of the consistency tests is in principle the same as that which other agents make?'. If I have no criterion but my own rule for consistency tests, then there is nothing that can guarantee I will evaluate moral reasons in the same way as other agents do. Thus, I could perfectly well have a personal morality whose reasons cannot be exchanged with others. In this view, there would be no intersubjective exchange of moral reasons, but only monadic agents.

This implausible account reveals a fundamental difficulty that Korsgaard's argument from agency comes up against. I will call it the problem of the normative bridge and will state it as follows: if, according to the argument from agency, the source of moral reasons resides in *me*, how could *other* persons be a source of moral reasons for me? And if they cannot be such a source, how can the argument from agency account for *moral* reasons? How can a personal morality made up of reasons we cannot exchange provide us with genuine moral normativity?

The problem of the normative bridge becomes particularly relevant when the argument from agency is extended to domains where publicness and intersubjectivity of reasons is even more essential than in morality, as in the legal domain. Such an extension can be found in Stefano Bertea's recent book, *The Normative Claim of Law*, where he develops a 'modified Kantian account' for the normativity of practical reason in general, and he argues (explicitly tracing his approach to Korsgaard's) that the normativity of practical reason can be grounded in a 'minimally necessary self-conception'[64] we have as human agents. This conception consists (in Bertea's own terminology) of reflectivity, rationality and autonomy. Bertea defends in his theory a unified conception of practical reason,[65] and so he concludes and argues from it that not only *moral* normativity but also *legal* normativity must be grounded in the minimally necessary self-conception.[66] Indeed, on his view the 'structure of human agency affects us in every aspect of our lives, extending its influence to the institutional frameworks in which we participate (including the institutions of the law as manifestations of practical reason)'.[67] This primacy that the minimally necessary self-conception is found to have over institutions plays a key role in Bertea's argument, particularly in his seeking to avoid an excessively abstract view of the self. In fact, given that institutions are grounded

[63] For a similar criticism, the reader may refer to E Watkins and W Fitzpatrick, 'O'Neill and Korsgaard on the Construction of Normativity' (2002) 36 *Journal of Value Inquiry* 349, 361.

[64] Bertea, n 1 above, 206.

[65] ibid 174.

[66] ibid 227.

[67] ibid 228.

in the features of human agency, Bertea can, on the one hand, concede that social life shapes our practical identity through institutions, and at the same time he can defend the view that the 'essential traits of human agency' cannot depend on social factors:

> This is because the very institutions in which we take part are governed by practical reason, and so the specific identities we take on in participating in such institutions supervene, and so are subordinate to, the identity shaped by the minimally necessary self-conception.[68]

The connection needed between the nature of institutions and the features of human agency is effected by way of a simple consideration: 'Institutions are not independent entities, rather they are the outcome of the interaction that takes place among those who bring them into being'.[69]

Now, it is clear that if the argument from agency aims at showing that institutions can be shaped by human agency (as Bertea's argument does) it must solve the problem of the normative bridge. In fact, when extended to the institutional domain, the test of consistency is an even more tenuous explanation of how others can prompt reasons in me than in the case of moral reasons. For if moral reasons stem exclusively from my own arguing within myself, it is difficult to see how we can have a public exchange of reasons, much less how institutions can be created that will embody the normativity of human agency. So if the argument from agency is aimed at concluding that there exists an entirely public dimension of practical reasons embodied in a given set of institutions (as Bertea argues), then this argument cannot avoid the burden of explaining how *other* people can be a source of such reasons, in addition to just *my* being such a source, and how the normativity stemming from different agents can be pooled together and solidified into something we can attribute to institutions.

As can be appreciated from the passage quoted at the beginning of this section, Korsgaard seems to see language as the main conduit through which to bridge normativity. In a later passage, she states that our recognition of others as human agents, and hence as sources of normativity, depends in some sense on our being capable of linguistic understanding:

> it is impossible to hear the words of a language you know as mere noise. In hearing our words as *words*, I acknowledge that you are *someone*. In acknowledging that I can hear them, I acknowledge that I am *someone*. If I listen to the argument at all, I have already admitted that each of us is *someone*.[70]

Can language solve the problem of the normative bridge, as Korsgaard seems to suggest? It depends on the conception of language we are dealing with. If the argument from agency appeals to language as a shared way of expressing reasons, then all the argument states is that agents can share semantic rules. From this

[68] ibid 232.
[69] ibid 232.
[70] Korsgaard, *The Sources of Normativity*, n 2 above, 143.

perspective, normativity would remain an inner process taking place within me as an agent, a process whose result can be expressed in such a way that others can understand it. As Alan Gibbard has noted, however, this solution does not guarantee a sharing of normativity, that is, it does not guarantee that moral reasons can be shared among agents:

> Suppose, then, I think of my reasons in my native English, a shared, public language that you too understand. Does this mean that we 'share our reasons' . . .? In one sense, it certainly does: if you think you have reason to enslave me if you can, you can tell me so, if you choose, and if I think I have reason to try to prevent you, then I can tell you that. What morality needs, though, is reasons we share in a different sense: roughly at least, that you have genuine reason to try to enslave me only if I have some reason to submit. (What morality requires more precisely is perhaps, as Korsgaard suggests, an ideal of a 'Kingdom of Ends': that our reasons all feed into a scheme of accommodation that we all have reason, all told, to join.) From our ability to talk together about your reasons and about mine, can we derive reasons we share in this strong sense?[71]

But language can play another role in the argument from agency. In *The Sources of Normativity*, Korsgaard very much insists on the inherently public character of reasons by appealing to Wittgenstein's private language argument. Quite strikingly, however, she uses Wittgenstein's approach more as an analogy than as an effective instrument, maintaining that practical reasons, *like* language, can be conceived as inherently public: 'if we have to grant that meanings can be shared, why not grant that practical reasons can be shared too?'.[72] Korsgaard's argument for the relationality of reasons depends not on language but on an essentially relational account of the self's structure. She argues in particular that reasons are inherently relational because they always involve at least 'two, a legislator to lay it down, and a citizen to obey', and these two she conceives as 'the two elements of reflective consciousness, the thinking self and the acting self'.[73] But it should be clear that this does not bear on the problem of the normative bridge, because on such a description, the relationality of reasons still involves just me, and no explanation is provided as to how it can be extended to others aside from me. Hence, on this interpretation, Korsgaard does not offer a convincing account of the relationality of reasons.

As mentioned, while Korsgaard finds that the inherently public nature of meaning can be useful in clarifying the relational nature of reasons, she does not provide an argument to connect these two. How, then, is it possible to fill this hiatus? The desired connection can be attempted by reframing the argument from agency so as to link it more closely to the argument from discourse, saying that reasons are inherently linguistic, and that agency must be conceived of as essentially a linguistic agency. On such a view, reflectivity is reinterpreted as a sort of inner argumentation, thinking is conceived as arguing within ourselves by the

[71] A Gibbard, 'Morality as Consistency in Living: Korsgaard's Kantian Lectures' (1999) 110 *Ethics* 162. For a similar objection, see also J Skidmore, 'Skepticism about Practical Reason: Transcendental Arguments and their Limits' (2002) 109 *Philosophical Studies* 121, 136.

[72] Korsgaard, *The Sources of Normativity*, n 2 above, 142.

[73] ibid 138.

use of language, and reflective agents are in the first instance argumentative agents. Normativity still comes from me, but its form is inherently linguistic, doing no more than providing argumentative weight, and so reasons can by their nature be shared with others. Wittgenstein's private language argument is conceived here not as an insightful analogy but as a crucial tool: as long as language cannot be private, and as long as argumentation is the way by which we evaluate reasons within ourselves, linguistic agents are built for an exchange of reasons.

So, just like the argument from discourse, so too must the argument from agency be reframed to address a crucial problem. In fact, it is the inherently linguistic and argumentative nature of reasons which provides the normative bridge the argument from agency needs to account for moral reasons. We find here again, as we saw in the last section – the same argument from linguistic agency that relieved the argument from discourse of the burden of the problem of autonomy.

VII THE ARGUMENT FROM LINGUISTIC AGENCY

We should by now be clear on what the dialectical structure is of the relation between the argument from agency and the argument from discourse. In order for the argument from discourse to answer the problem of autonomy, it must be reframed so as to become a variant of the argument from agency, thus becoming essentially an argument from linguistic *agency* – the emphasis here falls on *agency*. Conversely, in order for the argument from agency to answer the problem of the normative bridge, it must be reframed so as to become a variant of the argument from discourse, thus becoming an argument from *linguistic* agency – the emphasis here falls on *linguistic*. Hence, when the two arguments are considered in relation to the two afore-mentioned problems, they must be recast to stand together as a single argument. And this single argument revolves around the concept of linguistic agency.

Let me briefly summarise the features of this argument. The starting point is the same as in Korsgaard's argument from agency: as human beings, we are self-conscious beings, capable of evaluating our perceptions and impulses and asking whether they are good reasons for belief and action. However (and this instead draws on the argument from discourse), this process of deliberation is essentially linguistic, in the sense that the balancing of reasons I make within me is nothing more than an instance of linguistic argumentation: when I balance reasons, I perform speech acts in the language game of assertion and argumentation. We can reflect on and perform actions only if we can give ourselves arguments, and that entails following a definite set of rules. Thus, for example, we recognise the claim to truth that reasons advance and know that this claim must be tested against possible objections; we know that reasons must be justified; and we also know that ignoring a reason does not make it irrelevant.

These rules are doubtless normative for us, and the same holds when other agents advance reasons. We do not have any discontinuity here, such as is found in the argument from agency, because the reasons that *other* agents advance are not any different in nature from the reasons we advance within ourselves – in either case they are linguistic. They carry argumentative weight, just as ours do. And, again, we know that if we want to think and behave rationally with regard to these third-party reasons, we ought to treat them as we treat our own, recognising they have a claim to truth while not taking that claim for granted, by testing them against reasonable objections and considering possible counter-objections. This time, however, the rules of argumentation, which we recognise as normative within ourselves when thinking, define a mode of behaviour toward others based on the assumption that others are rational human beings like us, because they can offer reasons that do not differ in nature from ours. Hence, the rules of argumentation in this case become moral rules, and we, as linguistic agents, cannot but recognise the normativity of these rules.

So formulated, the argument from linguistic agency seems able to avoid the problem of freedom. In fact, while rationality involves recognising the rules of argumentation as normative, we are not forced to actually *follow* these rules when thinking, much less when dealing with others. We can behave and think as irrational agents, and we can choose to behave irrationally toward others as well. We could call this the 'communicative choice', and it is something with respect to which we are free.

The argument from linguistic agency seems not to fall subject to the problem of autonomy, either. In fact, the normativity of the rules of argumentation does not stem here from the pragmatics of language conceived as something coming 'from without' and thrust upon us since birth. We are linguistic agents – that is our constitution. The normativity of the rules of argumentation thus structures our rationality, and so it comes from within us. We are perfectly autonomous with respect to it.

Finally, the argument from linguistic agency seems able to solve the problem of the normative bridge. In fact, the linguistic nature of our reasons makes it so that the process through which we evaluate our own reasons and the process through which we evaluate the reasons of others are one and the same process – that of argumentation. On this view, no normative bridge is needed to communicate rationally with others, or to respect them as humans capable of argumentation.

It is unclear whether the authors who have supported the argument from discourse and the argument from agency could accept such a recasting of their two arguments in the form of the argument from linguistic agency. On the one hand, it is quite clear that Apel's and Habermas' insistence on pragmatics as the essential dimension of language is owed to their belief that linguistic actions are a fundamental form of action. But would they accept that *all* rational thinking and action ultimately resolves itself into linguistic action revealing a normative moral dimension, a kind of argumentation? Some passages by Apel seem to confirm such a view. In his seminal essay of 1973, for example, Apel says that 'all linguistic manifestations and, more than that, all meaningful actions and physical expressions of human beings (insofar as they can be verbalised) can be conceived as virtual arguments', and then he adds this comment in a footnote:

> One can interpret in this sense Wittgenstein's idea of the 'connection' between linguistic manifestations, actions, and physical expressions. Moreover, the thesis that *all actions* and expressive gestures *can in principle be verbalised* is suggested by Austin's discovery of 'performative expressions' and by its generalisation and radicalisation in J.R. Searle's theory of 'speech acts'. (emphasis added)[74]

It clearly emerges from this passage that Apel is casting Austin's and Searle's pragmatics as a general theory of action and rationality. And a very similar view, albeit with greater insistence on the process of forming intentional content, can be found in Pavlakos' account of the basic features of his pragmatic rationalism:

> Pragmatic rationalism . . . is the idea that there are deep standards (reasons) of cognition and action which, however, are embedded within our practices of judging . . . Given that pragmatic rationalism adduces the foundational level of judging, i.e., grammar, with an eye to explaining the deep structure of content, it follows that the property of being *a priori* must be ascribed to the rules of grammar.[75]

Grammar is conceived by Pavlakos as fundamental with respect to any meaningful thought and action, both conceived as essentially an instance of rule-following:

> In contrast to other conceptions of rule-following, the pragmatic view steers away from a relapse into dualism by enjoining the fundamental character of practice with respect to thought and action.[76]

As regards Korsgaard, there are passages where she seems to support a view similar to that advocated by the argument from linguistic agency, as when, in answer to the question: 'Why shouldn't language force us to reason practically together, in just the same way as it forces us to think together?',[77] she concludes with this remark:

> Human beings are a social animal in a deep way. It is not just that we go in for friendship or prefer to live in swarms or packs. The space of linguistic consciousness – the space in which meanings *and reasons* exist – is a space that we occupy together. (emphasis added)[78]

My impression, however, is that Korsgaard does not intend to commit to the view that reasons are inherently linguistic. The impression is reinforced on reading her recent *Self-constitution*, where she discusses at length the interaction and the publicness of reasons as necessary features of the self. But she still considers the appeal to Wittgenstein's private-game argument as no more than an analogy, and in commenting on the use she made of this argument in *The Sources of Normativity*, she writes:

> Many readers have a misimpression about how I intended that argument to go. I did not intend to suggest that the publicity of reasons can be *inferred from* the publicity of

[74] Apel, *Das Apriori*, n 15 above, 400 (author's translation).
[75] Pavlakos, n 12 above, 153.
[76] ibid 152.
[77] Korsgaard, *The Sources of Normativity*, n 2 above, 142.
[78] ibid 145.

> meanings. I meant rather to be making an argument from the publicity of reasons that is analogous to Wittgenstein's argument for the publicity of meaning. Wittgenstein's argument, as I understand it, is intended to show that meaning can't be normative at all . . . unless it is public. My argument was meant to show that reasons cannot be normative at all unless they are public.[79]

Moreover, when Korsgaard argues that 'action is simply interaction with the self',[80] a view quite close to that taken by the argument from linguistic agency, she also maintains that 'the requirements for unifying your agency internally are the same as the requirements for unifying your agency with that of others',[81] but she does not explicitly identify such requirements with language and argumentation.

In any event, I do not intend to enter into interpretive questions, because my concern is rather theoretical. The argument from linguistic agency, obtained by merging the argument from discourse and the argument from agency, seems to respond to important objections better than the two original ones. Hence, those two arguments, which are often treated and discussed separately as two distinct Kantian approaches to normativity, should instead be conceived as a single argument revolving around the necessary linguistic and argumentative nature of human agency and rationality.

VIII TWO FURTHER PROBLEMS: UNAVOIDABILITY AND NORMATIVE REGRESS

As much as the argument from linguistic agency may fare better than its two constituents separately considered, it cannot address *all* the charges that may be levelled against them. There are at least two other problems with respect to which this argument meets the same difficulties as the constituent arguments from agency and from discourse. In fact, these problems concern these arguments' transcendental structure, a structure they all share.

I will first discuss what I will call the problem of unavoidability, which is quite straightforward: is the starting point of the arguments from discourse and from agency really unavoidable? It could be argued, for example, that rationality and argumentation represent for human beings not so much an *unavoidable* perspective as one dependent on social, external, or in any event contingent conditions. True, if you are a rational agent, the moral norms implicit in argumentation will be binding on you – but rational agency need not be a necessary status.

This is a classic objection, and we have already seen how Apel and Korsgaard reply to it, arguing that rationality, reflectivity and argumentation are clearly unavoidable because they are presupposed from the start even by the sceptic who doubts them – recall Apel's passage where he says 'that only through an act of self-destruction can the devil become independent from God'. But this appeal to

[79] Korsgaard, *Self-constitution*, n 3 above, 196 n 12.
[80] ibid 204.
[81] ibid 202.

the presuppositions of the sceptical doubt cannot count as conclusive. As David Enoch has made clear, this answer presupposes a specific conception of scepticism and its role in philosophy:

> Skeptical challenges – some, at least, including the ones relevant here – are best seen, I think, as highlighting tensions within our own commitments, as paradoxes arguing for an unacceptable conclusion from premises we endorse, employing rules of inference to which we are committed . . . The philosophical challenge is not to defeat a real person who advocates the skeptical view or occupies the skeptical position (*what* view or position?) but, rather, to solve the paradox, to show how we can avoid the unacceptable conclusion at an acceptable price. If we must think of the situation in dialectical terms, we should think of skeptical challenges as ad hominem arguments, with all of us as the relevant homini.[82]

We need not agree with Enoch to see that there is a specific conception of scepticism implicit in Apel's and Korsgaard's retorsive arguments against scepticism about the primacy of reflection and argumentation. And that conception must be argued for by recourse to non-reflective arguments.

What I want to stress here is that the argument from linguistic agency does not, for its part, give us much more to go on in the way of a solution out of this quandary – it similarly assumes that the unavoidability of linguistic agency can be demonstrated by reflectively refuting scepticism about it, and so it cannot do much more than the arguments from agency and from discourse vis-à-vis the problem of unavoidability. It might be said that the coupling of discourse with agency does put the argument from linguistic agency in a better position to show the primacy and unavoidability of its starting point as compared with what the argument from discourse alone can do. But it is highly debatable whether linguistic agency can offer in this regard better arguments than simple agency.

Still, the problem of unavoidability is not so devastating as it seems. In fact, even if we were forced to concede that argumentative rationality is not an unavoidable necessity, we could still plausibly argue (as Robert Alexy does, for example) that linguistic agency conceived as argumentation is 'the most general form of life of human beings'.[83] This would lead to a sort of 'weak' transcendental approach similar to that defended, for example, by Jürgen Habermas.[84] This strategy would have us replace the ultimate moral foundation with foundation relative to linguistic agency, and as much as it would wind up weakening the original transcendental approach, it would nonetheless make for an impressive philosophical result.

But there is yet another problem to which the argument from linguistic agency does not provide anything new as compared with the two arguments it derives from, and this problem can have more serious consequences than that of unavoidability. I will call this the problem of normative regress and set it up as follows. Let

[82] Enoch, n 1 above, 183–84.
[83] R Alexy, 'Discourse Theory and Human Rights' (1996) 9 *Ratio Juris* 209, 217.
[84] Habermas, 'Diskursethik', n 59 above, 105.

us concede that agency or discourse is unavoidable for me as a rational agent, and let us also agree that there are rules whose normativity is constitutive of agency or of discourse. With these two premises, from my first-person perspective as an agent I cannot but recognise constitutive normativity to be binding. But the point of view from which the arguments from agency and discourse are put forward – the point of view from which constitutive normativity is analysed – is *not* that of an agent's first-person perspective. In fact, from an agent's perspective, constitutive normativity simply appears as grounded *ab origine*: it is part of our constitution as moral agents that we cannot but recognise certain norms or values as binding. But from the perspective of the arguments from agency and from discourse, normativity is grounded *because* constitutive: both arguments assume a theoretical perspective, one from which the constitution of agency and discourse are taken as objects of analysis, and both explain normativity by connecting it to this constitution. But in so doing they make normativity *dependent on* that constitution.

Let us concede that a similar perspective is possible. What matters here is that if this external perspective is possible for the arguments from agency and from discourse, then so is it possible for those who object to these arguments. And here the problem of normative regress arises. In fact, if I can come to know from an external perspective that something is normative for me because constitutive of my agency or of discourse, why then should I conclude that such a constitutive role is sufficient for me to recognise normativity as binding? I could simply reframe my question and ask 'why am I obligated to "bow" to agency or to discourse?'. In fact, why should I accept the constitution of agency and discourse as normative?

The point can be illustrated by going back to the ever-present example of chess. The rules of chess are binding for those who are willing to play chess. Playing chess is something we can do only on the condition of respecting the trust our opponents place in our not cheating, but we are bound to that respect only if we want to play chess with them. In this sense, constitutive normativity is normally conditioned, in that constitutive rules are normative only for those committed to the practice so constituted. Now, let me extend this simple consideration to the arguments from agency and from discourse. It could be argued that, just as in the case of chess, the constitutive normativity these arguments derive is relative to that which is constituted – it is relative to agency or discourse – and hence that no ultimate normative foundation can be established by way of constitutive normativity if the constituted practices are not already grounded in their own turn. This problem is illustrated by Enoch as follows:

> If a constitutive-aim or constitutive-motives theory is going to work for agency, then, it is not sufficient to show that some aims or motives or capacities are constitutive of agency. Rather, it is also necessary to show that the 'game' of agency is one we have reason to play. . .[85]

[85] Enoch, n 1 above, 186.

Clearly, it is not a straightforward parallel that can be set up between discourse and agency, on the one hand, and chess, on the other, since a fundamental difference intervenes between them. Chess is a practice we can willingly enter into and get out of, while the arguments from agency and from discourse are premised, as we have seen, on the basic point that agency and discourse are not optional: our status as rational agents is not (according to Korsgaard and Apel) something we can properly *choose* to have: indeed, in a sense, it might be argued that if we can choose anything, then we are already within the boundaries of agency. However, even if we decide to weaken these arguments in accordance with the problem of unavoidability, conceding that agency and argumentation are not unavoidable, we will still have to recognise that they are much more fundamental than contingent practices such as chess, at least insofar as the consequences of forsaking agency or discourse are much more serious than, say, those of choosing to play bridge rather than chess.

But does this difference make irrelevant the problem of normative regress? This is a debated question. Thus, for example, in *The Possibility of Practical Reason*, David Velleman discusses a variant of the argument from agency similar in many respects to Korsgaard's, and he recognises that agency and reflection are unavoidable when asking for reasons to commit to them:

> There may be, in some sense, an open question whether to be an agent, whether to get into or stay in the agency game. But of course someone who is not already in the game is in no position to entertain that question, because entertaining it entails thinking about what to do, which entails trying to bring his behavior under descriptions that would embody knowledge of what he was doing. Anyone who asks himself whether to get into the agency game is already in the game; and anyone who asks himself whether to stay in the game cannot answer in the negative without staying in it at least that far. Of course, such a person can leave the game in a final exercise of agency – say, by taking drugs or jumping off a bridge or just dozing off for a while. But reasons for someone to act are not reasons for him to start or continue functioning as an agent; they are reasons for him in so long and so far as he functions as such.[86]

But Velleman also recognises that such unavoidability is not sufficient to provide normative reasons for action:

> Yet the agent's inability to withdraw from his intellectual drives does not entail that he must approve of them, and it certainly does not entail that he must approve of them as that by appeal to which considerations qualify as reasons for acting. Even if the agent is inextricably identified with these drives, what gives them rational authority as opposed to brute motivational force?[87]

What, then, are we to make of such an agent who is, so to speak, 'captive' to agency? Can we really conceive of agents (or, to use Enoch's coinage, of 'shmagents') who accept that normativity is constitutive of their structure as agents and

[86] R Velleman, 'Replies to Discussion on *The Possibility of Practical Reason*' (2004) 121 *Philosophical Studies* 277, 290–91.
[87] ibid 293.

yet do not accept agency as a source of reasons? Is the problem of normative regress a genuine problem? According to Enoch, shmagents can exist in the same sense as alienated participants can exist in any practice:

> Think again about finding yourself playing a game of chess, and assume for now that for some reason you cannot quit – not that you should not quit but that you cannot quit. And assume that sacrificing a pawn is the thing you have most chess-related reason to do (it best promotes your chances of checkmating your opponent or some such). Well, do you have a reason to sacrifice a pawn? Not, it seems to me, if you don't have a normative reason to play or win the game, and this even if you can't quit. For you can continue playing or 'going through the motions', grudgingly, refusing to internalize the aims of the game. And absent some normative reason to play the game, there need be nothing irrational about such an attitude.[88]

Other authors, such as Luca Ferrero, do not agree with Enoch's analysis. In Ferrero's view, '[a]lienated participation in ordinary enterprises is a genuine possibility but not one that can be used to show that there is a problem with constitutivism'.[89] Ferrero finds Enoch's example of the 'grudging chess-player' to be miscast, because while we could conceivably not internalise the aim of chess and hence play grudgingly, if we consider ourselves captive to agency we necessarily must already have internalised reflectivity and the aim of agency. And in discussing Enoch's example of the shmagent, Ferrero comments as follows:

> The idea of a 'shmagent' is introduced by Enoch to show that there might be subjects who are indifferent to agency and would therefore need a reason available *outside* of agency to be convinced to take part in it. The inescapability of agency, however, shows that there is no standpoint external to agency that the shmagent could occupy and from whence he could launch his challenge.[90]

But it seems to me – let me stress this point again – that such a defence of the argument from agency is inconsistent with one of its fundamental presuppositions. Indeed, as was noted earlier, it is only from a 'standpoint external to agency' (in Ferrero's words) that normativity can be shown to be grounded as constitutive of agency, and then the question arises as to why this standpoint should be possible only for those who support constitutive normativity and not also for those who reject it.

I do not pretend the problem of normative regress to be a conclusive argument against constitutivism. I should only like to point out, instead, that there is not much more the argument from linguistic agency can bring in by way of a solution to the problem. In fact, shmagency and *linguistic* shmagency are not essentially different when it comes to the question of their possibility. The arguments for the impossibility of shmagency could be weakened, if at all, by recasting them as arguments for the impossibility of *linguistic* shmagency; conversely, if shmagency can be conceived as a possibility, I see no reason why *linguistic* shmagency should

[88] Enoch, n 1 above, 189.
[89] Ferrero, n 1 above, 313.
[90] ibid 311.

not also be so conceived. The reason why the arguments from agency and from discourse necessarily come up against the problem of normative regress even when reframed in terms of linguistic agency is that this problem points up an apparent inconsistency of them. Both arguments invoke the first-person perspective to solve the normative question, but they also invoke a sort of 'bird's eye view' over the structure of agency and of discourse.

The inconsistency could be worked out if the arguments from agency and from discourse managed to explain how the constitution of something can be fully analysed from within. This task seems particularly difficult where constitutive normativity is concerned because this normativity holds itself out as an answer to the normative question. According to this answer, agents should consider constitutive normativity as binding because they see it from within, in that they *are* that which is constituted. But if the perspective from which they consider constitutive normativity as binding is the same as that from which they can realise that this normativity is binding *because* constitutive of them, then it seems that normative bindingness can be relativised. And, if they can do so from within, then the arguments from discourse and from agency do not yield an ultimate answer to the normative question.

13

Tracing a Genealogy of Legal Normativity: Responsibility, Authorship and Contingency

SYLVIE DELACROIX

IF LAW CONSTRAINS us, if it somehow has a claim on our conduct or judgement, it cannot be out of mere habit or fear of sanctions. Unravelling law's normative dimension involves pinpointing exactly what would be amiss if it were so. This unravelling has taken many shapes in the course of jurisprudential history. Some of these accounts require faith, others may sound hollow; as my reading of past explanations has heavily influenced my own, the first part of this chapter briefly surveys the main elements of those accounts. In the second part, I outline what I call a 'genealogy' of legal normativity: instead of taking law's normative dimension as a 'given', it inquires into what makes it possible in the first place; instead of stripping it down to its 'essential' bones, it celebrates its 'contingent' flesh (by focusing on 'responsibility as authorship').

I A (VERY) BRIEF HISTORY OF LEGAL NORMATIVITY

A history has to start somewhere. If one needs to take a short-cut, a major shift or breaking point will prove helpful: if I were to choose a date marking the key transition period between what would be a 'pre-modern' and a modern[1] understanding of legal normativity, I would go for 28 June 1593.

On that day, the Paris Parliament upheld the devolution law which designated Henri de Bourbon the legitimate heir to the throne, despite his Protestant denomination. To counter the papal arguments (and the radical Catholic Ligue's) the Politiques[2] endeavoured to show that the Loi Salique was to be understood as the direct expression of God's will. Now, in order to promote the Loi Salique as the expression of a will that cannot be called into question, even by the Pope

[1] For more developments, addressing to some extent the controversy surrounding the term 'modern', see S Delacroix, *Legal Norms and Normativity: An Essay in Genealogy* (Oxford, Hart, 2006) 135.

[2] Referring to a group of jurists and intellectuals defending, for the most part, the idea of Gallicanism and, most crucially, arguing for a distinction between the state and religion, the expression 'Politiques' was mainly used by their critics, the radical Catholic 'Ligue', which called for the eradication of Protestantism in France.

himself, the Politiques could not merely argue that the order instituted by this devolution law 'imitates nature's order', which would make it conform to natural law. They had to present this devolution law as 'positive divine law', and by doing so to abolish the gap between nature and '*surnature*' – a contrast that is essential to the scholastic tradition.[3]

The Politiques' venture to incorporate a divine foundation *within* the legal corpus – instead of maintaining a distance separating law from its legitimating source – proceeded from the desire to lend man-made laws a normativity that would not have to pale before the invocation of divine authority, and would as such be able to resist assaults from the Church. The eventuality which neither opponent in this controversy fully anticipated, however, amounts to the fact that, by constructing this 'institutionalised' presence of God at the foundation of law, the Politiques may actually have provided for the possibility of its oblivion. Once secured in a fundamental, positive law, the link to transcendence traditionally conditioning law's legitimacy does not have to be constantly re-elaborated in a process testing the conformity of positive law to 'natural and divine law'.

Fortified by a normative dimension assuring it a new 'inviolability', the legal order can from then on develop itself in an autonomous way, away from the natural and divine order from which it traditionally derived its normativity. This new-found normative autonomy raises a problem which had until then been spared from legal thought: how can law derive from the arbitrariness of social and political practices the binding force necessary to ensure its normativity? As long as human laws were perceived as the mere adaptation of a superior kind of law which, in itself, eluded human ascendancy, the messy character of the practices bringing them about was of little consequence to law's normative force. Once human law is deemed to evolve independently of that superior order, however, its normativity seems somehow to have to arise out of the 'mess' of human affairs.

This challenge is eloquently encapsulated by Montaigne when he notes:

> Laws are often made by fools, and even more often by men who fail in equity because they hate equality: but always by men, *vain authorities* who can resolve nothing. (emphasis added)[4]

Because Montaigne refuses to grant law's empirical sources any other value than their strict fortuitousness, the normativity of law cannot rely on any justification linked to its birth, being too lightweight and tenuous in comparison with the 'grandeur' of what flows from it – the law in all its authoritativeness.

Given the disproportion existing between the object of his study and its sources, Montaigne seems to be willing to concentrate on the *established* authority of law, based on 'possession' and 'custom':

[3] It is indeed the gap between 'nature' and '*surnature*' that allows the scholastic tradition to speak of 'natural and divine law' while maintaining a tension between the two, as natural law expresses divine law while never equating it. Because of this tension, the scholastic tradition was able to construct the power to govern as legitimated by its link to God while nevertheless remaining under human scrutiny.

[4] M de Montaigne, *The Complete Essays* (MA Screech (trans), London, Penguin, 1991) III 13, 1216.

> laws gain their authority from actual possession and custom: *it is perilous to go back to their origins*; laws, like our rivers, get greater and nobler as they roll along: follow them back upstream to their sources and all you find is a tiny spring, hardly recognisable; as time goes by it swells with pride and grows in strength. (emphasis added)[5]

The 'peril' from which Montaigne wants to protect us consists in loathing the authority of law out of disgust for its tenuous and arbitrary beginnings:

> I once had the duty of justifying one of our practices which, far and wide around us, is accepted as having established authority; I did not wish to maintain it (as is usually done) exclusively by force of law and exempla so I traced it back to its origins: *I found its basis to be so weak that I all but loathed it* – I who was supposed to encourage it in others. (emphasis added)[6]

Knowing that the original weakness of law is not susceptible of being overcome, and wanting above all to avoid the 'wild opinions' aimed at denigrating the authority of law, Montaigne is faced with the necessity of 'reconstructing' it. According to Montaigne, the matter is first and foremost to see to it that the law does not only amount to the product of its historical birth, or at least that its authority does not flow from there. From this perspective, Montaigne puts forward 'The first commandment which God ever gave to Man . . . *the law of pure obedience*. It was a bare and simple order, leaving man no room for knowing or arguing' (emphasis added).[7] Such a reference is at the least surprising coming from Montaigne, as it indeed suggests a grounding of the authority of law in precisely the kind of ontological principle whose inaccessible and thus illusory character he emphatically denounced. Are we to understand this 'law of pure obedience' as the starting point for a natural justice of divine inspiration? Such an interpretation would be directly at odds with Montaigne's general perspective, and besides, it would directly contradict his explicit rejection of any kind of natural law justice.[8]

If, by contrast, one keeps in mind the Kantian formulation: '[law] is thought *as if it must have arisen not from men but from some highest, flawless lawgiver*; and that is what the saying "all authority is from God" means' (emphasis added),[9] this reference to a 'law of pure obedience' may be understood in a way similar to Kant's 'all authority is from God'. The point of such a reference would be to provide this supplement of authority without which thinking of the normative dimension of law does not seem viable, as it is desperately too grand in comparison to the weakness of its sources. From Kant's *as if* construction to Montaigne's legitimate fictions ('even our system of Law, they say, bases the truth of its justice upon legal fictions'),[10] the step is easily taken. The essential aim of both Montaigne's 'law of

[5] ibid II 12, 658.
[6] ibid I 23, 131.
[7] ibid II 12, 543.
[8] *cf* 'Nothing is just per se, justice being a creation of custom and law': ibid III 13, 1215.
[9] I Kant, *The Metaphysics of Morals* (MJ Gregor (trans), Cambridge, Cambridge University Press, 1991 (1797)) AK 6:319.
[10] Montaigne, n 4 above, II 12, 603.

pure obedience' and Kant's 'all authority is from God' is to provide the logical principle thanks to which one can theoretically establish law's normativity. From this perspective, one can understand the putative divine origin of Montaigne's first law as essentially aiming at cancelling its iterative character. The point of this law of pure obedience would above all consist in being ultimate, thus avoiding an infinite – and dangerous – regress in its motives.

At this stage, it is difficult not to mention a tempting parallel with one of the outstanding figures of twentieth-century legal positivism, Hans Kelsen. The ambition of founding the normativity of law on law alone, thus excluding any consideration of political or moral legitimacy, constitutes one of the striking features of the Kelsenian theory, which also gives a first norm – the Basic Norm – the task of founding the binding character of the laws flowing from it.[11] Both Montaigne and Kelsen choose to proceed on the basis of the acknowledgement that there is no remedy to our search for the sources of law's normativity but the necessity of a rigorous attachment to the law in its positivity. On this basis, the famous statement from Montaigne: 'Now laws remain respected not because they are just but because they are laws . . . If anyone obeys them only when they are just, then he fails to obey them for just the reason he must!',[12] may be considered one of the cornerstones of legal positivism, underlining the necessity of distinguishing between law's bindingness and law's justice.

While, in the case of Montaigne's theory, the initial law-creating practices were set apart in consideration of the danger they represented for the layman (who couldn't but be disgusted by their precarious and arbitrary appearance), in Kelsen's works a similar kind of danger is at stake, involving the more-than-ever threatening *surrender* of law to politics. Having thus excluded any appeal to either moral or factual considerations, Kelsen is left with the task of accounting for the normativity of law 'from within', without appealing to any external element. This ambition to define an autonomous legal 'ought' ultimately fails.[13] Kelsen's rejection of the classical natural law model indeed commits him to locating the source of legal normativity *within* human activity, while his methodological dualism[14] rules out any reference to the very 'fabric' of human activity – factual and moral elements.

What about Hart? He does not endorse Kelsen's methodological dualism, and one of the main factors distinguishing Hart's theory from Kelsen's lies in his

[11] It is worth noting here that in Kelsen's work this first norm ultimately takes the form of a *fiction*, asking us to proceed *as though* the law were irreducibly normative.

[12] Montaigne, n 4 above, III 13, 1216.

[13] This is bluntly put. For a full, detailed analysis, see Delacroix, n 1 above, ch 2, 27–60.

[14] Kelsen's methodological dualism may be seen as a continuation of the work of his predecessors (such as Laband and Jellinek), which aimed at freeing legal science from the 'vice of methodological syncretism', the illegitimate combination of different methods of cognition. Kelsen nevertheless radicalised this trend by supporting an expansive version of methodological dualism, separating the worlds of normativity and facticity by an 'insuperable abyss', corresponding to two independent spheres that are epistemologically unbridgeable.

embrace of the *social facts thesis*, ie 'the claim that while law is a normative social practice it is made possible by some set of social facts'.[15] Hart nevertheless does not elaborate much on the link between the initial social practices and the normative dimension of law. His accounting for the difference between coercion and obligation by reference to the 'distinct normative attitude'[16] typically associated with the use of the word 'obligation' presupposes law's normative dimension. Its focus is on the surface phenomena flowing from the fact that law is normative, not on what it takes for law to be normative in the first place. His late reference to a conventionalist framework to explain the emergence of the rule of recognition is made in passing, in a brief passage of his Postscript[17] – as if the study of the context of social interaction allowing and conditioning law's normative dimension were unlikely to yield any significant insight as to the meaning and properties of law itself.[18]

II TRACING A GENEALOGY OF LEGAL NORMATIVITY

From a 'downstream' perspective, explaining legal normativity involves considering its impact on individuals, its potential conflicts with other forms of normativity, but never what conditions its possibility. By contrast, the ambition of a genealogical account of legal normativity is to challenge its axiomatic status. It does so by considering the web of social and cultural practices that enable law to bind us, and hence have a claim on our conduct and/or judgement.

[15] J Coleman, 'Incorporationism, Conventionality, and the Practical Difference Thesis' in J Coleman (ed), *Hart's Postscipt: Essays on the Postscript to the Concept of Law* (Oxford, Oxford University Press, 2001) 116.

[16] This distinct normative attitude 'consists in the standing disposition of individuals to take such patterns of conduct both as guides to their own future conduct and as standards of criticism which may legitimate demands and various forms of pressure for conformity' (HLA Hart, *The Concept of Law*, 2nd edn (Oxford, Oxford University Press, 1994) 255).

[17] 'But the theory remains as a faithful account of conventional social rules which include, besides ordinary social customs (which may or may not be recognised as having legal force), certain important legal rules including the rule of recognition, which is in effect a form of judicial customary rule existing only if it is accepted and practiced in the law-identifying and law-applying operations of the courts' (ibid 256).

[18] As if, more importantly, any such inquiry into its conditions of possibility would inevitably grant the concept of normativity a metaphysical status it should not, and cannot have. His inscription within a philosophical context dominated by JL Austin, weary of abstract essences whose metaphysical status is supposedly independent of linguistic usage, comforted Hart in his reluctance to question what conditions law's normativity. Given his scepticism as to the possibility of preserving the objectivity of values without adhering to some form of moral realism (a metaphysical option he was committed to rejecting), Hart had every reason to keep looking downstream, as opposed to the social practices lying 'upstream' in relation to law's normativity. For more developments see S Delacroix, 'Meta-ethical agnosticism in legal theory: Mapping a way out' (2010) 1(2) *Jurisprudence* 225–40.

A What Makes Law's Normative Dimension Possible in the First Place

A fairly instinctive way of making sense of things is to ask about their origins. If one is not familiar with this or that institution, one will inquire about the circumstances or phenomena that brought it about, and gave it its present shape. This effort can be characterised by two contrasted attitudes, translating very different expectations when inquiring into the origins of a phenomenon. One possible attitude seeks to trace the 'pedigree' of a given phenomenon. In that case, one expects to be able to assign it a single, fixed point of origin, generally with a view to legitimising or justifying that phenomenon.

By contrast with the pedigree approach, there is no end to a genealogical enquiry into the origins of a phenomenon. As it progresses 'upstream', a genealogy reveals a conjunction of diverse processes which cannot be brought back to a singular origin. Whether they confirm or downplay the perceived legitimacy of the phenomenon in question, these processes are exposed for the sake of challenging common perceptions.

From this perspective, Montaigne's own quest, challenging the classical natural law model, initially had all the traits of a genealogical endeavour. Its potential to radically undermine law's accepted authority, based on the belief in the existence of natural laws, however, drove Montaigne to take a striking turn and ultimately rely on a pedigree approach rather than a genealogy. Montaigne's grounding the authority of law in a 'law of pure obedience' – the 'first commandment which God ever gave to Man' – is indeed meant to 'save' legal normativity from the peril of its contingent beginnings. This safety comes at a price: the alleged divine origin of this law of pure obedience can be deemed a form of 'surrender' on Montaigne's part. The quasi-tautological character of its formulation – obedience to the law would be justified by a law of pure obedience – confirms the necessity of avoiding developing any interest for this last and ultimate law, and yielding to law's authority on the basis of 'obedient faith'.

This attempt to turn attention away from what is meant to 'stand as' the ultimate grounding of law's normativity is a trait characteristic of a certain kind of legal positivism. From the perspective I briefly exposed above, Kelsen's Basic Norm, like Montaigne's 'law of pure obedience', comes across as a stop-gap measure. The reality it is meant to avoid – the context of social interaction that brings law into being, and maintains it as a *normative* practice – is precisely what a genealogy of legal normativity seeks to highlight.

B Celebrating the Contingent Part of the Story: Responsibility as Authorship

The interaction of individuals within a community will bring about desires of various sorts. Beyond the obvious physical ones, there will also be desires related to one's self-image (the desire to have a good reputation, for instance), and desires related to the possibility of getting on with one's projects without any interference, as well as the possibility of securing the fruit of these projects. These desires, once coordinated, will give rise to formal and informal rules. Nothing is typically legal in this scenario. What is sometimes deemed to characterise a legal system as a distinct form of normative order is a certain degree of sophistication, as a set of rules organised around some meta-rules or 'rules about rules'. This formal characterisation, however, does not even begin to account for the reason why we resort to law as a distinct form of social organisation. While it is easy to point at law's formal assets and show the way in which it may greatly improve a 'primitive' disciplinary structure, for instance, the story cannot stop there. One can only start to get an idea of why people adhere to legal standards and treat them as normative if one aims at a broad, all-encompassing picture of the various aspirations which a community may seek to realise through law.

Although culturally dependent, these aspirations are not commonly reducible to the mere desire to secure the possibility of non-violent social interaction. Whatever its content, there tends to be a programmatic element meant to encapsulate what that particular society sees as a 'better' way of living together. Relying on the possibility of peaceful coexistence as a presupposition, this programmatic element typically combines instrumental concerns and moral values. Far from being confined to the actual creation of a legal system, this element shapes its evolution and is key to understanding law's normative dimension.

For law's normativity, its capacity to impose some non-optional mode of conduct upon us is concomitant to the project we want it to serve. Instead of considering it as a 'given' established once and for all, provided the officials' minimal commitment condition is verified, law's normativity gains in being understood 'dynamically'. Each time an individual is led to assess law's normative claims in the light of morality's demands, each time a judge is led to rearticulate what we want law for – these cases contribute to shaping the socio-cultural fabric enabling law's normativity. While it would considerably diminish, and maybe cancel law's efficiency as a social institution if such practical deliberation were to be entered into each time an individual is confronted with law's demands, the total absence of such deliberation would in turn transform legal rules into mere habits devoid of any normative meaning.[19]

Once confronted with the demands of morality or prudence, the reasons provided by law may sometimes, on balance, fail to give rise to an obligation. Does this rob law of its normative force? Answering this question positively would equate the concepts of normativity and obligation and hence forego the possibility

[19] One could consider the hypothesis of a totalitarian legal regime whose propaganda is aimed precisely at rendering any kind of practical deliberation on the part of its subjects seemingly irrelevant or pointless. As long as this propaganda still has a point – that is, as long as there are still some individuals out there who will assess law's demands as part of a broader picture including other requirements – one may still speak meaningfully of law's 'normative' dimension. As soon as the possibility of practical deliberation disappears, however, the normative dimension of law becomes illusory, an empty-sounding concept.

– and necessity – of civic responsibility. Answering this question negatively, on the other hand, would imply that law's normativity consists in its making a difference in the subject's practical deliberation, no matter how successful or 'conclusive' law's reasons ultimately are. If law were to systematically fail to give rise to an obligation, being consistently defeated by other types of reasons, there would, however, be a sense of unease in still considering it as 'normative' – and in still considering it as 'law' *tout court*. This is what prompts authors like Marmor to specify that 'at the very least . . . the idea that law is a normative social practice suggests that law purports to give rise to reasons for action, and that at least some of these reasons are obligations'.[20]

Far from being detrimental to law's normative dimension, every opportunity to assess law's claim to bind us (hence rearticulating the project we want it to serve) is vital to maintaining legal normativity 'alive', so to speak, in touch with the material that first triggered its emergence: the changing demands of morality and prudence. These efforts of assessment and articulation depend, in turn, on our conception of normative agency: assert the need to track the truth of ethical judgements to some independent moral 'entities' conditioning their objectivity, and you will get a different understanding of what it is we are doing when we dispute law's authority in the name of moral values. Tracing the truth of moral judgements back to our own social practices rather than conditioning it to their accurately tracking some independent entities not only affects the nature of disagreement, it also changes the nature of our responsibility when, as law-makers, judges or citizens, we 'take the law into our own hands' and confront it with our moral expectations.

When it is contaminated with subjectivity, a reference to morality will not be able to provide the comfort of a Sartrian 'screen' we may safely hide behind; the responsibility we take is a matter of authorship rather than the mere implementation of an external source safely removed from the contingencies of human activities. McDowell aptly captures this qualitative difference when he argues: 'If something utterly outside the space of logos forces itself upon us, we cannot be blamed for believing what we do'.[21] When we deem morality to be such an 'external' source, we not only avoid the possibility of a certain kind of 'blame' (as McDowell puts it) but when we confront the law with our moral expectations, we basically confront a man-made institution, with all the contingency it implies, with a robustly independent reality.

Of course, we must be careful not to fall for a dualist caricature. The alternative to a 'robustly independent' morality need not be the voluntarist fiat associated with a certain kind of existentialism. The sense of authorship arising from an account of morality highlighting its response-dependent character may come with a pre-set, non-negotiable 'text' or 'content': one way of unpacking it consists in working out what the 'committed we' – our common humanity – entails. As a

[20] A Marmor, *Positive Law and Objective Values* (Oxford, Oxford University Press, 2001) 25.
[21] J McDowell, *Mind, Value, and Reality* (Cambridge, MA, Harvard University Press, 1998) 181.

daily endeavour, this unpacking process is shaped by the way we answer the 'unspoken ethical plea of the other' (to use Levinas' language).[22] As this answer is always in the process of being reformulated, our common humanity may be said to be a work in progress, structured around one unalterable moral fact: our inalienable dignity, and our concomitant responsibility for the other.

In this account of normativity, the concept of responsibility operates in two distinctive ways. While, on one hand, it constitutes the anchor of our commitment to morality,[23] it also encapsulates, on the other hand, the 'plasticity' of that commitment: its substance is shaped by the way we answer the other's summons to responsibility. This malleability in turn engages a distinct, proactive kind of responsibility – responsibility as authorship.

This malleable dimension is key to a genealogy of legal normativity. A genealogical endeavour won't stop at the cheerful acknowledgment that we are all equally dignified human beings who are committed to treating each other as such (maybe throwing in some coordination strategy for good measure). While normative agency is key, it doesn't get us very far if our purpose is to understand what enables law to bind us on a daily basis. The nitty gritty that gets us there will be shaped by all sorts of aspirations and desires. Some of them will be mundane (the desire to move around the country safely, for instance), and unlikely to yield much controversy. When it echoes deep-seated aspirations touching upon our very understanding of personhood, however, law's power to bind us will hinge upon the kind of deliberation at play in tragic civil disobedience cases or dramatic revolutionary circumstances. Legal theory's ability to shed light on law's normative dimension depends on its success in weaving together both those mundane and tragic deliberative backgrounds.

III CONCLUSION

The fact that laws are made by men and women has always been an inescapable truth. My emphasis on the '1593 turn', highlighting legal normativity's progressive detachment from the 'natural and divine order' traditionally grounding it, was meant to point at a significant change in the understanding of what conditions law's normativity: instead of having to be *derived* from a higher order eluding human ascendency, legal normativity is hence meant to be *brought about* by us, morally short-sighted human beings.

Montaigne's candid engagement with the challenge brought about by such a conceptual change, and ultimately his resorting to a bypassing strategy – the 'law of pure obedience' – inaugurates a trend that will permeate twentieth-century legal positivism. This trend consists in separating, rather than combining, law's

[22] E Levinas, *Totalité et Infini: Essai sur l' Extériorité* (La Haye, M Nijhoff, 1961).

[23] Our common humanity entails a certain responsibility towards fellow human beings: we are all summoned to acknowledge each other's dignity, whether we like it or not and whether we heed that summons or not.

social and normative aspects into two distinct explanatory targets. The existence of law is accounted for by reference to some conventional framework of interaction. Law's normativity is explained in terms of the difference it makes in individual practical deliberation: this explanation presupposes the possibility of legal normativity. It proceeds from the assumption that law is indeed normative to then consider how this manifests itself.

Yet law's normative dimension is not a 'property' that is somehow mysteriously attached to law. Law's power to bind us is concomitant to the project we want it to serve. Each time this project is reformulated, confronted with the demands of morality or prudence, law's normativity is concomitantly 'brought about'. While this quotidian construction presupposes our inalienable dignity (and concomitant responsibility for the other), it also engages a distinct sense of responsibility: responsibility for the way we answer the other's ethical plea, for the substance we give to morality, for our answer to that crucial question: 'how do we want to live together?' (and hence the substance we give to law). Given the contingency inevitably introduced by this 'responsibility as authorship', as I have called it, it may be tempting to keep it safely apart form one's account of normativity.

Yet that contingency is precisely what makes the concept of normativity worthy of philosophical discussion. To be confronted with a 'norm' does not necessarily entail that one approves (or disapproves) of it, that one will follow it, or that one has an obligation to do so. All it entails is that one is either committed to it (whether that commitment is the product of an act of will or the culmination of a set of circumstances) or that it is part of a system deemed normative in virtue of some people's commitment to it. If that system, like law, typically serves a moral task, one cannot make do with the 'systemic' commitment of a few to understand its normativity: one has to build our daily endeavour to rearticulate that moral task into one's account of normativity, whether that story be called a genealogy or otherwise

Index

www.ingramcontent.com/pod-product-compliance
Ingram Content Group UK Ltd.
Pitfield, Milton Keynes, MK11 3LW, UK
UKHW020238290926
15470UKWH00002B/606

9 781849 462389